ALSO BY STEVEN WATSON

The Birth of the Beat Generation: Visionaries,
Rebels, and Hipsters, 1944–1960

The Harlem Renaissance: Hub of African-American
Culture, 1920–1930

Strange Bedfellows: The First
American Avant-Garde

PREPARE FOR
SAINTS

STEVEN WATSON

 RANDOM HOUSE NEW YORK

PREPARE FOR SAINTS

Gertrude Stein, Virgil Thomson, and the
Mainstreaming of American Modernism

All rights reserved under International and Pan-American Copyright Conventions. Published in the United States by Random House, Inc., New York, and simultaneously in Canada by Random House of Canada Limited, Toronto.

All acknowledgments of illustration sources appear on page 371.

Library of Congress Cataloging-in-Publication Data
Watson, Steven.
   Prepare for saints: Gertrude Stein, Virgil Thomson, and the
mainstreaming of American modernism / Steven Watson.
        p. cm.
     Includes bibliographical references and index.
     ISBN 0-679-44139-5
     1. Thomson, Virgil, 1896– Four saints in three acts. 2. Stein,
Gertrude, 1874–1946. 3. Modernism (Aesthetics)—United States—
History—20th century. I. Title.
ML410.T452W37   1998
782.1—dc21   98-17496 CIP MN

Random House website address: www.randomhouse.com

Printed in the United States of America on acid-free paper

9 8 7 6 5 4 3 2

First Edition

BOOK DESIGN BY CAROLINE CUNNINGHAM

To Robert Atkins,
for all the years together

CONTENTS

Act I

CONCEPT

"Miss Gertrude Stein: Of Paris and Broadway," by William Cotton, full-page illustration for *Vanity Fair*, May 1934. Attendant saints include Pablo Picasso, Alice B. Toklas, Carl Van Vechten, Henri Matisse.

Introducing
Four Saints in Three Acts

In early February 1934, a red velvet curtain slowly parted in the Wadsworth Atheneum's intimate subterranean theater. After a long drumroll, the stage began to fill with black singers draped in richly colored vestments. Artfully posed beneath feathered trees and beaded arches, the ersatz sixteenth-century saints began to sing:

> To know to know to love her so
> Four saints prepare for saints.
> It makes well fish.
> Four saints it makes well fish.

The 299 members of the audience who heard these words to the orchestra's vigorous oompah rhythm could use no conventional measure to evaluate what they were seeing and hearing. Even the opera's title, *Four Saints in Three Acts*, was misleading: there were more than a dozen saints and four acts. Nor did anything that followed the opening chorus offer more

One of Al Hirschfeld's earliest caricatures, of *Four Saints in Three Acts*. (Copyright © Al Hirschfeld. Art reproduced by special arrangement with Hirschfeld's exclusive representative, the Margo Feiden Galleries, Ltd., New York.)

than a hint of meaning. The libretto told no coherent story, the staging and costumes were deeply eccentric, and most of the lines made no apparent sense. The cellophane set, brilliantly lit to evoke a sky hung with rock crystal, defied comparison to anything the audience had ever seen. The music was too naïve, too simple, and too American for an opera. Yet when the final curtain fell, many found themselves caught between tears and wild applause. Later they found that they could no more explain their extravagant reactions than they could the opera they had just seen.

After its move to Broadway two weeks later, it became difficult to recapture the novelty of that evening. *Variety* reported that the opera had appeared in more newspaper columns than any production in the past decade. Nationally broadcast over Columbia Radio, the phrase "pigeons in the grass alas" entered popular vocabulary. Along Fifth Avenue, Bergdorf

Goodman and Elizabeth Arden rushed *Four Saints* motifs into their Easter store windows, and Gimbel's advertised a new line of patterned linen tablecloths called "Instead of," "After a While," and "Have to Have," phrases taken from the libretto. Against all odds, *Four Saints in Three Acts* became the longest-running opera in Broadway history and America's most legendary, and unlikely, performance collaboration.

|||

Gertrude Stein wrote the libretto, and Virgil Thomson set her words to music. Florine Stettheimer designed its fantastic sets and costumes, John Houseman made his debut as theater director, and Frederick Ashton sailed from London to choreograph dancers whom he recruited from Harlem's Savoy Ballroom. Chick Austin, director of Hartford's Wadsworth Atheneum, produced the opera to christen the first architecturally modern wing in an American museum.

For some the opera was a onetime brush with modernism; for others a vehicle for long-overdue recognition. For all involved it remained a touchstone. Chick Austin's wife, Helen, called it "the great period." Thirteen years after the opera's premiere, high-bohemian hostess Constance

Four Saints invades Gimbel's and other Fifth Avenue stores, Easter 1934.

Askew sweepingly declared its collective importance for her generation: "It *does* stand for the best part of our lives."[1] The elaborately intertwined lives of the collaborators provide a window onto the brilliant generation that defined modern taste and stylishness in the early years of the Depression.

|||

The eldest of the collaborators, sixty-three-year-old Florine Stettheimer, became the first American painter to participate in a stage production, extending Sergei Diaghilev's practice of inviting artists to design sets and costumes. The opera offered Stettheimer a chance—the only chance in her life—to see her work realized on a lavish scale.

Four Saints opened six months after the publication of Gertrude Stein's *The Autobiography of Alice B. Toklas.* Stein had always desired *la gloire*, and, at sixty, she had finally been transformed from an object of ridicule into a best-selling author. Yet, as the waves of publicity for *Autobiography* and *Four Saints* engulfed her throughout the opera's runs in Hartford and New York, Stein couldn't write. She had at last found fame in her native land, but lost her literary identity.

Virgil Thomson used the opera's success to storm the citadel of America's musical establishment—what he called the "German-American musical complex"—which had excluded him. Thomson's music did not fit the dissonant vogue of the contemporary avant-garde, and those who championed modern music had largely ignored him. He would look back on the opera as a pivotal moment in his career.

For the black cast, the opera was a landmark event. Never before had African Americans been cast in a work that did not depict black life. Never before had they been paid for rehearsals. And never before had an all-black cast performed in an opera before white audiences.

For thirty-three-year-old impresario and museum director Chick Austin, the night of the opera's premiere was the pinnacle of his career. With *Four Saints* he inaugurated the world's first architecturally modern museum wing and simultaneously staged America's first Pablo Picasso museum retrospective. Friends and colleagues called him the three-ring-circus master of modernism. He wedded stylishness and modern museum practice, daring and caprice, and in the process transformed Hartford into "the New Athens."

Director John Houseman referred to the opera as "the womb of my career."[2] He had previously supported himself by selling grain futures and when Thomson invited him to join the team in the midst of the Depression, he was broke. In a stuffy Harlem church basement and in the sleek offices of the Hartford museum he absorbed enough hands-on experience to become a producer. He would demonstrate his resourcefulness on stage and in film for the next fifty years.

For the youngest of the collaborators, choreographer Frederick Ashton, the opera began as a lark, a chance for a free ticket from London to New York. Accustomed to classically trained ballet dancers, he found that working with the black cast became—on both sides—a process of cultural and corporal transmission. Ashton borrowed for his new choreography from classical ballet and the religious rituals of his childhood in Peru. As Thomson put it, "He knew how nuns moved."

|||

Four Saints in Three Acts was both an outrage against theatrical convention and a product of its stylish times. Its success epitomized the mainstreaming of modernism. Unlike America's first brush with modernism, the Armory Show in 1913—conceived, organized, and installed by disenfranchised artists—the success of *Four Saints* was the calculated work of a new generation of cultural tastemakers. The constellation that drove the opera forward—museum professionals, high-bohemian society, and commercial producers—played little role in the avant-garde's pioneering era in the 1910s. But when the Museum of Modern Art opened in 1929, critic Lloyd Goodrich observed, "Modernism today has reached a stage much more subtle and difficult than in the old crusading days when black was black and white was white."[3] By the mid-1930s, modernism entered realms formerly considered *derrière-garde:* the opera, the museum, and the ballet. This book describes that transition.

In the seven years between its inception and production, *Four Saints in Three Acts* became the crossroads of Harvard and Harlem, Paris and New York, the Upper East Side and Broadway's theater district. The opera embodied the transatlantic love affair between Paris and New York that inspired two expatriates to create a self-consciously "American" work. Its production developed hand in hand with the largely homosexual constellation of Harvard-trained art professionals who would define modernist taste in America.

The production's premiere came at a pivotal moment when modernism moved from its marginal position in the avant-garde into that citadel of high culture, the museum. With its move to Broadway, *Four Saints* went one step further, transforming American opera, and Broadway, in the process.

The opera's casting represented the apotheosis of the period's Negro chic and signaled the movement of black performers from lively revues and hackneyed melodramas to the fashionable opera stage. Summing up the opera's confluence of fashion, art, and revolution, society columnist Lucius Beebe called *Four Saints* "the fanciest and most utterly Bedlamite flag-raising within recent memory."[4] Beloved and subversive, *Four Saints* remains the watershed American collaboration that redefined performance possibilities for generations to come.

A half century later Virgil Thomson observed, "It couldn't have happened before, and it couldn't have happened after." By reconstructing the events leading up to the opera premiere, this book gives a behind-the-scenes look at a seminal moment in the history of modernism. Prepare for saints, prepare *Four Saints*.

CHAPTER 1

The World of
27, Rue de Fleurus

On an evening in early January 1926, Virgil Thomson and George Antheil walked south across the Luxembourg Gardens to a quiet, angled street in the Sixth Arrondissement. Passing through a glass-gated entrance, they crossed a courtyard and stopped before the double wooden doors of 27, rue de Fleurus. The address was by this time legendary as the residence of Gertrude Stein and Alice B. Toklas. As a friend of Thomson's observed, "A summons to her home was an invitation to present oneself to Mont Blanc." Stein had extended an invitation to George Antheil, the younger and better known of the two American composers, who had in turn asked Thomson to accompany him for "intellectual protection." Thomson was the more eager of the two to accept: he had admired Stein's *Tender Buttons* since his undergraduate days at Harvard. He quoted it in his letters and had recently experimented with setting some of it to music. Although he had never met Stein in person, Thomson already felt an intimacy—and a compatibility—with her words.

The studio of 27, rue de Fleurus, when Gertrude and Leo Stein shared the apartment.

Since the maid was away in the evening, Alice Toklas answered the door herself and directed the two men through book-lined halls and into a tall studio room. A motley assortment of porcelain figures, alabaster urns, and curios and liturgical figures cluttered the tables and floor. At the center of the room stood Stein's solid oak desk, littered with pencils and French school notebooks. Visitors' eyes were drawn to the puce-colored walls, filled with canvases by Picasso, Matisse, Cézanne, Gris, and others —what Stein called the "collection of the worthies." When Ernest Hemingway had first entered the room a few years earlier, he had observed, "It was like one of the best rooms in the finest museum except there was a big fireplace and it was warm and comfortable."

Stein frequently rearranged the paintings, and when one of them ceased to engage her, she relegated it to the back room known as the *salon des refusés*. No matter how the constellation shifted, Picasso's *Portrait of Gertrude Stein* always commanded a central position on the wall. The portrait provided visitors with a striking image of their hostess two decades earlier. The young Stein was leaning slightly forward, one hand planted on her thigh. She wore a loose brown robe and, around her neck, a white scarf pinned at the throat by a small coral brooch. Her monumental girth filled the canvas. Flat and masklike, her head seemed transplanted. Her hooded eyes gazed out with imperious intensity.

Below the painting, seated in a generous, chintz-slipcovered armchair, was Gertrude Stein in the flesh. That flesh was not as ample now as it once had been, but her bearing had retained its papal authority. Alice Toklas sat across from her in a carved, doll-like chair. "I saw two old ladies sitting by the fire," Virgil Thomson recounted to a friend. "They were waiting, and I couldn't help thinking of the line: Will you come into my parlour? said the spider to the fly."

In the mid-1920s, Stein dressed in corduroy skirts, tweed waistcoats, and embroidered vests. She wore heavy thonged sandals or carpet slippers and her thick brown hair was piled in a coil on her head. One visitor compared the overall impression to "the homely finish of a brown buckram bean-bag."[1] Her conversation was punctuated with a laugh so large that it filled the room. "As it gradually dwindled into chuckles and appreciative murmurs," recalled her young friend the writer Bravig Imbs, "the silence that followed seemed golden with sunlight."

At that first meeting in 1926, Thomson strategically used his time alone with Stein to impress upon her both his broad knowledge of art and culture and his particular appreciation for her work. He reminisced about World War I and the doughboys, whom Gertrude adored, he spoke about Erik Satie's musical composition *Socrate*, but he directed his most winning comments to Stein's experimental work *Tender Buttons*, which he had first encountered in 1919 and soon read aloud to amuse his Harvard classmates. Stein was especially pleased when he mentioned his attempts to set her words to music.

Thomson was twenty-nine when he met Gertrude Stein. "I still had a baby face in those days," he recalled decades later, "which led to my being thought to be even brighter than I was."[2] His auburn-tinged hair was already thinning, accentuating his high forehead, and his pale blue eyes could seem alternately unprepossessing and piercing. He spoke in full declarative sentences, issuing pronouncements with surprising authority. A newspaper described him as "an elderly cherub, albeit an acerbic one," and W. H. Auden later compared him to an intimidating butler at an English country house.[3] Thomson could show off shamelessly, but there was glee in his knowledge and audacity in his manners, and his aspirations to stylishness balanced his homespun directness. A friend summed Thomson up: "With him there may be pose, but never bunk."[4]

Stein, who liked to cast her friends as historical figures, soon decided that Thomson resembled his namesake, Virgil, author of the *Aeneid* and Dante's guide in *The Divine Comedy.* In both the classical figure and his modern counterpart she saw precision, taste, and a lofty, admirable propensity to associate with the great.

Alice Toklas remained in the background that evening, smoking cigarettes in an ivory holder. All newcomers passed through Alice; she was known as the "sieve and buckler" and deftly acquired information about each guest's family, connections, and education. She discharged her interrogation with such charm and dispatch (often the whole exchange lasted less than three minutes) that her victims frequently remained unaware of just what was at stake. Despite the elliptical restraint of her vocabulary ("compromise" for "seduce," "impure" for "bisexual," "inadequate" for "dead drunk"), her shrewd evaluations were uncompromising.[5]

Antheil never again appeared at 27, rue de Fleurus—James Joyce and Ezra Pound's informal sponsorship may have put him irrevocably in the rival camp. The couple's feelings about Thomson were more complicated. Thomson later recalled that "Gertrude and I got on like Harvard men." At the close of the evening, she warmly commanded him, "We'll be seeing each other."

But they did not. Nor did the two women respond to a postcard that Thomson sent them that summer. Nearly a year would pass before Thomson would visit 27, rue de Fleurus again. The length of that delay suggests the breadth of Alice's purview. Neither her Guerlain tuberose perfume nor her painted, almond-shaped nails could mask her willpower. As Thomson would later advise friends, "Keep your eye on Alice."[6]

|||

When Virgil Thomson met Gertrude Stein in 1926, they shared a common disappointment at being inadequately appreciated and a determined ambition to alter their state. As Stein later wrote to Thomson, "Neither you nor I have ever had any passion to be rare, we want to be as popular as Gilbert and Sullivan if we can, and perhaps we can."[7] But the two were at opposite points in their professional lives. Thomson was just embarking on his composing career; none of his works had been published or performed, and his name was virtually unknown. Stein had four books to her name, the first published seventeen years earlier. Her name was all too well known and almost invariably ridiculed.

"The name of Gertrude Stein is better known in NY today than the name of God!" Mabel Dodge exclaimed in 1913, at the time of the Armory Show. A salon hostess and celebrator of modernity, Dodge was partly responsible for that first surge of recognition. Publicizing both Stein and herself, she printed copies of Stein's abstract work "Portrait of Mabel Dodge at the Villa Curonia," in 1912, bound in flamboyant Florentine wallpaper, and circulated them at the Armory and among the trendsetters who attended her influential "Evenings" at 23 Fifth Avenue. For a special Armory Show issue of *Arts and Decoration*, Dodge wrote a piece that linked Stein's intentions to those of modern artists and provided a vocabulary for understanding Stein's hermetic writing:

> In a large studio in Paris, hung with paintings by Renoir, Matisse, and Picasso, Gertrude Stein is doing with words what Picasso is doing with paint. She is impelling language to induce new states of consciousness, and in doing so language becomes with her a creative art rather than a mirror of history.[8]

The first public parodies of Stein's work appeared at the same time, in newspaper columns and in such books as *The Cubies' ABC* (1913). Dodge had linked Stein's revolutionary language to the Cubists, and her detractors used the connection to ridicule her:

> I called the canvas *Cow with Cud*
> And hung it on the line
> Altho' to me 'twas vague as mud
> 'Twas clear to Gertrude Stein.[9]

These extreme and divergent reactions reflected a pattern that would continue for decades, even after her death. Stein's handful of defenders made sweeping claims for her revitalization of American language, while her detractors considered her work quoted verbatim a ready-made parody. As her friend Robert Coates noted, Stein's name became "a tag for anything from 3 A.M. at the Select Bar to Communism."[10] To fans she represented literary freedom and modernity. "She is like yeast, the yeast that makes the bread," Carl Van Vechten said in 1928. "One might perhaps say that her poetic medium is the forerunner of a changed language."[11] But neither the jokes nor the acclaim brought her the readership that she craved.

An abidingly loyal friend, art critic Henry McBride, described the paradox of Stein's career: "There is a public for you, but no publisher." There were, in fact, several publishers, but they were small and paid little. As her friend Louis Bromfield put it, "Being caviar never interested her."[12] She wanted to be ham on rye, to be listed in *Who's Who*, to be published between hard covers, and most of all to appear in a large-circulation American magazine such as *The Atlantic Monthly*.

Stein herself had financed the publication of two of her books (*Three Lives*, in 1909, and *Geography and Plays*, in 1922). A tiny Greenwich Village press called Claire Marie published *Tender Buttons* in 1914, and Robert McAlmon's Contact Publishing Company brought out her masterwork, *The Making of Americans*, in 1925, in an edition of five hundred. Shorter pieces appeared on both sides of the Atlantic in the small-circulation avant-garde publications known as "little magazines." While many of these are now regarded as the apex of an inspired period (among them were *Camera Work*, *The Little Review*, *Broom*, *Rogue*, *The Soil*, the *Transatlantic Review*), their readership was small. The only glossy magazine that published her work was Frank Crowninshield's *Vanity Fair*. Stein's literary reputation was jarringly out of scale with her self-evaluation: she believed, quite simply, that she possessed the most creative literary mind of the century. A month before she died, she summed up her ambition: "I always wanted to be historical, from almost a baby on, I felt that way about it."

Stein tallied up publishers' rejections in a notebook, itemizing them like an accountant. By the time she met Thomson, the list was long, and the growing pile of unpublished manuscripts filled her large Spanish armoire. Although editors' polite—and sometimes not-so-polite—rejections inspired doubt that her work would ever be appropriately appreciated, Stein never doubted the work itself. To the worst rebuffs she reacted with booming laughter. But her thirst for recognition from conventional quarters is attested to by her persistent volley of submissions to *The Atlantic Monthly*. Ellery Sedgwick, its editor, outlined the problem of finding an American audience: "Here there is no group *literati* or *illuminati* or *cognoscenti* or *illustrissimi* of any kind." His subsequent rejections described her work as a picture puzzle to which few had the key. After nearly

Henry McBride by Peggy Bacon, c. 1930.

importance: "For the valuable position of Henry McBride as critic depends upon his persistence in time, and his insistence over extended time on certain elements of freshness, elegance and humanity."

McBride's invaluable perspective on the preparation of *Four Saints in Three Acts* reflected his closeness to several key participants. He had known Gertrude Stein since the summer of 1913 and promoted her thereafter in his column whenever possible. He had encountered Florine Stettheimer through her oil-painted portrait of Marcel Duchamp's thirtieth birthday party in 1917, and he joked in print that he was miffed at not having been invited. He soon became a regular at the Stettheimers', where he heard Virgil Thomson sing the opera in 1929 and again in 1932. McBride wrote about it at greater length than anyone, and with more intimacy.

Near the end of his long life, McBride noted that fifty young artists called him "Uncle Henry." He bore a similarly avuncular relationship to *Four Saints* as its all-important observer and encourager.

Henry McBride began writing art criticism for the New York *Sun* a few months before the 1913 Armory Show. At the advanced age of forty-six he embarked on a new career, and for the next four decades, he kept his eyes open to the art of the twentieth century. He wrote weekly art columns for the *Sun* until 1950; he was the art critic for *The Dial* throughout the illustrious tenures of Scofield Thayer and Marianne Moore (1920–1929), and he was the editor of *Creative Art* (1930–1932). His last published work for *Artnews*, written in his mid-eighties, examined such younger artists as Mark Rothko and Jackson Pollock, and he concluded his career saying, "a new cycle begins." Lincoln Kirstein best described McBride's a decade of submissions the editor threw up his hands: "We live in different worlds." Was it possible to bridge them?

|||

The delicate equilibrium required to sustain Stein's writing depended on those closest to her. In the early years her older brother Leo had provided it, but when she began to outshine him, he ridiculed her repetitive style. After a decade of living together at 27, rue de Fleurus, he moved out in 1913. "A prophet can support not being honored in his own country when other lands sufficiently acclaim him," he later wrote, "but when the acclamation otherwise is faint the absence of support at home is painful." For the rest of Stein's life, support was supplied by Alice Toklas. By the time Virgil Thomson entered Stein's life, the partnership was firmly established, the rules well understood, and the daily rhythms irrevocably set—all in service of Stein's writing.

Stein reported (as Alice) in *The Autobiography of Alice B. Toklas* that when the two women met, Alice heard the tolling of an internal bell: "I may say that only three times in my life have I met a genius and each time a bell within me rang and I was not mistaken." Alice's recollection was characteristically less grand but more precise. She remembered Gertrude's childlike, dimpled hands and the sculpted mass of her head. She described her that September afternoon in 1907 as a golden-brown presence in a brown corduroy suit wearing a large round coral brooch from which her voice seemed to issue: "It was unlike anyone else's voice—deep, full, velvety like a great contralto's, like two voices."

When she arrived in Paris at the age of thirty, Alice was at a dead end.[13] After studying to become a pianist and performing in two recitals, she had given up her music career, and she had no desire to marry. Serving as Gertrude's secretary gave her purpose. She moved into 27, rue de Fleurus in August 1910. When Leo moved out, three years later, Gertrude and Alice jointly exorcised his ghost, selling three Picasso paintings to Daniel-Henri Kahnweiler in order to renovate the apartment. They replaced the gaslights with electricity and built a covered walkway between the studio and their private living quarters in the adjoining *pavillon*. They replaced Leo's furniture, plastered over the door to his bedroom, and transformed his study into the *salon des refusés*.

|||

Gertrude Stein and Alice B. Toklas, Aix-les-Bain, summer 1928.

In her quietly tenacious way, Alice became irreplaceable. At the beginning of the relationship Gertrude took note of the control that fueled Alice's adulation: "She is docile, stupid, but she owns you, you are then hers." Leo Stein, admittedly not a neutral party, described her as "a kind of abnormal vampire who gives more than she takes."[14] Toklas not only governed the regular domestic rhythms that were essential to Stein's creativity but supplied her with intelligent and rarely qualified approval for the results. Sometimes she appended encouraging notes to the manuscript. "Sweet pinky," she wrote in the early years of their relationship. "You made lots of literature last night—didn't you. It is very good." She transformed Stein's loose, slanting, barely legible script into neat typescript and sent off manuscripts to potential publishers. Alice was often described as a "faithful companion," as one might describe a family dog, but this restrained vocabulary cannot capture the emotional and erotic ties between the two women. Nor does it suggest how important Toklas was to Stein's writing industry.

Often cited as a historical model for lesbians, Stein and Toklas never spoke of their relationship publicly. Although many of their female friends were lesbian, they avoided self-consciously lesbian gatherings such as those of Natalie Clifford Barney. Even after Stein's death, her old friend Etta Cone claimed not to believe that "there was something *between* Gertrude and Alice." Yet the erotic ties between the women appear in Stein's coded writings, such as "Lifting Belly." On the surface, the relationship reflected a traditional hierarchical model of dominating husband and self-effacing wife. In the sphere of the tea table and of general household management, Alice's authority went unquestioned. She also served as the couple's official memory—it was, Janet Flanner observed, "as exact as a silver engraving"—and despite Gertrude's irritation that Alice was always right, stories were eventually told in her version.

Using Alice as her mouthpiece (and echoing Flaubert), Stein wrote, "Gertrude Stein says that if you are way ahead with your head you naturally are old fashioned and regular in your daily life." The daily household rhythm began at six, when Alice rose and cleaned the drawing room, to prevent servants from breaking her porcelain figurines. She spent the rest of the day marketing, polishing the furniture, and embroidering handkerchiefs with dime-sized "rose is a rose is a rose" motifs. Stein awoke at nine and spent the morning writing playful letters and reading. After bathing and eating her dietetic lunch, she would drive around Paris in Godiva, the two-seater runabout Ford they bought in 1920, or walk through the tortuous streets of the Left Bank. Her sole job was to write, and by then she had developed the concentration to write, even in Godiva's high front seat, letting the street sounds mix with the verbal rhythms in her head. During these afternoons, when words were poised between spontaneity and development, she would pencil them in schoolchildren's copybooks, called *cahiers*. "Before you write it must be in your head almost in words," she later told her friend Thornton Wilder, "but if it is already in words in your head, it will come out dead."[15]

After four, friends would visit for tea or dinner. Since there was no telephone in the house, guests dropped in at prearranged times set in small engagement books or communicated by *petits bleus*, notes delivered the same day through the Paris post office's system of pneumatic tubes. These social interludes provided Stein respite from her word-filled day and offered her a chance to listen to the gossip and speech patterns of others. Stein retired by one o'clock, a few hours after Alice, only to repeat the same pattern the next day.

|||

Gertrude Stein is often assumed to have presided over the brightest worlds of the Paris avant-garde—in both the heroic pre–World War I years and the expatriate era of the 1920s. But it is telling to consider the sets to which she and Alice did not belong. They did not consort with the high-bohemian set surrounding Étienne de Beaumont, who staged Les Soirées de Paris, or attend the musical soirées organized by the Comtesse de Polignac. They were not part of the hard-drinking café life common among Montparnasse writers and artists. They rarely attended Diaghilev's Ballets Russes, nor visited the stylish café Le Boeuf sur le Toit, where Jean Cocteau's circle gathered. After Sylvia Beach chose to publish James Joyce, they abandoned Shakespeare and Company. They actively avoided Ezra Pound and had little to do with either the Surrealists or the group of composers known as Les Six.

Since Stein rarely ventured out to meet the movers and shakers of the avant-garde, guests frequently came to her. The regular visitors at 27, rue de Fleurus included only a few women, most of them lesbian (the Duchesse de Clermont-Tonnerre, Janet Flanner, Mildred Aldrich, Janet Scudder). But the preponderance were young men; Stein would later de-

Ezra Pound was the period's most self-consciously energetic promoter of modernist literature. He promoted his band of protégés through several little magazines (including *The Dial, The Little Review,* and *Exile.*) Whatever sympathy he felt for Stein's writing dissipated when they met in person and competed to dominate the conversation. A few desultory meetings later, Pound accidentally broke a chair at 27, rue de Fleurus, and Stein refused to see him again. Each relished the opportunity to ridicule the other in print and conversation.

T. S. Eliot's position as editor of *Criterion* gave him the opportunity to publish Stein. When he solicited from her a piece in November 1924, insisting it be her latest thing, she titled her submission "A Description of the Fifteenth of November." Eliot recognized the power of her writing, but it alarmed him: "It is not improving, it is not amusing, it is not interesting, it is not good for one's mind. But its rhythms have a peculiar hypnotic power not met with before. It has a kinship with the saxophone. If this is the future, then the future is, as it very likely is, of the barbarians. But this is the future in which we ought not to be interested." Eliot declined to publish sections of *The Making of Americans.*

William Carlos Williams supported Stein in print, naming her to his personal pantheon of modernists, and subsequently credited her with fomenting "a revolution of some proportions." But their first meeting in September 1927 proved disastrous. Stein asked Williams what she should do with her mountain of unpublished works. Dr. Williams replied with excessive candor, "If they were mine, having so many, I would probably select what I thought were the best and throw the rest into the fire." Stein responded with fury. "A writer's writing is too much of the writer's being; his flesh child," she said. "You may, but of course, writing is not your metier, Doctor." Stein instructed the maid not to admit Williams if he ever called again: "There is too much bombast in him." Stein and Williams never saw each other again.

Stein regarded **James Joyce** as her most formidable peer and *Ulysses* as one of the three greatest novels of her generation, adding that his influence was "local." Virgil Thomson observed that the rivalry was inevitable, since "viewed near by, they appeared as planets of equal magnitude." When Shakespeare and Company published *Ulysses,* Stein informed Sylvia Beach, the bookstore's proprietor, that henceforth she and Miss Toklas would borrow all books from the American Library. Although Joyce's informal headquarters at Shakespeare and Company was only a few blocks from her home, neither made an attempt to arrange an introduction. When they did finally meet at a party in the thirties, Joyce was nearly blind and had to be led to her. "How strange that we share the same *quartier* and have never met," he remarked. Gertrude looked at him and replied, "Yes."

scribe the late 1920s as "the period of being twenty-six." Some were writers (Glenway Wescott, Robert Coates, Bravig Imbs, René Crevel, Max Ewing, and later Paul Bowles and Charles Henri Ford); some were painters (Pavel Tchelitchew, Christian Bérard); many were expatriates, from the United States and Russia; and most were homosexual.

In addition to Alice's little cakes and colored liqueurs and Gertrude's earthy humor, the habitués sought her informal sponsorship. Stein's imprimatur did not confer chic, as did Jean Cocteau's; nor did it spell immediate publication in little magazines, as did Ezra Pound's; nor did she offer financial support, as did Étienne de Beaumont. But Stein's approval mattered. She reaped some of the credit that belonged to her brother for discovering modern artists, and her continuing friendship with Picasso provided celebrity by association. Since she represented the extreme pole of literary abstraction, her work and opinions seemed to point the way toward the next stage of modernism. She used her power to single out for praise such writers as F. Scott Fitzgerald, Ernest Hemingway, Charles Henri Ford, Parker Tyler, and Robert Coates; and artists Pavel Tchelitchew, Eugene Berman, Christian Bérard, and, most enduringly, Francis Rose. With the exception of Fitzgerald and Hemingway, none of these have entered the canon.

What attracted Stein to these young men? As Picasso observed with characteristic modesty, her new discoveries could never rank with the prewar discoveries of Picasso, Matisse, and Gris. Publisher and writer Robert McAlmon concurred, "She accepts too readily the adulation of people that a person of healthy self-confidence would dismiss at once as parasites, bores, or gigolos and pimps." Protective distance was built into Stein's relationships with her protégés. She was less competitive with artists and composers, and preferred writers at the very beginning of their careers. "A virgin page is such fun," she remarked to a World War I doughboy. "One does like to know young men even though as soon as that they are not any longer young," she wrote. "As soon as one really knows them they are not any longer young."

The threat of a protégé becoming a peer is reflected in her relationship with Ernest Hemingway. When they met in February 1922, he was twenty-two and she forty-eight, and she was a grand dame. Their relationship soon accelerated beyond that of mentor and protégé. Stein became the godmother of Hemingway's first child, and he became her admiring reviewer ("the most first rate intelligence employed in writing today"), and he proofread the galleys for the early installments of a projected serial publication of *The Making of Americans* in the *Transatlantic Review*. He also recalled, perhaps factitiously, a mutual sexual attraction between them. When the element of competition was added—Hemingway curried literary friendships with Joyce and Pound and garnered excited attention in print and in gossip—their relationship finally unraveled, just as Thomson came into her orbit. His entrance evoked a ditty that Stein and Toklas liked: "Give me new faces new faces new faces I have seen the old ones."[16]

Virgil Thomson:
Roots in Time and Place

"Show me I am from Missouri," began Gertrude Stein's first piece about Virgil Thomson.[1] Her lead word, "show," applied to Thomson in multiple ways. He showed himself plainly as a foursquare American, had grown up in the Show-Me State, was a show-off in his manner and showy in his clothes. Proud of his state of birth, Thomson rarely missed a chance to bring it up and chose it as the site of his burial, although he had not lived there since the age of twenty-two. He often declared, "I come from Missouri, which is the home of Mark Twain and Harry Truman, and the stubborn boys."[2]

Virgil Garnett Thomson was born in Kansas City, Missouri, on November 25, 1896. A half century later, his fellow musician and critic Peggy Glanville-Hicks analyzed his astrological chart. Although Thomson had no patience with astrology, which he considered mumbo jumbo, he kept this reading throughout his life:

Your emotions are not so much controlled as they are natural adjuncts to practical wishes. . . . You are rarely bored, or boring, but you can wear others, and yourself, out by the ferocity of your attack on life. . . . Your sense perceptions are acute, swift, probably accurate and you are voluble in expressing what you take in. . . . [You take] infinite pains with the little things that underlie success, and plug along at a hopeless cause until lo and behold! it amounts to something. . . . You are less introspective than most. You want to see the tangible evidence of success, and like it best if the rest of the world can see it too.3

Thomson grew up in a modest two-story frame house at the edge of Kansas City. By the turn of the century, the bustling city lay at the edge of eastern culture's reach. The starting point of the Santa Fe and Oregon trails, Kansas City mixed the brassy independence of a frontier town with the amenities of culture, touring Wild West shows, religion, and open vice. Thomson's father worked as a civil servant and served as a deacon at the Calvary Baptist Church. His mother, a housewife, was a sociable and energetic hostess. Virgil's first memories include his family's bay-windowed parlor, a cozy room he recalled as the setting of his earliest performances on an upright piano. Relatives and neighbors applauded his musical precocity, which at first consisted of loudly pounding the piano, pedal down. He aptly named his first explosive improvisation after the Chicago Fire of 1871. By the age of five he could read notes and play songs and dances.

On entering first grade, Thomson learned a lesson that would remain with him throughout his life: although he would inevitably lose in a physical fight, he could settle scores and vanquish enemies with his

Virgil Thomson at the age of twelve, Kansas City, 1909.

sharp tongue. In first grade Virgil saw his first play, *Miss Petticoats.* The spectacle so enthralled him that he insisted on reenacting it that night before going to sleep. Throughout his childhood and adolescence he turned to the theater, at first in the company of his sister, later as a candy seller and usher, and finally as a piano accompanist to silent movies. When he was not working, he watched from the audience. Thomson loved everything about theaters: their spires and cupolas, their heavy curtains and ornate chandeliers, the costumed audiences and brightly painted scenery, the oasis of fantasy and impersonation. Between the Auditorium and the Convention Hall, the city provided a cultural center for the region, and between 1909 and 1917, Thomson saw nearly every show that came to town, from stock theater and musicals to touring operas and ballets.

When he was not in theaters, Thomson played the organ, not only for the Calvary Baptist Church, which his family attended, but for anyone who would pay him. Although he enjoyed his professional status and relished the liturgical repertory, he never confused his musical appreciation with faith. His piano teacher recalled that as a teenager he had abruptly stopped a discussion of religious dogma: "We are musicians and do not need that," he said. "We get our emotional satisfaction from our Muses."[4] His varied musical diet included the classical repertory assigned by his teacher, the schottisches and polkas he performed for his sister and her friends, and all the ambient music one heard in turn-of-the-century America: banjo ditties, parade band tunes, ragtime, the oompah sounds of summer band shells, and the lilting melodies of Sunday parlor socials. This repertory of indigenous Americana would later form the basis of his musical vocabulary.

Thomson was an A student, a voracious reader, a disciplined music student, and an enterprising accompanist. He felt less connection to his classmates than he did to the adults in his life, most notably a homosexual church tenor who directed him to his most important music teacher, Geneve Lichtenwalter. He regarded his peers as clay to be shaped by his erudition and taste. "Virgil wasn't at all reticent about the fact that he expected to be a great man someday," one friend recalled. The only question was whether he would make his mark as a writer or as a musician.

After graduating from high school, Thomson attended a newly founded junior college, Kansas City Polytechnic Institute, where he organized a group called the Pansophists. The pretentious name, its all-male membership, and its chief activity of debating the advanced issues of the day all reflected Thomson's developing persona—as did the fact that he not only founded the club but appointed himself president, published its magazine, entitled *Pans*, and wrote its preamble:

> If you wish a distinction between character and personality, let us say that personality is a mask one wears in public; character is the mask one wears to oneself. . . . Democracy is a device to insure the survival of the unfittest, a plan to reduce the world to uniformity, a synonym for mediocrity. All men are not equal; they should merely be given an equal chance to prove their superiority.

His worldview blended Wildean dandyism and Nietzschean self-assertion and coupled posturing with invective. His classmates regarded him as an arrogant, talented oddball. His criticism, a friend recalled, "was always delivered with a combination of omniscience and patronage that was hard to take."[5] But take it they did; Virgil's cocksure leadership and his self-evaluation as a budding genius went unquestioned.[6]

During World War I, Thomson briefly served in the National Guard. He spent most of his military duty in Oklahoma's landlocked Camp Doniphan, his first taste of close living in a community where erudition counted for little. He wrote to his mother of his difficulty communing with his fellow soldiers: "It is as if some active psychic influence extended from them and monopolized my mind, for I can't think properly or feel like my own self as long as any of them is around, whether he talks or not."[7] He preferred the dissonant sounds of the military band tuning up to their finished performances, likening the practice sessions to the symphonies of modern composers.

In 1919, after the war ended, Thomson headed for Harvard, where, because of his years in junior college and in the military, he was older than most of his classmates. He had hoped to find his niche in a world of culture at Harvard, but his undergraduate years proved lonely. He was chided for his "uppishness," and his secret homosexual feelings for classmates caused him discomfort. Unaccustomed to being anything but a leader, he was ill equipped to hear the Music Department chairman berate his work in harmony, counterpoint, and fugue. "It takes a good deal to get down to my sentimental skin," he wrote to a friend at the age of twenty-three, "through all the callous layers of my deliberate and temperamental egotism." At the age of twenty-three, Thomson composed his first formal piece. He set Amy Lowell's poem "Vernal Equinox" to music, foreshadowing his interest in the words of strong lesbian women.

A few years later Harvard would be animated by an adventurous group of students that would support modernism in general and Thomson's opera in particular. They would treat him as a wise and worldly elder, schooled in the politics of the cultural world. But in the early 1920s, Thomson enjoyed no such position, and his most consequential educational experience happened outside the formal curriculum. His tutor, S. Foster Damon, introduced him to a thick sheaf of Erik Satie piano music and to Gertrude Stein's slim volume *Tender Buttons*.

The Liberal Club, a three-story frame house just off campus, provided Thomson with the closest thing to a progressive community at Harvard. Less exclusive than Harvard's other "finals clubs," it welcomed Jews, leftists, and nonmonied young men. In addition to teas and afternoons of bridge, the Liberal Club offered a reading room stocked with avant-garde magazines and books. In this cheery atmosphere Thomson met some of the key figures in his life: Briggs Buchanan, for whom he developed an unrequited infatuation; Henry-Russell Hitchcock, who would become a close friend; and Maurice Grosser, who would become his lifelong mate.

In his second year at Harvard, Thomson became the assistant conductor of the Harvard Glee Club. The position gave him the status and community he had missed, and, most important, it introduced him to Paris. In hindsight, Thomson relegated Harvard to the "Jumping-Off Place for Europe."

|||

Thomson arrived in Paris in the middle of a June night in 1921, driven through its deserted streets perched on the top front seat of a four-horse omnibus. He never forgot that experience. "It does not happen many times to anyone," he wrote, "but when it does, it stamps upon a color-photographic image the memory of something personally possessed." Paris would be his primary residence for the next two decades. As he later wrote to a friend, "I do well here. Elsewhere in Europe I should feel lonely. In America I should go mad." His first visit to France lasted fourteen months, some of it on the road with the Harvard Glee Club; then he went back to

Cambridge for a final year. He returned to Paris in September 1925 for an open-ended stay that would continue, with several trips to America, until the Second World War.

A snapshot of Thomson shortly before his longer emigration to Paris suggests the state of his professional and personal life. He could have pursued his professional life in America as a performer, teacher, or writer about music. Most promisingly, he had written long articles—including "The Cult of Jazz," "The Future of American Music," "How Modern Music Gets That Way"—for America's most stylish magazine, *Vanity Fair*. The editor, Frank Crowninshield, appreciated them sufficiently to pay $100 for each and to issue an open invitation for Thomson to write more. These and early articles for *The Boston Evening Transcript* and *The American Mercury* showcased the assured opinions, pithy and outrageous generalizations, and plainspoken, witty voice that would inform his later career as America's premier music critic. Thomson was also offered two positions, one as an organist in Kansas City and the other directing the Music Department at the University of South Carolina. He declined the security of these jobs for the more glamorous financial uncertainty of Paris. "I was leaving a career that was beginning to enclose me," he later wrote. "I was leaving also an America that was beginning to enclose us all, at least those among us who need to ripen unpushed."

Part of Thomson's necessary ripening was sexual. He wrote privately about his homosexuality in the homeliest terms: "If I habitually choose turnips to asparagus, that taste is largely a matter of indifference to my neighbors. With exactly equal indifference do I regard the varieties of sexual habit manifested by my friends."[8] Nearly twenty-nine, he had yet to experience a sexually fulfilling relationship. He expressed his homosexual desires only in coded language and struggled with his physical unattractiveness. While he feigned indifference about his sexuality, it was actually a source of intense loneliness. Paris offered an ideal stage for exploration. The city's many settings for homosexual encounters ranged from bicycle paths in the Bois de Boulogne and the Bois de Vincennes to fancy cross-dressing balls at Magic City. Maurice Grosser, who would become Thomson's lover, recalled that "in Paris one's source of income was regarded as a private matter, but the details of one's sex life were treated as public property."

|||

Harvard Glee Club, Milan Cathedral, summer 1921. Thomson is dead center in the light suit, holding the boater hat.

In 1925, a month before he sailed to Paris on his second and longer trip, Thomson described the discomfort he felt in his native land: "By uncomfortable, I mean I'm a misfit. I'm not a vegetable, a salesman, or a joiner. Paris, as such, is bunk. But, my God! So is America." Paris offered good food, cheap rent—and, most important, a community of working musicians, writers, and artists of which he could become a part. He told a friend that he wanted to study with music teacher Nadia Boulanger and noted that he had begun to set Gertrude Stein texts from *Tender Buttons* to music. ("The Stein things also mature slowly," he wrote, "because they are a knotty problem.")

His previous visit had inspired Thomson to idealize artistic collaboration. "I believe concerted music is greater than any solo performance," he wrote a friend, "team work for the production of something beautiful being, if not the highest end of man, at least symbolic of nearly all that we consider good." In private notes to himself written shortly before setting off for Paris, Thomson showed a more hard-boiled attitude. "As for society and team work, etc. work in a team if it's your prompting," he wrote. "If not, do your own bidding."[9]

These notes, penciled on stray pieces of paper in the summer of 1925

George Antheil (12, rue de l'Odéon, beginning 1923): American avant-garde composer.

Natalie Clifford Barney (20, rue Jacob, throughout the 1920s): Writer, celebrator of lesbianism, organizer of a largely female salon.

Sylvia Beach and Adrienne Monnier (18, rue de l'Odéon, 1921–32): Domestic partners and booksellers. Beach ran Shakespeare and Company and Monnier ran La Maison des Amis des Livres, across the street.

Black Sun Press (2, rue Cardinale, 1927–early 1950s): Run by Harry and Caresse Crosby; published books by James Joyce, Hart Crane, Ernest Hemingway, and Ford Madox Ford.

William Aspenwall Bradley (5, rue St.-Louis-en-l'Ile, throughout the 1920s): adventurous literary agent whose clients included Gertrude Stein, Ezra Pound, Edith Wharton, and Natalie Clifford Barney.

Nadia Boulanger (taught at the École Normale de Musique throughout the 1920s): Influential teacher of American composers, including Virgil Thomson, Aaron Copland, and Walter Piston.

Café des Deux Magots (place St.-Germain-des-Pres and rue Bonaparte): Transatlantic gathering place of artists, writers, and intellectuals throughout the 1920s.

Café de la Rotonde (103, boulevard du Montparnasse, beginning 1924): International hangout, nightclub, and gallery.

Café du Dôme (108, boulevard du Montparnasse, beginning 1898): Montparnasse hangout for American expatriates.

Alexander Calder (22, rue Daguerre, in 1926–28; studio at 7, rue Cels): American sculptor.

Harry and Caresse Crosby (19, rue de Lille): Writers and publishers of Black Sun Press.

e.e. cummings (46, rue St.-André-des-Arts): American poet, novelist, and artist.

Nancy Cunard (2, rue Le Regrattier): English poet, heiress, editor of *Negro* anthology, and publisher of the Hours Press.

Stuart Davis (50, rue Vercingétorix, 1928–29): American artist.

Dingo Bar (10, rue Delambre, beginning 1924): Hangout for American expatriates.

John Dos Passos (45, quai de la Tournelle, ca. 1920–21): American novelist.

Isadora Duncan (9, rue Delambre, 1926–27): American dancer.

F. Scott Fitzgerald (58, rue de Vaugirard, 1925): American novelist and chronicler of the Jazz Age; wife, Zelda Fitzgerald.

Ford Madox Ford (32, rue de Vaugirard): English novelist, essayist, and editor of the *Transatlantic Review*.

Ernest Hemingway (74, rue du Cardinal-Lemoine, 1922; 74, rue du Bal Musette, 1922–23; 113, rue Notre-Dame-des-Champs, 1924–26; 6, rue Férou, 1927): American novelist.

Hours Press (15, rue Guénégaud, 1929–32): Founded by Nancy Cunard; published Ezra Pound, Laura Riding, and Samuel Beckett.

Le Jockey (127, boulevard du Montparnasse): A transatlantic hangout run by painter Hilaire Hiler.

James Joyce (5, boulevard Raspail, 1920; 71, rue du Cardinal-Lemoine, 1921–22): Revolutionary Irish novelist.

Mina Loy (11, rue Campagne-Première, 1923–1930s; studio on rue du Colisée): English poet and artist.

Man Ray (studio at 31, rue Campagne-Première, 1922–23; studio at 8, rue du Val-de-Grâce, 1929): American photographer and painter.

Robert McAlmon (8, rue de l'Odéon, 1922–26): American writer, publisher of Contact Editions (1923–29), financed by his wealthy wife, Bryher. Contact published Stein, Hemingway, Mina Loy, and William Carlos Williams.

Gerald and **Sarah Murphy** (23, quai des Grands-Augustins; studio at 69, rue Froidevaux): Gerald was an American painter and set designer; both were transatlantic hosts.

Cole Porter (13, rue Monsieur, throughout the 1920s): American composer; lived with **Linda Lee.**

Ezra Pound (rue de Seine and 70 bis, rue Notre-Dame-des-Champs) American poet, editor.

Shakespeare and Company (8, rue Dupuytren, 1919–21; 12, rue de l'Odéon, throughout the 1920s): Run by Sylvia Beach, this bookshop and lending library was a center of transatlantic literary activity. Beach published James Joyce's *Ulysses* in March 1922.

Le Select (99, boulevard du Montparnasse, beginning 1925): Expatriate gathering spot.

Gertrude Stein (27, rue de Fleurus, throughout the 1920s): American writer; lived with **Alice B. Toklas.**

Virgil Thomson (20, rue de Berne, 1922–23 and 1925–26; 17, quai Voltaire, 1927–40): American composer and music critic.

The Transatlantic Review (29, quai d'Anjou, beginning 1923): Magazine edited by Ford Madox Ford, with Ernest Hemingway (briefly) as unpaid assistant; published Pound and Eliot and serialized Stein's *The Making of Americans*.

transition (6, rue de Verneuil, 1927–1930s): Magazine published by Eugene and Maria Jolas; published Stein and Joyce.

(Acknowledgments to Kiki's Paris: Artists and Lovers *by Billy Kluver and Julie Martin)*

and called "Maxims of a Modernist," show Thomson-on-the-brink-of-Paris as a canny, irreverent, pugnacious young man. He must not diminish the Gallic hardness he had worked so hard to develop, he had earlier written a friend: "It *is* my virtue."[10] At this early stage, Thomson articulated his own strategy: "As for the fighting spirit and strength, etc. don't *fight in* every battle you see. Concentrate on a few. But don't avoid them all."[11]

During his first and second trips to Paris, Thomson quickly infiltrated the city's avant-garde and came to know the newest generation of writers, artists, and musicians. Through his friend Bernard Faÿ he met Jean Cocteau and the composers grouped together as Les Six (Georges Auric, Darius Milhaud, Francis Poulenc, Arthur Honegger, Louis Durey, and Germaine Tailleferre). Erik Satie was the composer who interested him most, but Satie died before Thomson could "get inside" his music. In his capacity as a music reviewer, Thomson attended ballets by the Ballets Suédois and heard performances of Debussy, Schoenberg, and Berlioz. At fashionable bars he ate thick *foie gras en croute* and despite his lack of money learned to drink champagne for luxury and whiskey for style. He knew but rarely frequented Montparnasse, where the American expatriates settled, as it reminded him too much of Greenwich Village. He browsed at Sylvia Beach's Shakespeare and Company, where he was soon granted free book-borrowing privileges and invited to readings where he met James Joyce, Ernest Hemingway, e.e. cummings, and Ezra Pound.

During his periods of intense composing, Thomson's vicarious social life depended on the stories of his roommate, Eugene McCown, a Missourian painter who played piano from ten P.M. until two A.M. at the recently opened Le Boeuf sur le Toit. This was "the rendezvous of Jean Cocteau, Les Six, and *les snobs intellectuels*," as Thomson described it, "a not unamusing place frequented by English upper-class bohemians, wealthy Americans, French aristocrats, lesbian novelists from Roumania, Spanish princes, fashionable pederasts, modern literary and musical figures, pale and precious young men, and distinguished diplomats towing bright-eyed youths." Hearing of this world close up but secondhand, gaining entrance to Paris salons through his friendship with Bernard Faÿ, Thomson began to understand the Parisian interconnections among bohemia, art, aristocracy, and money.

Thomson's new life in Paris was not all social. He set about composing by prescribing for himself two practical methods. The "unrest cure," consisting of high living, rich food, and irregular hours as an avenue for getting new ideas, was followed by the "rest cure," a period of carrying out these ideas in disciplined and ascetic regularity.[12] And so his raucous Parisian social life was followed by midwestern industry, counterpoint practice, and music composition.

His music teacher, Nadia Boulanger, provided rigorous instruction in counterpoint and harmony. Boulanger's fourth-floor apartment at 36, rue Ballu, became the center for young American composers, beginning with Thomson's generation and continuing decades later to Philip Glass's. Looking back on her life when she turned seventy-five, Thomson observed, "Being midwife to developing musical nations would seem to be her basic role."[13] In the 1920s, she invited selected students, including Aaron Copland and Walter Piston, to take tea and cake each Wednesday afternoon, after which they would perform modern scores by Stravinsky and Schoenberg. Although Thomson later derided her musical taste as sentimental and rejected her maternal advances, she helped engender his self-confidence in composing. "Nadia made me understand that writing music was like writing a letter," he wrote. "All you had to do was to say what you had to say clearly and stop."

|||

One who studied with Boulanger, shared a room with the pianist at Le Boeuf sur le Toit, and knew Les Six, Sylvia Beach, and Jean Cocteau could not be described as unconnected. But Thomson was not a joiner, a disciple, or a celebrity. "I shall practice my trade," he wrote to Briggs Buchanan in anticipation of his Paris life. "If I practice it competently, I shall make money."

Thomson's 1925 arrival in Paris—after three years' absence—proved to be tense and difficult, and he described his first month as "miserable." He had an unrelenting cold in the chest; his baggage was lost in transit; he had neither satisfactory room, heat, nor piano; he missed two article deadlines; and a street hustler he picked up gave him a black eye. But he did not wallow in his misfortune. In a characteristic mix of pluck and denial, he applied himself to his trade by beginning to compose a symphony. He evoked his world brilliantly in a letter written a few months before meeting Gertrude Stein and Alice B. Toklas:

> 1920 is finally démodé and there is nothing to take its place. *Surrealism* has not been as fecund as one hoped. Everyone has gone

out hunting for an idea. Gide has gone to Africa. Étienne de Beaumont to America, Stravinsky (at last) to Russia. I, for one, welcome a dull season. I shall probably work from *ennui*. Nadia and I are engaged in a search for my character. With usual clairvoyance she comes right to the point at the second interview. "In spite of the fact," she says, "that I am acquainted with you as a talented musician, a charming person, and an incredibly intelligent young man, I have the feeling of not knowing you at all inside." Imagine the effect of that on an already turbulent and unhappy mind.

A few months earlier, in his "Maxims of a Modernist," Thomson had discriminated between love and affection: "Love is the anticipation of a successful marriage. Affection is the feeling we entertain toward persons who are useful to us in a more limited way." Using his own definitions, he experienced both that fall, thanks to a fortuitous encounter over coffee on the terrace of the Deux Magots. Thomson recognized at the adjoining table the attractive features of Maurice Grosser. He had met Grosser at Harvard's Liberal Club a few years earlier, but they hadn't been more than acquaintances. It was not until his season of crisis in Paris that he pursued the relationship. Seven years younger than Thomson, Grosser was a nonpracticing Jew from Huntsville, Alabama, who had come to Paris to paint. He consorted with modernists but painted technically assured figurative canvases that were not overtly modern; this avoidance of the current fashion was one of their only points in common. Virgil was sharp, Maurice was soft-spoken; Virgil was pudgy, Maurice was sinewy; Virgil delivered opinions ex cathedra, Maurice withheld judgment; Virgil was ordered, Maurice messy; Virgil self-assured, Maurice fidgety and insecure; Virgil homespun, Maurice courtly; Virgil felt discomfort about his homosexuality, Maurice reveled in his sexual feelings. Before the year was out, Thomson invited Grosser to share a tiny upper-floor flat overlooking the Seine. It had no bath and barely enough room for an upright piano, but in the corner was a small double bed. It was there, Grosser later recalled, that "Virgil and I shared many passionate moments together."[14]

Although Thomson described Grosser's domestic affection that first winter as pleasant, he wrote to Buchanan, "Mental intimacy impossible, however." But Christmas Eve of 1925 marked the beginning of a sort of marriage that lasted for sixty years. Thomson liked to boast of "26 years of

Left to right: Nadia Boulanger's students—Virgil Thomson, Walter Piston, Herbert El-well, and Aaron Copland—before a concert, 1926.

sex" with Maurice. After that ended they remained close friends and continued to talk constantly, until Grosser died from AIDS complications in 1986.

Thomson's second fateful encounter took place on the rue de l'Odéon at Shakespeare and Company, where he stumbled across a photograph of George Antheil. Four years younger than Thomson and an ardent self-promoter, Antheil already possessed a high profile; Thomson later described him as "the literary mind's idea of a musical genius—bold, bumptious, and self-confident." His piano concert two years earlier at the Théâtre des Champs-Élysées had caused an uproar, and Ezra Pound had found him worthy of a book entitled *Antheil and the Treatise on Harmony*. Thomson soon met him in the flesh and they quickly became allies. Both composers were out of step with the musical establishment, as Antheil recalled, "in that we both returned to a direct simplicity almost Satie-like in its complete cut away from the prevailing Debussy-Ravel-plus-early-Stravinsky mode of the day."[15] Their connection was cemented by their mutual marginality. Antheil urged Thomson to stop writing and devote himself full-time to composing: "I believe in you more than I believe in certainly any other American, and perhaps even a lot more of other nationalities."

Thomson's alliance with Antheil didn't last long, but it started the chain of events that led to *Four Saints in Three Acts*. Curious about so high profile a composer, Gertrude Stein invited Antheil to visit her house. Antheil, in turn, knowing of Thomson's interest in her writing, invited him to come along. The two composers crossed the Luxembourg Gardens to 27, rue de Fleurus, where this story began, as Alice opened the wooden door and ushered them into the canvas-filled studio.

CHAPTER 3

Virgil and Gertrude
Write an Opera

A few months after he met her, Virgil Thomson wrote to a friend, "Gertrude Stein has been impressive and unconsciously encouraging. She takes for granted many of the same things that I do." He had just finished setting to music her early poem "Susie Asado," but he was not yet satisfied enough to show it to her. He pursued his goal cautiously. "I didn't want to be pushy or anything but casual about it," he recalled. "I thought I would just wait and see what happened." He was especially sensitive to Alice's coolness toward him. Understanding that friendship and reputation were linked, he did not contact the two women again until he had made his musical debut in Paris. Although he lacked the fame and repertory to sustain a full evening of his own compositions, he was pleased to be included in a special concert devoted to young American composers. Sponsored by the Société Musicale Indépendente, the concert was dominated by students of Nadia Boulanger—including Aaron Copland, Walter Piston, Theodore Chanler, and Herbert Elwell—and Thomson successfully lobbied to include his friend and supporter George Antheil. The concert offered Thomson the ideal vehicle for promoting his career: the audience included both musicians and intellectuals, Americans and French. His dissonant *Sonate d'Église* drew more attention that evening than any other piece. Some in the audience even whistled. "My Church Sonata has had rather a *succès de scandale*," he reported. "Musicians, Catholics, and atheists were pleased. The unbelieving were shocked."

His musical stock on the rise, Thomson sent Gertrude Stein and Alice Toklas a postcard. In early December 1926, he sent another note to "Miss Stein" asking if she was in Paris and if he could visit.

Thomson was invited to an intimate Christmas Eve party at 27, rue de Fleurus to honor their visiting friend Sherwood Anderson. In a reluctant bow to "getting modern," the two women had just installed electric radiators, which, added to a roaring fire, made the atelier toasty warm. Anderson appeared in a stylish scarf, and the small assembled group sang carols, flanked by a Christmas tree and a large cake, decorated with ribbons and blazing with candles. That party was only one of Virgil's holiday celebrations. He counted two Christmas dinners ("turkeys from Lyon as big as sheep and plum puddings from London and mince pies from a swell nigger-restaurant"),[1] an eggnog party, and a dance with the hard-drinking Montparnasse set at Nancy Cunard's.

This "unrest cure" was followed by several days of the "rest cure" that yielded his most productive periods: "Excepting for the Xmas celebrations now finished and slept off no excitements, no emotion, no drama, no vice," Thomson reported. "No artists, no snobs, and no thrills. Not even people. . . . Only simple behaving and quiet working, and not thinking to speak of."

|||

Thomson came out of seclusion on New Year's Day and walked through light rain from rue de Berne to 27, rue de Fleurus. He carried with him his musical composition for soprano and piano, "Susie Asado," and a note: "Here is a New Year greeting from my own mechanical bird. . . . It is a beginning."[2] Thomson had long imagined Stein's words set to music and this first completed song, ninety seconds long, was lyric, playful, and funny.

"Gertrude was wonderful to set to music because there was no temptation to illustrate the words," Thomson observed. "For the most part you didn't know what it meant anyway, so you couldn't make it like birdie babbling by a brook or heavy heavy hangs my heart. My theory being, and I still hold it to be true, you had to set it for the way the grammar went and for the clarity of the words. If you make the words clear for pronunciation, then the meaning will take care of itself."

When Thomson knocked on the large wooden door with "Susie Asado" in hand, Hélène, the maid, informed him that no one was in. He left the musical manuscript with her. Alice and Gertrude were actually at home (but not At Home), engaged in a task that could not be interrupted: Alice was cutting Gertrude's hair. Never having done so before, Alice sheared warily and fastidiously all day long. Calmly reading, Gertrude made a discovery that afternoon: "I found that any kind of a book if you read with glasses and somebody is cutting your hair and so you cannot keep the glasses on and you use your glasses as a magnifying glass and so read word by word reading word by word makes the writing that is not anything be something. Very regrettable but true." This activity proved less mundane than it sounds, for it gave rise to the new look that Gertrude would retain for the rest of her life. It also gave rise to Ernest Hemingway's theory that the haircut marked "a turning point in all sorts of things."[3]

Near the end of the marathon session Sherwood Anderson turned up and found his friend looking remarkably different. There was now only a cap of iron-gray hair adorning her monumental skull. Anderson observed that Gertrude now resembled a monk; the two women were pleased. (When Picasso saw the haircut a few days later he sputtered, "And my portrait," but then gazed at his painting of Stein, recovered his composure, and said, "After all it is all there.") Others soon applauded Stein's new appearance—there are many references by correspondents to her looking "beautiful." Stein looked ever more like an imperial ruler; she had become the modernist patriarch.

Hemingway linked her haircut to the onset of menopause and the beginning of her new "patriotism" about homosexuality. In Hemingway's retrospective interpretation, Stein began to believe that only homosexuals were capable of creativity, and he claimed that she tried to convince him that he was a latent homosexual. "She lost all sense of taste when she had the menopause," he wrote after she died. "Suddenly she couldn't tell a good picture from a bad one, a good writer from a bad one, it all went phtt."[4]

Meanwhile, on that first day of 1927, Hélène delivered Thomson's musical manuscript. Alice, who could read music without the aid of a piano, announced her pleasure in the song and Gertrude was gratified at seeing her words set to music for the first time. She immediately dispatched a letter to Thomson:

> I like its looks immensely and want to frame it and Miss Toklas who knows more than looks says the things in it please her a lot and when can I know a little other than its looks but I am completely satisfied with its looks, the sad part was that we were at home but we were denying ourselves to everyone having been xhausted by the week's activities but you would have been the xception you and the Susie, you or the Susie, do come in soon we will certainly be in Thursday afternoon any other time it is luck but may luck always be with you and a happy New Year to you
>
> always
> Gertrude Stein.

It was Stein's first letter to Thomson and signaled an opening of the friendship. Stein also wrote a more private reaction to that day. During the winter of 1926–27 she was making frequent entries in a notebook that she later titled A Diary. "I like to be told not to go to the door. It is very nice to have words and music and to see them at the same time when by accident it is where they need it best. Most and best." In this brief passage we learn both that Alice told Stein not to go to the door and that Stein seemed genuinely and immediately open to the idea of music enhancing her words.

|||

Setting Stein's words to music freed Thomson's musical development from the dictates of Nadia Boulanger, from conventions learned at Harvard, and from the fashion of dissonant modernism. "I had no sooner put to music after this recipe one short Stein text," Thomson recalled, "than I knew I had opened a door."

That door was both musical and social, for his gift of "Susie Asado" provided the catalyst for his new friendship. When Gertrude Stein's *petits bleus* contained warm messages from "Alice" (no longer "Miss Toklas"), he interpreted it as a most hopeful sign that he would be admitted to the inner circle. As snatches from Gertrude's "A Diary" indicate, Virgil became a regular visitor that January and February: "the day before Virgil was asked and the day before Virgil was asked," and later, "Everyday a little greeting from Virgil."[5] Even Hélène, the maid, wondered why Virgil was asked to stay for dinner so frequently. By the end of February he set another Stein text, "Preciosilla," to music, perhaps as a means of ensuring his place in Stein's affections in preparation for the most important question: Would she write an opera libretto that he could set to music?

Thomson proposed the opera at a moment when Stein was especially open to the prospects of collaboration. In her notebooks of 1927, Stein wrote, "Collaborators collaborators tell how in union there is strength."[6] Is it a rhetorical command? A statement of confident faith? A means of seeking self-assurance? Around the time she wrote this, she discussed the possibility of collaborating with Pablo Picasso on *A Birthday Book*, to be published by the art dealer Daniel-Henri Kahnweiler. With Sherwood Anderson she had discussed the possibility of creating a joint volume about Ulysses S. Grant, and her statement about collaboration includes puns on "U.S." Grant in "union." Both potential collaborators were old friends, and both possessed a brighter public profile than Stein. Stein's six-year bond with Anderson—shortly after Sylvia Beach had introduced them, Anderson had written an appreciative preface to *Geography and Plays* in 1922—was especially useful at this moment. His novel *Dark Laughter*, although of negligible literary value, had recently gone through eight printings in its first nine months. At this point in the career of Stein, who had stacks of manuscripts sitting in a large armoire, joining forces might increase the chance of seeing those manuscripts published. Yet neither of these two projects ever moved beyond the planning stages.

A few months earlier, Kahnweiler had commissioned and published a limited edition of Stein's *A Book Concluding with As A Wife Has A Cow. A Love Story*, with four lithographs by Juan Gris. (One couldn't say "illustrated by" Gris, for his work was conceived independently.) From 1923 to May 1927, Gris and Stein developed an increasing intimacy, but only on the page. They did not meet once during the entire collaborative process. Nonetheless, the experience was positive for Stein, who declared it "perfect."

An opera was a different story. "She was not by nature what we would call musical," Thomson observed. "She used to say music is for adolescents."[7] The composer, not Stein, would be the one to gain by the association, and members of her inner circle were not universally fond of Thomson. His waspish wit could be bullying, his unmitigated self-confidence exhausting. Alice was observed "darting little poisoned arrows whenever she could." Years later she tartly remarked that "the young Virgil showed sweetness and light only in his music."[8] Pavel Tchelitchew, a reigning favorite in Stein's court, dismissed him as a *"malin"* (smart aleck), while his lover, pianist Allen Tanner, judged his music superficial. But Gertrude defended Thomson. "He frosts his music with a thin layer of banal sounds to put people off, but what's underneath is very pure and special," she said. "You can say what you want, you will hear of Virgil Thomson yet."

By March, Gertrude agreed to collaborate. But how would she and Virgil Thomson agree on a subject? Thomson recalled that they divided the task in an apparently balanced way: Virgil suggested the opera's theme, and Gertrude chose its setting and dramatis personae.

Thomson proposed the theme of "the working artist's life, which is to say, the life we both were living." Although he never intended the opera to be a twentieth-century *La Bohème*, he wanted to take off from an experience that was common to both librettist and composer. Stein embraced the theme and endowed it with religious reverberations; she believed that the purity of the artist's devotion to art reflected the immaculate conditions of the religious life, that genius was analogous to sainthood, and that artists and writers expressed contemporary spirituality before it appeared in the society at large.

Determining how to embody that theme proved more difficult. As Thomson recalled, he ticked off some historical precedents in music: "I thought we ought to start where opera started, Italian opera seria, which has a serious mythological subject with a tragic ending. After Wagner had covered the field of German and Scandinavian mythology, we'd best stay out of that. But history exists in our mind as mythology—after all, the difference between Little Red Riding Hood and George Washington isn't all *that* great." Since American history fascinated Stein, she suggested that the opera be built around George Washington: Thomson vetoed the idea on the grounds that eighteenth-century characters in wigs all look alike. "Eventually we had come to saints," Thomson recalled. "Spanish saints might be just fine."

"In American religion there are no saints and no shrines," Stein pointed out. "There is no Heaven, because there is only 'up.'"[9] She repeatedly described *Four Saints* as an opera about Spain and the Spanish landscape. The opera's geography was not literal, but Spain provided Stein

Virgil Thomson and Gertrude Stein examine the score of *Four Saints in Three Acts*, ca. 1929.

with a field of associations, a rich interior landscape. Spain signified her two dearest friends, Picasso and Gris, who were emblematically modern. "Cubism is a purely Spanish conception and only Spaniards can be cubists," she wrote. Since Stein always considered her own writing a manifestation related to Cubism, writing about Spain became a way of writing about herself.

Stein also saw a comparison between America and Spain. "Americans," she wrote, "are like Spaniards, they are abstract and cruel. They are not brutal they are cruel."

Finally, Spain recalled the golden summer of 1912, when she and Alice had traveled through Spain, visiting Madrid, Avila, Toledo, and Barcelona. In the church of Saint Teresa at Avila they had seen a chapel covered in beaten gold and ornamented in coral. In a nearby shop they had found pastries arranged and mounted in caramel and meringue to resemble the cathedral. This fantasy landscape so fascinated Alice that she announced, "I am enraptured with Avila and I propose staying." Stein decided to feature Saint Thérèse as the opera's central figure. Saint Thérèse is simultaneously an evocation of Alice and of Stein, the mystic bride of Jesus transformed into the bride of Art. ("Thérèse" was one of Gertrude's nicknames for Alice, which explains Stein's decision to use the French spelling.)

Saint Thérèse would be matched with Saint Ignatius Loyola, although the two had lived in different centuries and thus had obviously never met. Thomson was uneasy about the lack of historical connection and at one point suggested, "Let's scrap Loyola and find a real rival."[10] But he soon overcame his qualms about historical inexactness, thanks in part to his "joke theory" that good things came in twos. The idea of "complementary pairing" appeared in his letters of the time and much later in his autobiography.[11] That spring of 1927, Thomson gave his fullest expression to the dualities that ruled Paris:

> Bérard, Joyce, and Antheil stand for representation, depiction, emotion, the "true to life" effect. Their shapes are borrowed. Tchelitcheff, and Gertrude and I represent play, construction, interest centered in the material, nonsense, magic, and automatic writing. Between the tabloid newspaper and Mother Goose. Between culture and anarchy. The law and the prophets. Kant and Spinoza. Duty and pleasure. The stage and the home.

Within Thomson's broad thematic conception Gertrude was able to find an arena of her own interest. On March 26, 1927, she wrote to Thomson that she had "begun Beginning of Studies for an opera to be sung. . . . I think it should be late eighteenth-century or early nineteenth-century saints. Four saints in three acts. And others."

||||

In Spain in 1913, Gertrude Stein had begun to write plays, and even at that time her conception of theater subverted nearly everything one expected from an evening at the theater. There was no story to follow. Lines were often unassigned, a character could be animate (a person) or inanimate (a city, a telephone). There was no sequential time, only the continuous present. As she wrote shortly before beginning the opera, "Never describe as a narrative something that has happened."[12] A play could be a list, a group of objects, sentences.[13]

At the time she began *Four Saints*, she had not written a play for four years and had not attended the theater for much longer—and she had never written "an opera to be sung." She drew from early memories of live performances in the theater, the opera house, and the circus. As a child she had attended "twenty-five-cent" operas, and during her Radcliffe years she had briefly immersed herself in Wagner. But she had subsequently "concluded that music was made for adolescents and not for adults . . . and besides I knew all the opera anyway by that time I did not care any more for opera." In the theater she had seen everything from *Uncle Tom's Cabin* to Buffalo Bill's traveling show to Sarah Bernhardt playing Camille, and she recalled the comfort of hearing Bernhardt declaiming words with no recognizable meaning. It was not the verbal content she recalled but the atmosphere: theater was "like a circus that is the general movement and light and air which any theater has, and a great deal of glitter in the light and a great deal of height in the air."[14]

Stein conceptualized theater as the creation of experience through word constructions, not representations of past experience, anecdote, or plot. She likened *Four Saints* to a landscape, where many elements are presented simultaneously, stretching to the horizon without a center. One discovered it piece by piece rather than following a predetermined path. In 1934, Stein wrote, "In *Four Saints* I made the Saints the landscape. All the saints that I made and I made a number of them because after all a great many pieces of things are in a landscape all these saints together made my landscape."[15] Like the elements of a landscape, she wrote, saints do not *do* anything; they just *are*.

Stein began the libretto in March 1927 in a notebook entitled "Avia," and the first line—"To know to know to love her so"—invokes not only Saint Thérèse but also Alice. This magical touchstone allowed her to overcome her anxiety enough to write (an early line reads, "Come panic come. Come close").[16] Her usually prolific production began at a crawl. She called it "A Narrative of Prepare for Saints." After a month she had completed only five pages of printed text and had been unable to bring the central saints onstage together. Her writing progressed more quickly when Thomson left Paris for a trip to the south of France. Working alone at night, she completed her part of the opera without contact with her collaborator. She filled five notebooks, with about eight lines written on each page, and after Alice typed them up, she sent Thomson the text in mid-June. On June 17, Thomson wrote her, "Thank you for the saints. For each and ever and all."[17]

|||

That April, while Stein was writing her libretto, Thomson was setting to music her three-thousand-word piece "Capital Capitals." Far more ambitious than his setting of "Susie Asado," it functioned as a sort of tryout for composing the opera, and he proudly reported to Stein that "the capitals sound like exactly one million dollars, one full twelfth of a dozen, no less."[18] Linked to Stein's, his career gathered force. That spring, *transition* offered to publish Thomson's settings of Stein. The Duchesse de Clermont-Tonnerre suggested that a performance would be the perfect *divertissement artistique* for her Grande Semaine party on June 21.

Virgil had drilled four male soloists in the antiphonal music for "Capital Capitals" and asked Stein to be present at the rehearsals ("I do need your moral effect on the singers").[19] The duchesse held her costume party in the garden behind her eighteenth-century gatehouse, with a quartet of hunting horns hidden behind the bushes announcing the guests' arrivals along paths lit by blue cup candles and Chinese lanterns in the trees. Thomson described the guests: "All French people at the duchesse's. More dukes than you could see for the ambassadors. Not the Princesse crowd. Cocteau came to see me more or less as their representative, I presume." Virgil and the soloists performed "Capital Capitals" promptly at 11:30; the performance lasted exactly twenty minutes. As one of the singers had not shown up, Virgil sang the part while playing the piano. The music was vaguely interdenominationally sacred; it reminded actress Fania Marinoff of a Jewish synagogue, caricaturist Miguel Covarrubias of a Mexican church, and Jean Cocteau of the Catholic liturgy. Cocteau commented, "At last a table that stands on four legs, a door that really opens and shuts."

Gertrude and Alice had delayed their departure for Belley in the south of France for a month. Stein reported to Thomson that the wait had been worthwhile: "We are happy about your music, and it means a lot to me that I like the variations and the children as much as the Capitals. We are both happy about it this Alice and I are."[20]

When Virgil Thomson received Stein's libretto in June 1927, he turned the text over and over in his head. "Anything can be set to music," he later asserted. "A text may be in prose or in verse or in some style in between. . . . It can also be as clear as a love-call, as obscure as the transcript of a mystical state, as abstract as an exercise for vocal practice." That said, Thomson was overwhelmed by the magnitude of his task. Since Stein had not consistently assigned parts to individual singers, the libretto looked to him like "one compact mass of words."[21] With her words unlinked to their usual place in sentences, their sense meaning gone, without narrative shape or links to identifiable emotion, he was forced to rely on sound and rhythm. He later wrote that the text added up "to a quite impressive obscurity." Essential to the collaboration was Thomson's absolute respect for that obscurity: "The two things you never asked Gertrude, ever, were about her being a lesbian and what her writing meant."

||||

Stein's subsequent comments about the opera allow one to track some of her associations. Lines about her two lead saints, for example, were inspired by things she saw in a store window: still photographs of a girl becoming a nun evoked Saint Thérèse, while a figurine represented Saint Ignatius. Repeatedly asked to explain the opera's most quoted passage—"Pigeons on the grass alas"—Stein responded straightforwardly:

> That is simple I was walking in the gardens of the Luxembourg in Paris it was the end of summer the grass was yellow I was sorry that it was the end of summer and I saw the big fat pigeons in the yellow grass and I said to myself, pigeons on the yellow grass, alas, and I kept on writing pigeons on the grass, alas, short longer grass short

longer longer shorter yellow grass pigeons on the grass pigeons large pigeons on the shorter longer yellow grass, alas pigeons on the grass, and I kept on writing until I had emptied myself of the emotion. If a mother is full of her emotion toward a child in the bath the mother will talk and talk and talk until the emotion is over and that's the way a writer is about an emotion.[22]

She described a passage about "a magpie in the sky" as a vision of the Holy Ghost. The magpies in Avila looked as if they were standing stationary and flat against the sky, she explained, so that they resembled the bird that symbolizes the Holy Ghost in Annunciation pictures .

After years spent studying Stein's texts, scholar Ulla Dydo wrote of the opera, "Spain and Picasso and Gris and mortality and visions and art and singing, the saint's death to the world and the life in Christ—it all comes simply and essentially together."[23] However richly Stein's themes and references resonated in her own mind, her system of signification was private; Edmund Wilson described her writing as "registering the vibration of a psychological country like some human seismograph whose charts we haven't the training to read."[24] (Even the word portrait that Stein did of Thomson yielded scant meaning to its subject, both at the time it was written and fifty-five years later, when he was questioned by his biographer.)[25]

Thomson decided to set to music everything Stein had written, including her stage directions. He turned Saint Thérèse into two figures so that he could write duets, and he changed the two-syllable Thérèse to Teresa so that he could gain an extra syllable. Stein graciously allowed this, although it altered the rhythm. Thereafter it was Saint Teresa. He assigned lines to lesser characters and created a small, mobile chorus and a larger stationary one, as well as two lay figures, the Commère and Compère, to comment from the sidelines like end men. At the time he received the libretto, Thomson was between flats and consequently had no piano; he improvised the opera in his head. "The saints are singing," he wrote Stein two months before he began composing at the piano. "Gaily praising their maker and trying not to be too catty to one another."[26]

III

Without the narrative and significance usually provided by a libretto, Thomson depended purely on the sounds of Stein's words. He looked to musical traditions that stretched back to medieval times, when the desire to merge words and music had produced liturgical chants tied to the rhythms of Latin. Opera, a later secular version, had first been sung in Italian around 1580, in French by the middle seventeenth century, in German by the late eighteenth, and in Russian by the middle nineteenth. But opera music had not yet been written that comfortably fit the rhythms of English, although a number of composers had attempted it (*pace* Handel). Thomson observed, "It is as if we bore it, all of us, an unrequited love."[27] Thomson saw his task clearly defined: to set spoken American language to music.

On November 1, 1927, Thomson moved into a new flat at 17, quai Voltaire, and rented a piano. The next day he began a regular schedule of composing. Five flights up, Thomson's octagonal flat had all the charms of a bohemian garret without forgoing luxurious living. North light flooded through his high windows onto the golden tan carpet and mahogany Louis-Philippe furniture, and from his window he enjoyed a view of the Louvre, the Opéra, the Sacré-Coeur, and, below him, a small piece of the Seine. In the morning he improvised at the piano; he took a break at noon while his neighbor practiced the violin, and bathed and shaved. Afternoons were spent running errands and walking the city streets, returning at five for more composing and dinner. He went to bed early, rose early, and began his routine all over again.

The day Thomson began composing, he wrote a letter to Briggs Buchanan proclaiming his feeling that Parisian modernism had come to a dead end. What Thomson saw as a dull season ahead had its bright side, however; a crack in the modernist orthodoxy made possible a new generational approach. Thomson was not the only one to believe it was time for something new—the previous January, shortly before Thomson had proposed the opera collaboration to Stein, Jean Cocteau had informed him that a new generation of creators was emerging, and around the same time Marcel Duchamp's mistress, Mary Reynolds, had remarked, "The good chaps are beginning to get together again."

Thomson felt that modernist music—saturated with dissonance, descended from the pre–World War I triumvirate of Stravinsky, Schoenberg, and Debussy—had arrived at its end point. "I had a moment of truth if you wish in which I said, 'This is old-fashioned and there is very little profit to be derived in trying to continue it beyond its recent masters. What I had better do is to write as things come into my head rather than with a preoccupation of making it stylish and up to date, and it was by the discipline of spontaneity, which I had come in contact with through reading Gertrude Stein, that made my music simple."

Thomson drew on his repertoire of musical associations: the patter of Anglican chant and the booming choruses of the Harvard Glee Club, marches and parlor dances, children's games and Gilbert and Sullivan. Most of all he thought of American hymns. "When you reach down in your subconscious, you get certain things," observed Thomson. "When Aaron [Copland] reaches down, he doesn't get cowboy tunes, he gets Jewish chants. When I reach down, I get southern hymns or all those darn-fool ditties we used to sing: 'Grasshopper sitting on a railway track.'" (Thomson did find a problem with his method: "Jingle Bells" frequently crept into his compositions.)

Thomson employed what he called "plain-as-Dick's-hat-band harmony," hymnbook cadences, a single melodic line with plain choral accompaniment. On first hearing, the score sounded simple and folksy. But, one scholar observed, "it is more like a fine, multi-faceted diamond than a simple rectangular transparent window pane."[28] The opening section of the opera, for example, sounds like a waltz vigorously played at a fairground. But it quickly changes to a minor key, and the accompaniment switches meter. What starts off as a waltz soon becomes a musical comment on American rhythms. Beneath its apparently simple surface are finely calculated repetitions of musical phrases associated with syntactical units, bits of neo-Baroque recitative, and melodic lines that shift as the meter shifts. "I'm not a naive composer, you see, and neither was Satie," Thomson later warned. "My simplicity was arrived at through the most elaborate means."

With Stein's words unmoored from syntactical meaning, Thomson's compositional architecture had to shape the theatrical narrative as clearly as possible. His apparent simplicity animated the text and provided shape, climaxes, and stretches of run-along patter. "You can't be advanced all over the place," Thomson remarked. "What that text needs is clarity, and it needs music to help it run along. Obscure as it is, if you add further musical complexities, it is like putting sand in a gear. You don't want to make friction, you want to eliminate friction."

Thomson placed Stein's libretto for Act I on his music rack each morning that November and improvised harmonies on the piano and sang each part. He did not write down a note. "I don't mean that her writing *lacks* music; I mean that it *likes* music," he wrote. When the melodies began to come out the same way each day, Thomson knew it was time to set the work to paper. For the first ten days in December, he sketched his improvisations from memory, setting down the vocal parts and figured bass lines, leaving harmonies for a later point. In just over one month, he finished a performable piano score of the opera's first act.

Thomson invited a dozen carefully chosen friends for a Christmas night champagne and lap supper party. Among the guests were Alice and Gertrude; Henry-Russell Hitchcock and his Harvard architect friend Peter Smith; Tristan Tzara, the former leader of Zurich Dada; and the young French poet Georges Hugnet. Thomson built his lavish meal around three culinary gifts from his patron Mrs. Chester Lasell.[29] Prepared by the former cook for King Edward VII, the box of Christmas goodies included a Stilton cheese soaked in port wine, a *foie gras en croute*, and plum pudding. Thomson added to this a salad of mâche, beets, celery, and peeled walnuts, a huge truffle-embedded chicken aspic creation in the shape of a bird with four wings, and champagne. "It was too beautiful for anything and heavenly to eat," Thomson reported to his sister. But he ate little before sitting down at the piano to play the score he had unconsciously memorized. For half an hour he sang all the saints' parts in his light tenor voice. Given the company, he worried that his music might be dismissed as backward-looking. But when he finished, Thomson recalled that "they had all undergone a musical and poetic experience so unfamiliar that only their faith in me (for they were chosen friends) had allowed them to be carried along, which indeed they had been, as on a magic carpet." Thomson's one-man performance was the first of the many performances that Henry-Russell Hitchcock would dub "the Paris production."

Gertrude Stein's first letter after that Christmas blithely tossed off the opera's first-act premiere. "Otherwise there is no news," she wrote Carl Van Vechten, ". . . and beside I have written an opera and a rather amusing young American is making it put on the stageable."[30]

|||

Thomson's composition of the next acts proceeded so smoothly during that winter and the spring of 1928 that he recalled the period as a blessed point in his life and 17, quai Voltaire, as a magic locale. Money came from his two patrons: Mrs. Chester Lasell sent him $125 a month in appreciation for medical advice that had saved her life, and Gertrude Stein's supporter Emily Chadbourne provided $1,000 to encourage the collaboration. For a brief period, Thomson did not have to worry about money.

Friendships were budding during that period. Visiting writers included André Gide and young Scott Fitzgerald, who drunkenly stood on a stove and nearly toppled off. Bernard Faÿ brought princesses and writers; there were neo-Romantic painters, including Christian Bérard, Eugene and Leonid Berman, and Kristians Tonny; and women including *New Yorker* columnist Janet Flanner [aka Genêt] and Mary Reynolds (Duchamp's companion, known as the American queen of Montparnasse). Thomson played leisurely games of *plafond* (a card game) and ate delicious, cheap meals carried up five flights by an energetic waitress dubbed "Yvonne the Terrible." Thomson's afternoons were filled with leisurely walks through the city with his voluble guide, Henry-Russell Hitchcock, who was in Paris writing his first scholarly pieces on modernist architecture. Thomson had new clothes from Lanvin and a trim waistline, thanks to workouts with a Russian gymnast. He had never composed so assuredly, and the opera proceeded steadily. "Nothing seemed to be going on," Thomson recalled, "because everything was going right."

Thomson took advantage of his career momentum—and the financial largess of his patrons—to organize a concert devoted entirely to his own compositions. Staged on May 30, 1928, at the Salle d'Orgue of the Old Conservatory, the concert included his "Variations and Fugues on Sunday School Hymns," "Capital Capitals," Georges Hugnet's "Le Berceau de Gertrude Stein," and songs set to French texts by the late Duchesse de Rohan. The singers performed perfectly, and both the tony audience and the press responded with lively praise. But silence followed. Thomson was not to be adopted by the French musical tastemakers. (Years later, expressing surprise at Thomson's power as a critic, Darius Milhaud recalled that "in Paris he was just that little man in a dark suit.") Two weeks later Thomson wrote Stein that everyone considered the concert a great success, but there were "no echoes" and the Left Bank cafés were filled with "my American rivals."[31] He would voice his feelings of exclusion from the musical establishment throughout his life, blaming sometimes Jews and at other times "the German-Austrian musical complex" or the Metropolitan Opera, but the theme persisted. "Nobody said so in my presence," Thomson wrote years later about this 1928 concert in Paris, "but I could feel it, smell it, know it for true that my music, my career, my position in the whole time-and-place setup was something the French power group did not choose to handle."

The French musicians of Les Six were friendly but not inviting. The same pleasantly noncommittal response came from that inveterate French career maker Jean Cocteau, who praised Thomson's music but did nothing to promote it. A few years earlier, Thomson had left the womb of Nadia Boulanger's circle of young American composers. Ezra Pound had once suggested to Thomson, "If you stick around with me, you'll be famous," and James Joyce later invited Thomson to compose music for a ballet based on *Finnegans Wake*, but Thomson could not brook Pound's dominating presence, and he rejected Joyce's invitation because he knew that he could not be simultaneously aligned with both Stein and Joyce.

On July 1, 1928, Thomson headed south for a tiny Basque village called Ascain, with the opera's fourth act still to be completed. Each morning he walked closer and closer to the Spanish border, but he refrained from crossing. Along the way he stopped in Catholic chapels with gilded Madonnas and polychrome wooden saints, mass-produced religious charms and brightly painted altars. "This is an extremely God's-country sort of country,"[32] he wrote to Stein on his second day. Three days later he saw San Ignacio (Spanish for Saint Ignatius). Quoting the opera, he wrote to Stein, "And he was handsome and thirty-five between thirty-five and forty-five and alive and he had a black beard and was singing an aria."

After completing the score on July 19, 1928, Thomson finally allowed himself to cross the border into Spain. The landscape reminded him of Texas. "And the Spaniards are all enclosed like Americans and very sad though not about anything in particular and they are very sweet and gentle and they like you," reported Thomson. "They are really very tender."

Although he finished composing the opera in July, he could not hear it on a piano until he returned to Paris in the fall. In Paris he played it over and over and wrote to Gertrude, "And wasn't I surprised it is very swell and full of inspiration and variety and I can only hope it isn't as bad as my contentment would indicate." The opera was completed.

Stein and Thomson's joint creation went against all conventional stereotypes about the collaborative process. Theirs depended on artistic sympathies and trust, but also on privacy and differences. In age and geography, in levels of understanding. "Gertrude was twenty-two years older than I," Thomson observed. "That was a gap big enough for Gertrude and me to talk across. Anything less would have made for difficulties."[33] Stein worked alone and collaborated in the only way that she could imagine, creating a libretto that was uncompromisingly hers. She made no bow to the practical needs of stage production. Thomson composed with minimal consulting. The collaboration was a clean, independent affair. Thomson wrote, "Beauty is not a product of opposing forces, which neutralize each other, but of vector forces, which combine." Years later, he expanded on that theme: "Collaborative art, I knew from instinct and experience, can only give a good result when each man offers to the common theme, through his own working methods and at a proper time, his own abundance. . . . These must come out of each man's own technique. An artist cannot be ordered about or hypnotized, but he can be fecundated by another's faith. Here lies the difference between live art and the commercial, that in live art everybody trusts everybody else."

But an opera unproduced was only slightly more tangible than an opera unwritten. Bravig Imbs, who had heard the "Paris production," expressed a common opinion: "I was pretty certain at the time that . . . he was writing posthumous music. It seemed most incredible in 1928 that an opera by Gertrude would ever go on the boards—just as it seemed incredible that the wave of prosperity should ever break."

A Transatlantic
Love Affair

Written by two Americans living in Paris, *Four Saints in Three Acts* embodied the complex nature of that transatlantic love affair: the mutual fascination between Paris and New York that reached its height at the time of the opera's birth, fueled by the confluence of dynamism and pageantry, high and low, old and new. The best experimental magazines and avant-garde books were published in Paris but written by Americans; the French language heard in Montparnasse was peppered with American slang; the stylish advertisements of the day counseled, "A Lanvin gown in the *tonneau* . . . and the tires by Goodrich."[1] To embrace one's identity as solely French was backward-looking, to be strictly American was provincial; the truly modern were transatlantic. *Four Saints* was American by intention and American in its sound and rhythm. But it could never have been written in America.

Thomson often quipped that he went to Paris in order to write about Kansas City; the distance from home allowed him to discern American qualities more clearly. Stein provided the richest description of the freedom she felt to be American while geographically and culturally separated from her native home:

> It is very natural that every one who makes anything inside them-selves that is makes it entirely out of what is in them does naturally have to have two civilizations. They have to have the civilization that makes them and the civilization that has nothing to do with them. . . . The Renaissance needed the greeks [*sic*], as the modern painter needed the negroes as the English writers have needed Italy and as many Americans have needed Spain and France . . . when it is another civilization a complete other a romantic other another that stays there where it is you in it have freedom inside yourself which if you are to do what is inside yourself and nothing else is a very useful thing to have happen to you and so America is my country and Paris is my home town.[2]

The French and the Americans nurtured romanticized images of each other. The themes of the Old World versus the New, dramatized in the novels of Henry James and Edith Wharton, acquired new dazzle after World War I, when the cult of the new became the rage. Up to that time the romantic composite that signified "America" to Europe was comprised of images of Niagara Falls and the Grand Canyon, Wilbur and Orville Wright, Buffalo Bill, and Thomas Edison. During the 1920s, that classic composite assumed new forms with astonishing rapidity. The reciprocal stereotypes of New York and Paris developed in those years served altogether different purposes: Americans invoked Paris as the site of personal and aesthetic reinvention, while the French invoked New York as the center of a new world order. America's version of Paris meant coming of age, falling in love, finding one's sexual identity, acting out bohemian rebellion: "Paris" became a vital postadolescent stage, a life passage, just as a tour of Italy had been to earlier generations of Germans, French, and English. If "Paris" was a nostalgic watercolor of artists enjoying cheap meals on the bank of the Seine, "New York" existed completely in the present tense. It was big, vibrant, public, and full of possibility. Above all, it was new. "Paris" provided the crucible for modernizing one's self, while "New York" was the crucible for modernizing twentieth-century civilization. "There is a group of lyric poets who think they have composed a poem by writing 'Manhattan,'" one European critic observed. That poem, com-

Al Capone
Arrow collars
Fred Astaire
Automats
Josephine Baker
Barbette
Beauty contests
Billboards
Bobbed hair
Brooklyn Bridge
Burlesque
Cafeterias
Cellophane
Charlie Chaplin
The Charleston
Chewing gum
The Chrysler Building
Cigarette lighters
Coca-Cola
Cocktails (especially sidecars
        and Manhattans)
Comic strips
Cosmetics
Cowboys
"Legs" Diamond
Dime stores
Drugstores
Engineers
Eversharp (pencils)
Elevators
Factories
Flappers
Fords
Frigidaires
Gadgets
Gangsters
Gas stations
George Gershwin

Gillette safety razors
Grain elevators
Harlem
Hollywood
Hot dogs
Hygiene through technology
Indoor plumbing
Jazz
Buster Keaton
Kodak cameras
Krazy Kat comic strip
Charles Lindbergh
Lunch counters
Martinis
Florence Mills
Daily News
Nick Carter detective stories
Nickel-plated cocktail shakers
"Palookas"
Parker pens, especially Duofold
Pistols
Cole Porter
Pullman cars
Quaker Oats
Ragtime
Sailors in bell-bottom pants
Speakeasies
Subways
"Sugar daddies"
Tabloid newspapers
Tap dancing
Frederick Winslow Taylorism and
        industrial efficiency
Texas Guinan
"Toasted" cigarettes
Vim
Waffle irons
Mayor James J. Walker

posed in the wake of World War I, reached its height of popularity in the late 1920s.

Before World War I, the transatlantic pilgrimage had been unidirectional: from New York to Paris. But in the decade between 1919 and 1929, European artists, writers, musicians, and society figures made the reverse crossing; among them were Osbert Sitwell, Lady Mountbatten, Darius Milhaud, Marcel Duchamp, Étienne de Beaumont, Federico García Lorca, the Duchesse de Clermont-Tonnerre, Llewelyn Powys, Fernand Léger, Samuel Courtauld, Frederick Kiesler, Ford Madox Ford, and A. R. Orage. "For the first time," F. Scott Fitzgerald noted, "an educated European could envisage a trip to New York as something more amusing than a gold-trek into a formalized Australian Bush."[3]

A visit to New York was perceived as an assault, a brilliant physical experience: cacophony, size, and brash exhibitionism. It was the first world capital created not on a human scale but on an industrial one. "New York's supreme beauty, its truly unique quality, is its violence," observed French writer Paul Morand. "Violence gives it nobility, excuses it, makes its vulgarity forgettable." The tangible sense of a culture run riot came most intensely to Europeans while visiting Times Square. Here the horizontal tube of subterranean railway met the vertical shaft of skyscraper; men catapulted over one another in an animated Spearmint Gum ad, while red and blue neon proclaimed CHEVROLET; horns honked and light glinted off Checker cabs; a lighted strip of news flashed around the angled New York Times Building. To its visitors the city looked like a cosmic stage theatrically illuminated. One looked west to the stepped-back profile of the McGraw-Hill Building and overhead to blimps trailing long advertisements over the Hudson River. From the piers where Europeans arrived and departed, New York's jagged skyline resolved into a perfectly engineered grid of modernity, inspiring grand metaphors. Architect Erich Mendelssohn regarded its garishness, its gigantism, and its futuristic qualities as signs of a modern-day Babylon, and Salvador Dalí described it as "my Egypt" with soaring pyramids of democracy.

Those who did not experience America in the flesh experienced the New World through the industrial artifacts that invaded French culture, through the new habits of living *"à l'américaine,"* and especially through the movies. Even Gertrude Stein, who never attended a movie throughout the 1920s, observed encroaching Americanism in new bathtubs, jazz, advertising slogans, skyscrapers, and revived interest in sports.

At the time *Four Saints in Three Acts* was being completed, the English-language, Paris-based magazine *transition* asked twenty-four European writers to describe the encroaching influence of "The Spirit of America." En masse, their responses reflect Europe's postwar attitude of attraction-repulsion toward the New World—not only because they saw America's effect on their own civilization but also because Europe seemed to be entering a period of decadence and decline. Some regarded Paris as "an archaeological city," while New York was "inhabited by the strongest race in the world." The French envisioned America as the wave of the future, as inevitable as the changing seasons; one could see the evidence in one's kitchen as well as at the cinema, while sipping a Manhattan or dancing a Charleston, while hearing salty American slang or reading about assembly-line factories. "It is the American rhythm that carries the planet today," concluded Régis Michaud. "It is irresistible, whether you regret it or not."

Remaking their identity in the wake of World War I, Parisians filled the vacuum left by a declining aristocratic social order with a search for "modern" types, such as Wall Street tycoons, flappers, and black dancers. Their elegant accoutrements for daily living, which reflected an age of servants, gave way to technological gizmos. (As writer Marcel Brion observed, "An American kitchen consecrates the defeat of Second Empire furniture.") They embraced the new, raw personal qualities—spontaneity, raucous laughter, and a vigorous gait—that would previously have been considered *de trop*. Describing something as *"très américain"* suddenly became a compliment. "We saw the America they wished us to see," writer and editor Malcolm Cowley recalled in 1934, "and admired it through their distant eyes."[4]

As early as 1909, poet-boxer-polemicist Arthur Cravan wrote from Paris, "To be an American, therefore, is to have a status."[5] But this reverse status invariably represented the French romance with newness or low culture and low life. As for art, George Antheil expressed the widely held belief that America was still in the "baby-garde" stage. The "America" constructed in the European imagination fell into a clear pattern: vulgar over genteel, popular culture over high culture. The Charleston, the Lindy Hop, and hoofing were applauded; "serious" dance was ignored. Vaudeville revues and Josephine Baker's extravaganzas fascinated, while legitimate theater rarely made its way across the ocean. Advertising graphics of gigantic billboards and the shorthand of cartoon strips provided spurs to visual invention, while American painting was rarely shown in French galleries. Jazz and spirituals were heard, along with Cole Porter and Irving Berlin, but few were interested in "serious" American composing. Parisians applauded street slang over parlor diction, tabloid newspapers over literary quarterlies. The French admired the construction technology derived from the repeating regular forms of American grain elevators and factories, but Le Corbusier expressed the prevailing attitude toward architecture: "Let us listen to the counsels of American engineers, but let us beware of American architects."[6] Formal American cuisine was ignored in favor of hot dogs and Coca-Cola. Everywhere the artifice of lowbrow authenticity replaced the artifice of gentility.[7]

|||

Several avant-garde works performed in Paris during this period—including *Parade, Within the Quota,* and *Ballet Mécanique*—portrayed "America" in broad cartoon strokes and primary colors.[8] The French avant-garde thought such stylization resonated with America's brash youthfulness, and these performance works suggest available models for an "American" opera written in Paris. They also embody the signifiers of "America" that Stein and Thomson avoided in creating *Four Saints in Three Acts.*

Parade was produced in 1917 by Sergei Diaghilev, written by Jean Cocteau, designed by Pablo Picasso, composed by Erik Satie, and choreographed by Léonide Massine. Among its characters were the "Little American Girl" and an American sideshow barker. Dressed in a navy-blue sailor suit and white pleated dress bought at the Williams Sportswear Shop, the American girl was inspired by Mary Pickford. She rode a horse, caught a train, drove a Model T Ford, snapped pictures with a Kodak camera, and played cowboys and Indians. The American barker wore a stovepipe hat à la Abraham Lincoln, cowboy chaps on his legs, an oversized holster and gun belt across his chest, a skyscraper on his back, and a train's cowcatcher on his torso. Satie's music (not all used in the first production) evoked Irving Berlin's Tin Pan Alley sound and incorporated mechanical sounds (sirens, typewriters, gunshots, a klaxon).

Within the Quota, produced in 1923 by the Ballets Suédois, with score by Cole Porter, story and set by Gerald Murphy, featured an innocent Swede who travels to New York and encounters a millionairess, a black vaudeville dancer, a shimmying jazz baby, a Prohibition agent, a cowboy, a sheriff, and America's Sweetheart. It ends happily with the principals dancing as movie cameras film them. All of these adventures are performed before a curtain with huge headlines selected to capture the "quintessence of Americanism": ("Boycott All Syndicate Hootch," "Ex-Wife Heart-Balm Love-Triangle," "Unknown Banker Buys Atlantic").[9] The musical inspirations for Cole Porter's ballet score included ragtime jazz, burlesque cadences, a Salvation Army chorale, and taxi horns.

George Antheil, the man who had introduced Thomson to Stein, wrote several homages to America, including a 1930 opera entitled *Transatlantic*. The most famous of them, *Ballet Mécanique*, premiered in Paris in 1926 and in New York in April 1927.[10] The black-and-white backdrop featured a huge spark plug rising against the night sky between two skyscrapers. One American critic called it a representation of America, "a dream of niggers, skyscrapers and glittering polished surfaces, rising up for thousands of feet."[11] The sound was simultaneous and mechanical, and Janet Flanner observed that it sounded like three people at once, "one pounding an old boiler, one grinding a model 1890 coffee grinder, and one blowing the usual seven o'clock factory whistle and ringing the bell that starts the New York Fire Department going in the morning."[12] *Ballet Mécanique* caused a melee between its supporters and detractors in Paris, but New York's audiences were unmoved.

Stein and Thomson knew all three of these performance works, if only by reputation. Some of the collaborators, notably Antheil and Picasso, were close friends, and Satie was a model for Thomson. Yet the opera Stein and Thomson created could not have been more different. It included none of the prevailing signifiers for "America."

Just as Stein's conception of theater subverted all expectations for the theater—characters, sequential time, plot—so Stein and Thomson's opera went against both popular and avant-garde expectations of an "American" work. The setting was not America but Spain; not urban but indeterminately rural. No picaresque tale is told, no anecdotes are given or topical references made. The time is not the present but the distant past. The musical idiom was inspired not by jazz, which Thomson called "our native gin," but by hymns. Yet those present at one of the many "Paris productions" instantly recognized that they were hearing an American opera. (Russian expatriate composer Nicolas Nabokov thought he had just entered a Baptist church.) A year after Stein died, Toklas wrote a friend, "Isn't

Gertrude the essence of U.S.?"[13] Like Gertrude, *Four Saints in Three Acts* was the essence of America, embodying not its anecdotes and history but its sound and structure.

Although she lived in Paris for most of her adult life, Gertrude Stein spoke only rudimentary French. She treasured the vernacular of the American soldiers she met during World War I. Believing that a growing nation in transition spawned the most vigorous speech, Stein claimed that Americans had pioneered modern writing. The monosyllabic rhythms that run through *Four Saints in Three Acts* reflected her belief that Americans had mastered the most basic vocabulary: "Americans can do and express everything yes everything in words of one syllable made up of two letters or three and at most four."[14]

While she believed that American English was burdened by dead nouns attached to even deader adjectives, she discovered other sources of vitality in the language: "In the verbs there is life in the prepositions and adverbs too and very much in the conjunctions. As an example the most vigorous expression in American speech is that composed of two words—'And how.' It is full of emotion and it says everything that needs to be said."[15]

Stein's conception of the theater experience as something always moving also linked the opera to her observation "that it is something strictly American to conceive a space that is filled with moving, a space of time that is filled always filled with moving."[16]

In composing *Four Saints*, Virgil Thomson fashioned his prosody to distinctly reflect the American language. Other Americans had written operas evoking their native land. Like the transatlantic versions of America, they stayed on the surface: wilderness frontier backdrops and Native American life as romantically evoked in Victor Herbert's *Natoma* or Charles Wakefield Cadman's *Shanewis, or the Robin Woman*. When the most recent attempt, Deems Taylor and Edna St. Vincent Millay's *The King's Henchman*, opened at the Metropolitan Opera in 1927, Thomson huffily dismissed it as "a so-called American opera." Thomson evoked his native land by tuning his ear to the rhythms of American speech. Stein's text, Thomson wrote, "forced me to hear the sounds that the American language really makes when sung."[17] Drawing from his bank of musical memories, Thomson summed up his experience composing the opera: "A Jew and a Protestant turn out a Catholic opera about Spain in the 16th century and in the course of writing that music I came into practically total recall of my Southern Baptist upbringing in Missouri."

CHAPTER 5

Virgil Thomson
Visits America

In late November 1928, shortly after celebrating his thirty-second birthday, Virgil Thomson boarded the *Ile de France* in Le Havre, bound for New York. Short, pudgy, and pink-cheeked, he wore a stylish Lanvin black-and-red overcoat, bought in anticipation of his first American winter in four years. For his transatlantic passage, Thomson chose the newest addition to the French line, advertised as "A Step in Advance of the Modernist." Even from his shared third-class cabin, Thomson enjoyed the elegance of transatlantic travel, drinking the ship's complimentary Médoc in the Salon Mixte, and promenading in the open air. He wrote to Stein, "The boat is really very handsome from the toppest pink officer to the lowest Lalique port-holes, in the dining hall there are only the rarest of rare woods and the most variegated india-rubber. Cuties in red trousers run our errands, huskies from below box daily for our pleasure, domestics are of the most amiable, barbers of the most competent, and there are primeurs at table and quails in jelly and foie gras a volante."[1]

From the deck of the *Ile de France* Thomson took in Manhattan's changing silhouette. Midtown skyscrapers now complemented lower Manhattan's lofty man-made peaks. Observing the increasingly vertical profile of the city, the novelist and critic Carl Van Vechten wrote to Stein that "towers have sprung up on every hand, until New York begins to resemble in the twilight a greater and more glittering San Gimignano."[2] The new skyline featured vertiginous slabs, some stripped of all ornamentation, and the Waldorf-Astoria—a victim of Prohibition and the decline of fashionable society that had filled its glittering and now empty ballrooms —was about to be demolished, to be replaced by the tallest building in the world, the Empire State Building.

Watching the comings and goings of the transatlantic set was one of the social pastimes of the era, when Walter Winchell and other gossip columnists made a business of identifying prominent voyagers. Thomson's professional stature did not yet merit appearance in such columns, and he was largely ignored as he descended the gangplank in New York. In America, Thomson hoped to ferret out promising production venues and sources of financial support for the opera. Whose hand should be held, whose bottom tweaked, whose ear engaged, whose pocket invaded? The biggest question of all: Was America ready for a modernist opera?

On arrival, Virgil Thomson reported to Gertrude Stein that New York's bootleg liquor had improved. This was only one symptom of the city's stylish hedonism at the height of its prosperity, less than a year before the stock market crash altered everything. *Vanity Fair*'s advertisements reflected the drive that many newly prosperous American consumers felt to modernize themselves stylishly. Lord & Taylor announced that it was "ready to design modern [furniture] ensembles to meet the individual needs of its clients," the new Childs restaurant on Lexington Avenue billed itself as "modernistic," the Dynamique Creations firm offered, as alternatives to Sheraton and Hepplewhite, modern furniture that reflected "the vivid personalities of a new American people," while the venerable purveyors of sterling silver Reed & Barton were promoting a new line in which "modern decoration are applied, *sensibly*." The cautious approach implied by the advertisement's italics signaled the limits of America's embrace of modernity. In the name of fashion, progressive New Yorkers were ready for the new—but they were unlikely to embrace anything more modern than Art Deco. The baffling spectacle that Thomson wanted to bring them was a long step beyond the safe newness of stylish decors.

At the moment of Thomson's arrival, New York was anything but the cultural center of the world. Thomson ranked its musical milieu inferior to those of Berlin, Paris, Vienna, Prague, and Rome. "Coming from Paris to the United States is like going from Paris to Spain," he later observed. "New York and Barcelona are not capitals. They are large sea-ports, jumping-off places for Europe, receiving points for foreign merchandise, centers of violence and talk."[3]

A few monied collectors were building collections of modern art—within a year three of them would found the Museum of Modern Art—but the number of commercial modern art galleries was in decline. The robust community of artists and writers that had provided an audience for the modernist experiments of the 1910s could no longer be assembled, in part because the bohemian nexus provided by Greenwich Village had long ago yielded to commercialism, in part because many of the more enterprising writers, artists, and musicians had left for the cheaper and more convivial artistic community of Paris. "I spent all my time listening to the whistles of the midnight-sailing liners, and having people come in and get drunk and weep about Paris," wrote Robert Coates, a friend of Gertrude Stein, "until finally I decided that I'd be better off in New York to *be* in New York, uptown, where they wear straw hats and Kupenheimer clothes and read the *Graphic*."[4] The rallying events of the late-1920s avant-garde included such isolated events as the Société Anonyme's 1926 exhibition of modern art at the Brooklyn Museum, the Provincetown Players' 1928 production of e.e. cummings's *Him*, and Jane Heap's Machine Age Exposition of 1927. A pale reminder of the heyday that followed in the wake of the Armory Show, they hardly constituted a robust movement.

|||

In those days, Virgil Thomson's collaboration with Gertrude Stein was much on his mind. He had twice reread her "Portrait of Virgil Thomson," which she had recently written and mailed to him. The portrait opened:

> Yes ally. As ally. Yes ally yes as ally. A very easy failure takes place.
> Yes ally. As ally. As ally yes a very easy failure takes place. Very
> good. Very easy failure takes place. Yes very easy failure takes
> place.[5]

Stein's opening lines reflected her recent alliance with Thomson, and the leading trope was joyfully positive. But the refrain at the end of the paragraph introduced a note of doubt. What might that failure be? Or was Stein simply evoking the truism that it is easy to fail? When Thomson wrote to Stein in early February, he ignored any hints of failure or breaks in the relationship and stuck to the barely decipherable middle paragraph, telling Stein that he enjoyed its texture, a "great variety of sentences and a really concentrated progress in those parts which is I suppose what we mean by profundity or deep thought anyway."[6]

|||

On the evening of February 15, 1929, Thomson embarked on his American campaign for *Four Saints in Three Acts*. Carl Van Vechten had invited a dozen potentially influential guests to hear Thomson sing the opera in the apartment he shared with his wife, actress Fania Marinoff, at 150 West Fifty-fifth Street. "I think you had better come, don't you?" Van Vechten wrote *saloneuse* Muriel Draper. "The audience will be worthy."[7] It included Alma Wertheim and her husband, Maurice Wertheim, patrons of art, music, and theater; composer Max Ewing; and poet Witter Bynner. Salon hostesses were most prominently represented: Muriel Draper, sisters Ettie and Carrie Stettheimer, and the legendary prewar Greenwich Village hostess Mabel Dodge Luhan. Among Van Vechten's handpicked group only Alma Wertheim was directly involved with promoting music. But Van Vechten was an inveterate networker who understood that tastemakers were essential to the success of any cultural enterprise. As Thomson later observed, "Tastemaking is a big show."

Virgil Thomson arrived at Van Vechten's apartment at seven o'clock, the rest of the guests at nine. In the foyer was a mirrored tabletop supported by a kneeling blackamoor youth, a tribute to Van Vechten's highly publicized fascination with African Americans. The guests moved into the drawing room. At a time when modern interiors of the day were tending toward Art Deco combinations of white-painted plaster and shiny chrome, Van Vechten mixed raspberry, purple, and turquoise, and his clutter of ceramic cats, Venetian glass paperweights, and calla lilies on a glass-topped table suggested a happy marriage of the Gay Nineties and the Jazz Age. Once the group had disposed of their most recent gossip, Virgil Thomson sat down at the Knabe piano and sang *Four Saints in Three Acts* in what might be described as the opera's informal American premiere. Many of the guests quickly entered into the spirit of the music. Van Vechten was

Virgil Thomson, photographed by J. Sibley Watson, the publisher of *The Dial*, in his home in Whitinsville, Massachusetts, 1928.

so pleased that Stein's words sounded "so right & inevitable in music" that he cabled Gertrude Stein the next day to announce that "EVERYBODY LOVED IT."

The response was actually more equivocal: Witter Bynner considered the music wasted on the text, while others privately doubted that it could ever be put onstage. "Carl is trying to interest someone to perform it," wrote Max Ewing the next day. "I doubt that anyone will, it is so mad."[8] No one could match the characteristically outsized reaction of Mabel Dodge Luhan: she announced that *Four Saints in Three Acts* would devastate the conservative Metropolitan Opera as completely as Picasso had destroyed the painting of the past.

After the performance, Van Vechten introduced Virgil to Harlem. With a few other guests they taxied nearly one hundred blocks uptown to the Rockland Casino, Uptown's largest dance hall. They made their way to a box overlooking the dance floor to view one of Harlem's most venerable institutions, the annual drag ball, sponsored by Hamilton Lodge No. 710 of the Grand United Order of Odd Fellows. "Of course, a costume ball can be a very tame thing," reported the black social newspaper *The Inter-State Tattler*, "but when all the exquisitely gowned women on the floor are men and a number of the smartest men are women, ah then, we have something over which to thrill and grow round-eyed."[9]

Virgil's party gazed down at the dance floor as a procession of men and a few women promenaded beneath the colossal crystal chandeliers and a sky-blue ceiling. Newspapers estimated that the crowd numbered three thousand. The women were dressed in drab, loose men's suits (not a tuxedo among them), and the men plumbed the possibilities of feminine extravagance. Senoritas in black lace and red fans paraded down the dance floor, followed by a bride in canary satin and calla lilies, soubrettes in backless dresses and huge spangles, and a creature called La Flame, who wore only a white satin stovepipe hat, a red-beaded breastplate, and a white sash. Virgil had attended Mardi Gras drag balls at Magic City in Paris, but he had never seen anything like this. Like Harlem itself, the drag ball offered a racially mixed arena in which propriety was turned on its head. Van Vechten reported to Stein three days later that Virgil "behaved very well, but in spite of that I think he was a little astonished."

After the ball they carried the party to Lenox Avenue, where Van Vechten danced with singer Louis Cole, who was in drag, and then they went on to Pod and Jerry's Cabaret. Along the way, one of Van Vechten's

The façade of the Alwyn Court, which Carl Van Vechten called "the Château Stett-heimer."

black friends picked up a millionaire who offered the party a ride in his sleek Hispano-Suiza. When Mabel Dodge Luhan's remark about *Four Saints* obliterating the Metropolitan was recounted, he wailed, "Mustn't do that, what'll I do on Thursday nights?" (Van Vechten thought the inter-change so perfect that he not only immediately recounted it to Gertrude Stein but also appropriated it for his new—and final—novel, *Parties: Scenes from Contemporary New York Life.*) Reflecting her voracious desire for conventional recognition, Stein wrote to Virgil that she hoped they would "get on the radio and the gramophone yet and have royalties and buy a prize Bedlington terrier and a telephone and pay for my new Ford car, perhaps."[10]

At the opera's first performance, only two of the Stettheimer sisters had been present, for an ironclad rule in the Stettheimer family held that one of the three sisters must remain at home with their mother. On that evening of February 15, the task had fallen to Florine. Ettie insisted that Thomson must meet the absent sister, and within the week she invited him to tea. On February 22, Virgil walked to the southeast corner of Fifty-

Interior of Florine Stettheimer's studio (top) and the Stettheimer apartment at Alwyn Court, site of regular salons from 1915 to 1935. Guests included Marcel Duchamp, Carl Van Vechten, Georgia O'Keeffe, Charles Demuth, Muriel Draper, Leo Stein, Elie Nadelman, Edgard Varese, Marsden Hartley, Henry McBride, Edward Steichen, Alfred Stieglitz, and Paul Rosenfeld (photographs by Peter Juley).

eighth Street and Seventh Avenue, bearing flowers. Standing before the French Renaissance facade of the Alwyn Court, its arched entryway ornamented with sinuous salamanders and cherubs and fleurs-de-lis, Thomson immediately understood why Van Vechten dubbed the Alwyn Court the "Chateau Stettheimer."[11] It would be difficult to outdo the opulence of the Stettheimers' domain, with its gold moldings and glittering chandeliers, undulating folds of red taffeta curtains, crystal punch bowls, and extravagant bouquets. "It was all a kind of camp on elegant New York houses inhabited by artists," recalled Virgil Thomson. "And in their terms it was a kind of joke about the German royal style."

The eight dinner guests arrived precisely at 7:00. At 7:30 they sat down to a dining table laid with antique Italian altar cloths and Crown Derby porcelain, lit by chandeliers. In Van Vechten's words, "it looked like a room in a royal palace."[12] Carrie Stettheimer's seven-course meal began with mushroom timbales, moved to halibut in aspic and poussins in orange and jelly trimming, and concluded two hours later with meringue and fresh strawberries. In addition to Thomson and the Stettheimer sisters, the guests included composer Aaron Copland, artist Georgia O'Keeffe, Van Vechten and Fania Marinoff, publisher Joseph Brewer, art critic Henry McBride, and Theatre Guild producer Philip Moeller.

Another dozen or so people arrived after dinner for the evening's main event. Thomson sat down at the piano and began to sing:

> Four saints are never three.
> Three saints are never four.
> Four saints are never left altogether.
> Three saints are never idle.
> Four saints are leave it to me.
> Three saints when this you see.
> Begin three saints.
> Begin four saints.

Sometimes cracking in excitement, Thomson's flutey voice and precise diction rendered every word hearable, if not decipherable. He sang all the parts—from Saint Teresa and Saint Ignatius on down through Saint Settlement, Saint Plan, and the minor saints. Even played on a single piano, the music was amiable, lively, and evoked a midwestern church. Accustomed to the standards of the Theatre Guild, Moeller reportedly treated the performance as an amateurish musicale and chatted until he was firmly hushed. Thomson reported to Stein that "he was mad he hadn't thought of it himself and he bit his fingernails in fury all during."[13] But the others appeared to be swept along and pressed Thomson for an encore. Virgil complied with a song composed in homage to Gertrude Stein. Set to a suite of six poems by the French poet Georges Hugnet, it was called "Le Berceau de Gertrude Stein, ou Le Mystère de la rue de Fleurus" (The Cradle of Gertrude Stein, or the Mystery of the rue de Fleurus).

The song featured Gertrude drawing her dreams in chalk, driving home in her Ford called Godiva, sitting on a rose-colored sofa. "We've forgotten how to dance," Virgil sang. "Gertrude, Gertrude, Gertrude, we've lost the mood. Gertrude, Gertrude, teach us again how to dance."[14] Each time Virgil sang the heroine's name, it came out exaggeratedly Frenched-up as "Jhairtroodah." The audience laughed, perhaps more at the encore than at the opera, for Thomson took the liberty of hamming up Hugnet's text. Carl Van Vechten and Henry McBride—Americans who had championed Stein's writing for the past sixteen years—were particularly sensitive about the laughter that evening. "We roared with enjoyment," McBride wrote Stein, "but Carl Van Vechten, who sat opposite me, pulled a serious face and shook it at me reprovingly, as though to say, we were not taking it in the right way."[15] McBride also wrote to Stein that he had been most impressed by Thomson's "imperturbability combined with a perfect pitch."[16] Looking back at that evening years after the salon had ended, McBride declared the one-man musicale the most memorable of all the Stettheimer sisters' gatherings.

III

When Virgil Thomson saw Florine Stettheimer's paintings, first at the Alwyn Court tea party and a month later in her studio, he immediately sensed an affinity between her sensibility and that of his new opera. "She was scandalous in the same way that Gertrude was scandalous," he later remarked. "You didn't always know what she was up to." By applying colors over thick impastos of china-white oil paint, she created the sensation of intense light coming from within. Her high-keyed colors, her gilt furbelowed frames, and her willowy figures were sometimes described as naïve, but the more discerning found in her paintings the refined gaiety and humor of Jazz Age Manhattan and the excitement of a Woolworth's window transformed.

Florine Stettheimer, ca. 1930.

Before he met Florine Stettheimer, Virgil Thomson had separately considered Pablo Picasso and Christian Bérard to design the opera's sets and costumes.[17] But when he saw Stettheimer's paintings, he immediately knew that he had found the ideal collaborator. He imagined onstage her bright colors and flashy, spangly textures, radiating the light that reminded the painter Charles Demuth of "our beaches, at noon when the sun blazes in July out of a cloudless sky."[18] Stettheimer would bring neither fame nor stage experience to the collaboration, and she repeatedly expressed ambivalence about participating, but Thomson would not give up.

Years later, when asked to explain the affinity between Stettheimer's paintings and the opera, he said, "Florine's paintings are very high camp, and high camp is the only thing you can do with a religious subject. Anything else gets sentimental and unbelievable, whereas high camp touches religion sincerely and its being at the same time low pop. People who have been cured of an eye disease put little toy eyes in front of a statue of a saint. And then the world of tinsel can only be sincere."

Thomson did not formally invite Florine to join the team until two days before he sailed back to France. He returned to the Alwyn Court and performed the opera for her alone. "He sang the whole," Florine confided to her diary the next day. "He makes the words by Gertrude Stein come alive and flutter and in sound have a meaning. He wants me to do the visual part of the opera."[19]

|||

The Stettheimer sisters' salon provided an ideal site for promoting the opera. The piano was well tuned, the decor opulent and fantastically theatrical, and, most important, the carefully selected audience was both aesthetically adventurous and socially connected. The Stettheimers' crowd barely overlapped with the society patrons who occupied opera boxes at the Metropolitan; gathered here were the supporters of America's avant-garde. The Stettheimers' regular guests included not only McBride and Van Vechten, but Marcel Duchamp, photographer Alfred Stieglitz, Georgia O'Keeffe, critic Paul Rosenfeld, Charles Demuth, and Muriel Draper.

The three sisters—Carrie, Florine, and Ettie—had launched their salon in 1915, after a decade-long sojourn in Europe. Just as they began entertaining, New York became a mecca for wartime expatriate artists and writers who found at the Stettheimers' a style that felt convivial and familiarly Continental.[20] In those early years in New York, Ettie Stettheimer published an intellectual coming-of-age novel called *Philosophy* and enjoyed flirtations with both Marcel Duchamp and sculptor Elie Nadelman. Carrie began furnishing a now-legendary dollhouse whose twelve rooms were filled with needlepointed rugs and carved settees and whose walls

Cut-paper silhouettes of the Stettheimer sisters in a 1933 Christmas card by their close friend artist Carl Sprinchorn. Left to right: Florine, Ettie, Carrie.

such artist friends as Duchamp and William Zorach furnished with minia-ture paintings. Florine had the first solo exhibition of her paintings in 1916 at the Knoedler gallery in New York. As Ettie wrote in her diary that year, these were "exciting days for the Stettheimer family."[21]

One could find adventurous guest lists in other New York salons of the World War I period—Mabel Dodge's or later Muriel Draper's—but only the Stettheimers' lasted from the 1910s to the 1930s. It mixed nine-teenth-century propriety, the opulence of the banking world, and the edgi-ness of twentieth-century modernism. At the center, Henry McBride wrote, the three hostesses "enacted the roles of Julie de Lespinasse, Mme. du Deffand, and Mme de Staël in modern dress."[22] By the time Virgil Thomson entered the orbit of the Alwyn Court, the salon's most adventur-ous period was over. Now in their late fifties, the sisters had settled into an elegant stasis. "They were preserved," Thomson observed, "like royalty."

The sisters' entertaining provided ideal subject matter for each of the three sisters. In Carrie's extravagant dollhouse rooms, in Florine's witty paintings, in Ettie's intellectual *romans à clef*, the Stettheimer sisters por-trayed the court life of America's high-bohemian society that flourished be-tween the wars. Florine described her high-bohemian entourage in a scrap of verse: "Our Picnics / Our Banquets / Our Friends / Have at last a raison d'être / Seen in color and design / It amuses me / To recreate them / To paint them."

III

On March 29, 1929, shortly before 5 P.M., Virgil Thomson again boarded the *Ile de France*. This time he found the corner of his third-class cabin filled with tins of caviar, bouquets, boxes of candy, a bottle of champagne from Florine Stettheimer, and a wire from Carl Van Vechten that read, "HAIL AND FAREWELL DEAR VIRGIL."[23]

During Thomson's four-month stay in the United States, he had renewed many old ties. At his alma mater, the Harvard Glee Club, he performed a scene from the opera, and he reported to Stein that he was no longer considered "a bad boy."[24] On a visit to Kansas City, he absorbed the political wisdom of his ninety-seven-year-old grandfather, caught up with his mending, and asked himself, "I'm home at last and am I glad? All is calm and sweet and quiet."[25]

Most important, Thomson had planted the seeds for America's first grand scale *Gesamtkunstwerk*: he found his first collaborator and converted several vital supporters. Shortly before the composer's departure, Henry McBride wrote to Gertrude Stein, "But Virgil Thomson really is a wonder. I never saw such self-possession in an American before. He is absolutely undefeatable by circumstances. When singing some of the opera to me he was constantly interrupted but never to his dis-ease; he would stop, shout some direction to the servant, and then resume absolutely on pitch and in time. We all pray that the opera will be given."[26]

Act II

TASTE

Young Harvard
Moderns

Although Stein and Thomson created the opera together, the task of getting it onstage fell entirely to Thomson. Stein encouraged from the sidelines but, not surprisingly, did little else. She knew nothing of the world of opera production, and the publication of her complete libretto in the June 1929 *transition* provided her with some sense of completion. In Europe, Thomson tried to promote a production in such disparate venues as the Hessiches Landestheater in Darmstadt, Germany, and a stylish theater in Monte Carlo.[1] Neither plan worked. Where could he go? What doors could he open? In the midst of the Depression, America offered meager possibilities for *any* composer. Thomson casually inquired of the Music Fund whether there were any position for him in his native land. The response was chilling: "I think you are mistaken in supposing that there is a place somewhere for composing as a serious full-time occupation in the present state of American music."[2]

With his canny instinct for cultural politics, Thomson quickly understood that those who supported the progressive edge of high culture in

American art would be found in museums and galleries. "It was the art world that was interested in *Four Saints*," he observed, "not the musical world or the literary world or the theatrical world." No one understood the affinity between Stein's writing, the opera, and the art world better than the art critic Henry McBride. In 1934, he wrote in *The New York Sun:*

> Gertrude, from the beginning, always has been "one of us," to the confusion, at times, of the literary contingency, who never quite understood the frequency of Gertrude's appearance in art journals, and suspected—perhaps not without reason—that we were putting over some of our values on 'em. And Virgil won't mind being adopted by us, either, since his great forerunner, Erik Satie, was always more apt to be encountered in the studios of the artist than in the corridors of the Salle Pleyel; and Virgil himself keeps to a like itinerary and gets more heated in a discussion of Picasso's latest than in a dissection of a new opus by Hindemith. . . . So probably it was inevitable that the artists took him over and decided to own him.[3]

Within the art world resided a constellation of young men, all graduates of Harvard in the late 1920s, who became America's promoters of modernism. Without their efforts, *Four Saints* would not have been produced. Nor would it have achieved the cachet that ultimately made it a popular success.

The key figures among this band of Harvard modernists were Alfred Barr, A. Everett "Chick" Austin Jr., Henry-Russell Hitchcock Jr., Kirk Askew Jr., Lincoln Kirstein, Philip Johnson, and Julien Levy.[4] In letters to one another they referred to themselves as "The Friends" or "The Family," and this suggestion of a sort of cultural mafia was appropriate. This handful of Harvard men set the course of "official" modernist culture in America's most prestigious institutions for nearly half a century.

Their importance to the success of *Four Saints* can be described in terms of concrete contributions—one produced it in his museum, and another organized the salon that became *Four Saints'* clubhouse and purveyor of cultural chic. But their influence extended beyond such tangible contributions. By founding pioneering modernist institutions and disseminating modernist taste, they created the milieu in which the opera could be produced and appreciated. The interaction of the group's many ventures, ranging from ballet to architecture to Surrealism, spurred both creators and audiences. *Four Saints* is best understood as a key element in the complex gestalt promoted by the Harvard modernists: a high point of their enterprise. Philip Johnson called its premiere "the most important night of the decade."

|||

Harvard was an unlikely spawning ground for modernism. The quiet, staid campus hearkened back to its august tradition and was in every way an appropriate backdrop to Charles Eliot's greeting to the incoming freshman class in 1926: "Flee introspection," the ninety-two-year-old former Harvard president counseled gravely. He then died a few days later.[5] Although freshman Lincoln Kirstein misheard his injunction as "Free introspection," the vast majority of Harvard's student body followed his counsel and were studiously trained to avoid the personal, the radical, and the modern. Rich and wellborn, embedded in the archaic social customs of Gold Coast clubs and boiled shirts worn to coming-out parties, "The Lads," as Kirstein called them, were anachronisms out of the nineteenth century.

In the *Harvard Crimson* that fall, Alfred Barr, who was then a graduate student in art history, pronounced himself shocked to find nothing modern in "places which have a deserved reputation as centers as alert cultivation of the Seven Arts."[6] Not a single painting by such masters as Cézanne, Gauguin, Seurat, or van Gogh, not to mention Picasso or Duchamp, could be seen in Boston or Cambridge, where the history of painting stopped at Impressionism and sculpture ended with Rodin. When the Boston Art Club dipped its toe into the exhibition of modern art with a mild show of Picasso drawings shown against plain white walls, Boston's shocked response led the club to "purge itself of modernism" and promptly cover the walls in mouse-colored velvet.[7] In his doctoral exams, Barr reported, ninety minutes were devoted to fifteenth- and sixteenth-century Italian painting, one minute to "modern art." The most recent artist mentioned was the late-nineteenth-century salon painter Adolphe Bouguereau.

But by the end of the 1920s, there were three prominent arenas for budding modernists at Harvard.[8] Only one of these, Paul Sachs's Museum Course, was part of the curriculum. The other two—*The Hound & Horn* magazine and the Harvard Society for Contemporary Art—had been created by students and were devoted exclusively to the art and literature of the twentieth century.

SHADY HILL: THE BIRTH OF THE MUSEUM · PROFESSIONAL

On a sun-dappled hillock a thousand yards northeast of Harvard Yard stood a white Federal-style mansion with pleasantly wide verandas commanding views of thirty-four acres of oak, beech, and pine. Coming up the winding driveway produced, as Henry James recalled, "very much the effect of a sudden rise into a finer and clearer air." It reminded Dante Gabriel Rossetti of one of the heavenly destinations in *Pilgrim's Progress*.[9] Shady Hill reigned as the headquarters of cultural tastemaking in nineteenth-century America, when it was known as "the Cambridge Parnassus."[10] Its first resident, Charles Eliot Norton, had taught the first art history courses in the United States; subsequent residents Walter and Louise Arensberg became America's most advanced collectors of modern painting, in the wake of the Armory Show. But it was Shady Hill's final resident, Paul Sachs, who played the most important role in the rapprochement of art and museums; he was the "kingmaker."

Sachs first made his way to Shady Hill in 1899 as an undergraduate, tongue-tied when he stood in the presence of Charles Eliot Norton. He knew already that he wanted to pursue a career in art history and collecting, but he would wait years to do so. From his graduation from Harvard in 1900 until his purchase of Shady Hill in 1915, Sachs followed his father's orders and worked on Wall Street in the family firm, Goldman Sachs. He was by all accounts a competent bond salesman, but his passion for collecting would not fade. Drawings, prints, and engravings began gradually and secretly to accumulate in black boxes. Sachs's position in the financial world offered him an intimate perspective on the collecting activities of captains of industry and finance. He could enter their mansions, handle their rare books, majolicas, bronzes, and Oriental porcelains, and scrutinize their paintings and tapestries.[11] As he recalled, "There wasn't a single night that I didn't prepare for the future that I thought might never come."

At the outbreak of World War I, Sachs bought Shady Hill, and Edward Forbes hired him as the associate director of the Fogg Museum. Shortly thereafter he began teaching graduate students. In these two positions Sachs provided precisely the bridge figure needed by the burgeoning museum world. He was a man of affairs and a devoted connoisseur who knew the worlds of finance and academe intimately. A member of a prominent family in the "Our Crowd" Jewish financial world, he was connected to money and society. Although his taste reflected the past, he embraced the developing interest in collecting modern art. Only once, on being offered the directorship of Boston's Museum of Fine Arts in 1919, was he tempted to leave Harvard. His friend William Ivins prophetically counseled, "Where you now are, you occupy the most important strategic point in America in the art game. The museums and the thought of the future will be controlled by men whom you train, through whom you can spread the doctrine over the land."

Sachs was short, rotund, voluble, and occasionally explosive and was once described as a cannonball adorned with a Phi Beta Kappa key. His elegant but unobtrusive dress—"the best tweeds," a friend recalled, "but never so you would notice"—reflected his subtle display of power. Sachs bred a generation of future stewards of high culture at the pivotal moment when modernism became respectable in institutions.

|||

Museums devoted exclusively to art and open to the public were fairly new on American shores; in Europe they could be traced back to the French Revolution (when the Louvre Palace had become a museum), but in America the first museums were not established until the late nineteenth century. Throughout the century, museums ranged from patron-sponsored galleries to the commercial "dime museums" and peep shows flourishing in the Bowery. Their displays of tantalizing miscellany fit Dr. Johnson's original definition of the museum: "A Repository of learned Curiosities." Next to paintings and sculpture the museumgoer might find a sled from Friesland, stuffed birds perched in their natural habitat, mastodon bones and buffalo horns, wax figures of presidents, Japanese lacquerware, live rattlesnakes, painted panoramas, fossils, and embalmed freaks of nature. Museums appealed to many audiences before the terrains of highbrow and lowbrow, art and natural history came to be separated.

America's new museums served a ragtag assortment of functions—as cabinets of curiosities, storage bins for the rich, emporiums of culture, clubs, civic sanctuaries, gymnasiums for the development of taste, attics for all, educational laboratories, and visual reference collections.

These new institutions were driven by the great industrial fortunes that fueled the golden age of museum patronage in the United States. The great new American collectors included such industrial titans as Andrew Carnegie, Henry Clay Frick, Andrew William Mellon, J. Pierpont Morgan, and John D. Rockefeller Jr. and his wife, Abigail. Together they established a genteel, hegemonic, Europhile culture of libraries, theaters, schools, orchestra halls, statuary parks, and museums. The emporiums of culture embodied the didactic purposes to which art, between the Renaissance and the twentieth century, was typically put: "We aim at collecting materials for the education of the nation in art, not at making collections of objects of art," Charles Perkins of the Boston Museum of Fine Arts said in 1870. "That must be done at a later stage of national development."[12]

As the century drew to a close, the rhetoric became less that of the schoolroom and more that of the pulpit. In a process that one historian called "the sacralization of culture," art and science museums were split, original works replaced the ubiquitous plaster casts, and aesthetics gained ascendancy. As the secretary of the Boston Museum put it, "A museum of science is in essence a school; a museum of art is in essence a temple."

The nation's first public museum of art, the Wadsworth Atheneum, opened in Hartford, Connecticut, on July 31, 1844. Housed within a turreted Gothic Revival fortress of cream-colored granite, this center of culture embraced art, natural history, literature, and Connecticut history. The Atheneum's architect accurately described it as the nation's foremost institution "to provide for the arts of civilization a characteristic and permanent home." For a twenty-five-cent entry fee, the local populace was encouraged to refine its taste and improve its character through contact with art. In its early years, despite its lofty moral purposes, the Atheneum drew few visitors to its art gallery's dimly lit chamber. An elderly attendant sat by the door, knitting and guarding the collection, which initially consisted of seventy-eight paintings, one miniature, two marble busts, and one bronze sculpture. The occasional visitors tiptoed in, sniffed the musty air, whispered reverently, and rarely returned for another visit.

Around the turn of the century, a banker and an Episcopal clergyman banded together to rescue the museum from its moribund state. The Reverend Francis Goodwin spearheaded the effort, while his cousin J. Pierpont Morgan and his family provided money. In 1910, when the massive Morgan Wing opened, the museum began a new era: a former librarian was brought in and served for seventeen years as its first director, and the prominent Goodwin family led the board for the first half of the twentieth century. The Atheneum's fledgling collection now included everything from paintings and jewelry to furniture and firearms, an imposing new building in the approved English Renaissance Revival style, and a stable administrative structure. The Atheneum was well poised to take advantage of the moment when private art collections would be passed along to museums.

III

Paul Sachs anticipated a problem when he arrived at Harvard in 1915. The private collections that had been assembled by nineteenth-century captains of industry and finance would soon enter museum collections in a great wave. Who, he asked, would lead these cultural treasure houses, "when the time came that every prosperous, self respecting municipality in the land would wish to boast a museum of its own?" Surveying the ranks of museum directors, he found mostly artists, collectors, and architects, poorly paid, lacking art historical knowledge and the administrative skills necessary to run a museum. "Before [Sachs's] time, to work in an American art museum had been a casual avocation for the rich or a cruel sacrifice for the dedicated," observed John Coolidge, a later director of the Fogg Museum.[13] "A museum director had to be a *gentleman* interested in art but not an ideologue—a man of conviction but not expected to impose his conviction." Without a budget for acquisitions, directors could ill afford to display the temper to refuse gifts. Museum director Francis Henry Taylor called them "those flattering High Priests of culture."[14] The Metropolitan imported European art historians and critics such as Sir Caspar Purdon Clarke, Roger Fry, and William Valentiner when they needed individuals who could wed art-historical knowledge to museum practice. Sachs knew that American museums by the 1920s would house world-class collections and would need native-grown curators and directors. Only after Sachs's teaching did the "museum director" become a recognized profession.

In 1921, Sachs introduced a course at Harvard that he called "Museum Work and Museum Problems," which became known as the "Museum Course." Twice weekly, Sachs invited graduate students into his living room at Shady Hill to examine his art collection and his books. Connoisseurship, built around the close study of the art object, was his art-historical modus operandi. He devoted much of the class to hands-on administrative issues and shared with his students the mail that crossed his desk: exhibition announcements, auction previews, catalogs. He let them browse through the two black loose-leaf notebooks he kept in his hip pocket, listing private collectors and art dealers, each carefully annotated with their areas of collecting. He arranged field trips to the homes of collectors and then quizzed his students about the work they had seen, in sequence, on the walls. He offered homely bits of advice: directors should leave their office doors open to communicate availability; they should cultivate the habit of shifting from foot to foot to avoid physical fatigue on long museum forays; above all, they had to learn to make the right noises in the presence of collectors.

"He invented the profession and formed its standards," said his colleague John Coolidge, "and *not* just the American version of the profession." Sachs recommended that his students collect in unfashionable areas and strongly discouraged collecting personally in areas that overlapped with their professional curatorial responsibilities. He advised that a museum's permanent collection could act "as a stabilizer or measuring rod against which temporary exhibitions might be projected and evaluated." He stressed the importance of museum publications at every level—from scholarly treatises and catalogs to popular gallery lectures and succinct wall labels. While he encouraged the cultivation of positive relationships between curators and museum trustees, he also emphasized the separation of their respective functions.

After the academic year of 1926–27, the Museum Course met in the living room at Shady Hill for one of its weekly sessions and at the Fogg Museum for the other. The class members who attended a farewell dinner that year included Alfred Barr, A. E. "Chick" Austin Jr., Agnes Rindge, Henry-Russell Hitchcock Jr., R. Kirk Askew Jr., and Jere Abbott. Sachs strongly encouraged collegiality among his students. He knew that their professional success would depend in part on cooperating with one another after they had left Harvard, but he could not have known then that their collective impact would shape the course of modernism in America.

THE HOUND & HORN

Some of the Harvard modernists became involved with *The Hound & Horn*, a prototypical small modernist magazine that published work mainstream magazines would not print. Rejected by the editorial board of the *Harvard Advocate*, Lincoln Kirstein and his classmate Varian Fry conceived *The Hound & Horn* in 1927. As Fry recalled, they both valued Stein and Joyce, Stravinsky and Picasso, "and we felt that Harvard undergraduates ought to know more about them than they did. It was to hail the new and glittering world they and their influences were creating, and to bid

Cover, *The Hound & Horn*, Vol. 1, No. 3, Spring 1927
(designed by Rockwell Kent).

farewell to the stodgy in the nineteenth century and its heavy hand on the twentieth."[15]

The first issue of *The Hound & Horn* appeared in September 1927—its cover was by Rockwell Kent, its elegant typography designed by Bruce Rogers, and its name taken from an early poem by Ezra Pound. Calling itself "A Harvard Miscellany," the magazine aspired to publish the best material it could find, without allegiance to any social or literary coterie. The opening editorial offered an amiable, well-mannered disclaimer that could not have been more different from an avant-garde manifesto. But the editors did have an agenda, outlined in a passage from the first piece to appear on its pages. "How many contemporaries have modern ideas and how few have modern feelings!" wrote Henry Marston. "It is really up to the artists and thinkers of the present age to help us over this chasm."[16] The contributions that followed addressed precisely that task. Henry-Russell Hitchcock contributed a provocative piece on "The Decline of Architecture," illustrated with Jere Abbott's photographs of the Necco factory building. A homoerotic painting by Maurice Grosser, entitled *Narcisse Noir* (and quoting Manet's *Olympia*), presented a scantily dressed black man smoking a cigarette. Books by James Joyce, H.D., Wyndham Lewis, D. H. Lawrence, and Ford Madox Ford were reviewed, and a generous sampling of avant-garde magazines from Paris and London (including Ezra Pound's *Exile* and T. S. Eliot's *The Criterion*) were described. The modernist aesthetics of Clive Bell and Roger Fry were compared favorably to those of John Singer Sargent, whose decor of the Boston Public Library had been commissioned by Kirstein's father. It was not such a miscellany after all.

Due largely to the energy of Kirstein and the financial support of his father, *The Hound & Horn* appeared each quarter for the next seven years, like clockwork, and its record of publication was impressive. By 1929, when both *The Little Review* and *The Dial* folded, *The Hound & Horn* became the leading modernist magazine in America; its purview encompassed literature, dance, photography, architecture, design, film, and art. Eventually overcoming its Anglophilia in letters and its Francophilia in art, the magazine challenged the perception of America's colonial status in the world of arts and letters.

THE HARVARD SOCIETY FOR CONTEMPORARY ART

The third modernist outlet in 1920s Cambridge was the Harvard Society for Contemporary Art. Founded in reaction to the absence of twentieth-century art in Boston's environs, the society was sparked by Lincoln Kirstein's initiative, Alfred Barr's advice, and Paul Sach's cooperation. The three met on December 12, 1928, over dinner at Shady Hill. Barr was serving as Kirstein's academic adviser at the time and shared with him his excitement about the modern art he had seen over the past year on a Sachs-funded tour of Europe. "He was a very puritanical, Presbyterian character," Kirstein observed of Barr. "But he was very good for me, and he believed in enthusiasm—very remarkably."[17] Combining his own executive drive and Barr's vision of what was possible, Kirstein proposed to Sachs a way of exhibiting twentieth-century art at Harvard. Kirstein was not

John Walker III, Lincoln Kirstein, and Edward M. M. Warburg, founders of the Harvard Society for Contemporary Art, 1929.

drawn to Sachs—he later remarked, "I thought he was a squirt and an awful man"—but he recognized that the older man was intellectually receptive and provided a necessary link to the Fogg Museum. Sachs regarded the idea of a Harvard Society for Contemporary Art as "healthy" for young people and useful as a training ground for the next wave in art collecting. By supporting the new society, Sachs could sanction exhibitions of controversial modern art without involving the Fogg Museum in the fray. Sachs's involvement lent credibility to the new organization and brought it a distinguished board of trustees that combined, in roughly equal parts, art history and money.[18] Kirstein enlisted two other undergraduates, Edward Warburg and John Walker III, to help run the society. "It's my brain, Eddie's money, and Johnny Walker's social contacts,"[19] Lincoln commented at the time.

In Rooms 207 and 208 of the Harvard Cooperative Building, known as the Coop, at 1400 Massachusetts Avenue, the three undergraduates created an exhibition space. The location, overlooking a bustling Harvard Square intersection, placed the society outside the ivied bastion of academe. They painted the walls white and silvered the ceiling, scavenged marble columns from a recently folded ice-cream parlor, topped them with thick slabs of monel (a nickel-and-copper alloy), and furnished the room with tubular steel café chairs. Like Katherine Dreier's Société Anonyme and A. E. Gallatin's Museum of Living Art in New York, this casual setting provided a vital link between avant-garde revolutionaries and modern institutions. The society's declared purpose was "to hold exhibitions . . . which are frankly debatable."[20]

Less than three months after its founding dinner at Shady Hill, the society mounted its first exhibition. Featuring the work of living Americans, the exhibition provided the germ of and model for America's multidisciplinary modernist art institutions. By the brochure's second page, Kirstein had roundly and impatiently declared the "uselessness of all categories," a cardinal feature of the society. The opening exhibition included not only painting and sculpture but also decorative arts. Placing an oil painting by Arthur B. Davies next to a cocktail tray by Donald Deskey was perhaps the exhibition's most radical move, and an indication of the society's future assault on traditional aesthetic hierarchies.

One could end a trip to the Harvard Coop with a look upstairs at the first American exhibitions of Isamu Noguchi or Alexander Calder. The exhibits ranged from modern German printing and Buckminster Fuller's (then known as Richard B. Fuller) Dymaxion House to American cartoonists (drawn largely from the pages of The New Yorker and Vanity Fair). Their show of modern photography (which included not only "art" photographs but also photos from the daily press and aerial photos) foreshadowed the founding of a photography department in the Museum of Modern Art, and their exhibition of works by Bauhaus masters predated any American museum show by a decade.

The society moved quickly, cheaply, and with a minimum of formal organization. Decisions were made over lunch at the local Schrafft's, and the undergraduates then hit up friends of the trustees for loans of works. The few New York galleries that exhibited modern art—Valentine, Kraushaar, Downtown, Reinhardt, John Becker, and Weyhe—eagerly loaned works in order to cultivate a new generation of Harvard-educated modern collectors. In contrast to the present day, when arranging loans occupies an army of professional intermediaries and a flotilla of forms, loans were arranged then by handshakes between gentlemen. The costs for mounting a series of groundbreaking exhibitions was astonishingly low. The society spent $7,288 during its first year. The most expensive show, "Derain, Matisse, Picasso, Despiau," cost $724.33, and the cheapest, devoted to Buckminster Fuller's Dymaxion House, was mounted for $56.66.

The Harvard Society for Contemporary Art could have grown only in the fertile soil that brought together Harvard and Wall Street, Jews and WASPs, society and academe during a period of swelling economic prosperity. "I was always chronologically in luck," Kirstein explained, for he founded the society at the moment when the rich began to support modern art. At the same time the society opened, Mrs. John D. Rockefeller Jr., Mary Quinn Sullivan, and Lizzie Bliss began the discussions that would lead to New York's Museum of Modern Art. The conjunction was not coincidental. That there were few outlets for modernism in either New York or Boston made utterly clear that its advocates would have to create their own institutions. Lincoln Kirstein and Alfred Barr led the way.

What later came to be called "The Family" or "The Friends" was just beginning to cohere in the late 1920s, but the electricity of those personal connections created a vibrant, if circumscribed, arena for the young Harvard modernists. "Somehow it was the air," Philip Johnson recalled. "That was one time when there was *air* there. The Harvard thing."

ALFRED BARR JR.

Spindly, pale, intensely earnest, Alfred Hamilton Barr Jr. arrived at Harvard as a doctoral student in the fall of 1924. As an undergraduate at Princeton he had studied medieval art—painting, sculpture, architecture, crafts—as the principal archaeological record of a civilization. As a graduate student at Harvard he brought that synthetic approach to the twentieth century, which he described as "our amazing though none too lucid civilization."[21] Before he finished his graduate work, Barr had already begun

Alfred H. Barr Jr. at age sixteen. Museum of Modern Art. Copyright 1998 The Museum of Modern Art. *"That reasonable air of his is deceptive. It's just the sugar-coating on the pill of absolute certainty."* (Philip Johnson)

to introduce lucidity to the study of modern art. He was Harvard's pioneer preacher of modernism.

Alfred Barr's father, grandfather, and uncle were Presbyterian ministers; his homes were church parsonages, and his ministerial vocation seemed predetermined. There are few more trenchant examples of nineteenth-century religious faith transfigured to twentieth-century faith in art. The "minutely observing scholarly temperament" that art historian Meyer Schapiro commemorated at Barr's death,[22] the catholic taste he would

MODERNIST LITERACY ACCORDING TO ALFRED BARR

To assess the knowledge of students in America's first course on modern art (Wellesley, 1927), Alfred Barr administered the following quiz; Frank Crowninshield reprinted it in Vanity Fair *in August 1927.*

What is the significance of each of the following in relation to modern artistic expression? [Note: Barr's answers to **bold** items appear on the reverse of the page.]

1. George Gershwin
2. Max Reinhardt
3. Henri Matisse
4. *The Hairy Ape*
5. Miguel Covarrubias
6. James Joyce
7. John Marin
8. **UFA**
9. Alexandre Archipenko
10. **Roger Fry**
11. The Zoning Law
12. Alfred Stieglitz
13. *The Cabinet of Dr. Caligari*
14. Aristide Maillol
15. The Imagists
16. Jean Cocteau
17. **Saks Fifth Avenue**
18. *Petrouchka*
19. **Harriet Monroe**
20. Paul Claudel
21. **Gilbert Seldes**
22. Franz Werfel
23. **Gordon Craig**
24. Forbes Watson
25. **Oswald Spengler**
26. Luigi Pirandello
27. *Les Six*
28. The Sitwells
29. **Edgar Brandt**
30. (Who wrote this?) Thou art come at length more beautiful than any cool god in a chamber under Lycia's far coast than any high god who touches us not here in the seed years; ay than Argestes scattering the broken leaves
31. Polytonic
32. **The Barnes Foundation**
33. Wyndham Lewis
34. **Frans Masereel**
35. Frank Lloyd Wright
36. George Antheil
37. **John Quinn**
38. *Sur-realisme*
39. Arnold Schoenberg
40. ***Aria da Capo***
41. **John Alden Carpenter**
42. **Frankl**
43. Vsevolod Meierhold
44. Harold Samuel
45. Fernand Léger
46. **(Who wrote this?) "Silence is not hurt by attending to taking more reflection than a whole sentence. And it is said and the quotation is reasoning. It gives the whole preceding. If there is time enough then appearances are considerable. They are in a circle. They are tendering a circle. They are a tender circle. They are tenderly a circle."**
47. Suprematism
48. *Das Bauhaus*
49. Le Corbusier–Saugnier
50. **Richard Boleslavsky**

8. **UFA:** German moving picture company. Perhaps the only great film producers who frequently sacrifice commercial for artistic values, Universum Film Aktiengesellschaft.

10. **Roger Fry:** Organizer of the first Post-Impressionist Exhibition in England—the most brilliant English art critic supporting the modern aesthetic attitude (*ma non troppo*).

17. **Saks Fifth Avenue:** Through its advertisements and show windows, this department store has done more to popularize the modern mannerism in pictorial and decorative arts than any two proselytizing critics.

19. **Harriet Monroe:** Editor of *Poetry,* matriarch of Chicago poets.

21. **Gilbert Seldes:** Editor, dramatic critic, author of *The Seven Lively Arts* in which the relative qualities of Beethoven, George Gershwin, and Puccini are clearly discerned.

23. **Gordon Craig:** "Old master" of the modern theater and the modern woodcut.

25. **Oswald Spengler:** German philosopher. In his *Der Untergang des Abendlädes* (The Decline of the West) he proves by cumulative analogy a cyclical theory of history and the decadence of our civilization. If, however, decadence is the "inability to create new forms" the

personalities and works of art included in this questionnaire are at least attempting a refutation.

29. **Edgar Brandt:** Distinguished for his wrought iron in the modern manner.

32. **The Barnes Foundation:** Merion, Pennsylvania. A privately owned institution for education in the aesthetic appreciation of the fine arts.

34. **Frans Masereel:** Modern Belgian artist known primarily for his woodcuts.

37. **John Quinn:** American lawyer and bibliophile who before his death was the most emancipated among the great American collectors of modern art.

40. *Aria da Capo:* Early play by Edna St. Vincent Millay.

41. **John Alden Carpenter:** Composer of American ballets, *Krazy Kat* and *Skyscrapers.*

42. **Frankl:** New York. One of the very few firms exclusively devoted to the designing and manufacture of modern furniture which makes "no compromise with reminiscence."

46. **Who wrote this?:** Gertrude Stein.

50. **Richard Boleslavsky:** Of the Russian theater, now director of the Laboratory Theatre in New York City.

demonstrate as a museum director, the love of history that imbued his scholarship—these outlines of a distinguished career can be seen even in Barr's childhood diary accounts. "Alfred was a connoisseur from the beginning," recalled one of his oldest friends. "The amazing aspect was that he was a connoisseur of just about everything."[23]

To study the art of the twentieth century, Barr forged his own path, aided by a handful of modern art exhibitions in New York and reproductions of modern art in *Vanity Fair* and *The Dial*. Although he remained uninterested in modern art, Paul Sachs encouraged his students to write about it and even created an impromptu fellowship that allowed Barr to travel to Europe in 1927–1928. As Barr's wife, Margaret, would observe after his death, "Alfred got there without a chaperon."[24] He instead chaperoned others: Lincoln Kirstein, his advisee, and Philip Johnson, his friend. "I seem to have achieved some of the enthusiasms and much of the tactlessness of the evangelist," he wrote to Sachs along the way.

At Wellesley in 1927, Barr taught America's first systematic course on modern art and architecture, requiring that students answer a "Modern Questionnaire" to be considered for the course. Since texts about modern art were few and hard to come by, Barr relied on his own ingenuity. On his budget of two hundred dollars, he assembled color reproductions from *The Dial*'s portfolio and from gallerist J. B. Neumann, and he used everyday materials at hand. His class rounded up examples of modernist design in current periodicals and advertising. They rode the Boston and Albany trains to experience H. H. Richardson's railway stations; they took field trips to see the modern vernacular architecture of the Motor Mart and the Necco Factory; they scoured five-and-dime stores to select a dollar's worth of the best-designed items. Divided into "faculties," each student developed a specialty in movies, theater, graphic design, or music. In class they discussed Diaghilev's Ballets Russes, Fritz Lang's *Metropolis*, and George Antheil's *Ballet Mécanique*. For their final exam they turned in a take-home essay and then listened to Jere Abbott and a friend play Ravel, Milhaud, Debussy, and Stravinsky at twin pianos. "Those were really mad, glorious days," Abbott recalled.[25]

Paul Sachs put forth Barr's name for the position of director of a new museum being planned in New York, the Museum of Modern Art. Barr initially demurred, suggesting that Sachs himself should be the director. But he closed his letter to his mentor in a tone of fevered gratitude for the opportunity: "This is something I could give my life to—unstintedly." The unheard-of twenty-seven-year-old scholar was summoned to Mrs. John D. Rockefeller's summer "cottage" in Seal Harbor, Maine, for an interview. She concluded that his knowledge "would make up for his not having a more impressive appearance." He got the job.

During that un-air-conditioned August, Barr wrote a manifesto for a modern museum that reflected his Wellesley course: "In time the Museum would probably expand beyond the narrow limits of painting and sculpture in order to include departments devoted to drawings, prints, and photography, typography, the arts of design in commerce and industry, architecture (a collection of *projects* and *maquettes*), stage designing, furniture and the decorative arts. Not the least important collection might be the *filmotek*, a library of films."[26] When the Museum of Modern Art brochure appeared that August, Barr's grand vision had been edited to the very mild: "In time the Museum would expand . . . to include other phases of modern art."[27] But, Barr recalled, his ambition did not die: "The 1929 plan went underground and did not reappear until 1932."[28]

HENRY-RUSSELL HITCHCOCK JR.

During his childhood in Plymouth, Massachusetts, Henry-Russell Hitchcock Jr. constructed elaborate sand castles on the beach, and before he reached adolescence he was drawing house plans. His father, a doctor, assumed that his son would become an architect, while his mother thought he should become a teacher. Perhaps his mother's aspiration and his having grown up in Plymouth predisposed him toward history. As Hitchcock recalled, "Plymouth was, and still is, peculiarly historical-minded and backward looking."[29]

Hitchcock arrived at Harvard in 1921, completed his undergraduate work in three years, and stayed on an extra year to study at the School of Architecture. He found nothing architecturally modern or useful at Harvard but was inspired by the lively seminars in architectural history conducted by Kingsley Porter in the Fine Arts Department. "He has all along been a puzzling person to me," Paul Sachs wrote of Hitchcock as an undergraduate. "He has a mind, but as you say, not the least of a method. I think he has the making of a scholar rather than that of a practicing architect." Hitchcock spent the summer of 1922 working his way to Europe on a cattle boat, then traveling from Glasgow to Sorrento, mostly by bicycle. He experienced buildings by standing in front of them and examining them

Henry-Russell Hitchcock, freshman photo, Harvard, 1921.

closely, like a connoisseur. His protégé Philip Johnson later observed that Hitchcock was "an 'eye' scholar"[30] who feasted on buildings as the impetus for his elegant prose. After graduation, he again traveled to Europe to see buildings, this time in preparation for an ambitious and massive study of the use of brick through the ages.

By the time he enrolled in the Museum Course in 1926, Hitchcock had changed course from architecture to architectural history. He felt most at home in the Fine Arts Department, which introduced him to the constellation of Harvard modernists enrolled in the Museum Course at Shady Hill. Friends and colleagues have repeatedly observed that words were Hitchcock's métier, but if such a portrait suggests a classroom academic, it neglects Hitchcock's highly cultivated sensuality and appreciation of popular culture. He loved good clothes, food, wine, and sex. He wore red, he spat, his gestures were big and his talk loud. He could be exuberant and wearing. Acknowledging that he was "not wholly untouched by the tabloid,"[31] Hitchcock wrote in *The Hound & Horn* about Proust, Ruskin, and movie fan magazines. "Would that I had more of your equable temper and were less easily excited by *impressions de corps, de coeur et de l'intelligence,*" he wrote to Virgil Thomson. "Weak soul that I am I repose if I am permitted from time to time on friendly bosoms to gain a little serenity which gained I go forth to receive new stimulation's."[32]

His first article, published in the premier issue of *The Hound & Horn* in 1927, bore the Spenglerian title "The Decline of American Architecture." He observed, "For what passes today for architecture is but a blonde wig and gold teeth;" he wrote, "no ghost, rather, but a soulless imitation of its former body; it were better such illusions of second childhood were at once dispensed with, and the possibility of a future without architecture frankly faced."[33] He feared that architecture had reached an impasse now that the best American buildings were anonymous and virtuous primarily in their grasp of engineering. He wrote to Alfred Barr that he believed the Western world was undergoing "a period when even architecture is a symbol if an unconscious one of the *crise de l'intelligence.*"[34]

Hitchcock had remained remarkably unaware of modern architecture until 1926. At the Exposition des Arts Décoratifs held in Paris in 1925, for example, he had missed Le Corbusier's epochal Pavillon de l'Esprit Nouveau and Alexander Rodchenko's Reading Room. It was only after reading Le Corbusier's periodical *L'Esprit Nouveau* and through his close relationship with Peter Van der Meulen Smith, a Harvard friend, that Hitchcock grew familiar with the new vocabulary of architecture.[35]

In Alfred Barr's Wellesley class on modernism, Hitchcock delivered the first lecture of his long teaching career. He championed factories and laboratories that eschewed architectural ornament and personal signatures but teased out some radical implications: "If indeed this theory be correct, there can be no such thing as a 'modernist'—that is aesthetically-conscious-contemporary—architect, and the very presence of an architect in our civilization is an anachronism."[36] In the February 1928 issue of *The Arts* magazine, Hitchcock published his first important examination of modern architecture, "The Architecture of J. J. P. Oud." The article displayed Hitchcock's magisterial grasp and intellect, and it would rivet at least one reader, a Harvard undergraduate named Philip Johnson. A few months later Hitchcock's article on "Four Modern Architects" appeared in *The Hound & Horn*, and it was here, in his description of Peter Smith, that he first used the term "international style."[37] Hitchcock's book *Modern Architecture*, published in 1929, marked his full conversion to modernism. Dedicated to Peter Smith, it illustrated one of his projects on the title page.

The book provided a grand historical perspective that began in 1750 and concluded with the "New Pioneers" of the 1920s. When Alfred Barr reviewed the book in *The Hound & Horn*, he observed that Hitchcock had already established himself "as very possibly the foremost living historian on the subject."[38]

PHILIP JOHNSON

Pampered and energetic, Philip Johnson matriculated as a Harvard undergraduate in September 1923. In his high school yearbook, his fellow students had elected him most likely to succeed and had written, "How we envy that youth (he's only sixteen, too) his brains." A great deal had already transpired in the young man's life. His older brother had died when Philip was two, and at twelve Philip had told his family of his physical attraction to men. A year later he traveled to Europe, where he saw Chartres Cathedral and would recall, "I was so moved I don't know why I wasn't dead."[39] He was almost handsome, too. A chiseled cleft chin and intense eyes saved his patrician features from prettiness. He seemed the picture of golden, privileged youth.

Johnson, however, felt anything but lucky. His freshman academic performance proved indifferent, and he was shunned by the most prestigious of Harvard's clubs. Before his first year was over, his father presented each of his children with their inheritance. While his sisters received a relatively stable commodity—downtown Cleveland real estate—Philip received stock in the Aluminum Corporation of America. The boom of the 1920s made him a rich man, wealthier even than his father. In the summer of 1924 he motored through Europe in his new Peerless motorcar. When he returned in the fall, he rented fancy quarters and treated potential friends to theater and music. But his largess was followed by a trough of agitated depression. Performing poorly in classes and unable to cope with his secret infatuation with a freshman, he wept, feeling overwhelmed by excessive stimuli. The neurologist he consulted diagnosed cyclothymia (now called bipolar disorder), told the undergraduate he should not worry since it was common among people in the arts, and prescribed rest. In March 1925, Philip retreated to the Johnson family's three-thousand-acre farm, where he alternately read detective novels and cried. After a few months the cycle turned, the depression lifted, and he returned to school in the fall.

Philip took extravagant new quarters, bought a Mason and Hamlin grand piano, and found a personal hero in philosopher Alfred North Whitehead. For months at a time he studied hard, and he experienced his lack of academic focus as testament to a wide-ranging intelligence that could encompass music, mathematics, philosophy: "I like to think I am not narrow enough to get all A's in my courses." Periodically he discerned oncoming depression, as tangible as an approaching storm. He would collapse emotionally, cycling ever more rapidly through affective swings. During these low periods he could sustain neither class work nor friendship. "The sense of failure was appalling," he recalled, "and nothing fails like failure." Johnson requested leaves of absence in the spring of 1925 and the fall of 1927 and took extended trips abroad. Between these leaves, the readjustment they required, and the varied academic paths he pursued, Johnson spent seven years as a Harvard undergraduate. Only near the end of this period did he find his direction. "The failure in all these things," Johnson recalled, "made my epiphany all the more epiphanous."

He ascribed his "Saul-Paul conversion" to architecture to two events that happened near the end of his tenure at Harvard. The first was reading Henry-Russell Hitchcock's essay about the living Dutch architect J. J. P. Oud. Published in *The Arts*, the essay began, "Architecture should be devoid of elements introduced for the sake of ornament alone: to the engineering solution of a building problem nothing should be added."[40] This functionalist philosophy, illustrated by seven photographs of geometric, unembellished structures, riveted Johnson. "I had to drop everything and be in architecture," Johnson said. "I was totally fearless and without tact or finesse, so I just bulldozed my way in wherever I could find a door. Alfred Barr was the door."

When Johnson met Barr in June 1929, the two experienced an electric connection. The undergraduate looked up to Barr as an intellectual mentor. The two were convinced that a new kind of architecture—later named International Style—would mark the inevitable direction for the twentieth century. As Johnson recalled, they also shared a missionary zeal: "We were both Calvinist mono-maniacs, and all for converting the world."

By the time Johnson finally graduated from Harvard in the spring of 1930, pushing twenty-four and feeling himself lagging behind his younger classmates, he had accomplished a great deal. He had found the vocational direction that would dominate his life. He had survived his cyclothymic mood swings. As his stock continued to rise and he became a

Philip Johnson, freshman photo, Harvard, 1924.

millionaire, he was able to personally finance his modernist zealotry. Most important, he had met the two men—Alfred Barr and Henry-Russell Hitchcock—who would guide him. "Neither of them was sensible," Johnson recalled. "They were gurus and gods and exciting visually."

Directly after his graduation from Harvard, Johnson met Hitchcock in Paris, and they embarked on a life-altering tour of Europe. Johnson contributed his Cord convertible and Hitchcock his brilliant monologue as they drove from one country to the next in search of modernist buildings. Along the way they saw Oud's buildings in The Hague and Stockholm's huge modern exposition hall designed by Erik Gunnar Asplund. Johnson felt that his most important education had finally begun: "There is no one with the visual acuity of Hitchcock in architecture, before or since, no books, no nothing equals him. Drove me crazy. Because I thought I had an eye. He was always better. It was his eye, his pure ordinary eye. He could just see through buildings and see what they were about and what the influences were and where they came from. That was clear at once, the first day, when we started out."

Seventeen-year-old Julien Levy arrived at Harvard in September 1924. Thin and dark, with handsome features that prompted his future wife to compare him to a Persian miniature, Levy was bright and high-strung. His indulgent mother thought he was a genius, while his hardheaded father, who ran a real estate firm that prospered during New York's building boom of the 1920s, hoped he would pursue a practical vocation. But from his high school days it became clear that he could not focus on an ordered regimen of study. He moved from the rigorous Ethical Culture School to the Roger Ascham School, a progressive Scarsdale day school seemingly more compatible with his imagination, academic insecurity, and need for what he called "individual research."

Supported by his mother's belief in his writing talent, Julien planned to major in English at Harvard. But his literary ambition was derailed when he received a D in freshman English. He recalled that his cavalier treatment of commas and his habit of inventing verbs "got pretty sour treatment." Julien's mother consulted Paul Sachs, whose wife she knew, and Sachs called Julien in for an advisory conference. Julien's major would make no difference to his ultimate career, Sachs counseled. The fine arts, however, promised small classes and individual work, an ideal refuge for creative loners. Levy soon began making trips to Shady Hill, where he became one of the few undergraduates admitted to the Museum Course. He quickly developed a horror of museums—stable institutions were anathema to his rebellious character. He could tolerate just so much of Sachs's administrative how-tos, and the prospect of negotiating with trustees exceeded his limited patience. "I judged myself as somebody incorrigibly rebellious against the kind of tact and politesse it takes," he concluded. "Somehow or other I have to be my own boss."

During his years at Harvard, Levy fostered instrumental friendships with Harvard modernists who would soon help establish him in the art world. He was tutored by Henry-Russell Hitchcock, he submitted pieces to Lincoln Kirstein's *The Hound & Horn*, he studied with Chick Austin in the "egg and plaster course," and for a Fogg Exhibition of modern art in student collections he lent Alfred Barr works on paper by Klee, Chagall, Schiele, and Campendonk. Another fine arts professor, Chandler Post, encouraged his interest in movies, which led to a fascination with photography.

Swept along by each ensuing whim, Levy rarely finished anything he started, including his Harvard baccalaureate. During his senior year he dropped out to become an errand boy for the then-Bronx-based Columbia Studios in order to be near Gloria Swanson. Looking back on his life a half century later, he observed, "I didn't have discipline, but I found my way somehow into the most extraordinary, lucky coincidences."

The most fortuitous of these connections happened in 1927, when Levy met Marcel Duchamp at the Brummer Gallery exhibition of Constantin Brancusi. When Julien revealed his interest in film, Duchamp replied, "Well, don't go to Hollywood. Come over to Paris and meet Man Ray. I'll get him to let you use his studio." Six weeks later, Levy was sipping Cinzano with Duchamp in the lounge of a boat headed for France. Levy had three hundred dollars in his pocket for raw film stock and the promise of Man Ray's collaboration and use of his studio. The next morning, he and Duchamp spied a westbound ship. Man Ray was on the boat, they were told, so the film project was off. "But our relentless propeller drove on," Levy recalled, "and as one expectation vanished behind us, another appeared ahead."

At 6 P.M. on Levy's first evening in Paris, author and publisher Robert

Julien Levy, freshman photo, Harvard, 1924.

McAlmon escorted him to Peggy Guggenheim's studio. In the golden haze of his memory, Levy recalled all of Paris being crowded into that single room: Natalie Barney, Jean Cocteau, Janet Flanner, André Gide, Ernest Hemingway, and James Joyce. In one corner, clad in plum silk, Isadora Duncan reclined on a couch, and from another corner Levy heard an offer of imported gin that promised instant inebriation. *"Il faut de l'eau fort, pas trop d'effort,"* responded Marcel Duchamp. "Speak-easy?" asked a handsome woman with iron-gray bobbed hair. "Why, if I ever tried to speak easily some policeman would come up and give me a really hard sentence."

Levy's ears pricked up at the acerbic authority of the speaker, the poet and artist Mina Loy. Earlier that day Robert McAlmon had described her daughter Joella as "the most marvelous *jeune fille* in all the world." When nineteen-year-old Joella entered Peggy Guggenheim's studio that evening, Julien thought she was "like light breaking through clouds." Two months later they were married.

Levy's first evening set the tone for his heady visit. "I had two very definite impressions, and they were both somewhat mystic," Julien recalled a half century later. "Number one, I felt as though I'd found where I belonged, so I was not surprised at all. And number two, I was full of hero worship which I didn't lose."

LINCOLN KIRSTEIN

The last of the Harvard modernists to matriculate, nineteen-year-old Lincoln Kirstein arrived in Cambridge in the fall of 1926. He presented an intimidating figure to his classmates: at 6 feet, 2½ inches, he was towering and lean, with a jagged profile. Friends recalled him as saturnine and clumsy, his brows intensely knit, and one friend said, "One doesn't love an eagle."

Representing the third generation in America of an upwardly mobile Jewish family, Kirstein seemed made for success. Lincoln's father, Louis Kirstein, had earned a comfortable fortune as a partner in Filene's department store, and Boston's high society had sanctioned him for his leadership of charities. In turn, he loyally championed Lincoln's mercurial interests, not only with his paternal pride but also with the financial support that made them viable. "My father gave me the idea that anything was possible," Kirstein recalled. "I mean that nothing was possible for him but

Lincoln Kirstein, passport photograph, ca. 1927. *"This was my passport, which would admit me to the cenacle of T. S. Eliot in London and Ezra Pound in Paris." (Kirstein)*

anything was possible for me."[41] Whatever course he would pursue, Lincoln felt the pressure of family support behind him.

Despite his obvious intelligence and wide-ranging curiosity, his early education proved problematic as he shifted from one private school to another. An early instructor warned his mother, "I must tell you that your son is fearfully scatterbrained and prone all too often to wander down imaginative bye-ways of his own devising," while a Phillips Exeter Academy headmaster simply dismissed him as "unsuitable." Today Kirstein would probably be diagnosed with a learning disability or attention deficit disorder; then, he simply observed that his mind "had had no chance to absorb 'normal' habits of intellection."[42] Alternatives to normal classroom work offered rich outlets for learning. He responded ecstatically to visual stimuli. He wrote, "I have a live eye; for me the visible world supersedes every other."[43] At the age of eight he founded a dramatics club called "Tea for Three" and served as its author, actor, and impresario. Although sports terrified him, he loved dance. At the age of ten, in a progressive summer camp, he learned to move to music in the style of Isadora Duncan. This early experience of dancing freely to a measured beat inspired his first vocational resolve: "I *would* be a dancer, that was all there was to it!"[44]

Kirstein required three attempts to pass Harvard's entrance exams, and his subsequent academic performance proved adequate at best. But this mattered little, for his life was outside the classroom. At night he circulated among Boston's Brahmin aristocracy, absorbing their manners, dynastic authority, and self-satisfaction. "I was the only Jew in Boston society," Kirstein recalled, "and I went to three balls a night."

Kirstein balanced this archaic social whirl with extracurricular activities that pushed the arts and letters at Harvard into the twentieth century—and provided him with what he called his "passport" to adventure in the arts. As a sophomore, he founded the *The Hound & Horn*; as a junior, he helped found the Harvard Society for Contemporary Art.[45] *The Hound & Horn* followed in the time-honored avant-garde tradition of magazines founded to promote modernism. The society served as a proto-modern museum, à la *kunsthalle* or Société Anonyme. These two enterprises quickly established Kirstein as a figure of extraordinary possibility. "I never felt like an undergraduate," Kirstein recalled, and he rarely acted like one.

The seminal encounters of Kirstein's undergraduate years took place not in Cambridge but in Europe. The first was in the summer of 1927 at the Institute for the Harmonious Development of Man in France, dedicated to the teachings of George Ivanovitch Gurdjieff. Following a ritualistic meal of baby lamb's brain and jerked bear meat, the Russian mystic initiated a series of toasts to his gathered company of followers, of which Kirstein was the youngest. He first toasted "ordinary idiots" and then "zigzag idiots," and after the sixth goblet of Armagnac he looked straight into Kirstein's eyes and said, "And, incidentally, Monsieur, to you."[46] The besotted neophyte heard nothing more that evening, but he felt that in a trillionth of a second an electric transmission had passed between Gurdjieff and himself. Looking back near the end of his life, Kirstein described this initiation as his first manic-depressive psychotic break (of which there would be many). Simultaneously "lurking in my mind and body was a sensation that here was the beginning of some important new adventure."[47]

For more than sixty years he would repeatedly describe Gurdjieff as "the most powerful influence of my life."[48]

The second encounter took place in Venice at the end of August 1929, when he spied a black-and-gold barge moored before a church. A bier banked with flowers was passing through the arched entry; a bass voice intoned a Greek Orthodox service. Silently he witnessed the funeral cortege as the gondola, now bearing the coffin on a raised catafalque, slowly disappeared up the Grand Canal. Reading the London *Times* the next morning, he discovered that he had witnessed the funeral of Sergei Diaghilev. "There was no more splendid background possible for the immediacy of this end of an epoch," Kirstein recalled. "Here was a fusion of life, death, and theater, which elevated one afternoon into the sunset celebration of an era."[49] In retrospect Kirstein looked on this event as an omen.

Kirstein graduated from Harvard in 1930. "I learned the assumption of authority at Harvard," he said sixty years later. But how to direct his considerable energies after graduation remained a mystery to him. He wanted to paint, and he wanted to write both novels and poetry. He wanted to be a professional horseman, and he wanted to be a diplomat. He wanted to dance. As he later recalled, "I was unformed, had no ideas, no instant philosophy, and I was very, very lucky."

CHICK AUSTIN

The Harvard modernist who most directly affected the production of *Four Saints in Three Acts*, Arthur Everett Austin Jr. abjured his given name at an early age. Virgil Thomson observed that it "was never more than a baptismal pseudonym," and his friends universally called him "Chick." He displayed the manners and panache of a cosmopolitan dandy. By the time he enrolled in Paul Sachs's Museum course in 1926, he had seen much of Europe, participated in George Reisner's archaeological dig in the Sudan, apprenticed himself to a Sienese master copyist (and forger) of Italian primitives, and studied wall paintings at the Mayan ruins of Chichén Itzá in the Yucatán. He was an only child, and his wide-ranging education had been the consuming focus of his mother.

The museum director's version of a stage mother, Laura Etnier Austin was consumed with collecting. She valued objects that others neglected (including side chairs with missing legs), was interested in architecture, and was obsessed with fanciful costume. Her developed sense of fantasy could be seen in everything from her anachronistic dress sense (all bustles, wide hats, and buttons) to her dishwashing habits (she used every dish in the house once before washing them all). In her son's eyes, her eccentricity represented fearlessness and daring. She had married a respectable middle-class doctor and medical professor, but as soon as he fathered a son she banished him from the house and devoted her energy to cultivating "the boy" or "boy dear," as she called Chick. (In his late years he said, "The saddest thing in my life is that I never knew my father," and he wished his children would call him "Pop" despite his un-"Pop"-like manner.) Chick's closets were filled with costumes bought by his mother on their travels. On one day he would wear lederhosen, on another a tartan shirt or sailor suit. "She instilled the idea that you could change your personality by changing clothes," observed Chick's daughter, Sally. From childhood well into middle age, Chick would climb into Laura's bed for confidential tête-à-têtes. Although she possessed all the traits of the smothering mother, she gave her son free range to become a daring aesthete and a powerful nonconformist. "She was consciously grooming him for his place in the world," observed Chick's son, David. "She drove him forward."

The education she provided included extensive travel in Europe beginning at the age of three and schooling in Paris, Dresden, and Lausanne. Exposed to the best architecture and art on the Continent, he developed the discerning eye for which he would become famous. After seeing masterpieces in Europe's great galleries, Harvard's art courses were little more than refresher courses. Austin skipped the required texts, attended classes only casually, and, not surprisingly, received middling grades. He spent his time at Harvard copying lantern slides and plaster casts. After a few years of formal training, Harvard-style, he concluded that "Taste was not encouraged."[50] Facing the likelihood that he would not graduate with his class in 1922, he decided to accompany archaeologist George Reisner on an expedition to Egypt and the Sudan.

Austin went back to Harvard in 1923 to complete his undergraduate degree but left shortly thereafter to study painting techniques with an Italian forger and copyist. He returned to Harvard in January 1924, and this time he stayed. He found his niche assisting Edward Forbes for the next three years in a course called "Methods and Processes of Painting." Popularly known as "the egg and plaster course," the hands-on course introduced budding art historians to techniques of the past, such as fresco and

Chick Austin, 1927, on becoming the acting director of the Wadsworth Atheneum.

tempera painting. Austin was an ideal teacher; it was his signature style to do *everything* hands on.

Austin wore his eclectic taste and sensibility as casually as his clothes, and his classmates thought of him as a man who never sweated, read, or toiled over his wardrobe. They attributed his knowledge to "osmosis" and his magnetic grace to privilege, breeding, and destiny. Lincoln Kirstein recalled his surprise on meeting Austin at Forbes's home in front of two early Renaissance Italian panel pictures: "He chatted of the Amico di Sandro or the Bernardo Daddi, or whomever the pictures were attributed to very much as we were wont to speak of Raoul Dufy or André Derain—competent professional artists of a certain epoch." Julien Levy remembered his first vision of Austin, teaching a group of freshman how to slake lime for fresco painting: "all in white, with white spattered on his hair and on his face, with an ambiguous smile, almost melancholy, as he faced his students."

|||

While Austin was teaching the "egg and plaster course," the trustees of the Wadsworth Atheneum were seeking a new museum director. Charles Goodwin, the president of the board of trustees, solicited the advice of Edward Forbes and Paul Sachs, and both recommended Chick Austin, "an attractive man with brains and good taste."[51] The trustees hired the twenty-six-year-old as "acting director." That they would do so without interviewing any other candidate suggests both Austin's winning charm and the casualness with which the search for a museum director was once conducted.

Austin assumed his post in October 1927 and found himself in an inhospitable milieu for his progressive ideas. The exhibitions—chintz, early New England bedding, shawls, Scottish clan tartans, linen damasks, and portraits of Hartford notables—could have been pulled from local attics. Hartford's newspapers often covered the museum's activities on the society page and devoted more space to the tea-pouring matrons at the openings than to the works on view. The city's closest brush with modern art had taken place in 1913, when the local Arts and Crafts Club staged a "fake" Cubist and Futurist show.

Unfazed, Austin told the press that Hartford would soon become the art center of New England and "the reputation of Hartford's artistic vitality will spread even to the foreign cultural capitals."[52] That Austin actually made good on this unlikely promise owed a great deal to his inveterate good fortune and his unsurpassed ability to woo Hartford's patrons. The same year that Austin became acting director of the museum, its trustees first considered adding a new wing, and the Sumner sisters donated money to help upgrade its art collection. The interest accruing from the two-million-dollar Sumner bequest was not enough to buy the Old Master paintings coveted by richer museums, so Austin cannily focused the museum's collecting on relatively undervalued fields: twentieth-century modern art and seventeenth-century Baroque.

During the first six months of his tenure, Austin staged two events that mixed art and society and set the tone for the Austin era at the Wadsworth Atheneum. He conceived his inaugural exhibition, "Distinguished Works of Art," as a concise history of all the plastic arts as seen through eighty world-class masterpieces. "As in schools and colleges," Austin told the press, "an introduction to the history of fine arts is always a necessary first course."[53] Austin's course stretched from the thirteenth century to the twentieth, and it encompassed painting, sculpture, and tapestries by Rembrandt, Hals, El Greco, Manet, and Whistler, among others. As the exhibition's centerpiece, Austin featured the museum's first Sumner Bequest purchase, Tintoretto's *Hercules and Antaeus*. Impressed as much by the paintings' collective value—more than three million dollars—as by their beauty, museumgoers crowded into the galleries in unprecedented numbers. The attendance for the first two weeks (35,000) surpassed six months' attendance in the pre-Austin years; the museum's hours were lengthened to accommodate the throngs attending its first blockbuster.

In the wake of his extravagantly successful debut, Austin announced his adventurous plans for the museum to the trustees. Of the four shows to be mounted in the next year, three would emphasize modern works, while the fourth, an exhibition of artists from the Connecticut Academy, was a tactful bow to civic pride. Austin planned to devote the Summer funds to the purchase of one major painting each year and to establish two or three rooms of world-class paintings.

To realize his plan, he depended on the support of Hartford society. In the spring of 1928, Austin planned his first fancy-dress ball to draw the rich and famous to the Atheneum. The museum was transformed into a Venetian palazzo featuring Austin's own painted views of the Grand Canal, the Bridge of Sighs, and other Venetian landmarks, illuminated by banks of electric candles. The event was conceived as a pageant in which Hartford's social elect would impersonate Venetian society of the eighteenth century in masks and powdered wigs, tricorns and brocaded bodices, all of which Austin designed himself. Articles and photo spreads appeared every day in the two Hartford newspapers for a full week before the event, describing what the revelers would wear as they were carried in on their sedan chairs. The event's tone—cosmopolitan, decadent, and glamorous —was something new to Hartford's elite. Austin's publicity-savvy approach was then unknown in the staid world of American museums. Concurrent with the Venetian fete, Austin opened an exhibition of modern French painting. Their juxtaposition established a pattern: by coupling the social forms of the past with the art of the present, he succeeded in slightly defanging modernism's latent antiestablishment threat.[54] He soothed Hartford's fear of new art by explaining to a newspaper reporter that "Fashion in art is very much like fashion in dress."[55]

The success of the fete was born out in the lavish articles on the newspaper's society pages. Once every important Hartford family—the Bissels, the Cheneys, and of course the Goodwins—had promenaded through the museum, Austin knew he could count on the local aristocracy in his campaign to link modernist art to high society.

On July 11, 1929, when Austin married Helen Goodwin, he entered Hartford's ruling elite. Helen's uncle, Charles Goodwin, was the museum's chief trustee. She believed in his genius and supported his ventures, even when they seemed too advanced for Hartford's taste.

By 1930, Chick Austin had largely accomplished his campaign to transform the Wadsworth Atheneum. Each calendar year began with an exhibition devoted to distinguished pre-twentieth-century art, but the remainder of the exhibition schedule was uncompromisingly modern.[56] In 1928, he founded The Friends and Enemies of Modern Music, whose inaugural concert included works by Stravinsky, Satie, Schoenberg, and others. Throughout the spring of 1929, he screened experimental films ranging from Fritz Lang's *Metropolis* to Sibley Watson's *The Fall of the House of Usher*. He installed Buckminster Fuller's visionary Dymaxion House in the spring of 1930 and also exhibited contemporary photography.

To modernize the museum, Austin relied on his Harvard friends. Henry-Russell Hitchcock worked with him at the Atheneum almost daily and was so frequently in the Austin home that he was known as "Uncle Russell." His opinions, printed in *The Hartford Courant*, provided a respectable academic imprimatur for Austin's activity. Kirk Askew, the New

York director of Durlacher Brothers gallery, offered a window onto the market for Baroque paintings, and his Sunday salons gave Austin a regular link to the movers and shakers. Lincoln Kirstein organized several of the Wadsworth Atheneum's exhibitions ("Buckminster Fuller's Dymaxion House," "Modern German Art," "Contemporary Photography"), each of which was imported from the Harvard Society for Contemporary Art. Julien Levy helped organize the Atheneum's Surrealist exhibition in 1931, and Alfred Barr provided a tie to the Museum of Modern Art, where he showed Austin's own paintings in 1930.

|||

Chick Austin was the member of the Harvard circle most instrumental in moving *Four Saints in Three Acts* toward production: he provided the theater and the sponsor, and he raised the money. The Harvard modernists wanted to promote the opera, Thomson observed, "because they had as yet no outposts for modernist prestige beyond the visual arts." Austin could not have moved so swiftly or audaciously without the support of his Harvard friends. They were *everywhere*: in galleries and museums, in film, photography, ballet, and architecture. How had such a small group attained such influence in so short a time?

Philip Johnson summarized that heady period succinctly: "It was a concatenation of Harvard and the homosexuals and modernism as a creed. And we were all believers in world improvement and the idea the world is fixable. And we were good Enlightenment thinkers." Many years later, in one of his last letters to Gertrude Stein, Thomson described what drove his modernist friends:

> It all comes out clear now what you meant last summer by "pioneering" which is just what we all, that is the little friends, have always been doing and maybe it isn't so easy for all of them though certainly it wasn't always so easy for us but any way it is the only thing any American can admit doing and respect himself because a pioneer is the only thing we can imagine ourselves being noble as or understand.[57]

A Personal Break,
a Commercial Breakthrough

Meanwhile, on the other side of the Atlantic, two developments in Gertrude Stein's life vitally altered the course of the opera's production. The first threatened to extinguish all hope; the second inadvertently prepared the way for its notoriety and eventual fame.

Stein and Thomson's collaboration had been clean. In the period immediately after the opera was completed, they maintained a partnership that was evenhanded and increasingly practical. What had begun in mutual admiration soon slipped into mutual promotion and shared friendships. By the end of the 1920s, Thomson's career was firmly linked to Stein's and to a lesser degree Thomson's musical settings gave Stein's words exposure. To jeopardize so symbiotic a professional bond would have been not only unpleasant but impractical. Thomson understood this and knew enough to back away at the slightest signs of turbulence. After minor quarrels he would apologize by sending nougats, his favorite Kansas City recipes, Gertrude's favorite yellow roses, and packets of dog biscuits for Gertrude's poodle, Basket. On receiving the flowers, Stein replied, "We may look upon them as a pleasure and a necessity."[1] Such conciliatory gestures were essential for the relationship to weather spats; Stein herself was constitutionally incapable of apologizing.

Stein wrote blithely about quarrels. As early as *The Making of Americans*, she observed, "Mostly every one does some quarreling"—one such fight being with Robert McAlmon, who published the book. In the wake of its publication, she observed in *The Autobiography of Alice B. Toklas* that "everybody quarreled. But that is Paris, except that as a matter of fact Gertrude Stein and he never became friends again." To never become friends again was a pattern for Gertrude Stein. Unlike many Parisian literary quarrels, her conflicts were neither casual nor ceremonial. As Alice observed, "When Gertrude was not interested, she was done."[2]

"Neither Gertrude nor I had ever wished to quarrel," Virgil wrote near the end of his life. Despite his wishes, despite his clearheaded sense of interpersonal relationships and his canny understanding of literary politics, Thomson walked right into a trap. From 1931 to 1933 they did not communicate. Thomson sometimes declined to discuss their long silence, saying, "It was all about other people." But how could these "other people"—Georges Hugnet and Alice Toklas—nearly derail a friendship, a professional bond, and an opera?

When the seeds of discord were sown in the spring of 1930, the feelings between Stein and Thomson were at their warmest. "No no I love you and we can tease each other always and always be happy and trusting," she wrote in March.[3] But it was around that time that Stein proposed to the young poet Georges Hugnet, whom she had met through Thomson in 1927, that she translate a series of his poems, *Enfances*, into English. This was an astounding proposal. Although she had taken pleasure in hearing her words joined to Thomson's music and had enjoyed seeing her words illustrated by artists, she had never before been so directly involved in another writer's words. Furthermore, although she had a comfortable speaking knowledge of French, it rarely entered her writing except through plays on words. Nor had she ever translated any other writers. With Georges Hugnet, however, she removed the usual boundaries.

Hugnet had founded a small press, Éditions de la Montagne, to publish his own poems. Soon he began to publish poems by Tristan Tzara, Pierre de Massot, and Stein, illustrated by such artist friends as Eugene Berman, Kristians Tonny, and Picasso. Hugnet's enterprise scraped by financially as long as no one took royalties and the publisher remained un-

Gertrude Stein, Georges Hugnet, and Basket in Bilignin, summer 1930.

paid. Stein applauded one of his pieces in *transition* ("strong, intelligent, lots of power"), and in the summer of 1928, Hugnet wrote an introduction to Stein's work that described her as a sui generis figure who had freed language. "One does like to be written about," Stein wrote Thomson, "but in him there is a freshness of comprehension that touches me to the heart."[4]

In 1928, with Thomson's assistance, Hugnet began translating Stein's words—selections from *The Making of Americans* and ten of Stein's portraits (*Dix Portraits*)—into French. By closely scrutinizing the text of Stein's self-proclaimed masterpiece and arranging for its publication, Hugnet entered the intimate terrain of Stein's words, just as Ernest Hemingway had a few years earlier. Hugnet was probably saved by the literal translation demanded by his limited English. "I have translated letter by letter and comma by comma,"[5] he wrote, thereby maintaining Stein's complete literary autonomy. "Our little Georges Hugnet 20 years old hair is turning white with the struggle," Stein wrote Van Vechten, "but it really does not sound so bad but it is a funny language not mine of course." To her great joy, the two books were stylishly designed and published in 1929 and 1930. Stein described the translations as "darn good."[6]

As the 1920s drew to a close, Hugnet became a member of Stein's inner circle. In March 1928, Hugnet, Thomson, and Kristians Tonny appeared at 27, rue de Fleurus bearing a gift for Gertrude. Hugnet had written the words, Thomson had set them to music, and Tonny had drawn a cover on silver paper. They called the song "Le Berceau de Gertrude Stein, ou le mystère de la rue de Fleurus," and its joyous, silly spirit embodied their familial affection and ability to tease one another. Six months later, Stein wrote a portrait of Hugnet that concluded, "George is in our ring."[7] She considered her portrait of Hugnet her most successful, even after she stopped talking to him forever.

The literary association had begun with Hugnet's translation of sections of her work, and it had gone so far as Stein writing a film script in French for Hugnet. Accompanied by Thomson's musical score, the collaboration, *Deux Soeurs Qui Sont pas Soeurs*, exemplified the closeness of the threesome. But to involve herself directly in the words and language of another writer was without precedent in Stein's career. Five years later, she explained the impulse that had led her to translation: "I did this not because of the poetry but because of the poet he had been very nice to me and I was grateful for it and so I wanted to make him happy and the way to show it was to translate the poetry of the young french poet."[8]

At this point in her relationship with Hugnet, in Virgil Thomson's words, "she went all emotional about him." Stein often used affectionate diminutives to describe Hugnet: "a cute kid," "a sweet kid," "an awfully cute soldier." She wrote him more than a hundred letters during their three-year relationship. And he sent her decorated letters in return: "Ah how I wish you were here: you could say the right things without my telling you what the trouble is, by intuition and true friendship."

In the tranquility of her summer home in Bilignin, Stein buried herself in *Enfances,* first reading each poem and then mirroring it in her own writing. She soon found herself doing more than literal translation. Hugnet's French became Stein's English, and in seeking an English equivalent to Hugnet's words she made discoveries about language that would affect her for the next several years, culminating in her abstract masterpiece *Stanzas in Meditation.* That October she described her accomplishment to Carl Van Vechten: "I have in it for the first time kind of solved the problem of modern poetry which torments them all, I kind of have invented a new music which is that and difficult well you'll see." When she mailed her translations to Hugnet, she expressed joy mixed with a note of vulnerability that was for Stein both rare and dangerous: "The translation is more like a reflection, a true reflection and from each moment to the next I am pleased with you and with me, and sometimes I am a little afraid but all the same I am pleased with you and with me."

When he received the translations in early July, Hugnet was vacationing and celebrating his twenty-fourth birthday. He responded to Stein's literary experiment: "This isn't a translation, it is something else, *it is better.* I more than like this reflection, I dream of it and I admire it. And you return to me hundred-fold the pleasure that I was able to offer you."

Thomson and Hugnet made separate visits to Bilignin at the end of the summer. Thomson brought his newly composed Sonata No. 3 "for Gertrude Stein," which accommodated her preference for using only the white keys on a piano. When Hugnet visited in September, they warily approached the question of how the two authors would be billed in her translation of *Enfances.* While Gertrude expected to be billed equally with Hugnet and wanted her versions to be called "adaptations" or "transpositions," Hugnet's basic English made it difficult for him to understand exactly how much Stein had embroidered his poems. Stein rejected his suggestion of "free translation." When Hugnet returned to Paris, he doubted she would again raise the proposition of coequal authorship.

"Your name beside mine would give the impression of a collaboration, when, don't you agree, there is no question of that."

Meanwhile, Hugnet and Stein devoted more pleasant time to the absent member of the trio, Virgil Thomson. They hatched a plan for Hugnet's Éditions de la Montagne to publish a one-hundred-page selection of Virgil Thomson's musical settings of texts, illustrated by artists. While not without its careerist dimension—such a volume would put not only Thomson into print but also Stein and Hugnet, whose texts he had set to music—the feeling behind this enterprise was remarkably generous. Stein planned to contribute eight hundred dollars to the venture, and Hugnet's father would contribute an additional two hundred. "I am awfully pleased that we are going to do you, you had done an awful lot for all of us," Gertrude wrote Thomson in the fall.[9] At that moment the triad was awash in warm feelings.

Virgil began negotiating which of his compositions to publish in the planned volume. The matter of selection and order proved ticklish. Hugnet wanted all the texts to be in French and declined to have his "Le Berceau de Gertrude Stein" appear between the works of two women (Stein and the Duchesse de Rohan). Stein insisted that she appear in English and wanted "Capital Capitals" instead of her *Deux Soeurs Qui Sont pas Soeurs*. Stein's letters to Thomson were firmly reasonable as to both aesthetics and business: "I am being quite thoughtful you see I want this book to do for you something like *Geography and Plays* did for me. . . . You see I want you shown at your best and want you salable to those who are your natural audience." But Hugnet was intransigent about his demands, and Thomson began to doubt that the book would ever be published. In the midst of the negotiations, Thomson took affront at the minor matter of Hugnet not giving him a free copy of a book of poems by his friend Pierre de Massot that he had published. It was an odd quarrel to pick and an odd time to pick it; Thomson reported to Stein that he had come down with a "frustration grippe."

Stein's and Hugnet's versions of *Enfances* were scheduled for publication, side by side, in the Winter 1931 issue of the American magazine *Pagany*. Hugnet arranged for gallerist Jeanne Bucher to publish them as a *livre de luxe* book with illustrations by Picasso, Tchelitchew, Louis Marcoussis, and Kristians Tonny. Stein simply thought of them as the "two Enfances," but Hugnet confided to Virgil his apprehension that his poems would be overshadowed by Stein's fame. "Really I have friends too strong for me," he wrote. Virgil thought the young poet was flexing his muscles, in light of recent recognition for his Éditions de la Montagne and a major literary award for a short story.

The clouds that had been gathering all fall broke one evening after Gertrude and Alice returned to Paris in November. In December at a circus performance, Hugnet showed Gertrude the subscription blank for the book. Stein's work was rendered as *"suivi par la traduction* [translation] *de Gertrude Stein,"* and Hugnet's name appeared in large type, while Stein's appeared below in ignominiously smaller type. She regarded this layout as disloyal and inaccurate. On December 17, she warned Hugnet, "This is quite a grave mistake my friend and our friendship together has always been very happy."[10]

The layout issue had seemed to Hugnet simply "a plain quarrel between *gens des lettres* about prestige,"[11] and he had responded by citing precedent from the French Authors League. When national lines were drawn in the literary feud, Stein felt overwhelmed by the opposition. Thomson perceived her as "terrified by Georges's rapid mobilization of the French intellectuals" and inadequate to wage a war. On December 18, 1930, she sent him a telegram threatening to withdraw the poems from *Pagany* and from publication by Jeanne Bucher if he did not agree to equal billing. She wanted her work to be called "Poem of Gertrude Stein on Poem of Georges Hugnet." When she encountered him three days later at Jeanne Bucher's gallery, Hugnet offered her his hand. When she declined to take it, the break became formal. That evening she wrote Virgil, "The last act of the drama was played this aft. You have been very sweet about not saying I told you don't imagine I don't appreciate it."

She withheld her manuscript and wired *Pagany* to stop publication. But the poem dominated the issue, filling pages 11 to 37, and the pages had been set in type. The only change she could effect was a new title, "Poem Pritten on Pfances of Georges Hugnet."

Hugnet was distraught and implored Thomson to negotiate. Imputations of disloyalty by both sides were inherent in such a task, and Alice's jealous intervention could also prevent a truce. Publishing the volumes of Thomson's songs depended on the two writers patching up their breach. Thomson understood this, guaranteed nothing to either side, and proceeded warily. Although he tried to show loyalty to both parties, such a position was impossible. Arguing too strongly on Hugnet's behalf, he alienated himself from Stein. He tried to patch up his misstep in a letter:

"Out of an overzealous and quite unnecessary loyalty to those absent I said an ugly thing to those present and that is worse because it hurt you whom I am ashamed to have hurt most of anybody and it was all so unnecessary on my part to hurt anybody especially my very dearest friend whom I love with all my heart."[12] The tone of his apology could not have been more ardent.

In the midst of these negotiations Thomson was planning an upcoming concert and wanted to perform "Le Berceau de Gertrude Stein," the song that had once bound the three together. The song no longer amused Stein. "I forgot to add that I would rather you did not do the Berceau at your concert," she wrote, "there was every reason for doing it the first time but there is no reason for doing a thing as intimate as that a second time now."[13]

Alice entered the picture a few days before Christmas by sending her own letter to Thomson stating Gertrude's position on the title: "This is

Alice intercedes with a sketch of a fair title page for *Enfances,* sent in a letter to Virgil Thomson, December 1930.

here definite—only—and first—and—last for all uses for the title of the book." Alice added her own requirement: "that these propositions are not offered to Georges but are offered by him to Gertrude—without any ifs or ands or further conditions—now or for the future." Her demands went beyond a matter of literary billing; they were a show of steel will. "You really are taking on too sweetly the difficulties only Georges can create," Alice wrote Thomson. "Don't please get worn out with it."[14] Thomson communicated this proposal to Hugnet shortly before Christmas, and after some posturing and face-saving in front of his new Alsatian mistress, Hugnet wrote on the top corner, "I accept." Now Thomson became the messenger.

Trudging across the city to 27, rue de Fleurus on a rainy Christmas Eve with Maurice Grosser, Thomson felt exasperated at his unenviable position. He was wary of the evening ahead. In preparation for this intimate holiday dinner and a piece of difficult business, he had wrapped up a white-framed Victorian lithograph featuring two young ladies on a swing. As if a portent of what was to come, he dropped the gift en route. The idyll of femininity now surfaced from behind shattered glass.

The two men entered the grand atelier to find their hosts in high spirits. Stein did not always appreciate Maurice Grosser's low-key manner, but this evening she felt warmly toward him. Grosser had created a scenario for the opera, and, as she was fond of saying, "Maurice understands my work." The foursome sat beside the fireplace, guarded by Wise Men from Provence and a crèche. The aroma of venison wafted from the dining room, and as they sat down to the octagonal table, on oversized Florentine chairs, a sense of well-being infused the small room. In the exchange of Christmas presents, Alice and Gertrude gave Virgil and Maurice stylish ties and scarves designed by Charvet. "When all the ceremonies had been accomplished and well-being established (for nobody had a power like Gertrude's for radiating repose)," Thomson wrote, "I brought out the paper." Gertrude looked over the new title page for *Enfances* and assented to the new layout in a completely relaxed manner. Passing it on to Alice, she asked, "What do you think, Pussy?" Alice surveyed Hugnet's two words of acceptance and said flatly, "It isn't what was asked for."

To restore an air of holiday camaraderie the matter was dropped, and at midnight the foursome warmly wished one another "Merry Christmas." But when Virgil awoke the next morning, he suffered from what he called his "usual frustration grippe." The mail the next day brought a neutral-sounding note: "When you come tomorrow will you bring with you my Mme Recamier, and Maurice plays and the Enfances. Thanks so much. Always, Gtrde."[15]

Virgil stayed home, wrapped his throat in flannel, nursed his cold, and practiced for his upcoming concert. The manuscripts were returned by messenger. When he resurfaced in mid-January, Thomson knocked on the door. Stein unexpectedly opened it and asked what he wanted, brusquely informing him that she and Alice were very busy. Virgil went away without having had a chance to invite the two women to his concert. He mailed an announcement a few days later and got no immediate response. On January 21, 1931, he found Stein's coup de grâce. Between the engraved "MISS GERTRUDE STEIN" at the top of her off-white formal calling card and "27, rue de Fleurus" at the bottom, she had penned in black ink: "declines further acquaintance with Mr. Thomson."

Thus Gertrude and Alice stopped talking to Georges Hugnet and Virgil Thomson. A few weeks later, suspecting complicity in the matter of the title page, Gertrude and Alice excommunicated Bravig Imbs with a businesslike telephone call. Alice had already cut off Kristians Tonny, this time in person. When he had politely inquired whether making contact would be desired immediately, she replied, "There was no need to make it at all as one had changed one's mind."[16]

Virgil and Gertrude had been drawn into a Parisian literary duel, and in flourishes of honor and pride, their friendship had been shot down in the cross fire. Thomson did not apologize, for he did not feel he had done anything wrong, and he took Stein at her word. "Gertrude, like a Russian monarch, felt deep remorse," noted Bravig Imbs, but she could not apologize.[17] Instead she wrote her own account, "Left to Right," which was published the next fall in the London edition of *Harper's Bazaar.* She described Thomson in warm terms: "Generale Erving [Thomson] was a writer, that is to say he had written not writing but something. That is to say we were writing we were writers who were writing. We were both very fond of him. He was never interfering but he knew everything and he always said something. I knew what he said and I noticed everything."

In her description she allies herself with Thomson as a fellow writer and grants him the privilege of her attention. She told the story of the break largely as it appears in this chapter (Thomson attested to the narrative's basic accuracy), except that Alice no longer figured in the power dynamics. Alice in fact remained invisible. Although Stein's reasons for turning against Thomson become no clearer from reading her story, she suggests her torn feelings about the break:

All this time I thought that it was all Arthur William [Georges Hugnet]. Perhaps it was and then perhaps I had better not have anything further to do with Generale Erving. Perhaps not. Perhaps I might think over everything. Perhaps I might remember everything. Perhaps Generale would come again and I would see him and I would not say anything. Perhaps he was worried about everything. Perhaps Generale would come again and I would tell him I was busy and could not see him. . . .

And now before I go out I always look up and down to see that none of them are coming. We were after that never friends or anything. This is all this true story and it was exciting.[18]

This marked the end of an era of young men in Stein's life, and she and Hugnet never again communicated. Shocked by the break, the young poet found company in the Surrealist camp. Beginning in 1932, he wrote several historical pieces about Dada and Surrealism and was associated with the group until the pope of Surrealism, André Breton, expelled him in 1938. At the end of January, Stein wrote to Carl Van Vechten, "Otherwise we have been having a nice peaceable time having really quarreled for keeps with all our young friends and there are lots of stories that will amuse you and will pretty well occupy us several peaceable days in the country. Paris rather wonderful and now the old Paris the before the war Paris is coming back so quickly it is more than ever wonderful, it is all so intimate again and so very lively."

A few months after the purge, in May 1931, Stein and Toklas published 120 copies of Gertrude's "mirrorings" of Georges Hugnet's *Enfances*. Hugnet's words had been completely expunged. Printed on antique Montval paper was the new title, which Alice had suggested: *Before the Flowers of Friendship Faded Friendship Faded*.

GERTRUDE STEIN WRITES TWO AUTOBIOGRAPHIES

It was no coincidence that the wave of excommunications coincided with the first fruit of Alice and Gertrude's brave publishing enterprise, Plain Editions. Their venture was grandly announced as "an edition of first editions of all the work not yet printed of Gertrude Stein." The undertaking, and its ambitious promise, provided Stein with the foundation of support that the young men in her court had previously supplied. Just two weeks before they banished Virgil Thomson, Gertrude and Alice published their first Plain Editions book, *Lucy Church Amiably*. Stein perused Paris's bookstores, and whenever she spied the book's blue cover in a shop window, she responded with "a childish delight amounting almost to ecstasy." Over the next three years more Stein works would be published by Plain Editions.[19] They did not include "all of the work not yet printed" by a long shot. But their publication provided a useful stopgap measure after Gertrude and Alice had exhausted all the conventional strategies of getting Stein's work published.

In the last few years, Payson and Clarke had been the only mainstream publisher to gamble on her work, publishing *Useful Knowledge* in 1928. When only 226 copies (of 1,500 printed) sold during its first year, Payson and Clarke declined to publish either a condensed 200,000-word version of *The Making of Americans* or her novel *Lucy Church Amiably*. A wave of rejection letters unpleasantly punctuated the end of the decade; they came from Little, Brown; Macaulay; Viking; Furman; and Harper's. The combined energies of her informal promoters—Carl Van Vechten, Henry McBride, Jane Heap—had not led to publication. Even her literary agent, William Aspenwall Bradley—one of the best literary agents in Paris, whom Stein had met through Ford Madox Ford—could not interest a commercial publisher. Only small presses published limited editions of her works.[20]

In 1930, when Stein and Toklas decided to publish themselves, their greatest asset was their collection of Picasso paintings. They sold his 1905 Blue Period work *Woman with a Fan* to art dealer Marie Harriman. Alice cried when Gertrude told Picasso of the sale, but she soon recovered and began to think like a publisher. What began as a work of love soon became concrete as she embarked on a new campaign of endless details, writing letters to bookstores, compiling inventory, and negotiating with printers and paper sellers. Above all, she learned how difficult it was to find an audience for Stein. The thousand-copy print run for the first two books was cut in half for the last three books, beginning in 1932. The only way Gertrude would find an audience was to write a book that was intended to be popular. "I am writing for myself and strangers," Gertrude had written on the first page of *The Making of Americans* in 1906. "This is the only way I can do it."[21] Now, urged Alice, she would have to write a book for an audience.

| | |

In late April 1932, just before she and Alice headed south for Bilignin, Gertrude was searching through the large Spanish armoire that held her unpublished manuscripts, when she came upon two identical forest-green notebooks. She opened the first to find, in her carefully penciled script from nearly thirty years before, the title "Quod Erat Demonstrandum." The notebooks—comprising her first novel, which had been completed on October 24, 1903—contained the thinly disguised story of her tangled affair with May Bookstaver; only the names were changed.

That relationship—Stein had seen Bookstaver from 1901 to 1903— had been the most painful, doubtful period of her life, and she had long ago buried her account of it below the ever-growing pile of manuscripts in the armoire. As Stein wrote in *The Autobiography of Alice B. Toklas*, "She was very bashful and hesitant about it, did not really want to read it." Instead she handed it to visiting novelist Louis Bromfield and suggested he read it. Perhaps she wanted to keep the manuscript safely away from Alice, but Alice would inevitably read it.

All too recognizable on the page was May Bookstaver, the Johns Hopkins student who had rejected Gertrude for a Bryn Mawr graduate named Mabel Haynes. Never having told Alice of the existence of this first novel or about the relationship, Gertrude disingenuously claimed she had forgotten about it. But in "Here. Actualities," a piece she wrote immediately after discovering "Q.E.D.," she noted, "The most exciting really the most exciting was finding the first thing that had been written and was it hidden with intention. Perhaps not on her birthday nor had it had a chance. There is no blindness in memory nor in happening."[22] She had remained silent about her love affair with May Bookstaver, even though she and Alice had exchanged such confidences when they fell in love. Gertrude's secret constituted a breach in the stringent rules of their relationship, and a few days later, when the two women headed south to Bilignin, the relationship described in the manuscript remained clandestine. Stein doubtless knew, however, that when Alice read it, she would not be pleased.

These six months of 1932 were some of the most quarrelsome in the long relationship between Stein and Toklas. They were also among the most productive of Stein's career. She wrote four plays, two short novels, several short pieces, an ambitious series of highly abstract stanzas, and an autobiography. The last of these writings, *The Autobiography of Alice B. Toklas*, most directly affected the success of *Four Saints in Three Acts*. The opera would not have achieved its notoriety had it not been preceded by the extraordinary publicity that greeted *The Autobiography*.

Stein's two long works from that 1932 residence in Bilignin—*Stanzas in Meditation* and *The Autobiography of Alice B. Toklas*—reflect the domestic tension between the two women. The first is highly abstract and among Stein's most difficult; the second is certainly her most inviting. The first abstractly evokes tension over the pursuit of fame; the second reports domestic amity. The battleground was words.

After Stein completed *Stanzas in Meditation* in late July, she continued to feel pressure to write the accessible, commercial work that would boost sales for the foundering Plain Editions. When friends had heretofore suggested to Stein that she write her memoirs, she had always responded, "Not possibly." The genre was beneath her, she said, for reporting stories would exploit her friends and herself, and it contradicted her enunciated principle that writing depended on the spontaneity and process of the absolute present. That summer, Gertrude suggested that Alice should write the memoirs. Call it *My Life with the Great, Wives of Geniuses I Have Sat With*, or *My Twenty-five Years with Gertrude Stein*, she suggested. "Just think what a lot of money you would make."[23]

But before Stein left Bilignin in November she had completed the memoirs that she had refused to write. What had happened? Now in her late fifties, Stein had reached the stage in life when it seemed more appropriate to look back. Several of her friends—Mabel Dodge Luhan and Muriel Draper among them—had recently published memoirs, and it became clear that many stories would be told about her circle, whether or not she did the telling. But her decision probably had more to do with Toklas's reading "Q.E.D." Toklas had finally read it and it had aroused her fury. In the contentious atmosphere of that summer, Stein struck a bargain both Faustian and conciliatory, for she could not function without Toklas's love and validation. "Shove is a proof of love," she declared. She would write an "autobiography" that would provide a new dimension to their collaboration.

Gertrude Stein with her dog Pepe, writing *The Autobiography of Alice B. Toklas*, fall 1932.

The first copybook notes show Stein struggling, starting sentences over, losing her point of view in convoluted sentences. The solution that came to her that summer was to write in Alice's voice, which she had listened to for twenty-five years. Its combination of odd humor, shrewd gossip, and crisp exposition was ideal for the memoir. Stein wrote in *Stanzas in Meditation*, "She will be me when this you see."

Among the hermetic sections that dominate the *Stanzas*, transparent passages stand out, evoking Stein's struggle with the competing demands of success, conciliation, and writing:

> Believe me it is not for pleasure that I do it
> Not only for pleasure for pleasure in it that I do it.
> I feel the necessity to do it
> Partly from need
> Partly from pride
> And partly from ambition.
>
> Not to be interested in how they think
> Oh yes not to be interested in how they think
> Oh oh yes not to be interested in how they think.
>
> Let me listen to me and not to them.

Stein grappled with the doubleness of *The Autobiography*. The first notebook showed Stein's characteristic discursive repetitiveness. But then the writing picked up, even though she was working in a style utterly foreign to her own: the tart, precise, economical voice of Toklas. Maurice Grosser believed that *The Autobiography* "was made up word for word of the stories I have heard Alice tell."[24] Thomson concurred that stories always ended up reflecting Alice's sharp and detailed memory: "Every story that ever came into the house eventually got told in Alice's way." Alice's direct intervention, through editing the notebooks, appears minimal.[25] But her presence, the sound of her voice in Stein's memory, was all-surrounding.

After Stein's death, Toklas commented that *The Autobiography* was the only work Gertrude had written for her. In writing the book, Stein affirmed her love for Alice, but it was not a simple valentine. *Stanzas in Meditation* gives voice to her resentment about sharing enforced fame:

After all I am known
Alone
And she calls it their pair

Stein characterized the writing of *The Autobiography* as the casual product of six weeks of autumnal beauty in Bilignin. Despite its careful appearance of effortlessness, the book's production provided her the means of editing her version of history and revenging herself on her enemies. It appeared to yield meaning yet hid a great deal. It announced her domestic relationship with Alice yet kept it private. It was a necessary conciliation and also a means to fame. It was both Stein's work and not her work. As Stein wrote in *Stanzas in Meditation:* "I wish to say/This is her day."

CHAPTER 8

Group Snapshot 1932:
The Harvard Moderns

In late November 1932, a few weeks after Stein completed her two auto-biographies, Virgil Thomson arrived in New York. He sailed third-class on the *Ile de France*, as he had done three years earlier. His fortunes had not improved in the intervening years; he was relying on a two-hundred-dollar loan from Philip Johnson to make the trip, and on the hospitality of John-son and other friends for his lodging. But Thomson considered the trip es-sential in light of his growing determination to get *Four Saints in Three Acts* staged. Since his last trip the Depression had deepened, the Metro-politan Opera had nearly gone under, and commercial art galleries were closing as quickly as they had opened during the boom years of the 1920s. And—perhaps most ominous of all—Gertrude Stein had stopped speaking to him.

Thanks to the ingenuity of Maurice Grosser, Thomson had cleared one difficult hurdle; he now had a series of playable scenes that trans-formed *Four Saints* from an oratorio into an opera. Grosser's scenario could not impose a plot or a narrative on the material, but he drew from the text enough suggestions for a series of vignettes. He called them "a train of images . . . a train of action."[1] They contained neither message nor story but were evocative enough to ground the music and words on stage. As Alice Toklas later commented, "It not only sounds like an opera but it looks like an opera."[2]

Grosser imagined the first act as a series of Sunday school entertainments. The second act became a lawn party, the third act a multiwalled version of Barcelona, and the final act presented the saints congregated in heaven.

Grosser had begun writing the scenario after Thomson's return from New York in 1929. He was an ideal scenarist. As Thomson's domestic companion, he had repeatedly heard him perform the piece, and because he was not a writer he was less likely to encroach on Stein's jealously guarded turf. A proficient painter of still lifes, portraits, and landscapes, his canvases were concrete but not literal; they reflected many of the allusive connotations of Stein's text. "Saint Teresa could be photographed having been dressed like a lady," for example, justified a scene in which a minor saint carried a large camera on a tripod and Saint Settlement delicately focused the lens on Saint Teresa on her throne. For other tableaux, Grosser took his inspiration from the rapture of Thomson's music, envisioning a dancing angel or sailors tangoing with their Spanish ladies.[3]

A close look at Thomson's date book during his five-month visit to New York in 1932–33 shows how and where he found the resources to stage the opera—in two overlapping groups that could be called the Harvard modernists and high-bohemian society. Their members made modernism chic; their cachet and cash made the opera's production possible. Together with the Museum of Modern Art and the School of American Ballet, *Four Saints* brought modernism into the settings of the old guard: the opera, the museum, and the ballet. "It shows how strong a need there was," Philip Johnson said, "and how strong a wave . . . coming along and breaking at the same point on the beach."[4]

|||

Jere Abbott met Virgil Thomson at the French Line Pier. After cabbing across town, they ascended five flights to Philip Johnson's duplex apartment. He had torn out walls and replaced them with translucent glass and floor-to-ceiling curtains on slender steel rails. Johnson described it to *House & Garden* as "designing in planes." The "living room" consisted of

Philip Johnson's International Style apartment, featuring Mies van der Rohe and Lilly Reich's furniture.

an austere white-walled chamber whose only ornament was a rubber plant. Tan raw silk covered windows overlooking the East River and pale ecru linoleum the floor. Mies van der Rohe's and Lilly Reich's designs dominated the room: chromium-and-pigskin chairs, a bookcase that was more beautiful than functional, and a rosewood table set with porcelain dinnerware by Porzellan of Berlin. A narrow Werkstätte der Stadt lamp with a partially sheathed bulb illuminated the ensemble. This apartment, the first of Thomson's several residences during his stay, offered the most programmatically Bauhaus interior in America at that time. When Johnson told a reporter that it was "a show apartment to counteract the terrible wave of modernistic apartments we now have,"[5] he meant to distance his design from the Art Deco style that was more often associated with modernity in America.

After a month, Johnson asked Thomson to leave. The apartment was not the sort of space that could easily accommodate an extra, and his manservant had threatened to quit if Thomson did not depart soon. "He

HARVARD MODERNS AND THEIR AFFILIATIONS

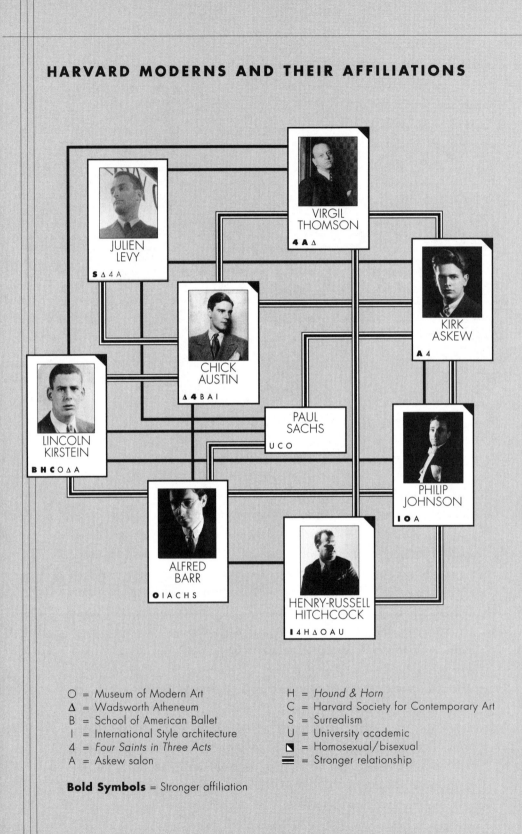

JULIEN
LEVY

S Δ 4 A

VIRGIL
THOMSON

4 A Δ

KIRK
ASKEW

A 4

CHICK
AUSTIN

Δ **4** B A I

LINCOLN
KIRSTEIN

B H C O Δ A

PAUL
SACHS

U C O

PHILIP
JOHNSON

I O A

ALFRED
BARR

O I A C H S

HENRY-RUSSELL
HITCHCOCK

I **4** H Δ O A U

O = Museum of Modern Art
Δ = Wadsworth Atheneum
B = School of American Ballet
I = International Style architecture
4 = *Four Saints in Three Acts*
A = Askew salon

H = *Hound & Horn*
C = Harvard Society for Contemporary Art
S = Surrealism
U = University academic
◣ = Homosexual/bisexual
≡ = Stronger relationship

Bold Symbols = Stronger affiliation

could charm the birds off the trees," Johnson recalled. "Unless he didn't like you, and then the viper's tongue came out. It was like living with Oscar Wilde." Thomson moved on to guest rooms at Kirk and Constance Askew's on East Sixty-first Street, Henry-Russell Hitchcock's in Middletown, Connecticut, and Chick and Helen Austin's in Hartford. Everywhere he saw the signs of his Harvard friends' success. Thomson ascribed his friends' rapid success to the newly advanced collecting habits of the rich, which connected them with curators and dealers in what Thomson called "the racket of art." The economics were basic, he explained; it took "a combine of collectors, dealers, and curators to establish a theory that historical values, artistic values, and commercial values are identical." (On hearing this summary, Lincoln Kirstein observed, "That is the Marxist view, and it was also accurate.") The Crash tightened the umbilical cord between wealthy collectors and the Harvard modernists and led to one of Thomson's pet theories: "You must remember the Depression scared hell out of the powerful rich. The shake-up of the rich in 1929 destroyed their confidence in their ability to run the art and literature world. We could do all sorts of things in places they thought they were running. They let their curators take over for a minute. For five to ten years the intellectuals were allowed to run things." What did they do?

ALFRED BARR JR.

Conger Goodyear, the Museum of Modern Art's president, described Alfred Barr in 1932 as "wearing out at the edges under the strain of three years of high-pressure work."[6] The physical reality was even more disturbing. When Paul Sachs lunched with him in early 1932, he observed that Barr's lips seemed thinner and his cheeks more sunken than usual and that his pallor suggested insomnia. Sachs expressed his concern and then cautioned, "Please do not think that these are the vaporings of an old fool. I say these things as an older and devoted friend, and because I have great faith in you." Barr had not slept soundly for a year and a half without medication, his digestion was poor, his eyes stung, he ground his teeth. When Sachs lunched with him again a few months later, he thought Barr was on the verge of a nervous breakdown and sent him to a "nerve specialist." The doctor prescribed a year's rest far away from the Museum of Modern Art.

Barr's deterioration dated back to the museum's opening on November 7, 1929. A smartly dressed crowd congregated in the lobby of the

Heckscher Building at Fifty-seventh Street and Fifth Avenue, then went up twelve floors to the exhibition of Post-Impressionist classics, "Cézanne, Gauguin, Seurat, and van Gogh." It was the first show in the world's first museum devoted exclusively to modern art. The Beaux Arts urge to decorate had given way to the modernist credo of spare white walls and perfectly proportioned volumes. For $12,000, the new museum had freshly plastered its ceilings and installed a bright and sophisticated lighting system and a few taupe velour couches. One historian described the rooms—with their thick walls, patterned ceilings, chamfered corners, thin marbleite base, naked picture rail, and neutral friar's cloth—as only "half-modern."[7]

The crowd of several thousand included a few artists and more collectors. Some of them had been severely hurt by the stock market crash just nine days before, but no one looked like it. Many leafed through the museum's first catalog, which Frank Crowninshield had rushed through priority printing at Condé Nast, bound with striking yellow boards and printed in sans-serif type. Jere Abbott conducted a personal gallery tour for Sir Joseph Duveen and was astonished to find Duveen's eye so habituated to art of the past that he could not distinguish a van Gogh from a Gauguin. A reporter from *The New Yorker* overheard one guest exclaiming that van Gogh's *Lady from Arles* was the spitting image of Mary Baker Eddy and another proclaiming his confusion that Gauguin's paintings depicted "all colored people."[8]

Exhibiting four Post-Impressionist masters was hardly a daring step in 1929; already by the mid-1920s, their paintings had become investments promoted by such blue-chip galleries as Knoedler and Wildenstein. (The ultramoderns of the moment, as identified by Barr in 1929, were Joan Miró, Pierre Roy, Otto Dix, and Jean Lurçat.) The Post-Impressionist canvases that had proved so shocking sixteen years earlier at the Armory Show now looked reassuringly traditional. "It truly makes us rub our eyes now that we have gone such a journey to see that we have arrived at the destination," wrote Henry McBride. "What was the insidious danger of it twenty years ago, or even ten years ago? Nothing more than that, that it was alive."[9]

Another journalist directed his attention to the dynamics of the assembled crowd: "For the first time in the history of the town society and art met and kissed each other without a single false move or gasp of surprise.

Alfred H. Barr Jr., by Jay Leyda (1931–33). (Gelatin-silver print, 4¾" x 3⅝" [12.1 x 9.2 cm.] The Museum of Modern Art, New York. Gift of the photographer. Copyright 1998 The Museum of Modern Art.) *"Our pituitary gland is called Alfred Barr."* (Conger Goodyear)

It was all done so charmingly, so naturally and with such distinction that for once the people seemed on a par with the ornaments on the walls."[10]

Of course, the charm depended on a finely balanced combination of taste, social chic, and money. Three wealthy art collectors—Abigail Rockefeller, Lizzie Bliss, and Mary Quinn Sullivan—had come up with the idea for a modern art museum in early 1929, and over the next nine months they gathered a team of art advisers (Paul Sachs, Alfred Barr, Jere Abbott, Conger Goodyear) and members of stylish society (Frank Crowninshield, Mrs. W. Murray Crane). Such a combination provided a multitude of resources, and it allowed the fledgling institution to weather the Depression and gradually change New York's taste for modern art.

Barr and his paid staff of three ran the enterprise from a single, poorly ventilated office, fifteen feet square and equipped with two typewriters and five telephones. Before the museum opened, Barr had prophesied, "At the end of two years, we should be able to discover whether New York really wants a Modern Museum, which may easily become the greatest of its kind in the world."[11] During those initial years, the museum went a long way toward fulfilling its promise. One of America's most controversial museums, it was also its sixth best attended. With Lizzie Bliss's death and the conditional bequest of her art collection in 1931, a substantial foundation was established for the institution's collecting future. Bliss's bequest included paintings by Cézanne, Matisse, Gauguin, Degas, Picasso, and Seurat. The institution had managed to successfully balance the solid financial base of the old guard (the trustees) with the adventurous ideas of young turks (embodied in the Junior Advisory Committee, which included Lincoln Kirstein, Philip Johnson, and Edward Warburg).

In December 1931, the museum's president told the press that "the experimental period of the Museum will come to an end with the present season." With this remark he announced the museum's move into new and larger quarters at 11 West Fifty-third Street, the site of the refurbished Rockefeller town house. The final two shows of the season—"Murals by American Painters and Photographers" and "Modern Architecture: International Exhibition"—revived the spirit of Barr's 1929 manifesto: to extend the museum's purview to all media of modern art.

The extraordinary achievement of those first years owed a great deal to the energies of what one called "a really evangelical team."[12] Barr's wife, Margaret, recalled the tone of the early days' informal meetings: "You felt an unbelievable vibration. It sort of centered around Alfred but, nevertheless, everybody was adding their contributions, reminding one another of things and saying 'we could do this,' 'we could do that.' It was absolutely electric."[13]

Alfred Barr encouraged a climate of rigor and adventure, and, by example, inspired his colleagues. At the time of Barr's death, Philip Johnson recalled his friend's most important characteristic: "his narrowly channeled torrential passion; at times a divine rage, at times a quiet concentration on his goal that was as inspiring and, yes, as frightening as his rages. Calvin had a true son."[14] Barr's zealotry was reflected everywhere in the museum, from the signs on the bathrooms and the catalog typography to the lapidary wall labels and modern furniture in the galleries. Barr simultaneously curated exhibitions, wrote catalogs, delivered lectures, traveled to Europe to secure loans, conferred with trustees, and inspired a young cadre of curators. Yet in his quest to create the world's greatest modern museum, he slowly fell apart.

A graphologist's report on his handwriting told the story in a nutshell: "The new always beckons, he will always follow the same pattern: seduced by yearning toward an unreachable, always receding *fata morgana*." Barr's high school yearbook described him at sixteen as "a sincere nut of the silent but deadly type."[15] At thirty, Barr had funneled that sincere nuttiness into the creation of a seminally important modern institution.

JOHNSON, HITCHCOCK, AND THE INTERNATIONAL STYLE SHOW

The museum's final exhibition in the Heckscher Building, "Modern Architecture: International Exhibition," opened on February 9, 1932. Philip Johnson, its chief organizer, was undergoing an operation, but his cocurator, Henry-Russell Hitchcock, led guests through a miniature city of white mechanomorphic buildings that stretched through five galleries. Proceeding from the smaller galleries just off the elevator, visitors passed a series of maquettes—an aluminum apartment building, a glass-and-plywood school, a papier-mâché housing development—on low platforms. The meticulously crafted models accompanied architectural elevations comprehensible only to experts (although Hitchcock never lacked explanatory words) and a frieze of black-and-white photographs, uniformly enlarged to three feet high. In the main gallery were models for houses designed by Frank Lloyd Wright and J. J. P. Oud, and featured at the center

Henry-Russell Hitchcock, by George Platt Lynes, 1935.

Philip Johnson, dandy-provocateur, January 18, 1933, by Carl Van Vechten.

were projects designed by Le Corbusier and Mies van der Rohe, the masters most revered by Hitchcock and Johnson respectively. "Mies was too cold and simple for Hitchcock," recalled Johnson, "and Corbusier was too much of a painter for me."

The exhibition encompassed the work of forty-six architects from fifteen countries, ranging from a gas station and a drugstore to factories and department stores. On this polyglot display of industrial-style metal spandrels and horizontal ribbon windows, pipe-rail parapets and glass screen walls, the two curators had imposed a modernist vision for building in the twentieth century. As Alfred Barr asserted in his introduction to the exhibition catalog, "The confusion of the past 40 years, or rather of the past century, may shortly come to an end."[16]

Supplanting a century of architectural disarray with a unified modernist polemic required both scholarship and propaganda. The process had begun in the summer of 1930, when the exhibition's two curators had motored through Europe.

In the months following his European tour with Johnson, Hitchcock wrote the text for *The International Style: Architecture Since 1922* and the catalog for "Modern Architecture: International Exhibition." These two books not only placed modern architecture within a historical context but made it seem the inevitable outcome of history. (Their proportions—two parts words to one part pictures—characterized modern architectural discourse, which from the outset consisted largely of theoretical discussion.) Hitchcock brought to the study of architecture an integrated approach and comprehensive sweep; his embrace of architectural idiosyncrasy and variety made the text all the more persuasive. The ideas were all Hitchcock's, Johnson recalled, but transforming the scholar's architectural logorrhea into readable prose depended on Johnson's discipline. "He didn't mind working, and I put him down at the table with some pencils. Two hours later there was some stuff," Johnson said. Without appearing to raise his voice or descend to polemical bravado, Hitchcock fashioned the intellectual backbone of a modern architectural canon.

Alfred Barr was an omniscient background figure. Separated by only a few floors in the same apartment building, he and Johnson constantly talked about modern art and architecture. "We were monomaniacs," Johnson recalled. "He was a Calvinist and I was too, so between us we were all for converting the world. A very dangerous American characteristic." Johnson wrote manifestolike articles that attacked those architects—such as

Joseph Urban and Norman Bel Geddes—whose popularizing brand of modern architecture did not fit within the narrow confines of his Bauhaus-derived doctrine. He considered them *moderne* rather than modern.

Describing himself as "the drummer and screamer-arounder,"[17] Johnson executed a splashy propagandistic stunt in the spring of 1931 that was perfectly in keeping with the tone and spirit of the avant-garde. When the projects of eight young modern architects were rejected by the Architectural League of New York's fusty but powerful show, Johnson organized the splinter group into a "secessionist" American Union for New Architecture. The attempt did not survive beyond its first meeting, but out of it grew an alternative show of "Rejected Architects." Their maquettes and plans were displayed in a West Side storefront lent by Julien Levy's father, and at Barr's suggestion Johnson hired a man to parade up Lexington Avenue in front of the league's exhibition at the Grand Central Palace wearing sandwich boards. "SEE REALLY MODERN ARCHITECTURE REJECTED BY THE LEAGUE AT 907 SEVENTH AVENUE," read the signs, prompting the league to have the sandwich man arrested. At this point reporters and critics jumped to the defense of embattled freedom of expression, and Johnson recalled, "We had a high old time, being mean to the establishment."[18]

"Modern Architecture: International Exhibition" and the simultaneous publication in 1932 of the catalog and *The International Style* provided the climax of the campaign. Hitchcock and Johnson's achievement was curatorial, scholarly, and above all polemical.[19]

Despite these feats and stunts, there was no groundswell of enthusiasm for the International Style. The exhibition attracted a relatively disappointing 33,000 visitors to the Museum of Modern Art before it began a two-year-long tour whose fourteen venues included the Wadsworth Atheneum as well as such department stores as Bullocks-Wilshire and Sears, Roebuck. But the exhibition and the publication of the books eventually became watershed events in the history of modern architecture in America. The transformation of the term—from "modern movement" to "modern architecture" to "modern style" to "international style"—also suggests how the leftist ideological roots of modern architecture were undercut and replaced by three formalist principles: (1) emphasis on volume enclosed by thin planes as opposed to static, heavy masses; (2) regularity of design as opposed to axial symmetry; (3) attention to elegance of materials and proportion as opposed to extrinsic ornament. This delicate balancing act—denuding aesthetics of their political foundations—allowed the upper class that supported the Museum of Modern Art to sanction modernist architecture without allying themselves to leftist politics.

Treating *The International Style* as a recipe book for building may have been a debasement of its elegant argument, but the authors certainly presented enticements to the docile, the doctrinaire, and the dutiful. They offered a manifesto reduced to three principles; proffered a specific list of dos (flat roofs, thin noncorroding metal window frames, sans-serif lettering) and don'ts (excess color, steel gargoyles, contrasting mortar, heavy mullions). They established a hierarchy of materials (moving up from stucco to glass brick to marble) and extended the absurdly formalistic promise that "Anyone who follows the rules . . . can produce buildings which are at least aesthetically sound."[20]

JULIEN LEVY STARTS A MODERN GALLERY

Shortly before Virgil Thomson's arrival in New York, the Julien Levy Gallery celebrated its first birthday. Its twenty-six-year-old, nattily dressed director bore the early marks of success. No matter that he had barely scraped by—launching a modern gallery during the Depression was itself a feat. The slight curve of his gallery's white plaster wall looked thoroughly modern, the friends at his openings embodied high-bohemian style, and—most important—the artworks that he exhibited were more advanced and eclectic than anything that could be seen in other galleries in New York. He not only showed photography (his first love) but also showcased the recent trends in modern painting after Cubism. "I *did* it," he said to himself on the opening of his first show, with a mixture of self-congratulation and awed surprise. After his abrupt departure from Harvard in 1927 and his impromptu trip to Paris, no one—least of all Julien Levy—had expected him to focus long enough to run a gallery.

When Levy had returned to America in the fall of 1927, he had established connections with the Paris art and literary world through Marcel Duchamp, Man Ray, and Mina Loy. His own country and especially his own family seemed backward and lackluster by comparison as he settled into the all-too-real life of marriage and soon fathered two sons. What niche would allow him to be stylish, carefree, and creative—and sufficiently stable to support his family?

Julien worked in his father's booming construction business for a year, and in 1930 he started working at Weyhe's Upper East Side book-

Julien and Joella Levy open their new gallery, 602 Madison Avenue, November 1931.

Julien and Joella Levy installing works in their new gallery, November 1931. *"I never did know how I got anywhere. I really seemed to follow my nose and my nose led into all kinds of things."* (Julien Levy)

store-gallery, where he sold books on the fine arts, along with a few prints and drawings. The position paid little, but it provided Levy an apprenticeship in running a gallery. Spurred by Erhard Weyhe's remark that, for a rich man's son, Julien was remarkably useful, the lowly assistant initiated an ambitious exhibition of Eugène Atget's photographs. At the same time he began to dream of owning his own gallery, which he saw as an extension of his "ingrained exhibitionism, for I am an exhibitionist, if only of other people's work."

Invoking Alfred Stieglitz's An American Place, Levy planned to call it "The Place of Levy." Stieglitz was both Levy's adopted mentor and the pioneering gallerist of American photography, and the eager young man spent hours listening to the loquacious figure in a black cape. "Stieglitz would wander around his gallery like a Western prophet or an Eastern guru," Levy recalled. On his twenty-fifth birthday, in 1931, Levy inherited the twenty-five thousand dollars his mother had left him in trust, and he dreamed of the pictures and objects he would buy to stock his planned "Art Shoppe." That summer he lived in Paris and made the arrangements for the first season of his gallery. He returned that fall with "almost an excess of material."[21]

Edgar Levy provided his son with a space in a building at 602 Park Avenue, just off Fifty-seventh Street. Julien devised an ingenious gallery design with one smoothly curving wall to set each work apart, encouraging the flow of traffic and, in Levy's mind, looking modern without slavishly evoking Bauhaus austerity. He thought that covering the walls with monk's cloth was distasteful, rejected the red velvet walls of blue-chip galleries such as Knoedler, and regarded as impractical Stieglitz's practice of re-plastering and repainting after each exhibition. Instead he ran two strips of molding two feet apart across the plaster walls, grooved so that photographs could float, sandwiched between two layers of glass.

The gallery's opening show of American photography was a success, or so he claimed. It was widely admired for its stylish installation, but nothing was sold. "Art has become here such a matter of fad," Levy wrote at the end of 1931, "that there soon must be a complete revulsion and the public will loathe the sight of any picture."[22] Julien quickly became adept at judging the evolving fashions of modern art, and his gallery became not just a place for art commerce but a site for screenings and parties.

Rotating his exhibitions every three weeks, Levy spotlit artistic trends faster than any of his few competitors.[23] After his death, Virgil Thomson

MODERN TASTE: WHAT NEW YORK SAW

MUSEUM OF MODERN ART (COMPLETE EXHIBITION SCHEDULE, 1929–1932)

Cézanne, Gauguin, Seurat, and
van Gogh (1929, opening
exhibition)
Paintings by Nineteen Living Amer-
icans (1929)
Painting in Paris from American
Collections (1930)
Weber, Klee, Lehmbruck, Maillol
(1930)
Forty-six Painters and Sculptors
Under Thirty-Five Years of
Age (1930)
Charles Burchfield: Early Watercol-
ors, 1916–1918 (1930)
Homer, Ryder, and Eakins (1930)
Corot, Daumier (1930)
Painting and Sculpture by Living
Americans (1930)
Toulouse-Lautrec, Redon (1931)
Memorial Exhibition: The Collection
of Miss Lizzie P. Bliss (1931)
German Painting and Sculpture
(1931)
Henri Matisse (1931)
Diego Rivera (1931)
Modern Architecture: International
Exhibition (1932)
Murals by American Painters and
Photographers (1932)
Persian Fresco Painting—Facsimi-
les of Seventh Century Fres-
coes in Isfahan (1932)
A Brief Survey of Modern Painting
(1932)

American Painting and Sculpture,
1862–1932 (1932)

INTERNATIONAL STYLE ARCHITECTURE: THE BIG NINE ACCORDING TO JOHNSON AND HITCHCOCK

Walter Gropius
Mies van der Rohe
Le Corbusier
Frank Lloyd Wright
Richard Neutra
Bowman Brothers
J. J. P. Oud
Raymond Hood
Howe and Lescaze

THE JULIEN LEVY GALLERY

* = American solo premiere

Surrealist Exhibition (1932)
Walker Evans (1932)*
George Platt Lynes (1932)*
Man Ray (1932)
Alexander Calder (1932)
Berenice Abbott (1932)
Max Ernst (1932)
Eugene Berman (1932)*
Joseph Cornell (1932)*
Lee Miller (1933)*
Mina Loy (1933)*
Pavel Tchelitchew (1933)*
Henri Cartier-Bresson (1933)*
Serge Lifar Russian Ballet collection
(1933)
Salvador Dalí (1933)*

observed that he had achieved his distinction early "by *being* early, which is the only way it can be achieved."[24] From the outset Levy possessed the best ear, the fleetest transatlantic organization, and the most eclectic sensibility of New York's modern galleries. Assessing the gallery's first three years, Joella Levy observed, "I have always insisted that Julien's great success came from his having all the artists across the pond. Because we could hang as we wanted, print what we wanted, all at top speed."

Levy showed young, now-classic photographers including Berenice Abbott, Henri Cartier-Bresson, Walker Evans, Lee Miller, George Platt Lynes, and Man Ray, as well as such older classic photographers as Nadar and Eugène Atget. (One of the only buyers was Kirk Askew, who bought a Nadar portrait of George Sand.) But he by no means stuck to photography alone. The Julien Levy Gallery is most famously linked to Surrealism —and the cover of his autobiography billed him as "The Man Who Organized the First Surrealist Exhibition in America." After that 1931 inauguration, he showcased such Surrealists as Max Ernst and Salvador Dalí.

Levy's gallery provided America's headquarters for a now-forgotten group of artists known as the neo-Romantics: Pavel Tchelitchew, Eugene and Leonid Berman, Christian Bérard, Kristians Tonny. Representing a figurative alternative to abstraction, the neo-Romantics are frequently characterized as modernist kitsch art, and Tchelitchew and Bérard may be best remembered for their stage design. Their paintings were avidly collected by the Harvard modernists in the early 1930s.[25] Julien Levy also showcased work that fit no school, such as wire sculptures and mobiles by Alexander Calder, figurative paintings by Mina Loy, photographic portraits by novelist Max Ewing, and collages and objects by Joseph Cornell. One might assume that Levy's stable of now-classic modern artists led to commercial success. In fact, his finances were precarious. Nor was it the famous artists who kept the gallery afloat. Sales of work by Eugene Berman and Massimo Campigli provided the gallery's bread and butter. Levy sustained heavy losses on his first two exhibitions of Dalí, lost money on Alberto Giacometti, broke even on Tchelitchew.

Levy began to show avant-garde films at the beginning of 1932, including Fernand Léger's *Ballet Mécanique*, accompanied by George Antheil's player piano roll, and Man Ray's *L'Étoile de Mer*, accompanied by John McAndrew at the piano. The following year, the gallery inaugurated an ongoing Film Society, which in 1935 melded into the Museum of Modern Art's permanent department of film. "Julien was always ahead of his time," observed Maurice Grosser, "and he had a movie camera before anyone else did."[26]

His mother-in-law, the poet and painter Mina Loy, provided access to that other side of the "pond," Paris, and served as the gallery's Parisian eyes and ears. Julien decided which artists he would show, but Loy often selected the individual works and negotiated the deals.

Julien's Harvard friends—primarily Chick Austin, Alfred Barr, and Lincoln Kirstein—provided essential connections to the museum world.[27] On Saturday mornings in the early 1930s, Edward Warburg recalled, they often toured the galleries along Fifty-seventh Street, embarking from Alfred Barr's apartment and ending the day at Levy's gallery. Joella's beauty, her industrious efficiency, and her Continental manner made her an alluring presence at the gallery, and more than one visitor fell for her charms.[28]

Like so many successful art dealers, Levy became a jack-of-all-trades. He designed graphically striking invitations and sometimes even wrote his own reviews, each tailored to the style of the art critic receiving it. He claimed to have pioneered the cocktail opening, democratizing Knoedler's practice of champagne in the back room for special customers and providing a magnet for conviviality. Most important, he created a milieu in which anything could happen. Of one opening, Henry McBride wrote, "The atmosphere was precisely that of the Boeuf sur le Toit back in the days when Paris used to be good."[29]

LINCOLN KIRSTEIN ZIGZAGS

Of all the Harvard modernists, Lincoln Kirstein in 1932 most resembled the protagonist of a picaresque novel. His orbit ranged from Harlem speakeasies to Oyster Bay estates, and from painter Robert Chanler's raucous bohemian parties on Nineteenth Street to the Brooklyn sailor bars along Sand Street. While each of the other Harvard modernists had found his niche, Kirstein zigzagged. As the title of a novel he wrote but never published suggests, he saw his vocational struggle as "A Choice of Weapons." Which would he choose?

Kirstein regarded Harvard as his launching pad and passport, his "luxurious playpen or laboratory," and his graduation in 1930 carried with it the weight of expectation. He remained in Cambridge until 1931 to run the twin enterprises of his undergraduate years: *The Hound & Horn* and

Lincoln Kirstein, by Carl Van Vechten, May 8, 1933, shortly before meeting George Balanchine. *"My brain is so full of plans that seem about to break through that I'm bursting. Every day seems to bring a new complication, a new friend, a new aspect."* (Kirstein)

the Harvard Society for Contemporary Art. By the spring of 1931, he had curtailed his involvement with the Harvard Society for Contemporary Art. As he plunged into the new, he struggled to rub out the patrician features of his past. "I killed all that," he said of his Boston and Cambridge upbringing. "I had to kill all that."

Kirstein moved to New York in 1931, where he continued editing *The Hound & Horn* from a pair of closet-sized offices at 10 East Forty-third Street, next door to Muriel Draper's home. But the leadership of the magazine was, he noted, increasingly "taken over by Southern Agrarians under the captaincy of [Allen] Tate, and finally by a mixture of Anglican Marxists(!), Trotskyites, and 'humanists.'" The mechanics of getting each issue out were turned over to a secretary.

Louis Kirstein continued to tolerate his son's mercurial shifts, expensive and odd tastes, and ambitious ideas about starting something new. All he demanded of his son in return was that he address the inevitable paternal question, "What leads you to suppose that you can really *do* it?" Following the obligatory and not entirely pleasant discussion, the elder Kirstein agreed to provide hands-off support for his son's invariably costly activities. *The Hound & Horn's* production expenses alone set him back about eight thousand dollars per year.[30] He lectured his son "that there were two kinds of energy: the energy to establish something and the energy to maintain it." He was all too aware that his son possessed primarily the former.

In New York, Kirstein shared a Greenwich Village apartment with an ex-cowboy. He dressed in Navy surplus sailor uniforms, took up boxing at the West Side YMCA (then, as now, a homoerotic milieu), and fraternized with firemen and sailors. These activities made up the strenuous program he called his "postgraduate education." His new friends embodied the grittily plebeian life that Kirstein regarded as more "real" than that of Harvard Yard and were certainly more physically attractive. "I was the worst physical snob in the world," he recalled.

In addition to flirting with burly men and New York lowlife, Kirstein was drawn into socialist politics through his infatuation with a sharecropper organizer. The dominant member on the Junior Advisory Council of the Museum of Modern Art, he initiated an exhibition, "Murals by American Painters and Photographers," that resulted in the museum's first major political controversy. One of the painted murals, by Hugo Gellert, depicted John D. Rockefeller, J. P. Morgan, and Al Capone behind a wall of money bags, the gangster wielding a machine gun. The trustees regarded it as "Commie stuff" but did not stop it from being exhibited.

Kirstein also served for a few weeks as Walker Evans's assistant, photographing New England architecture. Despite the chaos of his zigzagging, Kirstein's ultimate direction soon came into focus. "Whatever it was that lurked as an imaginative need," he wrote at the end of his life, "'ballet' stuck in my elementary judgment as a luminous magnet."

In the spring of 1932, Kirstein found himself looking into a mirror that stretched the length of former Ballets Russes choreographer Michel Fokine's drawing room. His hand on the barre, struggling to learn ballet's five classic positions, he saw in his reflection an awkward and unlikely dancer. His physical presence was gawky and stiff, his head large, his ears protruding. As his friend Eddie Warburg observed, "Lincoln was like a great dane with a tea table in the room."[31] But none of this really mattered. "He had no hopes of being a dancer," recalled Paul Draper Jr., Kirstein's fellow class member. "He did it long enough to figure out how tough a dancer must be, how mad you have to be to be a dancer."[32]

In Fokine's drawing room, he hoped to absorb dance by means that were corporal, historical, and mystical. He stayed on after class to interview Fokine, scribbling notes about his early years with Diaghilev's Ballets Russes. The reason for the interview and his presence on the barre was that he was writing a biography of Fokine, which was published in London two years later. "By birth, training, or merit I could never belong," Kirstein wrote of the ballet world, "but by association with Fokine, something might rub off on me."[33]

The two women most instrumental in guiding Kirstein toward ballet were Muriel Draper and Romola Nijinsky. Pointing young homosexual men toward their arena of greatest possibility was Muriel's métier, while Romola's strength was extracting money from balletomanes in the name of her schizophrenic dancer husband, Vaslav.

"I owed her much of whatever solid intellectual or moral development I may have made," Kirstein wrote of Muriel Draper, "and through her met the twin strata of society about which I was most inquisitive." She encouraged him to take risks, but she was also blunt. When he told her that he wanted to be a dancer, the pale, gold-turbaned woman with electric blue eyes responded that he was too tall, too old, and too rich. His talents, she pronounced, should be directed toward organization and man-

agement. Perhaps Draper saw in Kirstein someone who could fill the vacuum left by Diaghilev's death.

In the midst of Kirstein's chaotic sallies into high life and low life,
love life and politics, Draper provided consistency. They communicated
nearly every day. Although she was twenty-one years older and regarded as
a menace by Kirstein's parents, Lincoln even became romantically interested in her. The romance never flourished, but her role in his development proved seminal: "She became the judge and oracle of most of my
activity from the time I left Boston and Cambridge until I began to work
with the ballet."

Romola Nijinsky entered Kirstein's life in 1931 in the resplendent
drawing room of Mrs. William Vanderbilt, a patron of Diaghilev's Ballets
Russes. Speaking four languages, immaculately and expensively dressed,
Madame Nijinsky was both charming and steel-willed. Quickly sizing up
Kirstein's promising financial position and his fascination with her hus-
band, she soon swept him along in her schemes. "She was one of the san-
est people I have ever known," Kirstein observed near the end of his life.
"She lived off nothing and could manipulate anyone."

Romola Nijinsky was literally stateless (her passport had been issued
by the League of Nations), she slid from euphoria to suicidal feelings, and
her desperate schemes for survival constantly shifted as she was evicted
from one luxurious hotel after another. She proposed to write a biography
of her husband. No matter that Nijinsky's profound schizophrenia rendered him uninterviewable, no matter that Romola could not write—she
pushed on. To fill in the lacunae in Nijinsky's life, she engaged in seances
with an elderly seer called "Ma" Garrett, and to ghostwrite the book she
enlisted Kirstein.

Although she sometimes terrified and infuriated him, Kirstein freely
suffered her hysterical ups and downs over the next year. His new connection to Nijinsky, combined with his coincidental presence at Diaghilev's
funeral three years earlier, seemed a providential link. He later wrote, "I
felt endowed or, well, *chosen*." Romola introduced Kirstein to the manip-
ulative ploys one needed to run a ballet company, and she introduced him
to potential patrons. But her contribution to Kirstein's development had
little to do with concrete guidance and everything to do with a mystical
feeling of connection to a grand tradition: "She unlocked for me the closets, corridors, and subcellars of an edifice in which I would spend the rest
of my life."

Chick Austin as Osram, "the Sea-God of Magic," at the Wadsworth Atheneum, December 1944. *"Chick Austin was air and fire."* (Marguerite Yourcenar)

MAGIC AT HARTFORD

At eight-fifteen on a Thursday evening in mid-April 1932, Chick Austin stepped before a black velvet curtain, his abbreviated white jacket framed by a bright yellow proscenium arch, his figure illuminated by soft footlights. "I am the Great Osram," he majestically announced. Most of the audience seated in the barrel-vaulted tapestry gallery of the Wadsworth Atheneum were under ten years old. Accompanied by an upright piano, "Osram" snatched dozens of bright chiffon handkerchiefs and billiard balls from the air and pulled rabbits from hats and canaries from saucepans. Against a flamboyant backdrop, "Osram, The Man of Multiple Mysteries" was an ideal persona for Austin. "An important key to him is sleight of hand and concealment of mechanism," observed Austin's son. "You can only understand him in terms of theater." He had by then mastered many magic tricks, but his most implausible trick was the transformation of Hartford from the "Insurance City" into the "New Athens."[34]

By the time Virgil Thomson came to Hartford in December 1932, Austin's transformation of the Wadsworth Atheneum was nearly complete; under his guidance the museum had metamorphosed into an internationally renowned oasis of modernism. Only Alfred Barr's achievement at the Museum of Modern Art could compare. Yet their style could not have been more different.

The methodical, scholarly Barr was Paul Sachs's ideal. Chick Austin, by contrast, followed his instincts and tacked to the prevailing winds. But, as Barr later wrote Austin, "You did everything sooner and more brilliantly than any of us."[35] One of Austin's rare pieces of expressive writing, a description of the impresario of the Ballets Russes, reflects his own aspirations:

> With erudition and an unparalleled taste, he knit together the arts of painting, music, literature, acting, and choreography into a brilliant pattern, a triumphal procession, and set against it the eternal beauty of youth. Forever fortunate are those who were privileged to see the creations of Diaghilev. To them the joyful pangs of memory will be a constant proof that the twentieth century has known splendor devoid of vulgarity and taste kept inviolate from commercial degradation.[36]

In many respects Austin flouted the Harvard model of the museum professional. His only identifiable professional ability was his extraordinary connoisseurship. ("Chick's eye" became a legend among the museum world when he recognized Bernardo Strozzi's *Saint Catherine of Alexandria*, before it had been fully uncrated, as a replica rather than the original he had seen once eight years earlier.) His exhibition catalog essays are short and few, and he often used slangy vernacular language to describe his profession (e.g., he worked in "the art racket," beautiful paintings were "swell numbers"). "He was anti-intellectual by policy," Kirstein wrote, and Austin claimed, with slight exaggeration, that he read only *The Saturday Evening Post*. He could barely manage his own finances, much less those of an institution, and he showed little interest in becoming the custodian of other people's taste. The purpose of a museum, Austin joked, was "to entertain its director." (Virgil Thomson added: "And come to think of it, if it does not do that, God help us all!")

His formidable strengths as a museum director were the flip side of his professional shortcomings. Kirk Askew observed, "Psychologically Austin was a creative man *manqué*." He ran his museum like an artist or a poet, making decisions intuitively, ruling his small empire by enthusiasm and odd forays into new territories. Blurring the line between work and play, he incited his colleagues to follow suit—as Julien Levy put it, he "seduced them into unexpected achievement." Friends described him as "always at the ready," leaning slightly forward, talking rapidly, taking a drag on the Pall Mall cigarette that perpetually hung from his lower lip, his hand grazing the speaker's elbow. Austin's mannerisms provided the visible barometer of his enthusiasm. "Ecstasy did not embarrass him as it does so many Americans," Kirk Askew observed. His quivering receptivity was not mindless cheerleading; he grounded his judgments in the thousands of artworks he had witnessed since childhood. His friends asserted that Austin "got it" faster than anybody else in his generation.[37] Henry-Russell Hitchcock observed that Austin possessed "the happy talent of realization— sometimes almost impromptu realization—of ideas which others could cope with only more ploddingly and at a further remove from actuality."

Austin was not only a magician and a museum director but a hands-on creative practitioner. He ran a summer theater, designing its sets and acting lead roles; he danced (ballet) in the privacy of his office; he designed his own home and the interior of his museum; New York's Brummer Gallery and the Museum of Modern Art exhibited his paintings. His proficiency in these art forms ranged from inventiveness to doggedness, but the seriousness of his amateurism and the intensity of his participatory play earned him Virgil Thomson's praise as "a whole cultural movement in one man."

Fostering the latest waves of modernism offered one challenge and convincing his trustees to support him another. He assessed just how much the trustees could take, and then, as Lincoln Kirstein observed, "he administered discreet overdoses of piquant surprise." His most important potential ally was Charles Goodwin, who for twenty-eight years served not only as the museum's president but also as its treasurer. Through Chick's marriage to Helen Goodwin, he became "Uncle Charlie." Tall, handsome, and powerful, Goodwin had once run for governor of Connecticut on the Republican ticket, and his conservative New England style and complete absence of interest in art gave him and Austin little in common. The Goodwin family had once owned Hartford's fashionable Scarborough Street, where Chick and Helen Austin lived.

The Austin house on Scarborough Street, 80 feet long by 18 feet deep, inspired by the Villa Ferretti, photograph by Eugene Gaddis.

The Austins' house on Scarborough Street exemplified its owner: wacky in everything from the spontaneity of its conception to the extravagant objects that filled it. Impressed by the Villa Ferretti, a Palladian-style villa he photographed on his honeymoon in 1929, Austin asked Leigh H. French Jr. to copy the 1596 structure in wood on the site of a garden. Eighty feet long but only eighteen feet deep, the house resembled a stage set. Other Goodwins on the block skeptically called it "the pasteboard palace." With its theatrical interior, opulent first floor, and Bauhaus-inspired second floor, it embodied Austin's passion for the grand past and the austere present. As he joked to a friend, "The house is just like me—all façade."[38]

Carefully balancing a program of traditional and modern art at the museum, Chick managed to satisfy Uncle Charlie and the trustees while freeing himself to engage his modernist passions. "These pictures are chic," he said. "It is much more satisfying esthetically to be amused, to be frightened even, than to be bored."[39] When Thomson came to Hartford on December 19, Austin was facing the specter of boredom. The day before he had celebrated his thirty-second birthday; the anniversary had elicited an annual stocktaking: Now that he had transformed the museum, what battles remained to be fought?

Virgil Thomson performed sections of *Four Saints in Three Acts* for as many Friends and Enemies of Modern Music as could be squeezed into Chick and Helen Austin's shallow living room. Austin announced the opera with characteristic enthusiasm, claiming that it had brought Virgil Thomson fame in Europe. In fact, Chick had never heard a note of it and even botched its name on the invitation for the evening, which referred to the opera as "'Two or Three Saints' with lyrics by Gertrude Stein."[40] Ever since Henry-Russell Hitchcock had first spoken to him about *Four Saints*, Austin had wanted to produce it on a small scale, using a small orchestra from the Hartford School of Music, local choral groups, and his own sets.

During Thomson's visit to Hartford, Austin excitedly laid out a new and grander plan: he would stage the opera at the Wadsworth Atheneum, and the Friends and Enemies of Modern Music would sponsor it. This grand plan was, like Austin himself, "all façade." As John Houseman bluntly put it, "Certainly any contract Chick made was worthless, he never had any money." Nor did the Friends and Enemies have any experience producing on a grander scale than living-room musicales.

Formed in 1928, the society "has believed that contemporary music deserved a hearing and it has frankly recognized the valuable stimulating effect of controversy," according to its own literature. To these ends it presented performances of works by Stravinsky, Satie, Milhaud, Schoenberg, Hindemith, Antheil, and Ives. The Friends and Enemies met sporadically —a couple of times in 1929 and 1930, not at all in 1931, only once in 1932. But, as it later announced in the opera program, the society wanted to "offer to friends and enemies a new field of controversy."[41] By 1932, Chick Austin was the driving force of the Friends and Enemies, assisted by his wife as the organization's treasurer. Its sponsorship allowed Austin to move forward without being so directly under the thumb of the trustees. "Chick went ahead with the opera plan in the same way that he accomplished other things, by finding out whether anyone would try to stop him," Thomson wrote. "Then once inside a project he would rely entirely on instinct and improvisation."

Austin's enthusiasm reflected not only his appreciation for the opera but its strategic utility in enhancing his grand scheme for the new wing at the Wadsworth Atheneum. Chick even planned to make his opera debut in the third act, causing pigeons to appear and disappear and transforming a small tree into a bouquet of red feathers.

Constructing the new wing offered Austin the biggest challenge of his Hartford career. Money posed no problem; museum benefactor Samuel P. Avery Jr. had donated $225,000 for a new wing in 1918, and the combination of accumulating interest and the declining costs of Depression-era labor now made construction economically feasible. The problem was aesthetic. The trustees selected a Beaux-Arts-trained architect, Benjamin Wistar Morris, and his son-in-law partner, Robert B. O'Connor, to design a wing that would harmonize with the Morgan Memorial that Morris had designed in 1907. But Austin wanted to build the first International Style museum building in the world. While Morris and O'Connor were not entirely deaf to Austin's ideas, they provided a conservative—and cautionary—voice: "It can never be forgotten that a Museum sets a definite standard of taste in its community. . . . For the purely transitory, however alluring it may be at the moment, can only hinder in the long run that essential element among the Museum's functions, the development of good taste."[42]

Austin persisted with his campaign. Although Philip Johnson and Henry-Russell Hitchcock played no direct role in designing the Avery Wing, they influenced him from the sidelines. Hitchcock spoke with Austin constantly throughout the period of design, and Johnson's Miesian New York apartment offered inspiration. Equally important, their "Modern Architecture" exhibition moved from the Museum of Modern Art to the Wadsworth Atheneum at just the moment when the trustees approved the building plans. Since the Avery Wing's exterior was designed to complement the original museum buildings, the architects used Tennessee marble and bronze. Austin fought to make the interior more up-to-date.

Around the time Virgil Thomson performed his opera at the Austins' house, Chick delivered an impassioned speech to the trustees about the necessity for a modern design. Art history demanded that "a museum of living things" should reflect the present age. To interrupt pure planes and straight lines with columns and machine-made garlands was architecturally meaningless, even spiritually frivolous. Among his demands he included modern lighting, rectilinear balustrades, doors without transoms, and radiator grills. Should the trustees not agree, Austin offered to resign. "If, after five years, the trustees have no faith in me," he said, "then there is no point to my continuing as director." Austin knew that his design concerns would seem out of scale with his threat. (Would he really resign over skinny railings and some radiator grills?) But he knew he was right: "Perhaps I can be forgiven on the ground of my anxiety that the Avery building be as fine as I have tried to imagine it and excused for my insistence on details which may seem unimportant and irrelevant at the moment, but which I am certain are vital to the ultimate success of the building."[43]

When the trustees caved in, Austin was jubilant. He imagined not only the new wing but the events that would inaugurate it. Upstairs: the first Pablo Picasso retrospective in America.[44] Downstairs: *Four Saints in Three Acts.*

The World
of the Stettheimers

On December 25, 1932, five days after visiting Chick Austin in Hart-ford, Virgil Thomson was sitting at the Stettheimers' piano, regaling a small audience with selections from *Four Saints*. Among the Christmas guests at the Alwyn Court that night was Henry McBride, who reported that Thomson encored with Georges Hugnet's "Le Berceau de Gertrude Stein, ou le Mystère de la Rue de Fleurus." Thomson's top notes cracked in the performance because of a head cold, McBride wrote, but nonethe-less, "It was to die."[1]

Thomson performed virtually the same repertory he had played at the Stettheimers' in 1929, but the 1932 performance highlighted the changes that had ensued in the intervening years. Exactly two years and one day after Thomson had last seen Gertrude Stein, Hugnet's "Le Berceau de Gertrude Stein," now had, to McBride's ears, an edge of satire that he had not previously detected. Following Thomson's first *Four Saints* performance in 1929, McBride had written Stein that the guests all prayed that the opera would be produced—as if such an event would require divine intervention. After Thomson's 1932 performance, he noted with guarded amazement that "the opera really is to be given next year."

FLORINE DEMURS

Since Thomson had last seen Florine Stettheimer, in 1929, she had entered a seesawing commitment to the opera, and she had painted Thomson's portrait. Unlike her other models, Thomson became a disruptive agent: his invitation to bring Florine's art to the stage threatened the Stettheimers' tacit family rules about privacy and anonymity. Over the next few years, Florine's responses to Thomson's invitation reflect the tug between ambition and family pressure.

Consider her first diary entry mentioning the opera, after Thomson's private performance in 1929: "Virgil Thomson played his whole opera *Four Saints in Three Acts* to me today—it delighted me and his voice is so pretty—. He sang the whole—he makes the words by Gertrude Stein come alive and flutter and in sound have a meaning. He wants me to do the visual part of the opera."

She scrupulously erased her initial entry—"it is delightful"—and altered it to "it delighted me"—a slight change but an important distinction between a banal word of praise ("delightful") and the more subjective and committed phrase "it delighted me." She also changed "He sang it all" to "He sang the whole" and employed uncharacteristic emphatic modifiers ("so pretty") and poetic language ("the words by Gertrude Stein come alive and flutter"). This departure from Florine's usual dry, reportorial diary voice suggests a particular engagement.

Yet even in privately scrawled expressions she declined to pledge her participation unequivocally. Her next mention of the opera begins, noncommittally, "I may do Virgil Thomson . . ."[2] One's hope of reading her intentions are frustrated, however, for Ettie destroyed the next six pages of Florine's diary with a razor, as she revealed after her sister's death. Ettie's neat excisions bury parts of the story, but their existence suggests other tales about family privacy and will.

Florine may also have been uncomfortable about the opera's subject matter. Although she was Jewish, she could certainly respond to the opera's theme as a metaphor for a life dedicated to art. "We weren't being religious, but we were being artists," Virgil said. "Florine was being an

Florine Stettheimer in her garden, ca. 1916.

artist who knew how to handle materials and colors and little Sunday afternoon spectacles, saints and angels." Stettheimer voiced her antipathy to Stein's text publicly, even though McBride and Van Vechten, two of her closest friends, were Stein's most vocal American supporters. "I really haven't the least notion what she is talking about," Stettheimer told a newspaper reporter. She preferred the writings of Marcel Proust, whose novels she read in sequential rotation. "I am a Proustian, and surely there can be nothing farther from the style of Proust than that of Miss Stein."[3]

Ettie had published her novels anonymously as Henrie Waste (HENRIEtta WAlter STEttheimer) and repeatedly warned Florine that her participation in the opera must not publicly embarrass the Stettheimer family. Her fears reflect the family's social anxiety about its place in Jewish society. Through intricate intermarriages, the Stettheimers were related to several prominent Jewish families—the Seligmans, the Goodharts, and the Guggenheims—but they remained on the fringes of "Our Crowd." They did not have the fortunes of these families, the social position that money brought, the hope of marrying into a prosperous family.[4] On top of this, the Stettheimers had suffered a family scandal: around the turn of the century, their father had taken off and disappeared. He was erased from the family history, but the echoes of his desertion were felt long after. The three sisters assumed joint responsibility for protecting their mother from any further trauma,[5] and her subsequent illnesses and depression allowed her to control her daughters. One of them was expected to tend her at all times, despite the constant presence of capable servants.

The summer before she met Thomson in 1929, Florine wrote of her frustration in her diary with uncharacteristic directness: "This winter has worn me out very much. I look haggard and feel prostrated. I have had to watch time slip by while I sat in enforced idleness, [during] which I could have painted, because of the equal division of time to be home with mother."

"Three sisters are three sisters," Thomson remarked, echoing Chekhov. They enacted their separateness through costume and vocation. Each had a signature style: Carrie, gold and white dresses, pearl dog collars, and rhinestone tiaras; Florine, black satin harem pants and spangled net; Ettie, always in red and black. Each worked "in strict singleness," showing her creations to the other sisters only upon completion. By the time Virgil entered their lives, however, only Florine, nearing sixty, still actively pursued her vocation. After a decade of meticulously applying foils and satin, velvet and silk, Carrie seemed destined to leave her dollhouse unfinished. Ettie had stopped writing, and the flirtations that had enlivened her existence were over. Her last autobiographical novel, *Love Days*, evoked an era as poignantly preserved as a faded corsage.

"Carrie and Ettie were both sad ladies," Virgil said. "Florine was not sad." Ettie believed that stage design was Carrie's true vocation—the dollhouse a facile substitute—and only unfavorable circumstances had prevented her from finding success.[6] So when Florine received the invitation that had eluded her older, martyred sister, she was accused of encroaching on Carrie's territory.

| | |

Florine's participation in the opera forced her to traverse the land-mined terrain of publicity and commerce. After her 1916 solo exhibition at Knoedler, where she had failed to sell a single piece, she had effectively circumvented these troublesome issues by refusing to exhibit her paintings in commercial galleries. Although such prominent gallerists as Alfred Stieglitz and Curt Valentine proposed solo exhibitions, she confined her loans to noncommercial group shows.

She was reticent to expose her paintings beyond the cloistered atmosphere in which they had been created and was so averse to the idea of anyone owning her paintings that one of her wills stipulated they be buried with her. At Knoedler she had virtually re-created her bedroom milieu within the gallery space. She had been wounded by her first experience in a commercial gallery. In her journal she reported that few had asked to see the price list, and that dull humiliation was followed at the closing of the exhibition with two ruthless words: "Nothing sold." (Ettie echoed the sentiment in her own journal: "It's too bad she didn't make more noise and sell."[7]) Florine's friend Max Ewing reported that she asked two hundred and fifty thousand dollars for each picture. While Ewing may have exaggerated the price, he understood that it was an issue of control: "The result is that these magnificent masterpieces can only be seen by people whom Florine chooses to invite to see them."[8]

Yet Florine craved more widespread attention to her work. She invited journalists to private unveilings at the Beaux Arts Building, she subscribed to Romeicke's Clipping Service, and to her closest friends she expressed dismay at her relative anonymity outside the Alwyn Court. Florine considered her painting of Marcel Duchamp's thirtieth birthday party one more advertisement for an already famous artist, and on her six-tieth birthday in 1931 she confided her own desire for such an advertise-ment: "I had hoped to have a pendant for *La Fête à Duchamp. La Fête à Florine.*"[9] A year later she asked Henry McBride if she would ever be res-cued from oblivion.[10] "As for fame, you get it, as I often have told you, not by deserving it but by outraging public opinion," he replied. "But it is pub-licity that gets you into Radio City and such places."[11] *Four Saints* pro-vided an opportunity for publicity—without the nettlesome problems of commerce. To clear her mind of the complicated family pressures, Florine retreated to the sanctuary of her studio.

The light-shot, two-story studio in Midtown's Beaux Arts Building overlooked Bryant Park, which she referred to as "my garden." She de-signed furniture and accessories for her studio, incorporating great quanti-ties of red velvet, glass-and-gold tables, and a golden bowl bedecked with

Florine Stettheimer's lace bedroom, Beaux Arts Building, photographed by Peter Juley. Intimates saw connections between her bedroom and her decor for *Four Saints in Three Acts.*

gilt flowers. Carl Van Vechten observed, "Thaïs, Diane de Poitiers, or Ninon de Lenclos would have adored the place."[12] Cellophane curtains hung at the tall windows, a bust of George Washington occupied one niche, and a red carpet led upstairs to what she called "the lace bedroom." Here Nottingham lace stretched over the arched windows and two putti flanked her narrow, lace-covered bed. Thomson regarded her bedroom as an elaborate joke about virginity, and Henry McBride wrote, "The least observing visitors agreed that the studio and the pictures were all of one piece."[13]

In this otherworldly setting Florine arrived at her first decision about designing the opera. She wrote a brief poem, "To V.T.," which she never mailed—it was found on a scrap of paper after her death. It voiced her private struggle:

> The thrush in our elm tree top
> has been singing questions
> for days
> I feel clarified
> This is my clarification
> My role is to paint
> your four active saints
> and their props
> inside and out your portrait
> St. Gertrude will protect you all.[14]

To research the opera's setting—all of her paintings were inspired by specific associations—Florine consulted an encyclopedia. She found Avila illustrated by a photograph of stone lions chained down with real iron chains. Such literalness amused and inspired her, and reminded her of the stone lions flanking the New York Public Library, just around the corner from her studio.

Stettheimer had painted her portrait of Virgil Thomson in 1930, but she did not unveil it until April 13, 1931. Dressed in pink, shod in dainty patent-leather shoes, he sat at a light green piano with 4STS.3ACTS. 4STS.3ACTS.4STS.3ACTS.4STS.running above the keyboard. Looming over all was a mask of Gertrude Stein, manipulating four marionettes on a toy stage. In the upper corner, Carl Van Vechten knowingly observed to Thomson, was "a black *pansy*."[15] In the lower right a benign-looking lion

The Cathedral of Avila, whose stone lions restrained by real chains provided inspiration for Florine Stettheimer.

was chained to a circular red pillow. Each of the principals had banners: "St. Gertrude," "St. Thérèse," "St. Ignatius," and "St. Virgil." By adding a banner that proclaimed "Florine St.," she joined them in both the painting and the collaboration.

|||

As Florine proudly showed Thomson the portrait, she also informed him that she would not be able to design the opera; she had already used up all her inspiration on the painting. Thomson suspected that her refusal reflected family pressures: "Ettie had been at her and said you mustn't do this because it might be a failure. None of them wanted a failure. They were afraid of it. They had persuaded her to say she couldn't do it, and she kept saying to me, 'I put everything I know about that opera in your portrait.'"

Virgil simply refused to accept her withdrawal. He commanded her, "Get some new ideas." Fortunately, by the time he returned to Paris, she had changed her mind. But this would not be her last demurral.

OPPOSITE: *Portrait of Virgil Thomson* (1930) by Florine Stettheimer, oil on canvas, 97.2 x 51.1 cm. Art Institute of Chicago, gift of Virgil Thomson (1975.677).

CHAPTER 10

High Bohemia
and Modernism

"Little magazines" and "little theater," as they were dubbed in the 1910s, were frequently used to disseminate the avant-garde movement, but the notion of "little opera" seemed anathema. By nature a costly extravaganza, opera—even an opera as unorthodox as *Four Saints in Three Acts*—depends on the support of moneyed society. As critic Clement Greenberg observed, the avant-garde has always relied on a sympathetic class of patrons, "to which it has always remained attached by an umbilical cord of gold."[1] Virgil Thomson knew precisely where to go to find such gold.

In France he lunched with the Comtesse de Polignac and supped with the Vicomte de Noailles, and he consulted Étienne de Beaumont. Each of these functioned not only as a tastemaker but as an active patron and impresario of the avant-garde. Beaumont, for example, staged Les Soirées de Paris, costume balls on the lavish scale of opera. The Noailles financed and screened Salvador Dalí and Luis Buñuel's now-classic film *Un Chien Andalou* to scandalized response. The Polignacs commissioned modernist architecture—Le Corbusier designed their house—and staged musicales. These patrons devoted both money and organizational energy to adventurously modern undertakings, but all passed up the opportunity to stage *Four Saints*.

Elsa Maxwell dangled a more concrete promise of a production. An influential arbiter of international café society, she had been charged with promoting fashionable events in Monte Carlo's casinos and hotels. "Society as we know it must be in a very peculiar state," she once reflected, "if I, a girl from Keokuk, Iowa, and former vaudeville pianist, am acknowledged as one of its arbiters." After a long lunch with Thomson at the Ritz, she decided with great enthusiasm that *Four Saints* was a perfect event to kick off Monte Carlo's spring season. "Sounds big but God knows," Thomson wrote Stein.[2] After Maxwell canceled six engagements, Thomson gave up and turned his attention to finding support in America.

The New York opera crowd, however, was particularly ill suited to support *Four Saints*. The patrons of the Diamond Horseshoe boxes at the Metropolitan Opera represented elite WASP culture at its most backward-looking. Grounded in the rigidly codified society of the Four Hundred—so named by self-appointed arbiter Ward McAllister in 1891 because that number fit into Mrs. John Jacob Astor's ballroom—New York's upper crust longed for the bygone days of white tie, wilted linen collars, long gloves, and Lemaire opera glasses. "We have to be more exclusive in New York," observed Mrs. Astor, "because in America there is no authority in society."[3]

The opera house offered the venue for the most ostentatious display of class in a country that lacked the stamp of aristocracy. Just after the turn of the century, when Frank Crowninshield ranked signifiers of class, he listed an opera box first, followed by a steam yacht and town house, with known ancestors and culture bringing up the rear. But by 1930, the old guard was notably in decline. Highborn hostesses no longer entertained in the grand-ballroom style favored by Mrs. Astor, people of all classes mixed in speakeasies, and formerly aloof ladies clamored to be photographed by the press. As one doyenne sadly observed, "Society is a Nineteenth Century word in a Twentieth Century world."

Society's musical taste was in any case decidedly nineteenth century. After the Crash, opera was seen as especially vulnerable, and nervous jokes about "Operadämmerrung" proliferated. Not everyone would mourn the loss. As a 1933 *Vanity Fair* article concluded, "Opera, of course, is artistically on a par with the horse show."[4]

Virgil Thomson picnics with friends.

The New York counterpart to Paris's adventurous rich was progressively known as the smart set (in the 1910s), café society (in the 1920s), and high bohemia (in the 1930s). They were described by *The New York Times* as "the group which sets the pace in fashion, in genteel living and entertaining." This is where Thomson found his patrons and promoters—because to mount a production required both money and éclat. It included such hostesses as Muriel Draper and Constance Askew, gossip columnists such as Lucius Beebe, and editors such as Frank Crowninshield.

The postwar sea change in manners and social mores could be seen in fashion, music, slang, popular dances, and new publications. Cole Porter's lyrics and Peter Arno's *New Yorker* cartoons evoked Jazz Age society far more than Edith Wharton's novels. A doyenne of old New York, Mrs. Stuyvesant Fish, newly known as "Mamie," invited her friends to take up modern dances such as the Innovation, the Lame Duck, and the Half and Half. The term "gentleman" became a quaint throwback, while "gay,"

"Birth no longer is the prime requisite of society," observed **Mona [Mrs. Harrison] Williams.** She was walking proof. Born to a Kentucky horse trainer, she began her string of marriages at the age of nineteen. By 1926, she was married to her third husband, utilities magnate Harrison Williams, who was twenty-four years older than she and very, very rich. They lived in three houses: a Colonial brick mansion at 1130 Fifth Avenue, a Long Island country mansion with palatial gardens, and a vacation residence on Worth Avenue in Palm Beach. Mrs. Williams told the press that she spent $20,000 a year on clothes and considered it money well spent. Her trademark black-and-white couture photographed beautifully, especially against the zebra-striped banquettes of El Morocco, central headquarters of café society. Before long the press began referring to Mrs. Williams as "New York's smartest woman" (meaning well dressed), Cholly Knickerbocker dubbed her "Modish Mona," and Lucius Beebe called her the "Queen of Café Society."

The Four Hundred, café society, and high bohemia came together in the dapper figure of **Frank Crowninshield.** He had danced the cotillion in the Mrs. Astor's ballroom and joined the Knickerbocker Club, and he was called "the man-who-knows-more-celebrities-than-anyone-else-in-New-York." Near the end of his life, Crowninshield named his chief faults as an overweening interest in high society and "a perhaps preposterous liking for the new." It was precisely these "flaws" that made Crowninshield instrumental in the modernization of American society. By the 1920s and 1930s he would be acknowledged as America's *"arbiter elegantiarum."* The base of Crowninshield's tastemaking power was *Vanity Fair,* which he began editing in 1914. As Cleveland Amory observed, *Vanity Fair* was "America in mid-passage, as it were, between the old Four Hundred and the new Smart Set."

Crowninshield was widely considered to be one of the last of a vanishing species, a gentleman. He felt equally comfortable at El Morocco and in Mrs. Cornelius Vanderbilt's dining room, and he helped organize clubs that commingled the monied and working artist class, notably the Coffee House Club and the Artists and

Mrs. Harrison Williams, by Boutet de Mouvel, ca. 1930.

Frank Crowninshield, by Miguel Covarrubias; © 1942 The New Yorker Magazine, Inc.

Writers Golf Association. An enthusiastic promoter of modern artists to potential patrons, he became a linchpin between modernism and society. He served on the board of the Harvard Society for Contemporary Art and acted as one of the seven organizers of the Museum of Modern Art. While making way for the new he remained, as *The New York Times* put it in his obituary, "the undiminished and suave apostle of gracious living, elegant manner and true urbanity."

Alcoholic, monied, homosexual dandy **Lucius Beebe** was an ideal promoter of stylish society. Beginning on September 9, 1933, his weekly *New York Herald Tribune* column, "This New York," transformed the week's nightlife among the highborn and the amusing into purple prose. As rigorously as he chronicled the new society, he loved the affectations of the old. A friend observed that he cherished "a profound nostalgia for dead elegance." His role as social columnist seemed to legitimize his imperious manner and sartorial resplendence as he looked on New York's glittering night world both literally and figuratively through a monocle. Café society, Beebe announced, was the "only society that amounted to a hill of *haricots verts.*" With his gold-headed stick and preference for the Cunard line of ships over airplanes, his liking for English manners and Rothschild-sized Partagas cigars, his confusion with modern poetry and modern pictures, Beebe was a walking anachronism. As a Harvard-educated New Englander, a man of independent means, a "self-bespoke Londoner," Beebe had the credentials to be admitted to gilt-edged society. As a homosexual dandy who drank ostentatiously, society's doors would normally have been closed to him. But he defined smartness with great flair, and by the end of the 1930s even *Life* magazine featured him on its cover, emblazoned with the headline "Lucius Beebe Sets a Style."

FOREWORD

Caricature of Lucius Beebe, by Rea Irvin.

"amusing," "chic," and "smart" became newly prized qualities. El Morocco replaced Delmonico's as the place to eat; *Vanity Fair* replaced *Town Topics* as the magazine of choice. Birth no longer mattered, and the three generations it took to create a gentleman, per Ward McAllister's dictum, had been collapsed into one.[5]

The bridges among money, aristocracy, fashion, and art were built far more effectively by high bohemia than in the socially codified days of the Four Hundred. One could now have social aspirations without appearing in the *Social Register*. One could now be both a "gentleman" and a "chic personage," buy modernist art, frequent Harlem cabarets, and belong to the Cosmopolitan Club. Descending the social ladder was no longer regarded as "slumming" but as cosmopolitan adventurousness. "Rilda, my pretty, there's no such thing as a set any more and you know it," observed a character in Carl Van Vechten's novel *Parties*. "Everybody goes everywhere."[6]

In his song "Anything Goes," Cole Porter celebrated and satirized the dizzying social fluidity and the decline of propriety. But high bohemia's exhilarating freedom was balanced by stringent new prescriptions: cleverness, liveliness, and a new kind of culture and manners. High bohemia espoused liberalism in principle—Calvin Coolidge was regarded as a joke—but regarded political engagement as embarrassingly earnest. One had to be intelligent but not intellectual, serious but not earnest, progressive but not fad-driven, and above all amusing, unfazed, and cosmopolitan.

III

Although high bohemia constituted a very small island in the sea of American society, Virgil Thomson appreciated its strategic importance to *Four Saints*' success. As working artists, the opera's collaborators were anathema to old guard society. Its members regarded the arts as their possession by right of their class, but they rarely trafficked with those who purveyed them. Mrs. Winthrop Chanler declared, "The Four Hundred would have fled in a body from a poet, a painter, a musician, or a clever Frenchman."[7] What would they think of the homosexual, black, and Jewish collaborators on *Four Saints*?[8] By embracing precisely those groups that official society excluded, high bohemia catalyzed the development of *Four Saints in Three Acts*.

Lucius Beebe, a society columnist, was the most ostentatious dandy of high bohemia. In his weekly column for the *New York Herald Tribune*, "This New York," he described his subject as "Babylon-on-the-Hudson, sinful, extravagant, full of the nervous hilarity of the doomed."[9] Beebe wore a mink-lined overcoat with an astrakhan collar and doeskin gloves with a matching top hat, and carried a walking stick. Such nicknames as "Luscious Lucius" and "the orchidaceous oracle of café society" played on his homosexuality.[10] Beebe's bemused enthusiasm would go a long way to cementing the stylish popularity of *Four Saints*.

The undisputed capital of high bohemia was New York. The Stettheimer sisters' salon represented its conservative end, while Kirk and Constance Askew's gatherings embodied the middle and Muriel Draper's salon stood on the radical fringe.[11] These salonistes and the Harvard modernists worked hand in hand to champion the modernist chic of *Four Saints*. The opera could not have succeeded without them.

MURIEL DRAPER'S SALON

One snowy evening at the end of 1932, Virgil Thomson delivered a lecture at Muriel Draper's wood-framed house on East Fifty-third Street. An unadorned, barnlike space, it had makeshift wiring, white-and-gold tables, and a Charles Demuth painting on its exposed brick wall. Guests paid two dollars apiece to hear Thomson lecture on prosody and play selections from *Four Saints* on a grand piano that Henry-Russell Hitchcock had borrowed from Steinway. (Aghast that Muriel Draper had no piano, the Steinway representatives said that "she ought to have one whether anyone else did or not."[12])

The evening was in part a tribute to Muriel Draper's long friendship with Gertrude Stein, whom she had met in Florence before the war. When she had read Stein's "Portrait of Mabel Dodge at the Villa Curonia" in 1913, Draper had confessed that she understood nothing beyond the cover. But in the intervening two decades she had come to appreciate Stein's literary accomplishments. In Draper's unpublished magnum opus, "America Deserta,"[13] she wrote, "Gertrude Stein alone has created a style and content, from years of labor and intellectual ardor, which can be said to belong to the American people, and to be a natural utterance of their blood circulation."[14]

THE TRANSFORMATION OF FASHIONABLE SOCIETY

BEFORE 1920s	1920s–30s
Nobs	Chics
The Four Hundred	Café society
Delmonico's and Sherry	El Morocco
Ward McAllister	Elsa Maxwell
Society columnists	Gossip columnists
Mrs. John Jacob Astor	Mrs. Harrison Williams
Salon	Saloon
Old guard	Swells
"Cave dweller" society	Café society
Town Topics	*Vanity Fair*
Gobelin tapestries	Maxfield Parrish murals
Quadrille	Fox-trot

"WHAT THE WELL-DRESSED MIND WILL THINK" (1933)

- The low-brow is worthy of attention—Walter Winchell, Minsky Brothers burlesque, comic strips, dance marathons—though no longer as fresh as when discovered by Gilbert Seldes.
- Greenwich Village, Provincetown, and Taos are inhabited solely by face artists and real estate men.
- The jargon of psychology ("defense mechanism," "inferiority complex") should no longer be frequently used.
- San Francisco is the only American city to be mentioned aside from New York insofar as cosmopolitanism is concerned.
- No person of taste subscribes to a book club.
- Aesthetic dancing is always slightly ridiculous.
- Gutter slang is always welcome ("nuts," "lousy," "scram") but slang as a whole should be used discriminatingly because it so easily dates the user.[15]

Virgil's performance at Draper's was not exciting, and Hitchcock observed that he seemed to be less comfortable speaking than playing. Yet the pay for his tutorial helped him scrape by, and his performance increased the opera's visibility among the cognoscenti.

Muriel Draper made her living as an interior decorator. In the best of times she made money and spent it all. During the Depression she regularly fled the sheriff bearing eviction notices and struggled so frequently to keep the utilities from being cut off that her friends formed a "coal fund" to keep her warm and a "Committee for the Prevention of Moolie's Telephone Being Cut Off."[16] But she never did without her two servants, Maud and Mr. Cherry, who remained loyal even when she fell behind in paying them. Through thick and thin, she managed to entertain. As Thomson recalled, "Her divers domiciles remained for several years among the best New York had to offer as salons of arts and letters."

The motley set that Draper attracted included working-class laborers and body builders as well as London aristocrats and Parisian trendsetters, artists and writers, opera singers and cabaret performers, socialist organizers and Gurdjieff disciples. Her son Paul said, "She wanted to show that things could move without the social imprint." Muriel Draper's black maid was aghast, observing, "When the [bohemian] Hellstroms begin to act like the Vanderbilts and Emily Vanderbilt begins to act like a Hellstrom, it is *too bad!*"[17]

When society columnist Cobina Wright was promoting a new dress shop, she sought Muriel's imprimatur. When a young writer wanted to be published or to find a gallery to show Zelda Fitzgerald's paintings, he solicited Muriel's connections. New York's Gurdjieff community met in her rooms, and Marxist organizations in need of funds used her guest lists. She became an informal clearinghouse for musicians and found Paul Robeson his first singing teacher.

Every year on December 31, the fortunates who had received an engraved card announcing that Muriel Draper was At Home after eleven would gather in her vast barnlike residence. No less a critic than Edmund Wilson said that Draper's parties were his favorite in New York; others thought they were as epochal as the world war.[18] The evening's raucous events would be lubricated with bootleg gin and financed by anonymous contributions from friends. "I should never had believed it would be possible for such a variety of persons to come so near to spontaneous combustion without exploding," wrote one guest. "I participated during my mildly alcoholic wanderings in at least five near-conflagrations."[19]

Muriel Draper also presided, more tamely, over afternoon teas, held on Tuesdays and Thursdays from the mid-1920s into the 1930s. She would serve tea and a few Schrafft's cookies; as one guest summed up her culinary skill, "She knew how to make tea and cut bread." Alcohol was ruled out on these afternoons, for Muriel believed that conversation flowed when it relied solely on the synergy of pure imaginations encountering one another. "I felt as if I have been at Madame Verdurin's," remarked one first-time guest at her teas, "had all her habituals been replaced by interesting people."[20]

The young, bright, often homosexual, aspiring-to-be-worldly guests included writers, artists, and musicians. Critic Burton Rascoe described Draper's teas as "a salon in the grand style, although the grand style intensely modernized," and he reported that the topics of conversation included Proust, Picasso, antique furniture, and the newest color schemes. "I felt exactly like the man in the advertisement who has not devoted fifteen minutes a day to the classics. If only (I thought) I had devoted fifteen minutes a day to the cultivation of the aesthetic attitude!"[21]

Draper presided from an immense gilt throne with carved furbelows and a red plush velvet seat, and before this secondhand-store simulacrum of regality she set an oversized painted tea tray that provided the sole link to her wealthy home in Haverhill, Massachusetts. Her features were dramatic: a flattened nose, immoderately bright red lips, piercing blue eyes, and a blond English bang. Most striking of all was her silky, pale skin, luminous from across the room as well as close up. In London she was known as the "White Negress," and with this name the English expressed both their admiration for her outré style and their alarm at her exotic appearance.

Of all the high-bohemian salons, Draper's depended most upon the larger-than-life charisma of its hostess. She was "a flash of lightning in a somber world," wrote Lincoln Kirstein's sister, Minna, "one of the few large spirits in a meager age."[22] Framed by her ersatz throne, her eyes aloft, Muriel spoke in bursts that were both cerebral and colloquial, combining American and English accents, mixing mandarin pronouncements with sudden intimacy. She jumped precipitously from one topic to another without missing a beat. Lord Samuel Courtauld described her verbal ability as an "extraordinary power to make bricks without straw—or of focusing

The morning after a New Year's Eve at Muriel Draper's, with her gilt throne in the background. The guest list typically included the Askews, Heywood Broun, Bennett Cerf, Samuel Courtauld, e.e. cummings and Marian Morehouse, Walker Evans, Max Ewing, Frederick Kiesler, Alfred and Blanche Knopf, Lincoln Kirstein, George Platt Lynes, Princess Murat, Isamu Noguchi, A. R. Orage, Burton Rascoe, Paul Robeson, Esther Strachey, Mark Tobey, Carl Van Vechten, Fania Marinoff, Edmund Wilson, and Blanche Yurka.

the little point of value and disconsidering the rest."[23] With her penchant for hyperbole, her old friend Mabel Dodge Luhan declared her the most brilliant monologist since Oscar Wilde. "She made being American chic," observed one young friend, while Osbert Sitwell wrote, "She seemed a realization of the American spirit and might well have been the figurehead of a new race."[24]

Muriel combined ivory capes, embossed silver cloth, and accordion-pleated georgette; she wore the same 1920 Poiret dress for most of the decade. When she had no money, she bought $2.99 specials at Klein's and accessorized them with large velvet roses and jet-black beads. She often wound white turbans or silk stockings around her head.[25] Her elegance placed her above convention and beyond judgment. In his last years Henry James called her the only charming American.

Muriel's monologues, nearly as famous as those of her sister-in-law Ruth Draper, were disseminated by her court of young men. Her chief acolyte, Max Ewing, constructed a statue of "Muriel Enlightening the World." Standing beside an illuminated column, she holds a battle-ax in one hand and a light in the other, and a miniature loudspeaker protrudes from her head.

Virgil Thomson was not drawn to Muriel's combination of theatricality and dogma. He regarded her attempts to dominate artistic and intellectual circles as futile, for society considered her just a "playmate." But he valued her consummate skills as a hostess, which he attributed to her years spent in Florence: "The great hostesses, I've discovered, practically all had training in Florence. Muriel Draper, Mabel Dodge, Constance Askew, they all spent time in Florence. So there was a grace and relaxation which was very different from the kind of stiffness of the Rockefellers and their friends. And very different from the kind of rough-and-tumble of the bohemians. The bohemians and the rich lacked a general graciousness and intellectual openness. In Paris, you learn wit, in London you learn to crush your social rivals, and in Florence you learn poise."

In addition to her poise, the style of Draper's discussions contributed a passionately ideological edge to high bohemia. *Town and Country* warned that Draper was "a dangerous Nietzchean disguised as a turbanned Madonna."[26] Her beliefs mixed Marxist politics, Gurdjieffian mysticism, and libertarianism, and by the mid-1930s, her doctrinaire support of Russian communism drove away many friends. But in the early years of the Depression, most of them regarded her leftist politics as an expression of Muriel's undaunted faith during a difficult period. She regarded the Depression as a galvanizing moment, an opening wedge for revolutionary social change. "It's a time when we can do almost anything we damn please, really," she wrote Mabel Dodge Luhan, "because the world can be hypnotized into action as easily as it has been hypnotized into lethargy."[27]

Draper's brand of ideology linked politics to the arts and provided the

Muriel Draper, sketched by her protégé, Mark Tobey, no date, in a letter to her. *"You are, in all your virtues and in all your extravagances, the most American person I know."* (Gilbert Seldes)

catalyst for progressive change, if not revolution, in American culture. She championed an American ballet; she fostered the International Theatre Exposition, of which she was an honorary chairman; she promoted an all-Negro symphony orchestra; she cited steel-and-glass interiors as evidence of the engineer's new authority. Theories, causes, and projects were floated in Draper's rooms—called "the storm center of action"[28]—long before they found their way into the broader world. As one admirer wrote, "Muriel Draper is always at least 5 years in advance of everything."[29]

Both as hostess and as mentor, Draper provided a supportive haven for homosexuals, just as she did for political radicals and African Americans. By her son Paul's estimation, in her salon "there were perhaps more homosexuals per roomful than anywhere." Draper's extravagant clothes and theatrical pronouncements disinhibited them. When painter Mark Tobey anticipated exhibiting a homoerotic painting, he wrote to Draper, "I shall need to be near *you* when I show it."[30] When the prominent homosexual interior decorator Robert Locher was profiled in *Creative Art*, she wrote the article. And when the organizers of a Savoy Ballroom drag ball sought a judge, they would inevitably ask Draper. In her salon the discrepancy between sexual identity and its public expression was minimal—without "proper" guests to hide from and with few social rules to mediate, homosexuals and lesbians moved without social friction.

"One of Muriel's greatest gifts is for sending people off their balance while retaining a perfect balance herself in however dizzy an attitude," observed Max Ewing. "It amuses her to exercise this power."[31] She exercised her power especially with young protégés, who lived in fear that she might confront their overweening pretensions or circulate damning opinions about town. But when Muriel enthused volubly—Walker Evans recalled that she would say "Woooooo with accent on the third o"—she buoyed the creative young who filled her court.[32] Among the young men in her circle were Lincoln Kirstein, Mark Tobey, e.e. cummings, Walker Evans, Max Ewing, and George Antheil. Her judgments were unsparingly frank and owed nothing to charitable feelings, Kirstein observed: "It was a matter of whether or not she was attracted to the quality of their imagination." When she bluntly told Kirstein he was too old, too tall, and too rich to be a dancer, he initially felt as if she had slugged him in the stomach, but she was also generous in her advice and attention. "She told you what a young man should know," recalled interior designer James Amster. "It had nothing to do with facts—she had good talk and really no knowledge—but she gave me a firmament."

Many of her protégés welcomed, even savored, her dictatorial pronouncements, but Virgil Thomson could not tolerate her dominating influence. "Really talking seemed to mean that I must listen," he wrote, "and that I must accept her opinion as final on everything regarding art."

But for several less fully formed young men of that era, Draper conveyed maternal authority and provided the perfect foil for sharpening a modern consciousness. "I have often thought how useful Muriel Draper's salon was, and I don't think there has been anything like it since then," Lincoln Kirstein reflected near the end of his life. "Now it's about power. Then it was about talent and imagination."

SUNDAY AFTERNOONS AT THE ASKEWS

The most instrumental of the high-bohemian salons gathered every Sunday at five o'clock in the living room of Kirk and Constance Askew. Virgil Thomson had the good sense to make his headquarters in their brownstone at 166 East Sixty-first Street. During his visit of 1932–1933, he lived in their small second-story bedroom—so frequently used by visiting Harvard modernists that it was dubbed the "Hitchcock-Rindge Chamber"—and on Sunday afternoons he descended the stairs to a room filled with modernist movers and shakers. Virgil said, "The opera was managed and centered from there."

Held every Sunday during the "R" months, the Askews' gatherings were formally described as teas—although no tea was served—and sometimes more accurately dubbed the Askew Saloon. Paul Bowles called it "the only salon in New York worthy of the name."[33] Around five o'clock a few dozen people would enter through the double doors and the butler would deposit their coats in the library, beneath a Nadar photograph of George Sand and an early Max Ernst drawing. Guests entered the living room, whose tall bay windows looked out on a backyard patch of shrubbery. The large, L-shaped room proved ideal for circulating through what Thomson called "sort of a general come-and-go party." Traffic was impeded by a few large pieces of furniture: a high-backed Victorian couch, a Biedermeyer chest, and at the end of the room a black Steinway concert grand piano with an Alexander Calder mobile perched on top.

Bootleg cocktails were not served until six, but from then on they flowed freely. Five-gallon jugs of grain alcohol were delivered from the Central Drugstore, the bootlegger favored by the Park Avenue set, and the Askews' butler mixed grain alcohol with water and a small vial of juniper flavoring. Kirk Askew shook it up in cocktail shakers and, operating from the pantry off the living room, circulated through the crowd, dispensing gin and ginger ale. One guest from England noted that at the Askews he always got "roaring tipsy," while another was recalled drunkenly reclining on the floor as he gazed up and said, "Don't pity me."[34] The American cocktail party, a Prohibition institution, furnished the opportunity for informal and frequent mixing known as a runaround. "The booze flowed and everybody had a good time," said Thomson.

"Through these rooms circulated the 'notabilities,'" wrote John Houseman. "They flowed in slowly revolving eddies over the brown-purple carpet, between the massive Victorian furniture. From time to time this human stream seemed to get caught against some physical object—the tail of the piano or the curve of a love seat—or it would become congested around some particularly eloquent or glamorous guest." The Sunday-afternoon parade passed by a few fixed figures. Henry-Russell

Hitchcock frequently commandeered one of the corners, behind a brandy snifter and a demitasse, delivering a loud, authoritative monologue to a shifting audience. Political intellectual Esther Murphy would hold forth about leftist politics, standing before the fireplace. Virgil Thomson, in another corner, delivered urbane pronouncements about the state of modern culture. The rest of the crowd circulated, and by the end of an evening—guests began leaving by ten—one felt as if one had chatted with America's modernist elite. As Philip Johnson put it, "You *happened* at the Askews.'"

At a time when modern taste was just being codified, when standards were not professionalized, and when New York lacked a center for art scholars, modernists used the Askews' living room to pursue their related enterprises. Art world academics included Henry-Russell Hitchcock, Agnes Rindge, Richard Offner, and occasionally Paul Sachs. The Harvard circle that made up the social nucleus of the Askews' gatherings were the new museum professionals: Chick Austin, Alfred Barr, Philip Johnson, Jere Abbott, and Iris Barry. Art galleries were represented by Pierre Matisse, Julien Levy, Leila Wittler, Marie Harriman, and Valentine Dudensing, as well as such promising gallery secretaries as Allen Porter and John McAndrew. Artists Pavel Tchelitchew, Eugene Berman, Florine Stettheimer, and Maurice Grosser attended, as did writers e.e. cummings, Glenway Wescott, Max Ewing, and Charles Henri Ford; critics Henry McBride, Edwin Denby, Carl Van Vechten, and Gilbert Seldes; and performing artists Charles Laughton, Elsa Lanchester, George Balanchine, Joseph Losey, and John Houseman. Because the Askews spent their summers in London, there were often visitors from England, such as Elizabeth Bowen, Edward Burra, and Frederick Ashton. Beginning in 1932, Virgil Thomson added musicians into this mixture: Aaron Copland, Marc Blitzstein, John Latouche, and Paul Bowles. It was a heady guest list: short on money, long on talent and taste.

As Virgil Thomson observed, "The mechanism of taste forming is complex. You can't restrict it to art, you have to have a big show. Part of an effective salon is surrounding what you're doing with everything you can. The people at the Askews were not so much picture buyers, but talkers."

Kirk and Constance Askew declined to be listed in the *Social Register,* although they were eligible, and they did not care about the social eligibility of their guests. Professional accomplishment and advanced tastes were the hallmarks of an Askew guest. Julien Levy recalled that the parties "gave one a sense of belonging to an entertaining inside group." At the Askews' you might see black spiritual singer Taylor Gordon in the company of Muriel Draper or prominent black actress Edna Thomas arriving with her husband and her English lover, Lady Olivia Wyndham. The dress code for men was evening wear, either a dark suit or black tie—not a tuxedo, Kirk would instruct his grandson many years later: "Waiters wear tuxedos, gentlemen wear dinner clothes."[35]

The wider latitude for women was matched by a greater anxiety about hitting the precise note of chic embodied in a Lillie Daché hat or an Elizabeth Hawes dress.[36] Agnes De Mille was told that her dress was shabby, and when Iris Barry moved from London to New York, Philip Johnson immediately staked her to something suitable for the Askews'. Constance Askew set the tone. Her velvet dresses had short trains, and sometimes she wore a black taffeta dress designed for her by Charles Laughton, highly boned through the middle and with a train so long it had to be carried. Paul Bowles joked of its low back, "You could almost see everything, but not quite." She wore striking accessories: a pair of globe earrings half filled with water or a spiraling bracelet designed by Alexander Calder.

The talk at the Askews' was distinct from the "general conversation" heard before World War I at Mabel Dodge's or more recently at Muriel Draper's. Politics was heard most loudly in Esther Murphy's quarter of the room, and socialists Joseph Losey and Helen Carter promoted leftist politics, but the tenor of discussion rarely sounded an earnest ideological note. Henry McBride ascribed the hum at the Askews' to "the so-called brilliant set," and added, "If there is one thing more than another that wears me down it's being brilliant."[37] The focus was on what they were seeing, doing, and planning: the exhibitions, the plays, the articles, the affairs, the trips to Paris and London. As Philip Johnson recalled, "Those rooms were just the crossroads of the world for several years."

|||

Amid the stylish animation in their living room presided the host and hostess. Short, slight, and animated, Kirk Askew possessed, as Virgil Thomson wrote, "curvaceous facial forms that give him a carved-in-mahogany aspect which accorded well with his Victorian house." He convivially and aggressively introduced people, recycled bits of gossip heard on his art-world rounds, and tactfully broke up conversations that had run on too long—by his standards, about ten minutes. Julien Levy described this activity as "Kirk's system of invisible manipulation." He kept the festivities percolating.

The salon was essential to Askew's position in the art world, as well as to his own professional self-image. Around the turn of the century, his father had thrived in the saddlery business in Kansas City, where he had once lived next door to Virgil Thomson's parents. The family business had allowed Kirk (and his brother) to attend Andover and Harvard, but the saddlery business had declined with the advent of the automobile, and Kirk could no longer rely on family money to support himself as a gentleman or a scholar. He had to work but was something of a scholar manqué, and soon he chose art dealing, which was then regarded as more of a trade than a profession. To maintain his ties to the Harvard circle, he surrounded himself with professionals, scholars, artists, and writers. "He was on the fringe but wished he was in the center," Philip Johnson observed. "He collected people in hopes that some of their distinction might rub off."

Kirk's gallery, the Fifty-seventh Street branch of Durlacher Brothers, could not have been more distinguished. Paul Sachs considered the London-based Bond Street gallery "the most influential and knowing of European art firms," catering to the monied international clientele exploited by Joseph Duveen in the nineties. In January 1932, Kirk mounted a show of seventeenth-century Italian paintings and drawings that would initiate his pioneering role as a dealer of Baroque art. Denigrated by Charles Eliot Norton and John Ruskin—the taste arbiters of the second half of the nineteenth century—Baroque art saw a revival in the late 1920s. The fruitful complement of art historian, museum director, and art dealer (Arthur McComb, Chick Austin, and Kirk Askew) spurred the revival and gave credence to Askew's rationale for the nobility of art commerce. He placed the artist and the architect at the center of the visual temper of any age, followed by the scholar, the collector, and the dealer. "The happiest periods," he observed, "have been when all four worked in close collaboration."[38]

Constance Atwood McComb Askew provided the still center of the swirling crowd, receiving guests from a low blue couch. She had grown up in Stonington, Connecticut, and the Atwood Machine Company, the source of the family's money, was the largest factory in the world for manufacturing silk- and rayon-throwing machinery. Her early letters reflected her desire to leave the limited life of Stonington for a more cosmopolitan milieu. By her early twenties, she had found such a life in Florence, where

Constance Askew, high-bohemian hostess and exemplar of intellectual glamour, 1930.

Kirk Askew, art dealer and host, ca. 1930.

she saw great art and met the young Baroque art historian Arthur Mc-
Comb. Their marriage had produced one daughter but lasted just a few
years.[39] When Constance married Kirk Askew in 1929, he was eight years
younger than she and just starting out as an art dealer at Durlacher Brothers. Two years later, with the financial help of Constance's mother, the

Askews bought the house at 166 East Sixty-first Street. The stage was set for social theater, and Constance became its center.

Many considered Constance one of the most glamorous women of her generation. Although she stood only five feet, five inches, she had a commanding presence and exuded quiet charisma. The combination of her legend and her personality, observed a friend, "made you *feel* she was beautiful." Paul Bowles described her as "very feminine—almost exaggeratedly so," while actor Tonio Selwart recalled her intent listening and her seductive warmth. Her ability to establish the atmosphere of intimacy was due to her partial deafness. "Since not all her responses came through hearing," her eldest daughter observed, "she was sensitive to expressions, bearing, and other visual cues." Emily Hahn, a regular Askew guest and a biographer of Mabel Dodge Luhan, compared the two high-bohemian hostesses. "I think Constance had that still quality that Mabel *wanted*, a kind of genial complacency, always receiving."[40] Constance's grace was complemented by her playful delight in nonsense and her desire for adventure. "Even when she got tiddly," Virgil recalled, "she did it gracefully."

New Yorker writer John Mosher considered life at the Askews' "the acme of pleasant and easy and even brilliant living."[41] They constructed that life with elaborate care, mixing the regular rhythms of each day with the piquancy of elegant, rule-laden social life. "A beautiful woman must be kept busy," Thomson cautioned, "just like a beautiful young man must be kept busy. Otherwise they get in trouble."

Kirk began each day by putting on a three-piece Brooks Brothers suit and walking a few blocks to Durlacher Brothers. He alternated his workday between the gallery's two showrooms and the small mauve velvet-covered room at the end of the hall that was sometimes called "Kirk's lair." Equipped with an Empire sofa, two wing chairs, and a high-backed green velvet chair that doubled as a stand for paintings, this intimate room became a meeting place for friends and business acquaintances. As Philip Johnson recalled, "People met their future wives there." One dealer associate observed that Kirk made selling fun for both himself and his clients. He liked to shock people by saying things such as "Raphael is a bore" and promoting advanced artists within the conservative confines of Durlacher Brothers. Lunch was a daily ritual, always conducted Dutch treat so that Kirk could invite anyone on the spur of the moment. He would return home for late-afternoon tea.

Constance dressed before breakfast, after which she gave the day's instructions to the cook, the butler, the chambermaid, and the nursemaid. She spent the morning writing notes and reading books on a blue sofa in the library, and at 12:00 the butler brought in a glass of sherry. If she were going out to lunch—sometimes to Michel's, one of the museum world's favorite speakeasies—she wore a plain black silk dress, a John Fredericks hat, and pearls. She would return before 4:00, change into a velvet tea gown, and greet the close friends who had a standing invitation to drop in. Tea was served in the library promptly at 4:00. Kirk and Constance sat on blue sofas facing each other with English cigarettes in hand, and at 6:00 they switched to bootleg gin martinis. They dined either semiformally at 7:30 or formally at 8:00. Sometimes a second tier of guests was invited for 9:00 or 9:30, and they would be served alcohol, while the A-list would generally turn to something lighter, such as soda water and lemon.

The carefully ordered social life offered fertile ground for developing the calibrated sense of "in"-ness that was important to Kirk. An invitation to the Sunday afternoons (which about 1935 became Saturday nights) marked the first level of acceptance; Jane Bowles once lamented, "I think I might die if I wasn't asked to the Askew salon."[42] After each party, about eight people would be invited downstairs for a sit-down cold dinner and a postmortem of the party. The uninvited would carry the party on to Harlem. Kirk relished the activity of selecting the dinner guests, which he often accomplished in the middle of the Sunday cocktail party in such a way that it resembled being tapped for a Harvard club. This attention to initiation extended even to Constance's kiss. At the age of sixty-seven, upon reaching the status of being kissed by Constance, Henry McBride discussed the semiotics of her kiss: "Constance joined the ranks of those who now kiss me. To be kissed publicly promotes you to the inner circle. When a carefully rouged lady risks the maquillage in this fashion then the other people present understand definitely that you are there."[43]

The Askews' dress code, their Upper East Side address, the education of the guests, and the formal staff all set their salon apart from a bohemian gathering. A reprimand by the Askews' nurse suggested the delicate balance between social propriety and bohemian freedom: "You don't want anybody to be taking you for a little Third Avenue child," she warned one of the Askew daughters. "They were less than one hundred feet from Third Avenue," Virgil commented, "but Third Avenue was a barrier and a term." The hallmarks of WASP-prescribed manners coexisted with tolerance for eccentric behavior. The Askews' alcohol loosened things up considerably. Political commentator Esther Strachey, known as *"la pisseuse,"* could not hold her bladder after a few drinks. Nothing was said to her, but the butler periodically and discreetly appeared with a sponge. Jane Bowles moved from one man's lap to another, and occasionally two men privately "fooled around" in the bathroom or sneaked a kiss in the library.

It was at the Askews—another oasis for homosexuals—that homosexuals most carefully navigated the line between social propriety and sexual identity. A few blocks east, dotting Third Avenue, were gay bars, and on the other side of Third Avenue lay a residential enclave for homosexuals. But for the Askew set, Third Avenue was a social Maginot Line.

The fact that many of the Askews' male guests were homosexual or bisexual was not a secret, but alluding to homosexuality was bad form. "Everybody knew everybody was sleeping with everybody and nobody talked about it," Lincoln Kirstein sweepingly declared. "It was not a subject for gossip." Virgil Thomson described the rules of behavior most precisely: "It isn't a question of what you know, it's a question of how you behave. You did not camp at the Askews. If you rubbed their noses in it, you weren't going to be asked around." When Constance saw two young men kissing each other in the library, she would quietly order the butler to bring their overcoats.

Men sometimes came to the Askews as couples—for example, Monroe Wheeler and Glenway Wescott, Virgil Thomson and Maurice Grosser, Allen Porter and Tom Howard. But unlike at Muriel Draper's, those whose liaisons cut across class rarely appeared with their working-class companions.

Even the apparently heterosexual couples at the Askews' gave new dimensions to the term "mixed marriage." High bohemia accommodated unions that were flexible and sexually quietly open—"Come to think of it," remarked one frequent guest, "there was scarcely a normal couple in the room." Thomson called them "queer marriages," and he later proposed to enter into such a queer marriage with Philip Johnson's sister, Theodate. Witness the childless marriages of Lincoln Kirstein and Fidelma Cadmus, Paul and Jane Bowles, Carl Van Vechten and Fania Marinoff, Marc Blitzstein and Eva Goldbeck. Their marriages should not, however, be dismissed merely as hypocritical, respectable façades. The domestic rituals and emotional fidelity at their core were real and abiding. Even by the most conventional of measures, Chick and Helen Austin and Kirk and Constance Askew had "successful" marriages: they raised children, and they never divorced.

From our current perspective, the Askews seem to have encouraged a cosmopolitan version of "Don't ask, don't tell," but they would have experienced it as "Do more, say less." If their behavior reflected being in the closet, it was nonetheless an extraordinarily capacious closet, extending from Turtle Bay to Cambridge, to the Upper East Side, and, most important for *Four Saints in Three Acts*, to Harlem.

The Askew salon's contributions to the opera were instrumental. At the Askews', Thomson met John Houseman and invited him to be the opera's director. In the Askews' London home Thomson met another collaborator, Frederick Ashton, who would become the opera's choreographer; Constance sent him the telegram inviting his participation. The Askews provided the second-story bedroom where both Thomson and Ashton lived during rehearsals, and soloists auditioned in the Askews' living room. They initially contributed $100 toward the opera production, adding another $500 when the opera was about to run aground. Less tangibly, their eclectic and highly sought-after salon offered the ideal arena for gathering expectations.

In turn, the opera gave focus and breadth to the salon. "Although officially and overtly the main subject of the salon was the art world," Virgil Thomson observed, "the opera was a way of not being absolutely squeezed by the beginning pressure of the Modern Museum. And it was a way of taking up music without being really musical. You didn't have to have Schubert quartets—that was for the rich, or the very musical Jewish." John Houseman recalled the Askews' salon as the center of a magically fertile period: "The whole salon justified its existence as a result of that opera. *Four Saints* was the apotheosis of all that."

Modernism
Goes Uptown

In early 1933, Virgil Thomson traveled up to Harlem with Henry-Russell Hitchcock. Four years earlier, following *Four Saints'* first performance in the United States at Carl Van Vechten's, he had been introduced to Harlem in its pre-Crash heyday. Although Harlem's determined hedonism had diminished by the time of Thomson's second visit, it was still swinging. Guests at the Askews' often took their party uptown, a night at the theater was frequently capped with dancing in Harlem, a difficult day might be unburdened by the speakeasy gin or marijuana "reefers" available on 133rd Street. "To us," Lincoln Kirstein recalled, "Harlem was far more an *arrondisement* of Paris than a battleground of Greater New York."[1] Some took the A train, which offered a cheap subterranean journey. Others tax-ied through Central Park, their yellow cabs emerging from the foliage into a region where skin colors were darker and spirits seemed unfailingly brighter—at least in the glow of nightclub lighting and speakeasy inebria-tion that most white visitors knew. "Harlem is the one place that is gay and delightful however dull and depressing the downtown regions may be," wrote one uptown visitor to his midwestern parents. "Nothing affects the vitality and the freshness of Harlem."[2]

By the mid-1920s, Harlem had replaced Greenwich Village as the mecca of writers, performers, artists, bohemians, and the cosmopolitan chic. They flocked to "Jungle Alley"—133rd Street between Lenox and Fifth Avenues—to such recently opened nightclubs as the Cotton Club and Connie's Inn, which thrived by catering exclusively to a white clientele. By the end of the 1920s, even those who could not travel to Harlem could picture it. They read about it in magazine articles and gossip columns or in Carl Van Vechten's controversial best-selling novel *Nigger Heaven.* They played gramophone recordings of black vocalists and listened to the Cotton Club Orchestra on the radio. Harlemania attracted tourists from across the United States and visitors from Europe who were eager to mingle with—or at least witness—the exotic world they had constructed in their imaginations.

Color lines blurred, but a glimpse of a Cotton Club performance reveals the still carefully prescribed rules. The audience consisted of expensively dressed white couples eating overpriced Continental food and taking generous swigs from nickel-plated liquor flasks they carried in their pockets. Onstage were black performers and a scantily clad chorus line of women who were "tall, tan, and terrific" (hiring rules stipulated that performers be under twenty-one years of age; over five feet, six inches in height; and "high yaller" in complexion). The distance between audience and performer was no more than a few feet, but the separation between the paying and the paid, the dressed and the nearly undressed, remained total.

But such a snapshot is incomplete, for whites and blacks mixed in other places, sometimes only a few doors down from the lavish whites-only nightclubs. "Harlem is a magic melting pot," observed Harlem Renaissance novelist Wallace Thurman, "a modern Babel mocking the gods with its cosmopolitan uniqueness."[3] Harlem's attractions included the dancing, tray-twirling waiters at the mixed-race nightclub Small's Paradise. Cheap and raucous rent parties offered southern food in the kitchen and dancing in the living room to pay Harlem's inflated rents. Lesbian and homosexual cabarets featured performers such as Gladys Bentley in top hat and tuxedo, suggestively belting new lyrics to "Sweet Georgia Brown." At working-class speakeasies the predominantly black clientele danced to three-piece bands and drank a crude blend of bootleg liquor called "smoke." The largest and most democratic gathering spot was the Savoy Ballroom, where Fess

Williams's and Fletcher Henderson's bands sometimes competed, and on the vast burnished-maple dance floor, known as "The Home of Happy Feet," dancers outdid one another in stunning and acrobatic routines.

Although Harlem was popular to visit, those who challenged segregation by living there—such as the English publisher Nancy Cunard and her black lover, musician Henry Crowder—made headlines and shocked blacks as well as whites. Only between the hours of 10 P.M. and the early morning were the forbidden hedonistic impulses—liquor, jazz, dancing, marijuana, cocaine, and voyeurism—indulged. Harlem at night was the place to be, offering sweet abandon or, at the very least, overpriced frivolity. "Into two or three hours we concentrate the release from practical affairs," observed Gilbert Seldes, "which in another age might be spread over three weeks."[4]

And so on that night in early 1933, Virgil Thomson and Henry-Russell Hitchcock walked up Seventh Avenue to the Hot-Cha Bar and Grill, a small establishment one block north of Jungle Alley, at 2280 Seventh Avenue. The Hot-Cha, now best known as the spot where Billie Holiday was discovered in 1935, attracted a stylish crowd soon after it opened in 1932. Singer Elizabeth Welch recalled it as "a dive but an elegant dive. . . . It was ermine and pearls go to Harlem." (One French visitor, the Duchesse de Clermont-Tonnerre, amused the crowd when she requested *"une veille* Kentucky darkie song."*) Both Hitchcock and Thomson knew of the Hot-Cha's suave and boyishly handsome host, Jimmie Daniels, through Philip Johnson, who had introduced him to Berlin cabaret songs. In the midst of listening to Daniels's smoky, whispery tenor voice singing "I've Got the World on a String," Thomson recalled, "I had a brain wave. It suddenly hit me that he was singing so clearly and I could understand everything he said. He wasn't just vocalizing and adding a few consonants here and there, he was singing the *words*."

When Thomson exclaimed that he wanted to cast black singers in his opera, Hitchcock politely suggested that he should sleep on it and reconsider in the light of day. "We didn't mention it anymore," Thomson said, "but the next day I knew it was a very good idea and I did not abandon it."

Carl Van Vechten recalled Thomson's epiphany as occurring in another setting—in the lobby of Broadway's Lyric Theatre during the intermission of Hall Johnson's gospel musical *Run Little Chillun*. Whatever the location, Thomson's rationale for casting black performers, as Van

Vechten recorded it in 1934, was essentially identical: "They alone possess the dignity and the poise, the lack of self-consciousness that proper interpretation of the opera demands. They have the rich, resonant voices essential to the singing of my music and the clear enunciation required to deliver Gertrude's text."

Long before his "brain wave," Thomson had come to appreciate the sound of black musical speech. Seven years earlier, after visiting a Kansas City Negro tent revival meeting, he had written:

> I learned more about the rhythm of the English language in a half-hour than I had ever known before. Also African scales. You see the sermon was intoned. And fitted into a regular rhythmic scheme. Basic rhythm (clapping, swatting Bible, jumping) very simple. Complex syncopated rhythms to fill in the spaces. These determined by language, but sufficiently exaggerated that they are recognizable as interesting apart from the language. The extraordinary thing to me, however, was their aptness to the language.[5]

By the 1920s, some critics were talking about a "black voice" that they believed sprang from broader cheekbones and a different facial structure from whites'. These ostensible physiognomical differences gave birth to vocal qualities that were variously described as "warm," "deep," "smoky," "rich," "velvety," "deep-throated," "resonant," "emotional-sounding."[6] The words used to summon up the "Negro voice" are drawn from the vocabulary of feeling and touch. Thomson was among the first to describe black singers as notably articulate.

Even Carl Van Vechten—widely known as a promoter of black music and a godfather of black causes—expressed his skepticism about Thomson's plan to cast *Four Saints in Three Acts* entirely with black singers. Van Vechten stated that *Four Saints* had nothing to do with Negroes. Thomson tartly replied that it made no difference. "Think how many opera stars have blacked up to sing Amonasro and Aida. Why can't my colored singers white up for *Four Saints*?"[7]

Thomson's remarks were especially audacious in light of the discriminatory casting practices of the day. Black singers and dancers were hardly unknown on New York stages. In 1929, *Variety* estimated that about 300 women and 150 men were regularly employed in Harlem alone—and in 1933, at the time of Thomson's inspiration, Broadway's highest-paid performer was Ethel Waters. But black performers occupied a niche on the American stage that was as confined as it was conspicuous. Black revues had been a staple of the New York stage since the opening of Eubie Blake and Noble Sissle's *Shuffle Along* in 1921. Every year for the next decade they appeared, bearing such titles as *In Bamville, The Chocolate Dandies, Rang Tang,* and *Blackbirds of 1928.* The same recycled elements—plantation settings, giant watermelons, cotton pickers, and Zulus—offered a colorful but formulaic updating of minstrel shows.

Black characters also appeared in Broadway dramas, inevitably representing southern "Negro life." Such plays included Paul Green's Pulitzer Prize–winning *In Abraham's Bosom* and Dubose Heyward's *Porgy.* Onstage evocation of Negro life veered from primitive naïveté to lurid melodrama, relegating black performers to playing God-loving, capering naïfs in Marc Connelly's *The Green Pastures,* fervent gospel singers in Hall Johnson's *Run Little Chillun,* or Lenox Avenue sheiks and lubricious prostitutes in Wallace Thurman's *Harlem.*[8] The practice of "blacking up" white actors not only was done by such vaudevillians as Al Jolson and Eddie Cantor but also extended to the legitimate theater. Ethel Barrymore, for example, played the black protagonist in *Scarlet Sister Mary,* and Al Jolson campaigned hard to play *Green Pastures'* version of God.

As a general rule, the further up the ladder of high culture, the greater the resistance to black performers. Black Americans were applauded as stars in minstrel shows, cabarets, and revues, relegated to marginal characters in legitimate theater, and altogether excluded from opera. They got around this by forming their own opera companies. The Colored American Opera Company, performing as early as 1873, initiated a tradition of black opera companies, including the Aeolian Opera Company and the National Negro Opera Company, that continued until World War II.[9]

When it came to black roles within the classical repertory, such as Selika in Meyerbeer's *L'Africaine,* white singers were invariably cast. The jazz-player protagonist in Ernst Krenek's experimental opera *Jonny Spielt Auf* was played by a white singer in blackface, and as late as 1933, Louis Gruenberg's operatic adaptation of Eugene O'Neill's *The Emperor Jones* was cast with white baritone Lawrence Tibbett as the protagonist. The color line was broken when a black performer, Hemsley Winfield, danced the part of the Witch Doctor.[10]

None of this fazed Thomson. His plan challenged conventional casting practices in two ways: he proposed that black performers sing opera to a white audience in a white venue, and he wanted them to play roles unrelated to black life. This was seen as provocative, even outrageous. John Houseman described Thomson's method as "L'Audace, l'audace, toujours l'audace." But the time was ripe for this "audacity." Thomson's particular genius was to propose ostensibly revolutionary ideas that were completely in tune with the racial formulas of the times.

Both Thomson and Stein received African Americans socially, and Thomson received them sexually as well, but this did not prevent him from harboring many of the racist views of his childhood and times. To friends he recited a period homosexual ditty: "I went up to Harlem and I ended up with my end up in Harlem"; to the press he observed that black performers were ideal performers for his opera because they had no intellectual barriers to break down—they were satisfied with the beauty of sounds, he explained, and unconcerned with meaning. "Negroes objectify themselves very easily," he said. "They live on the surface of their consciousness."[11]

Stein's attitudes were more detached, for African Americans entered her life only occasionally. Her early story "Melanctha," portrayed black life, and writer James Weldon Johnson said she was the first white writer to depict black characters "as normal members of the human family."[12] At other times she cast them in roles that were anything but normal. Interpreting Carl Van Vechten's interest in American blacks, for example, Stein wrote in 1927, "It is not because they are primitive but because they have a narrow but a very long civilisation behind them. They have alright, their sophistication is complete and so beautifully finished and it is the only one that can resist."[13] Nearly a decade later, she expressed a similar belief that "publicity does not hurt them," that onstage "it is not acting it is being for them, and they have no time sense to be a trouble to them."[14]

Thomson and Stein offer fairly unsurprising variations on the tendency of the day to see black Americans as exotic "others," picturesque figures of desire and fear. As Josephine Baker once quipped, "The white imagination sure is something when it comes to blacks."[15]

Carl Van Vechten embodies the fullest expression of the era's conflicted construction of African Americans. An encouraging presence throughout the development of *Four Saints*, he hosted its first drawing room performance in America, he urged opera diva Mary Garden to play Saint Teresa, he cheered on the creative efforts of his friends Virgil, Gertrude, and Florine, and he wrote a program article explaining "How I

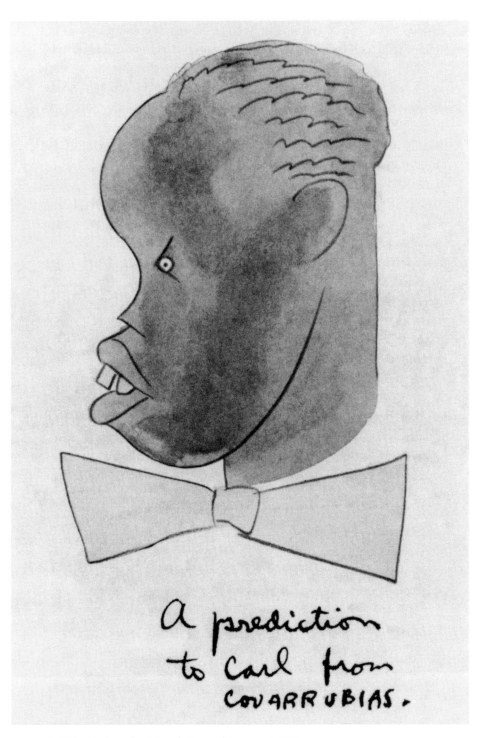

A prediction
to Carl from
COVARRUBIAS.

Carl Van Vechten, by Miguel Covarrubias, ca. 1927.

Listen" to the opera. While Van Vechten promoted the opera from the sidelines, he defined and purveyed the period's Negro chic from a more central position. He was the social linchpin and the chronicler of black and white Manhattan. Every night after twelve the tall, Iowa-bred, Nordic dandy with corn-silk hair and protruding teeth could be found investigating Harlem. He offered recommendations for the best clubs, the most authentic uptown dives, the ideal 6 A.M. eggs and double-Scotch breakfast, the latest black slang. As Andy Razaf's song "Go Harlem" directed its listeners, "Like Van Vechten, start inspectin." Through his integrated parties, his music and theater criticism in *Vanity Fair*, and his novel *Nigger Heaven*, Van Vechten popularly defined Harlem to a broad, white readership. Published in 1926, *Nigger Heaven* was greeted with mixed feelings by black Americans. Many could not tolerate the title, although Van Vechten intended it as a metaphor for Harlem; like the top-balcony "nigger heaven" sections of theaters, Harlem looked down on Manhattan. Van Vechten was variously dubbed "the undisputed downtown authority on uptown life" and "the white master of the colored revels," and his apartment was called "the mid-town office of the NAACP."

In 1925, when Van Vechten proposed a "Prescription for the Negro Theater," he replaced old clichés with updated stereotypes. Strike the comic darky and the plantation scene, cut the mammy singing about cotton bales, Van Vechten advised, and in their place stage a cabaret scene in Small's Paradise, orchestrate exuberant dancers performing the Black Bottom and the Hey Hey, present a vignette of upscale blacks on Strivers' Row, and offer a passionate jungle scene with bronzed men and women "as nearly nude as the law allows." Van Vechten's new Negro chic reflected not only his personal addiction to Harlem life but also a broader fascination. As one commentator observed in 1929, "To Americans, the Negro is not a human being but a concept."[16] Some black observers objected to the "jazzed-up" version of old stereotypes. The new Negro was presented as a naturally superior being, more virile, more American, and more spiritual than his white counterpart. From his position as an engaged observer of Harlem culture, Van Vechten helped to spread the romanticized images that dominated whites' descriptions of African Americans.

The racist stereotypes are familiar: blacks possessed innate spontaneity; the stage benefited from "instinctive Negro performers," who "harmonize instinctively," express their "deepest feelings in song," and are naturally "highly gifted" dancers. Van Vechten warned that performers could dilute those qualities through formal education. A Talented Tenth black protagonist in *Nigger Heaven*, for example, was described as having forfeited the "primitive birthright which is so valuable and important an asset, a birthright that all the civilized races were struggling to get back to—this fact explained the art of a Picasso or a Stravinsky."[17] His romanticized depiction of "intensely uncultured" African Americans reflected the feelings of loss that haunted white America in the postfrontier age. The noble savage was a familiar fallback for disaffected "civilized" man: lack of education was associated with the lost virtues of sincerity, physicality, joy, and spontaneity. "What a stroke of genius having Negro performers," Thomson's friend Yvonne Davidson wrote to him after seeing *Four Saints.* "We whites haven't enough simplicity to feel such rhythm."[18]

|||

Van Vechten shared the widespread belief that "primitive" expression lay at the heart of modernist aesthetics. He discerned in spirituals the roots of modern popular music and jazz, differing only in their instrumentation. Van Vechten undoubtedly picked some of this up from Paris, where the French linked African sculpture and Cubism and described Josephine Baker and the Revue Nègre as a "manifestation of the modern spirit."[19]

"If any race boasts a more interesting folklore than the American Negro I do not know what that race is," Van Vechten wrote. Highly attuned to the "American-ness" of Negro expressions, he repeatedly stressed the importance of accurately documenting blues songs, bawdy romantic ballads, work songs, and spirituals. He asserted that the "Negro race has given this country its only valuable folk music." He insisted on "authenticity" over musical education and was wary of training. He complained, for example, that the college-educated Tuskegee singers sang spirituals as if they were Bach cantatas, "the authentic Negro manner forty thousand leagues away."

Van Vechten's interest in excavating an authentic American expression, independent of Europe, was widely shared. Shortly after World War I, writer Waldo Frank's *Our America* initiated the investigation of "buried cultures" that made up the nation. This search took many forms: critics revived the novels of Henry James and Herman Melville, music ethnologist John A. Lomax recorded cowboy songs, curator Holger Cahill mounted an exhibition of American folk art at the Museum of Modern Art. But the artifacts and expressions most widely regarded as innately American were black: dances spawned in southern juke joints, rich slang, blues, and spirituals, and stories passed down as oral history. Shortly after Virgil Thomson decided to cast African Americans in his opera, he observed that America's folk culture "belongs to the Negroes . . . and the Negro remains the master of it, as of its bodily expression."[20]

Van Vechten shared the widespread belief that African Americans had special access to religious spirituality, so important to an opera about saints. The traditional schism between sacred and profane, essential to Puritanism, seemed to coalesce in the African-American "soul," and black church services offered a training ground for both religion and performance. Learned by rote and observation, undiluted by written notation, black spirituality was considered more "authentic." As commentator V. F. Calverton wrote, "He could express his soul, as it were, without concern for .grammar or the eye of the carping critic."[21] Often ascribed to the African-American "tribal" birthright, black spirituality was celebrated through song and chant, call and response, Bible slapping, foot tapping, and rhythmic swaying, in sharp contrast to the reserved style of Protestant services.

By casting black singers in his opera, Virgil Thomson got in the bargain a passel of fashionable New Negro stereotypes. Elegant and earthy, sensual and hedonistic, spiritual and authentic, black Americans loomed large as cultural icons of the Jazz Age. Thomson's revolutionary casting idea fit the opera like a glove.

Among the collaborators, the chief disagreement over the black cast concerned the display of flesh. That the body would be the arena for the conflict was probably inevitable. Commentators, including Van Vechten himself, invariably reserved their richest and most prurient vocabulary— about lips, flaring nostrils, rounded buttocks, sinews, skin tone, cheekbones, breasts, rump—for the black body.[22]

Florine Stettheimer worried that varied brown skin tones would sully the brilliant colors of her costumes, and she proposed painting the cast white or silver. In the summer of 1933, Virgil Thomson mailed her a newspaper clipping that suggested a novel alternative. A Haitian named Ismeon Dauphin who had ingested pulverized roiry flowers to cure asthma fell into a coma, went blind, and turned white, and when he regained his sight two months later his skin remained white. "It has all become very simple now," Stettheimer wrote Thomson. "We must feed them roiry flowers—no hand painting them before every performance."[23] Although this inter-change was obviously a joke, her concern remained a concern right up to the rehearsal period, and the plan to paint the cast white was even announced to the press.

In a letter from May 1933, by which time he was again communicating with Stein, Thomson described Florine's plan for costumes, including saints wearing transparent robes that revealed the bodies of the performers. Gertrude responded rapidly, "I suppose they have good reasons for using negro singers instead of white, there are certain obvious ones, but I do not care for the idea of showing the negro bodies, it is too much what the English in what they call 'modernistic' novels call futuristic and do not accord with the words and music to my mind."[24] Stein's

Avast, Ahoy and Belay, Mates!

"Avast, Ahoy and Belay, Mates!": The press seizes on Negro chic.

highly qualified syntax may reflect her ambivalence about Negro chic. "Futuristic" was for her an ugly word—the present was "sufficiently occupying." What were the "good reasons" for using a black cast? She may have been alluding to Thomson's and Van Vechten's attraction to black men or showing an appreciation of the spiritual qualities they would bring to the stage.

Thomson's description of Stettheimer's body-revealing inventions is suspect. None of the figures she later fabricated revealed the bodies beneath her cellophane robes. How likely was it that a woman concerned about covering even the cast's hands would design costumes that revealed entire bodies? The desire sounds more like Virgil, who favored any plan that would show brown skin. "We're like dead oysters," he later said. "Their color is live." He promised Stein that the performer's movements would be "sedate and prim" and that they would add the grandeur of classic religious art. Disavowing any interest in titillating the audience, he claimed to be interested only in keeping the stage unencumbered.

The richly textured layers of the singers' costumes—floor-length vestments, cowls, broad hats, and gloves—not only concealed their skin but also obscured the body's contours. Only in the opera's "sniplets," as choreographer Frederick Ashton dubbed the two fleshly *divertissements*, did the dancers reveal flesh. One of these, a dance in the second act about six angels learning to fly, featured women with bare midriffs, the shortest of skirts, and bare-chested, bare-legged men.

At just the right moment, *Four Saints in Three Acts* offered a casting revolution, daring and inevitable, at once libidinous and prim, wrapped up in a gauzy candy box of a setting.

Act III

SHOW

Negotiations and Exchanges

In the midst of his New York visit, while staying with the Askews at the end of January 1933, Virgil Thomson received a letter with a Paris postmark: "Miss Gertrude Stein, for whom, for some time past, I have been acting as literary representative, has learned indirectly of the project to inaugurate the new model theater in Hartford Connecticut in January 1934, with a production of the opera FOUR SAINTS. Naturally this interests her very much."[1]

The letter was signed by William Aspenwall Bradley, a respected literary agent whom Thomson had met at his concerts and at parties. The unenviable role of go-between now fell to Bradley, and he was charged with creating a contract that would structure the collaboration in legal and financial terms. Thomson had just passed the second anniversary of his break with Stein. Stein and Thomson knew that their best interests lay in successfully negotiating terms for a production; their recent history, however, demanded an intermediary.

On the afternoon of May 6, shortly after returning from New York, Thomson spent an afternoon with Bradley. Thomson proposed that he and Stein share equally in the opera's proceeds. He would later regret his proposal, but the feelings during this meeting were so warm that he wrote to Chick Austin, "Gertrude is being angelic about the opera," even envisioning the possibility of a new collaboration with her.[2] Bradley wrote to Stein that evening that Thomson showed friendly feelings, admiration for, and penetrating understanding of her work. He concluded: "Since the 'froid' between you seems to count for little or nothing in his attitude towards you, perhaps it would be possible for you, as well, to bury whatever little hatchet may be involved and to resume relations as in the past."[3]

That same evening, via Bradley, Thomson sent Stein the most complete blueprint of the opera's production:

> The negroes will, however, be painted white, at least their faces. The first act (living pictures) takes place on the steps of the Avila cathedral. Back-drop represents clouds, made of white cellophane gauze draped in puffs, with gold fringe. Cathedral made of contiguous strings of clear crystal beads with curtains of starched white Nottingham lace in the Gothic arch. The lions on the steps are gilded and chained by chains made of gilded paper links to a tulle Gothic rainbow. Rose carpet on the steps. St. Teresa in cardinal red velvet with red cardinal's hat and Nottingham lace veil. The second act decor is not yet precisely imagined, except for the May-pole dance. For this, the minor saints will be in bright colored robes, something like in Fra Angelico's pictures, with hats like gold halos on the sides of their heads and scarves wired to float in fixed folds (reading *Gloria in Excelsis* and similar mottoes), the robes also wired and transparent, revealing the negro bodies underneath. In the third act, the various visions will be built in low relief out of divers cloths and materials and raised from under the stage on a platform. Mr. Austin, who is a professional magician, will perform the miracles of sudden appearance and disappearance of pigeons and the flowering of a small tree into large bouquets of red feathers. With the exception of the storm-scene and one night-scene in the second act, the entire opera is played in white light."[4]

Among the ideas that would fall by the wayside were Florine's wired, mottoed scarves; the participation of the Hall Johnson Choir; Herbert Osborne as director; Chick Austin as magician; and painting the cast white.

Gertrude's objection to the transparent costumes, discussed earlier, was balanced by her sincere desire to get *Four Saints* onstage. "I like Virgil's original Sunday school ideas on the whole better," she wrote Bradley, "but still as it is up to them to make a success of the performance, I do not wish to be critical, the great thing is to get it done and successfully done both for his sake and mine."[5]

When the discussion focused on production decisions, Bradley wisely stepped out of the middle and asked the two to communicate directly. The foundations of renewed trust having been laid, the collaborators began to communicate without intermediary. On May 30, Thomson laid out his production's rationale to Stein:

> The colors and material she suggests are merely an amplification of the dazzling fairy-tale effect that is ordinarily aimed at in the construction of religious images out of tin and tinsel and painted plaster, and gilding and artificial flowers. . . . The negro bodies, if seen at all, would only be divined vaguely through long dresses. The movements would be sedate and prim, and the transparence is aimed . . . not at titillating the audience with the sight of a leg but of keeping the texture of the stage as light as possible. . . . I think the idea is worth trying, however. If it can be realized inoffensively, the bodies would merely add to our spectacle the same magnificence they give to classic religious painting and sculpture. One could not easily use this effect with white bodies, but I think one might with brown. My negro singers, after all, are a purely musical desideratum, because of their rhythm, the style and especially their diction. Any further use of the racial qualities must be incidental and not of a nature to distract attention from the subject-matter. . . . Hence, the idea of painting their faces white. Nobody wants to put on just a nigger show. The project remains doubtful, anyway, till I find the proper soloists.

On June 5, Stein responded with a cordial letter from Bilignin that concluded, "It all sounds very hopeful and about all these things I am quite ready to accept what seems best to those who are doing. The best of luck to us all."

But Stein and Thomson were not yet ready to sign the draft contract. Thomson objected that opera composers, under the standards of the French Authors League, normally received two thirds of royalties, not half. His argument reflected practical financial concerns—a composer has to pay for copying scores, an opera's score is less independently salable than its libretto—and he asked that his original proposal be revised to reflect that. Doubtless he understood that through such brinkmanship he was courting disaster.

Stein in turn objected to a phrase that Thomson had inserted. Production or publication would require acceptance by both parties, stated the contract, and Thomson added, "such acceptance not to be unreasonably withheld." Stein interpreted his insertion of this common "boilerplate" phrase as questioning of trust. She wrote Bradley, "It allows too much latitude to others beside it is taken for granted that we would consider our best interests."[6] Stein also reiterated that everything should be equally shared, asserting that the value of Thomson's efforts to mount the production were balanced by "the commercial value of my name." It was the first time in her life that Stein could invoke her commercial value. *The Autobiography of Alice B. Toklas* had begun four-part serialization in *The Atlantic Monthly* in May, and the response was overwhelmingly favorable. Stein was becoming a popular celebrity.

The rise in her commercial value touched on "a sensitive spot," wrote Thomson. In the next exchange of letters both Thomson and Stein dropped their cordiality.

Thomson to Stein, June 9, 1933:

> And dear Gertrude, if you knew the resistance I have encountered in connection with that text and overcome, the amount of reading it and singing it and praising it and commenting it I have done, the articles, the lectures, the private propaganda that has been necessary in Hartford and in New York to silence the opposition that thought it wasn't having any Gertrude Stein, you wouldn't talk to me about the commercial advantages of your name. Well, they *are* having it and they are going to *like* it and it isn't your name or your lieutenants that are giving it to them.

Gertrude Stein to Virgil Thomson, June 11, 1933:

My dear Virgil

Yes yes yes, but nous avons changé tout cela, however the important thing is this, the opera was a collaboration, and the proposition made to me in the agreement was in the spirit of that collaboration, 50-50, and the proposition that I accepted was in the spirit of that collaboration 50-50 and the proposition that I continue to accept is the same. When in the future you write operas and have texts from various writers it will be as you and the precedents arrange, but our opera was a collaboration, we own it together, and we divide the proceeds 50-50, and we hope that the proceeds will be abundant and we wish each other every possible good luck.

Always, Gtrude Stein

Gertrude and Virgil effected an informal compromise on June 19 and signed the contract four days later. They put their guns aside but not away. Thomson agreed to an equal split, and Stein agreed to Thomson's inserted phrase. The composer later explained to Bradley, "My ultimate capitulation was due to the necessity of her accepting an 'unreasonably withheld' phrase, the phrase itself quite unreasonably withheld, as you will remember, until I sacrificed some of my rightful royalties for it."[7] But in his correspondence with Stein he displayed none of the resentment he was feeling:

We now have, I think, a simple way of settling any differences that may arise without bitterness. As a matter of fact, we understand each other so well and our interests lie for the most part so close together that I am sure we shall always be mostly reasonable with each other anyway.

Snapshots:
Summer 1933

By the end of June, Gertrude Stein and Virgil Thomson had signed the contracts that signaled their wary rapprochement. Chick Austin had promised his museum as the venue for the opera, without any concrete plan for financing it, and construction of the subterranean theater in which it would be presented had begun. Florine Stettheimer had agreed to design the costumes and the sets. The chief obstacles had been overcome. A few snapshots from that summer and fall offer a picture of the collaboration just before the relentless demands of the opera took over our protagonists' lives.

The Autobiography of Alice B. Toklas appeared serially each month from May through August in *The Atlantic Monthly* and dominated Gertrude Stein's summer in Bilignin. She received letters from old friends and new fans and read about herself in numerous newspaper columns. Random House planned to republish *Three Lives*, and Bennett Cerf soon reported that Macy's alone had ordered 1,300 copies. The wave of success culminated in August with *The Autobiography's* publication by Harcourt,

Brace. The first printing sold out nine days before publication. The Literary Guild offered the book as one of its selections, it appeared on the bestseller list and on the cover of *Time* magazine, and it quickly ran through four printings. One young friend wrote that Gertrude was more discussed in Hollywood than Greta Garbo. For the first time Stein received real money for her writing ($8,495 in American royalties alone), and she felt so prosperous that she bought Basket a new stud collar and a custom-made Hermès coat. "I love being rich," Stein wrote, "not as yet so awful rich but with prospects, it makes me all cheery inside."[1]

The book's publication reified old antagonisms and created new fissures. Stein took revenge in print on her adversaries, skewering them deftly: Ernest Hemingway ("He looks like a modern and smells of the museums"), Ezra Pound ("He was a village explainer, excellent if you were a village, but if you were not, not"), and James Joyce ("The incomprehensibles whom anybody can understand"). About Virgil Thomson she was more equivocal, putting the criticism into Alice's mouth: "Virgil Thomson she found very interesting although I did not like him." Although Leo Stein enjoyed the sprightly gossip of the book, he was disturbed to find that he had been virtually eliminated and said that practically everything about the early years in Paris was "false in fact and implication." The biggest confrontations came from Gertrude's longtime painter and poet friends: Picasso, Matisse, Braque, André Salmon. *The Autobiography* so alienated them that Picasso stopped talking to her for two years. *Transition* published a special supplement of "Testimony Against Gertrude Stein." Her old friends objected not only to what they regarded as misrepresentation of events but to the fact that *The Autobiography* used the history of the avant-garde as fodder for gossip. Georges Braque was disturbed at her misunderstanding of Cubism, Henri Matisse silently shook his head in disgust, while Tristan Tzara found words for Matisse's gesture: "If the exploitation of man by man has found its shameful expression in the conduct of business, we have, up to now, rarely seen the application of this principle to the domain of art in the unexpected form of the exploitation of ideas. The memoirs of Miss Toklas furnish us with an opportunity to appreciate how far the limits of indecency can be pushed."[2]

Henry McBride, one of Stein's oldest and most loyal lieutenants in America, expressed concern about the fruits of her success. From the first serialization in *The Atlantic Monthly*, McBride knew the book was "doomed" to become a best-seller. "Doomed, is my word for it, not yours,"

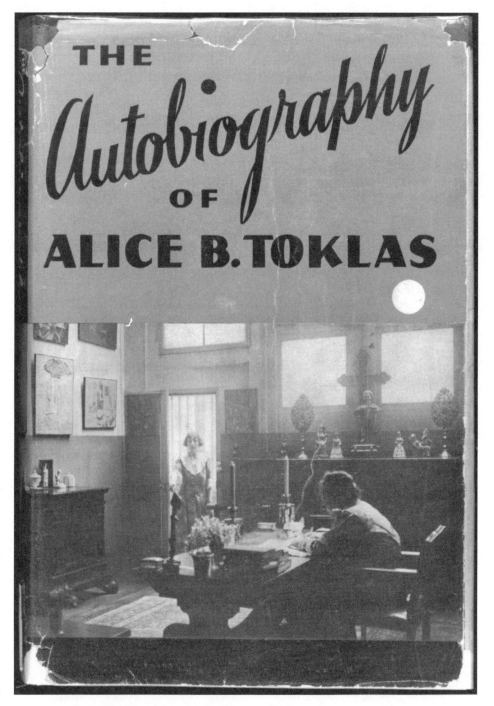

Cover of *The Autobiography of Alice B. Toklas,* published by Harcourt Brace, 1933 (cover photograph by Man Ray).

he wrote Stein. "I don't like giving you up to the general public and sharing you and Alice with about a million others."[3]

That summer in Bilignin, Gertrude walked and played with the dogs, Basket and Pepe, banged the piano and took trips in Godiva, and watched Alice hire and fire servants. But she did not write. For the first time in her life she became so preoccupied that words were no longer available to her.

|||

At the time Gertrude and Virgil signed the contracts in late June, Chick Austin was motoring from Hartford to Hollywood. He had stopped in Chicago at the Century of Progress World's Fair, buying a small De Chirico painting along the way. But this was not a summer of business for Austin; he simply wanted to escape Hartford and the exhausting rigors of the "architecture wars" connected with the Avery Wing. On the brink of staging his tripartite extravaganza—opera, Picasso exhibition, new wing—Austin expressed a desire to decamp. "I do wish I could get a job out here so we could move out for a while," he wrote his wife in July. "I'm still fed up with all the museum business. And I'm sure I'll never get anywhere in Hartford. They'll never pay me enough."[4] Prolonging his vacation as long as possible, he spent every day sunbathing on the Santa Monica beach. On his wedding anniversary, while on his return trip east, he gazed at the natural spectacle of the Grand Canyon and wired Helen a telegram: "Much love. Terribly sorry I can't be with you."[5]

|||

That same day, July 11, Lincoln Kirstein was delivering "a headlong onslaught" to George Balanchine in the kitchen of the Askews' rented Chelsea residence in London. It was their first serious meeting. "My information through Romola Nijinsky obviated any discussion with Balanchine; it was all predigested," Kirstein said. "I had known him a long time before I had met him."

Kirstein had spent the summer plotting this moment. On June 2, he had checked into the Hôtel Quai Voltaire in Paris, next door to Virgil Thomson. In early May, Thomson had reported that the Russian ballet companies were preparing to outdo each other in Paris, and Kirstein decided to witness the show. For the entire month of June he immersed himself in watching ballet, often seeking Thomson's advice. Three companies were performing, each competing for the legacy of Diaghilev's Ballets Russes: Léonide Massine's Ballet du Théâtre de Monte-Carlo was dancing in one theater; in the Théâtre du Châtelet, Serge Lifar offered an archaeological restoration of *The Spectre of the Rose* and his own ballet, *Jeunesse*; and George Balanchine had choreographed a program of four new works for an ad hoc ballet company called Les Ballets 1933.[6] Which one could spearhead Kirstein's plans for an American ballet? "I have never felt more certain of my own directions," he wrote to Muriel Draper after his first week in Paris. "It's here one can learn by participation really all the time."[7] Up close he witnessed Balanchine teaching mime to a young girl in rehearsals. From plush seats he applauded gala performances at the Châtelet, and over long meals at bistros he solicited the counsel of his American friends. Janet Flanner instructed him on Paris's competing salons; publisher Monroe Wheeler helped him sharpen his aims; and, most important, Thomson forced him to reexamine his plans for an American ballet in the tradition of Diaghilev. A week after his arrival in Paris, Kirstein described the situation in his diary: "Dickie Ames says everyone needs Diaghilev; there's no consolidating force around the considerable energy; split in tradition between Massine and Balanchine: Monte Carlo, reactionary; *Ballet 1933*, progressive; neither strong enough."

Kirstein quickly ruled Serge Lifar out of the running. He found him at loose ends, a narcissistic shell of his former self (Lifar and Jean Cocteau had aptly been used as models for advertising mannequins on the Champs-Élysées). But throughout his first month he remained torn between Massine and Balanchine. When it became clear that Massine had comfortably established himself with Monte Carlo, only Balanchine was left. Balanchine was a thin, tubercular twenty-nine-year-old whose career as a *demi-caractère* dancer had ended because of knee problems. His promise as a choreographer had been abundantly apparent in such early masterpieces as *Appollon Musagète* and *The Prodigal Son*, both of which he had choreographed for Diaghilev. Even after choosing Balanchine, Kirstein continued to express doubts; Balanchine was less serious than Massine, "satisfactory if not genius."[8] But his success in assembling and teaching a young company of dancers appealed to Kirstein.

Teaching was, in fact, the subject of Kirstein's passionate discussion in the Askews' kitchen on July 11. He planned to start a ballet school with a skeletal crew of Balanchine and two adolescent Russian dancers at its core, he explained heatedly to the choreographer. Later, he hoped it would evolve into a ballet company. He specified that it would include black and white dancers in nearly equal numbers. "I wish you were here to advise, to criticize, to tell me what not to do," Kirstein wrote Muriel Draper two days after meeting Balanchine.[9] "Within my hands seems to be my heart's desire and I'm so scared to do the wrong thing mechanically which might come up and hit me in the eye in six months' time."[10]

When he wrote to Chick Austin on July 16, too exhilarated to sleep, Kirstein was on the edge of mania: "My pen burns my hand as I write: words will not flow into the ink fast enough." Kirstein's handscript continued for sixteen pages. "This school can be the basis of a national culture, culture as intense as the great Russian Renaissance of Diaghilev," he prophesied. "But imagine it, we are exactly as if we were in 1910—offered a dancer only less good than an unformed Nijinsky, an incipient Karsavina. . . . Please, Please Chick if you have any love for anything we both do adore—rack your brains and try to make this all come true. We have the future in our hands. For Christ's sweet sake let us honor it."

| | |

Chick Austin had just arrived home from California, refreshed by his vacation, when he received Kirstein's letter. Before he even finished reading it, he brushed everything from his desk and shouted to a nearby volunteer, "We've got to get them, we've got to get them!"[11] Austin's fevered mind went straight to work. Perhaps dancers could rehearse in some of the museum's unused galleries? Perhaps pine planks could be laid over the stone floors of the Morgan Memorial? Perhaps George Balanchine could choreograph *Four Saints in Three Acts*? On July 26, Austin wrote back an enthusiastic reply, and by August 6 he had already solicited three thousand dollars (combined donations from Philip Johnson, art collector James Thrall Soby, Eddie Warburg, and Austin's assistant Paul Cooley). Austin wired, "MUSEUM WILLING. CAN'T WAIT."[12]

| | |

Lincoln Kirstein's two most respected advisers, Muriel Draper and Virgil Thomson, both derided his plan for establishing a ballet school at the Wadsworth Atheneum. Draper considered the museum a narrowly elitist base of operations, "a medium of prestige, passivity and gossip," and imagined the dancers forlornly stopping at a Hartford lunch wagon to eat a western omelette. Kirstein responded, "It's a hell of a lot better than the lousy way they've always had to get along wasting ¾ of their time in pointless intrigues, law-suits, and appearances at Polignacs or de Beaumonts. . . . You have developed such a keen gift for the use of the scalpel that its cutting edge can nearly sever the organ from the body as well as incidentally repairing the local injury."[13]

During the first weeks of Kirstein's visit to Paris, Thomson had been instrumental in furthering Kirstein's ballet plans by offering contacts and advice. "Virgil was a genius at social manipulation,"[14] he recalled, and the composer encouraged Kirstein's belief that a ballet company could succeed in America. Although France had shaped taste for the past three centuries, Thomson optimistically predicted that America would become the world's next cultural arbiter. But as the summer progressed and Kirstein's alliance with the Wadsworth Atheneum became more likely, Thomson grew more skeptical. Kirstein reported that Thomson questioned his aspirations to become a ballet impresario: "[Thomson finds] the role of entrepreneur too facile; my lack of any real taste shows that I am a 'creative,' not an 'appreciative' character." The intensity of Thomson's attack—he also called Kirstein "silly," "affected," and "mindless"—reflects a sense of threat. He was not pleased by Austin's suggestion that Balanchine choreograph *Four Saints*, nor did he relish the possibility that at this late date a ballet company might steal the spotlight from his opera. On July 21, Kirstein wrote in his diary, "He's so preoccupied with producing *Four Saints* he'd think I was trying to sabotage it with our ballet scheme for Hartford; he'd be right."

What Kirstein meant by this enigmatic diary entry is unclear. For a brief moment, Austin hoped to present the opera under the auspices of Kirstein's proposed ballet school. Did Kirstein hope that his ballet enterprise would thereby overshadow the opera? Did he hope to install Balanchine as the opera's choreographer? Did he want to overthrow Thomson's position as the chief authority among the Harvard constellation?

Plans were set for Balanchine to sail to America with a business manager and a pair of trained young dancers to demonstrate Balanchine's technique. They would form the tiny nucleus of the School of American Ballet. In mid-August, Kirstein and Balanchine stood at the corner of rue des Saint-Pères and rue Jacob, shook hands, and spoke of seeing each other next in America.

|||

Florine Stettheimer's puppet theater maquette for *Four Saints in Three Acts,* constructed in summer 1933. *"She built herself a little theater and filled it full of dolls and cellophane and feathers and crystal. She never put brush to paper." (Virgil Thomson)*

In the timeless world of the Alwyn Court that June, the three Stettheimer sisters celebrated Carl Van Vechten's fifty-third birthday. Carrie planned a dinner that consisted entirely of pink foods—from salmon and pink champagne to strawberry ice cream—served on a pink tablecloth, accompanied by pink flowers and heavy old-rose damask curtains trailing on the floor.

Carrie and Ettie soon left New York to summer in Atlantic City, while Florine stayed behind and prepared her studio for the summer heat. She removed the red velvet so that the studio was entirely white, gold, and silver, lit with 250-watt bulbs. Thomson had asked for a sketch of her ideas for the sets and costumes, but she resisted. "She knew that the purity of what she was doing depended upon not being a draftsman's idea," said Thomson. "Not a sketch, but a real toy." She constructed three shoebox theaters, about eighteen inches high and twenty-six inches long, in minute detail. For the beach scene she used dollhouse-sized clamshells and spiraling seashells, a strand of white coral for a bench, and palm trees made with feather fronds and rose ribbon–wrapped trunks. An arch that stood grandly behind Saint Teresa was made of tiny and large crystal beads. Behind them hung a large crinkled swatch of blue cellophane. In Maurice Grosser's words, it was "a Schrafft's candy-box version of Baroque."[15]

Florine fashioned the saints on wire maquettes, six inches tall, wrapped in cloth and brightly costumed. The faces all looked the same—crudely painted features on round cork balls—but the costumes were emphatically individualized. The Commère wore a red net skirt and a red sequin train, while the Compère wore black chintz. Saint Teresa was garbed in red velvet with a bobbin-lace bonnet beneath her broad sunbonnet. The dancers wore bits of metallic ribbon that curled up at the waist and matching anklets. The minor saints wore cream moiré silk surplices belted with white yarn, while the sailors wore aqua velvet buttons as tams. Each of the two dozen figures was rendered unique through a twist of metal foil, elbow-length white gloves, feathered anklets, bits of cherry-red taffeta, extravagant ruffs, satin toe shoes, bits of shiny chintz, or tiny pearl buttons.

But even after she had finished the toy theaters, Florine continued to harbor doubts about letting her doll-like sets be enlarged. When she revealed her doubts to Carl Van Vechten that summer, he wrote, "After what I saw yesterday in the way of cellophane and crystal, and pie pans, I think the Opera about Saints will lose a good deal if it loses your invaluable cooperation. Please don't let it."[16] Stettheimer wrapped her shoebox theaters in shawls and gauze and laid them away in domestic darkness on her closet shelf, awaiting Virgil Thomson's arrival.

|||

All summer long, Thomson desperately tried to reach the peripatetic Chick Austin for money to pay his copyist, whose task had to be completed by the end of summer for the opera to be produced on schedule. Thomson had requested $400 in early May, and when he had heard nothing by early July he called a "family council" that included the Levys, the Askews, Agnes Rindge, and John McAndrew. They agreed that Chick would eventually come up with the money, but that it might not be for some time. Thomson wrote to Austin, "I ask you my darling, I ask you is that any way to treat a guy?"[17] Philip Johnson and Jere Abbott lent Thomson $150 to keep the copyist going. "How on earth do you expect to put this opera on next winter if you can't raise more than $150 in all the six months that have passed since it was first informally agreed upon?" Thomson wrote Austin. "The score is advancing rapidly. So are my debts. I have given up my flat and pawned my silver. . . . I am at the moment on a farm in Normandy near Honfleur and hoping to wangle a visit or two out of somebody to fill in the weeks between now and when I can get a reply out of you."[18]

In August, Austin finally penciled Thomson a note from a New England roadside diner after his car broke down nearby. "Forgive me, darling," he wrote, "but if you were angry, I was worried as hell. I didn't know just where the money was going to be got this summer and I was completely broke or I would have sent it from my own meager store. . . . I'm not a rich art patron. I'm just a poor boy trying my damnedest to get that opera produced. Come soon please."[19]

|||

By the time Chick sent his note, Virgil and Maurice Grosser had sublet the flat at 17, quai Voltaire and left Paris. In July, Thomson went to London, and at the Askews' he met dancer and choreographer Frederick Ashton. At twenty-seven Ashton had a thin face that was lit up by the frank humor in his eyes. At that moment he was enjoying the opening of *After Dark*, a slick revue at the Vaudeville Theatre. Ashton had choreographed two of its dances and described one of them as "the love of an orchid for a cactus." Although Thomson had seen none of his choreography, he immediately took to Ashton's campy wit and intelligence. Thomson performed parts of the opera on the Askews' piano and described the collaboration to Ashton. "I said I think you should do this and do the other—just casually," Ashton recalled, and his ideas were in tune with Thomson's. When the composer asked whether Ashton could imagine staging the opera, the choreographer replied, "Oh, yes, and with delight." But nothing was decided.

Thomson and Grosser spent the rest of the summer on the island of Porquerolles, where living was cheap. Thomson scored the six hundred pages for an orchestra, maintaining a steady pace of ten pages a day. Since he had no musical instruments in this pastoral retreat, he could only imagine the sound his mixture of instruments—accordion, saxophones, strings, harmonium—would make, and he wrote Aaron Copland, "I only hope it sounds like I hope it sounds."[20] Maurice Grosser inked in the notes and then went off to paint the local sailors. By September, Thomson completed the score and sent it off to the copyist, confident that he had scored

Virgil Thomson and Maurice Grosser at the beginning of their decades-long partner-
ship, Paris, 1930.

it correctly, even without the benefit of checking his internal ear against a
piano. As soon as Austin sent him money ("Please wire today no fooling,"
he wrote Austin on October 19), Thomson would sail to New York. "When
I come," he advised, "everybody should be ready to get at the dirty work of
scene-building & dressmaking & rehearsing."[21]

||||

Before Virgil Thomson docked on October 31, his fears of being overshadowed by Lincoln Kirstein's School of American Ballet had subsided.
The school had already begun and ended its brief life in Hartford.[22]

On the late afternoon of October 17, George Balanchine and his
business manager, Vladmir Dmitriev, disembarked from tourist-class com-
partments of the S.S. *Olympic*. Greeted by Lincoln Kirstein, Chick Austin,
Eddie Warburg, and James Thrall Soby, they were whisked to duplex
rooms on the thirty-fourth floor of the Barbizon Hotel, where they gasped
at the panorama of lighted skyscrapers and the broad expanse of Central
Park. For dinner Balanchine ordered ice cream (which he took for true
American food), and until 2:00 A.M. he talked and drank bootleg whiskey

at the Askews'. Although Balanchine's English was limited, his responses —mostly "Swell" and "O.K. kid"—suggested his exuberance at finally being in America. It was the last untroubled moment that Balanchine, Kirstein, or Austin would feel that fall.

The Hartford Times proclaimed that Balanchine's arrival "may well develop into one of the most important cultural movements of the decade," and the next day the Dancing Masters of America met to organize their opposition.[23] Who cared about a cultural movement? they asked. This was competition! They were especially disturbed by the fact that students would pay nothing; were the Russians going to inject communism into the local dance scene? Chick Austin worked overtime to smooth the way. The dozen students who would enroll posed no threat, he told the press, and the new ballet school not only would present America's answer to Russia's Imperial Theater Ballet School but would develop "the newer possibilities which the American scene and the American rhythms may offer us."[24] Although he was talking through his hat, Austin reported to the local populace that Balanchine thought the Avery Wing's theater was as well equipped as any in Europe.

Within a week, all the plans for a ballet school had unraveled. Balanchine decided the theater was all wrong: the proscenium was too low, the auditorium too small, the floor too hard. There was no way to compromise on these brutal facts, and dealing with the parochial concerns of the indignant Dancing Masters of America proved dispiriting. Kirstein, Balanchine, and Dmitriev left Hartford and gathered in the Kirstein family's home; they talked while Balanchine played Negro spirituals on the piano, and by the end of the marathon discussion they decided a ballet school could not work in Hartford—nor would they take any part in Four Saints in Three Acts.

Kirstein and Balanchine decided to open the school in New York, perhaps switching their affiliation to the Museum of Modern Art (Eddie Warburg could be an effective agent in this plan, since his family had recently given the museum $100,000). "My historic or objective responsibility lay not to a closed past but a future possibility," Kirstein later wrote.[25] They still had to confront Chick Austin, who received the shattering news as well as possible; the local press reported the Russians' withdrawal as a disagreement about making the school a commercial operation. More personally, Kirstein worried about his damaged relations with Chick Austin and the circle of friends that gathered at the Askews' on Sundays. When

Philip Johnson refused to meet Balanchine, Kirstein was terrified of an ever-growing circle of rejection. "The small talk around New York has on successive Sundays after hours done its best to elevate it into a feud between you and me," Kirstein wrote Austin. "I hope there is nothing in this more than your justified resentment."[26]

Although Austin wanted to reconcile with Kirstein, he never shook the feeling that his museum's role in creating an American ballet had been insufficiently acknowledged. Two decades later, Austin wrote Thomson, "I have always been a bit miffed that Lincoln has never mentioned the fact that after all I had persuaded at one moment a number of Insurance Co. presidents that the thing they wanted more than anything in the world was to have a group of be-tutued ladies [and] extraordinary gents waltzing through the sacred purlieus of the good old Wadsworth Atheneum. I still think it's my greatest feat!"[27]

III

Chick Austin had no time to wallow in disappointment; the tasks ahead seemed nearly impossible. Construction was proceeding on schedule, but Austin still had to prepare for the two events that would inaugurate the new wing. He had not begun to raise the necessary ten thousand dollars for the opera. The trustees did not even approve his proposal for a Picasso retrospective until November 14, 1933, less than three months before the exhibition, the new wing, and the opera were to open. Alfred Barr applauded Austin's initiative and foolhardy courage in simultaneously mounting both a Picasso exhibition and an opera: "Either one would be enough for any ordinary mortal museum director."[28]

Confronting what lay ahead, Austin felt overwhelmed, and his priorities that November reflected his anxiety: he focused on minute details of the Avery Wing's interior. He corresponded with Philip Johnson, the head of his short-lived enterprise Art Inc., tracking down the ideal Miesian chest of drawers, the perfect tubular chair and chrome coat hooks, and suitable leather double couches for the galleries. He buried himself in samples of exotic veneers, bevels, and postcard racks and relished the possible colors that could be used for the fabric-covered gallery walls.

Austin did not mail the fund-raising solicitation letter for the opera until December 13, 1933, less than two months before the opening. The opera's name was printed in pink, and the salutation read, "Dear Friend or Enemy." Belatedly jumping into fund-raising, Austin appealed to all quarters of his life: art dealers, museum directors, Harvard friends, Hartford society. The budget was small enough that it relied neither on institutions nor on the very rich, and the mailing list was small enough that Chick's secretary, Eleanor Howland, typed them all without help. But they had to throw a net large enough to raise the necessary money. The budget that Houseman and Thomson drew up included vast amounts of cellophane and a dozen feather trees, musicians, salaries, and rehearsal and performance salary for the cast. Even with the collaborators working free, the budget came to ten thousand dollars, a considerable sum in 1934.

A month earlier, Austin had invited Gertrude Stein to loan several Picasso paintings for his exhibition and invited Stein and Toklas to stay with him for the *Four Saints* premiere. (Stein declined both invitations.) "I am convinced that you have found the only literary solution for opera in English," he wrote to Stein, "and that Virgil's music sets it off to perfection."[29]

Before Chick had raised any of the money, Thomson had already rounded up his team of collaborators. And, not incidentally, rehearsals had already begun in Harlem.

CHAPTER 14

Collaborators:
Not the Usual Suspects

When Virgil Thomson looked back on his handpicked team of collaborators—onstage and off—he observed that their two overriding virtues were lack of pay and inexperience: "It was everybody's *first time*. You see, in order to get something original and good you have to get somebody when he is *young*. After one or even one and a half successes, you are beginning to imitate yourself a little bit. And everybody worked free, except the cast. When you're not paid, you always do a good job, you're responsible, and there is no front office that can fire you. Or put his finger in your pie."

The artists whom Thomson chose had no experience with opera but were passionately idiosyncratic in their respective crafts. Driven by the fact that they were pioneers, they made it up as they went along. "Stage directors, designers, costumers, and choreographers, all working along different stylistic lines," Thomson later warned, ". . . will turn your work into a variety show."[1] But he knew that his collaborators' lack of theatrical experience would allow him to dictate his own style, thereby preventing chaos onstage and retaining his commanding position offstage.

|||

Virgil Thomson met John Houseman at the suggestion of his friend Lewis Galantière in late November 1933, on Houseman's first visit to the Askews'. By the end of that Sunday afternoon, Thomson considered him a likely candidate to direct his opera. "I thought he was out of his mind, frankly," Houseman recalled, "but I was eager, and the opportunity was a golden one." Houseman was thirty-one years old and had never directed a play in his life. Selling grain futures on Wall Street was his job, but Thomson quickly discerned other qualities in Houseman that would prove more important than theater experience: flexibility, cosmopolitan attitudes, an ability to deal with shifting finances, and, above all, taste. In Houseman's words, his opera-related experience was all part of "the education of a chameleon."

He had been born Jacques Haussmann in 1902 in Bucharest; by 1933 "Haussmann" had just begun to give way to "Houseman" (Thomson's notebooks of the day use both, for example, and Houseman signed his letters both ways). Known in his family as "Fat Jack," the youngster had been shuttled from grand hotels to shabby furnished rooms, where he had come to know extravagance but not security, and to English schools. By his teens he spoke several languages and had visited most of Europe's major cities; by his twenties he had become acquainted with the Bloomsbury crowd in London.[2] When he moved to New York, he quickly became involved with several prominent Greenwich Village residents: James Light of the Provincetown Players, e.e. cummings, and Edmund Wilson, among others. Entering his thirties, he became a successful grain merchant and married actress Zita Johann. By the time Thomson met him at the end of 1933, Houseman's grain company had declared bankruptcy, his wife had left him, and Houseman was living in garretlike servant's quarters on twenty dollars a week. At his lowest point in the Depression, Houseman was prone to self-flagellation in the third person: "He had had his big chance and muffed it." But the failure of Houseman's grain business also provided an opportunity to leave his respectable vocation for the theater. In less than a year he had coauthored four comedies. Although his writing was formulaic, his desire to establish himself in the theater propelled him forward, even though there was no immediate promise.[3]

John Houseman, by Lee Miller, 1934.

Drawn to Houseman's upper-class British accent and cosmopolitan upbringing, Thomson was taken with his observation that *Four Saints* sounded like something that Étienne de Beaumont could have produced at one of his Soirées de Paris.[4] Summing up Houseman's strategic virtues, Thomson observed, "His British rather wonderfully cool warmth, his considerate good manners, also British, and his elaborate cultural background in foreign letters and languages all went to make up a hand that he knew he could bid on."[5]

The opera production demanded someone with Houseman's intelligent flexibility to work with a temperamental crew. "I was there every minute, but my function was primarily as a producer," Houseman said, then discreetly qualified this remark: "In the *good* sense of a producer."

Houseman saw in Thomson "a small vivacious man several years older than myself, with a pale face, a piercing voice, precise articulation, and a willpower that became evident within thirty seconds of meeting." The next morning Houseman heard Virgil sing the opera, accompanying himself on a piano at the Hotel Leonori. Two days later, Virgil officially invited him to join the production—in exchange for no money, no contract, and many headaches. Houseman responded, "It would be fun to try." That he accepted immediately reflected both his vocational desperation and Thomson's charisma. And he had nothing to lose.

As Houseman described his task in hindsight, it sounded daunting: "We had ten thousand dollars and nine and a half weeks in which to find a cast, coach and rehearse them in two hours of unfamiliar music and complicated stage action, execute scenery and costumes, rehearse a new score, move to Hartford into an unfinished theater with an orchestra of twenty and a cast of forty-three, set up, light, dress rehearse, and open cold before one of the world's most sophisticated audiences. With the slightest theatrical experience I would have realized the impossibility of our task. In my total ignorance I assumed the job in a mood of irresistible euphoria."

|||

During the rehearsals of Houseman's forgettable comedy *Three and One*, he encountered "a pale-faced, garrulous, exhaustingly eager and ambitious young lighting expert." At twenty-four, Abe Feder was already one of the most opinionated lighting designers around. His sureness owed something to his character and something to the fact that his profession was just being born. The theater bug had bitten Feder at thirteen, when he had sat in a balcony and watched a magician called the Great Thurston make people appear and disappear behind black curtains. "But what really fascinated me was the lights. Colored, dazzling lights all over the stage! I went home in a dream. I have been obsessed with light ever since. Other boys played with footballs and postage stamps. I played with light."[6] He pursued his fascination by taking sandwiches from his father's delicatessen to the local theater, where he had a chance to observe the nuts and bolts of stagecraft.

At seventeen, Feder went to Pittsburgh to attend the Carnegie Institute of Technology, a center for theater training. Because of his middling grades at West Side High, he was admitted on probation. Feder recalled that his admittance depended on a letter from his high school principal, and it read something like this:

> My introduction to the young boy, as a freshman, was when he blew out the main fuse and when the police came they found this kid downstairs fooling around with some wire. From then on he was the bane of my existence. He was cutting holes in the ceiling and putting up curtains. All I can say is that he was the most talented kid during the four years he was there. I sure don't want him to come back here, but I really don't believe he will be a detriment.

Carnegie Tech offered no curriculum in lighting, which was not yet taught as a stage art, as the technical revolution that made the art of lighting design possible did not occur until the 1920s. One picked up lighting tips from electricians, and one of Feder's mentors at Carnegie Tech concluded, "He's going to have to learn on his own." He moved from Carnegie to Yiddish Theater projects in the Bronx, and the same month that Houseman invited him to join *Four Saints*, Feder had made his Broadway lighting debut with *Calling All Stars*.

"Lighting, it's in the marrow of my bones" was the way Feder explained his education. "To me light was something called the art of revealment." He embedded his art in the technical mastery of gels, amperage, and bulbs. When he encountered his collaborators on *Four Saints in Three Acts*, he found them lacking in any nuts-and-bolts grounding in the theater. The two exceptions were his friend Teddy Thomas, who helped light the show, and Kate Drain Lawson, who supervised the technical production of costumes and sets. "Thank god for Kate Drain Lawson," Feder said. "She brought law and order to that production."

|||

Thomson met *Four Saints'* conductor, Alexander Smallens, at the Askews'. Of all the collaborators, Smallens was the only one who was not new to the opera world. The forty-five-year-old musician had worked as the musical director of the Philadelphia Civic Opera and was currently assisting Leopold Stokowski at the Philadelphia Orchestra. Drawn to the project for its adventure and willing to conduct without a fee, he supported musical experimentation. He had conducted the American premieres of Prokofiev's *The Love for Three Oranges* and Richard Strauss's *Ariadne auf Naxos*, and he appreciated attempts to break down the American musical establishment. The most difficult thing about Smallens was his temper, and when rehearsals did not go smoothly he could lose his equilibrium. In the unflattering words of John Houseman, "Smallens was a bully and a shouter."

|||

At his first formal meeting with John Houseman, Virgil Thomson explained, "I don't really want them to act. I want them to be moved." But very few people in New York had any experience in directing opera, even of the most conventional sort, and none knew how to move singers. The star performers of the day generally owned their own costumes, developed their own interpretations, and neither required nor accepted much direction. "I knew it had to be done from scratch," Thomson recalled. He was guided by a memory of seeing Gluck's *Orpheus and Eurydice* in Kansas City, wherein singers from the Boston Opera Company had combined forces with Anna Pavlova and others had danced and mimed the story. Thomson had liked it so much that he decided to apply the "completely regulated spectacle" of the eighteenth-century opera-ballets to *Four Saints*. He thus required a choreographer not only for the two brief ballets but for the continuously patterned movements of the entire cast.

He recalled his meeting with Frederick Ashton a few months earlier and instantly decided to invite him to be the choreographer. Constance Askew paid for a cable communicating a parsimonious offer: Chick Austin

Frederick Ashton, by Lee Miller, 1934.

would pay steerage-class fare, in lieu of a salary Ashton would be given ten dollars a week pocket money, and the Askews offered him one of the twin beds in their second-story guest room, to be shared with Thomson.

When Ashton arrived, he faced the opera's challenge of choreographing movement for dancers who lacked formal ballet training; it was fortunate that not all the casts he had worked with had been as technically proficient as the Sadler's Wells dancers. In the fall of 1933, he had staged dances for a short-lived musical called *The Gay Hussar* and a ragtag charity show called *Nursery Murmurs*. The minimally trained dancers from Liverpool's Audrey Butterworth School had forced him to choreograph movements for amateurs. A dance colleague marveled at the lengths to which he would go to elicit the right movements from his dancers.

A year earlier, Ashton had had his first brush with black dance when he performed in a show called *High Yellow*. A trial run in reverse for choreographing *Four Saints*, it had offered Ashton the chance to dance a black role under the guidance of black choreographer Buddy Bradley. Ashton had not been convincing; producer C. B. Cochran observed that he had "remained a white man despite his make-up, and was far too self-conscious and absorbed with the fascination of 'snaky hips' to be convincing." (Snaky Hips, a dance that emphasized a wildly gyrating pelvis, had been popularized in the late 1920s by Earl "Snake Hips" Tucker.) But *High Yellow* had given Ashton the opportunity to assimilate liquid, swiveling movements into his own corporal vocabulary.

Perhaps the most relevant experience Ashton brought to *Four Saints* was his own childhood in Peru. Some of the sharpest images in his repertory sprang from his childhood, when, immersed in Catholic ritual, he had assisted in high masses in Lima's grand cathedral. As one of the few blonds in the congregation, he had been a favored acolyte. Ashton was, in fact, the only one of *Four Saints'* behind-the-scenes collaborators who could confront the opera's Catholic imagery without invoking irony or metaphor. Although he was not Catholic himself, the Catholic Church's rituals were second nature to him. Virgil Thomson was fond of saying that Ashton was the perfect choreographer because he knew how nuns moved in procession. One such procession formed one of his first memories at the age of two, and he later witnessed informal processions that ranged from bevies of nuns in long habits to plump women in bright, slit skirts and tango shoes. "The thing that a choreographer really needs is an eye," Ashton later said. "He has to do his training through his eye."

"Although we were supposed to be English boys and there was an English colony in Lima, I never thought of England at all," Ashton recalled. "It never entered my head." When he returned to England in 1919, he spoke English with a Spanish accent and experienced public school as "an absolute desert." At thirteen he saw Anna Pavlova on tour, dancing *Fairy Doll*, and later that evening he witnessed her stepping like a magical bird into a waiting cab. "She injected me with her poison, and from the end of that evening I wanted to dance," he recalled. "Coming from middle-class parents, it was a horrifying thought." In London, he took Saturday afternoon ballet lessons from Léonide Massine, spending a guinea (twenty-one shillings) per lesson from his thirty-shilling-a-week salary. When he tried to hide his dancing from his family, he became anxious, forgetful, and depressed. A doctor told his mother that unless he was allowed to dance he might end up in a psychiatric hospital. "That frightened her, and then she thought she'd better concede," Ashton recalled. "Which she did, though all my family were outraged and even she could never bring herself to tell anyone that I was dancing. She always said I'd 'gone on the stage' instead."

By December 1933, when Constance Askew cabled Ashton, inviting him to join the opera production, he had developed a prominent reputation in England. He choreographed primarily for Marie Rambert's Ballet Club but also worked for the Camargo Society and the fledgling Vic-Wells company. Critic Arnold Haskell called him "the first young choreographer of importance to have emerged since the end of the Diaghilev era." Ashton worked constantly, but the fact that he choreographed not only ballet but musicals and provincial charity shows suggests that he took many assignments to survive financially.

The premiere of Ashton's ballet *Les Rendezvous* on December 5, 1933, was a fashionable event—the audience included dress designer Elsa Schiaparelli, fashionable interior decorator Syrie Maugham, and actress Constance Cummings. Ashton read the glowing reviews just before he sailed the next day on the *Ile de France*. He crossed the Atlantic with Maurice Grosser, *Four Saints'* scenarist. Although Grosser had resigned himself to not seeing the opera for which he had written the scenario, at a propitious moment that fall he had sold a painting of an attractive sailor on Porquerolles Island. The sale had provided just enough to pay for the trip. On board Ashton and Grosser barely talked; it was a rough, cold passage, and they were mostly confined to their cabins. Ashton fantasized that he would be greeted by reporters and banks of orchids, but the *Four Saints* collaborators were too immersed in rehearsals and too poor for any such ceremony.

When Ashton and Grosser docked on December 12, rehearsals had already begun. Ashton was asked to choreograph two ballet *divertissements* (he called them "sniplets")—a brief second-act ballet in which the angels practiced flying and a third-act tango for sailors and their Spanish ladies.[7] Ashton needed to find three male and three female dancers. Harlem's clubs and revues boasted a surfeit of black dancers, but none trained in ballet's formal vocabulary.

Avoiding professional agents, Ashton was escorted through Harlem by Edward Perry, a black journalist with a nose for talent, and by singer Jimmie Daniels. He went to Lenox Avenue and 110th Street, where the Savoy Ballroom stretched a full block. "The Home of Happy Feet" was Harlem's largest and most democratic dance hall. Two bands played every night, so the music never stopped, and the vast burnished-maple floor (50 feet wide and 250 feet long) featured the best nonprofessional dancers in New York. Tuesday night attracted the most serious dancers, known as the "400 Club," who appreciated the expanse of floor available midweek. Ashton was unprepared for the explosive vitality and inventive range of the dancing he saw there. "Everybody went to the Savoy Ballroom, and very fancy stuff went on there," Thomson recalled. "That was the Lindy Hop school." Ashton saw couples Shim-Shamming and Trucking, dancing the Black Bottom and the Eagle Rock. Most of all he was amazed by the Lindy Hop, an updated version of the Texas Tommy that alternated a syncopated beat with improvised gyrating turns and breakneck pinwheel spins. When Ashton spied a promising dancer, Perry would approach him or her with a proposal to portray a dancing angel in a Gertrude Stein opera. "At first they thought we were pulling their legs," Ashton recalled. Within a week, Ashton had engaged three men and three women. One of the male dancers was a lifeguard at Lido Beach, one was a boxer, and one drove a taxi and played basketball. The trio of female dancers could execute "fancy" social dance, and one was the daughter of another cast member. None had formal training.

CHAPTER 15

Rehearsals
in Harlem

Rounding up a cast of black opera singers proved an even greater challenge. Thomson could not ask the Juilliard School who the best available singers were—it had nothing on black performers. Nor could the presence of a few prominent black opera singers—Roland Hayes, Marian Anderson, Caterina Jarboro—make up for the lack of a larger pool. Thomson and Houseman would have to look beyond the usual resources, to church choirs, cabaret and vaudeville performers, and professional black choirs. The most prominent professional choruses were the Hall Johnson Choir, the Wyn Talbot Choir, and the Cecil MacPherson Choir, but even in these groups few singers could sight-read music. "I made the mistake of asking to look at the music," one chorus member remembered, "and the others looked at me as if I had three heads." Others recalled the informal musical standards among professionals. Thomson had originally planned to use the Hall Johnson Choir. Its leader's musical education was impeccable, and he had presided over his choir since December 1925. He had composed the music for *Green Pastures* and, most recently, had written and directed *Run Little Chillun,* which Thomson had seen on Broadway with Carl Van Vechten in the spring of 1933. But Thomson foresaw problems with the choir: its members were, as a Hall Johnson Choir advertisement put it, "Like an Old-Fashioned Negro Camp Meeting." Reviews praised them as "crude," "energetic, earnest-acting," and "robust," with "sincerity and naïve skill." In *Run Little Chillun's* press release Helene Pons wrote, "I came upon these people dancing wildly, barbarically, with natural abandon. Here was primitive rapture, but withal such a joyous naivete."[1] This was not what Thomson had in mind.

Most members of the Hall Johnson Choir did not read notes, and learning their parts by rote for *Run Little Chillun* had required five months of rehearsal. Thomson had only three months until his premiere.

Like griot storytellers in Africa, like the blues at rent parties, like street slang, black church music depended on spontaneity; it was profusely embroidered with claps and shouts, dropped octaves, and rhythmic variations that could not be rendered in notes.[2] America's technically untrained musicians had offered the country some of her most important contributions. Writing to his mentor, Muriel Draper, George Antheil championed America's "illegitimate" and preliterate art: "The only great music are first the singing niggers, second the singing vaudevillists, and third Irving Berlin. None of these can write it down."[3]

Thomson and Houseman's recruiting lieutenant in Harlem was Edward Perry. A lean, chain-smoking, homosexual black man, Perry was widely connected and would subsequently be dubbed "the Elsa Maxwell of Harlem." He wrote articles in the *New York Amsterdam News,* helped organize A'Lelia Walker's Dark Tower gatherings, knew many of the leaders in the music and performing world, and, like Jimmie Daniels, belonged to the Edna Thomas–Olivia Wyndham circle.

Edward Perry led John Houseman and Virgil Thomson to Eva Jessye, a thin, thirty-eight-year-old black woman with conked hair, a forthright manner, and formidable credentials. "She was one tough cookie," a colleague observed, "and I don't doubt she had *reason* to be tough." The daughter of freed slaves, she had grown up in Kansas, less than a hundred miles from Thomson's birthplace. At the age of twelve, she had organized a girls' singing group, and from the age of fourteen, when she joined a university choir outside Kansas City, she had been drilled in note reading. She had studied music at Western University in Kansas, taught in Oklahoma public schools, and presided over the Music Department of Morgan State

Eva Jessye, by Lee Miller, 1934.

College in Maryland. When she moved to New York at the age of twenty-seven, she supported herself by ironing shirts and singing in movie theaters as a warm-up act for silent feature films. In 1926, she formed her own group of a dozen singers called the Original Dixie Jubilee Singers, soon re-named the Eva Jessye Choir. Singing the standard black repertory—songs such as "Massa's in da Cold Cold Ground," "That's Why Darkies Are

Born"—the choir became popular onstage and on the Major Bowes amateur hour. In 1929, she trained the choir for King Vidor's all-black film, *Hallelujah!* She was the first black woman in America to succeed as a choral director.

When Virgil Thomson met her in the thick of the Depression, Jessye's bread-and-butter jobs were Sunday-morning choral tours of the Baptist churches throughout the five boroughs of New York. The work was unglamorous but steady. Thomas Anderson, a member of her choir and later Saint Giuseppe in *Four Saints*, recalled being sent out to Brooklyn as the choir's advance man; he would step out of the subway and approach every church in sight, with leaflets advertising Eva Jessye's choir. Every Sunday, the choir members would gather at the subway, pay their nickel, and go to the morning's designated church. In the afternoon they would sing at Sing Sing prison, in Ossining, New York, and then go directly to the WOR studios, where they would provide the choral backup for "Thoughts at Sunset." At the end of the day Eva Jessye would wad up some bills and press them into the palms of her choir members in such a way that no one saw what anyone was paid. It was usually $2, transportation included.

When Jessye drilled her choir, as one choir member put it, "She had no mercy on you—you could sing it or you couldn't." Her hard-nosed drive prompted some to call her "Evil Jessye," but only behind her back. Her musical authority was never questioned. "She could be singing one song and tapping her foot another way and playing a different rhythm on the piano," observed chorus member Thomas Anderson. Knowing the cutthroat state of competition among black choruses, Jessye claimed that her singers could read music, which was not strictly the case. Some choir members had studied at black colleges, but their musical literacy ranged from the expert note reading of Altonell Hines, who held a music degree from Livingstone College and a master's degree in education, to the more characteristic level of Kitty Mason, who played Saint Cecilia in the opera. "I look at the notes and it helps me, but I don't read music per se," she said. "That's how I've always put it."

At the end of November, Virgil Thomson arrived at Jessye's three-story brownstone on West 133rd Street. The score he showed her was like nothing she had ever seen, but she was determined to get the job. "I knew they were in a pickle and needed us," she recalled, "just as we needed them." Jessye told Thomson her choir would see it the following morning at ten, and that he should return at that time to hear them audition. As soon as Thomson left, she called an emergency choir rehearsal for eight the next morning. Jessye stayed up with the score the whole night. The words meant nothing to her, but she found the music lucid, and she later declared, "I don't know any music that is any more *musical*." Early the next morning, she drilled her choir in the opening section of the opera. By 9:30, when they broke, the singers had survived the first shock of the words and could plausibly attack the music. Thomson arrived fifteen minutes later and greeted Jessye with the hope that the choir members would arrive on time. "They should be, since they're right around the corner at the drugstore," Jessye thought. "Well, they were on time, and they opened their copies of the music, as if they'd never seen it, and they hit that thing ninety miles an hour." Thomson exclaimed, "My God! I've never seen such note reading in my life!"[4]

Years later, Jessye visibly enjoyed recounting the tale of fooling Thomson, but Thomson never included it in any of his tellings of the opera's history and dismissed the ruse, saying that he always knew choirs accepted singers with different degrees of musical literacy. Eva Jessye recounts the story as evidence of her lifelong principle: "My motto was, and still is, 'What I may not know today I'll know tomorrow, because I always have the night between.'"

Performing the opera offered two breakthroughs for African-American singers. The first was musical. As Jessye put it:

> It was quite a departure, because up to that time the only opportunities involved things like "Swanee River," or "That's Why Darkies Are Born," or "Old Black Joe." They called that "our music," and thought we could sing those things only by the gift of God, and if God hadn't given us that gift we wouldn't have any at all. . . . With this opera we had to step on fresh ground, something foreign to our nature completely. Not like *Porgy and Bess* that came the next year—that was our inheritance, our own lives. But what did we know about the minds of Gertrude Stein and Virgil Thomson? We really went abroad on that.

The singers' second breakthrough was economic. In her demand that her singers be paid for rehearsal, Jessye was fighting a deeply ingrained system of discriminatory salaries, rampant kickbacks, and nonpayment of choruses during rehearsals. Actors' Equity payment guidelines had been granted to black leads only since *Show Boat* in 1927, and even then they were given the lesser pay due to "chorus equity."[5] But Jessye won her battle. Houseman decided to pay the cast fifteen dollars a week during rehearsals, although some chorus members recall being paid only ten. "It wasn't much, but it kept them alive," Houseman recalled. "And I think it was a great relief from singing hymns for a while." Rehearsal payment sprang less from humanitarian impulses than from the fear that the cast would disband during the two months before the production opened. This was no idle fear in the depths of the Depression: to keep *Run Little Chillun*'s seventy-five-member cast together, meals had been served at rehearsals. Some of *Four Saints'* cast members held side jobs to supplement their minimal weekly salary.

Jessye believed that her economic demand had inspired her conflict with Thomson. But money was only a small part of the problem. The two were natural fighters, and, although they had grown up within a hundred miles of each other, they lived in different worlds. "Eva Jessye would tussle with the Lord if he showed up in the middle of rehearsal," observed a colleague. Jessye regarded Thomson as effete, controlling, and condescending, and he summed Jessye up as "a woman who was very useful but a great nuisance."

Soloists auditioned downtown in the Askews' living room, where Virgil played the score on the grand piano. The leading role of Saint Ignatius went to twenty-six-year-old baritone Edward Matthews. The most classically trained member of the cast, he had dropped the study of medicine on the advice of Roland Hayes to become a classical singer. Matthews performed Handel concert recitals, toured with the Fiske Jubilee Singers, and sang on the Major Bowes program. Another principal role, the Compère, went to a vaudeville performer named Abner Dorsey, whose lyrical bass could effortlessly drop an octave. For the tricky role of the Commère, a performer was hard to find. More than one contralto looked at the words and ran for the next subway back to Brooklyn. Finally, Altonell Hines, a member of the Eva Jessye Choir, was elevated from the chorus to play the part.[6] The role of Saint Teresa II went to a contralto named Bruce Howard (a woman), whose lack of formal musical training was made up for by her rich voice and alluring presence. Handsome Embry Bonner was cast as Saint Chavez, not only because of his brilliant tenor voice but because he was the boyfriend of one of the Askew regulars.

But casting the central role of Saint Teresa proved troublesome.

Edward Matthews as Saint Ignatius, by Lee Miller, 1934.

Bruce Howard as Saint Teresa II, by Lee Miller, 1934.

Embry Bonner as Saint Chavez, by Lee Miller, 1934.

Thomson considered the renowned Marian Anderson, but she was not interested. On December 1, he auditioned the well-known soprano Caterina Jarboro but quickly realized she was likely to be a temperamental diva. When she withdrew early in the rehearsals, she suggested a friend. In early December a thirty-three-year-old singer named Beatrice Robinson Wayne reported for auditions after the rehearsals had already begun. She had graduated from a black college in Virginia, toured with an evangelical preacher, and even played an aproned maid at Radio City Music Hall, but to her the possibility of singing in an opera seemed "like a miracle."

She arrived in plain black mourning clothes. Her mother and aunt had just died, and her marriage had recently ended. Stocky and plain, her hair pulled into a bun, she limped into the room. Virgil Thomson took one look at her, twirled his amber cigarette holder, and said, sotto voce, "My God! She's dressed like she's dying." He handed her a score and snapped at her to stand near the chorus until her cue. She thought he behaved ridiculously. More than half a century later, she recalled that first audition: "Virgil was at the piano, and I'm standing up there looking at this thing, trying to make some sense of it. When he got to my part, I didn't fall into it like he thought I should have, so he turned his head like 'My God, what is this?' He made me mad. I said, 'What the hell is wrong with you?' I was ashamed because I never talk like that. Then he straightened up and said, 'Nothing, nothing, darling.' I looked at him and said, 'Well, why don't you play then, what are you waiting for? I don't know this. I've never heard this. I have to hear it in order to appreciate it.'"

Her rich voice effortlessly encompassed the top notes of a soprano and the bottom notes of a contralto; John Houseman said, "As soon as Virgil heard our lady, nobody thought about anybody else." Wayne and Thomson never fought again. She recalled, "That upsetment at the piano fixed it."

Rehearsals began the second week of that icy December of 1933 around Eva Jessye's baby grand piano on the parlor floor of her three-story brownstone on 133rd Street. The space proved too cramped, however, and a few weeks later the cast moved two doors down to the basement of St. Philip's Episcopal Church. The pride of Talented Tenth Negroes, St. Philip's was "the hoity-toity church of Harlem," designed in 1911 by Vertner Tandy, the first African-American architect licensed in the state of New York. The Episcopal worship service was more elevated than that of revivalist Baptist churches, and the impressive granite-and-brick façade

Beatrice Robinson Wayne as Saint Teresa, by Carl Van Vechten, March 9, 1934.

showcased stained-glass windows. St. Philip's offered the ideal meeting ground of Harlem and high bohemia, and it did the church credit to have both Eva Jessye and elegant downtowners as its temporary residents.

Entering the large church basement, Thomson worried that the black cast would fall ill. "The minute they felt a little cold, we turned up the heat," he said. "We kept them warm, and it was a very cold winter." With its radiators clanking continually, the stuffy basement became a semi-tropical island in the middle of wintry Harlem.

Each day, Thomson, Houseman, and Ashton took the Lexington Avenue subway to 135th Street. They walked west to St. Philip's in time for ten o'clock rehearsals. En route they saw Harlem by daytime in the depths of the Depression, an utterly different image from Harlem by night. "North of 125th Street, I found another world," recalled Houseman, "a world of poverty and desolation and fear where the winter winds seemed to blow twenty degrees colder than downtown and one could smell decay and despair in the uncollected garbage in the streets. But in our clean, stuffy church basement, all through Christmas and into the New Year, we were crowded and warm and secluded and busy."

Rehearsals ran from ten to two, followed by an hour-long lunch break and another two hours of rehearsal, ending at five. Punctuality was initially hard to enforce. While soloists sang from a tiny elevated stage, chorus members sat on wooden benches, whispering to one another. A group of men played gin rummy, and others clustered around the beautiful Bruce Howard; as Thomson recalled, "She was like a honey pot."[7]

Eva Jessye prepared the chorus, but not to Virgil's liking. "I discovered I couldn't let Eva Jessye take a rehearsal in my absence," he said, "because she knew the Negro singers but her rhythms were less subtle and elaborate than mine. And I thought it might get into one of those rowing-a-boat rhythms which do generate themselves in Negro life." Thomson would listen intently and strenuously correct: "I wrote the music, and I know what the note is. No scooping sopranos, please. The *note*." When he detected a word insufficiently enunciated, Thomson jumped up with a "No, no, no, no, no!" (More than fifty years later, three participants in the production each spontaneously mimicked Thomson's "No, no, no, no, no!" and each rendition sounded piercingly similar.) Then Thomson would clap his hands and flatter the cast outrageously and everything would be on course as Charlotte Alford, a short, energetic young black woman in thick glasses, banged away on the church's tinny upright piano.

Jessye sometimes bridled at Thomson's corrections, confident that she had a better idea of how to extract the most from her singers. "He was a musician, but I was a black person," Jessye said later. "I told him I had been a black person longer than him." The rehearsal's firm tone was set by Thomson, who kept tight command of every performer's style. "You can't just let singers pretend to act, to mug, stagger, or lurch," he said. "You tell them what to do, move them around becomingly, and act with the *voice*."

Thomson's tight musical stewardship reflected his fear that the opera would be perceived as gospel pageantry. "We were all in agreement right off that this was not a 'nigger show,'" Thomson said. "And you mustn't ever let it go that way." So when he came upon Eva Jessye conducting in a fashion that encouraged the choir to emphasize their gospel rhythms, he rushed in and took over. "You mustn't let them do that, for that takes all the education out of them," Thomson declared. "That's the way they go African."

The most recent all-black show on Broadway, Hall Johnson's *Run Little Chillun*, had elicited this response in *The New Yorker*: "But frankly I am getting tired of tom-toms and writhing and large ensembles depicting the more elemental forms of worship," wrote theater critic Robert Benchley, "and I see no reason why it isn't almost time now for Negroes in the theatre to behave almost as sensibly as white folks."[8] For *Four Saints*, the black performers carried the burden of behaving "as sensibly as white folks" while retaining the special character they could bring to the production.

Thomson's belief that Gertrude Stein wrote highly singable words was borne out in rehearsal. "The whites always kind of resisted Gertrude, whereas the blacks understood her perfectly well and took to it like ducks to water," Thomson said. He had encountered white singers who had refused to sing Stein's words, and he roundly declared he was not about to give a course in Gertrude Stein appreciation.

After the first week the cast began conversing in quotations from Stein and developing private jokes. When they sang, "If they were not pigeons what were they," a contingent would whisper, "Two black crows," referring to a popular black radio show of the period. A newspaper reported that by January the cast members were humming the opera when they arrived at the church basement each morning and as they left each night.

The cast learned Stein's libretto without the benefit of the conventional memory hooks of narrative, meaning, or association. Heavily weighted with vowel sounds, Stein's words were learned syllable by syllable, as if they were in a foreign tongue, wedded from the beginning to their musical setting. Beatrice Robinson Wayne learned Saint Teresa's part by humming it through every night in her bed. "What I wanted was to hear it, so I could get the connection whenever I was alone," she recalled. "If I heard it when I was alone, I would never forget it." For some chorus members, such as Kitty Mason, the sheer repetition transformed the words into meaningful passages: "You go through this thing day after day, and day after day you get something out of it—it wasn't altogether nonsensical."

Eva Jessye recalled the cast's pride in breaking both racial and musical boundaries: "They thought they were having a part in an invention." Thomas Anderson recalled the novelty of singing Thomson's music: "We wanted to prove that black people didn't have to only sing 'Massa's in the Cold Cold Ground,' and then fall on our knees and wave our hands about." (To demonstrate the point a half century after the fact, he got down on his knees in his New Jersey living room and waved his hands about.) "We always said, 'Well, we could sing if somebody gave us a chance.' Here was the chance. The proof was in the pudding."

|||

While Virgil Thomson became the group's taskmaster and John Houseman its genial top sergeant, Frederick Ashton arrived shortly after rehearsals began and soon assumed a unique position in the company.

Ashton quickly discovered that the dancers he had selected from the Savoy Ballroom had weak legs and that most of his ballet vocabulary was useless. "You see, none of them had ever been to ballet school," said Virgil Thomson. "They could dance like a house afire—shuffle along or jigs or taps or all that kind of thing. But the muscular control involved in sticking your leg out at a right angle and holding it there, and of whirling the whole body by getting up on one toe and opening and closing your arms—they knew nothing of that."[9] Ashton was dazzled by the dancers' plasticity and what he called "a kind of delicacy that was very touching." He created new, stylized movements that incorporated elements from both ballet and black vernacular dance and combined pelvic undulations, Charleston-like locomotion, and supple dips with the ballet vocabulary of pliés, relevés, and chassés. He recycled snippets of his most recent ballet, *Les Rendezvous*, and described his movements to one reporter as "a combination of Snake Hips and Gothic."

The scene in the opera that became the favorite of both the cast and Ashton—and later Gertrude Stein—was the four-minute-long procession in the third act. Resembling both a wedding march and a funeral cortege, the entire cast slowly swayed backward and forward, only occasionally taking a step, seeming to march without moving. Ashton and the cast found common ground in the shared physical vocabulary of religious pageantry. Ashton recalled, "That is why I did *Four Saints* well, because the action was not operatic but ritualistic and ordered, and not balletic but ceremonial and never has any production had to such a degree the beautiful leisure of a procession with its pauses, when the lifting of a hand and raised eyebrows is dramatic."[10]

The task of inventing new movements and teaching amateur dancers exhausted Ashton. His friend Edward Burra reported, "Madame A disappears up to Harlem at 9:30 each morning & returns a grey and white shadow screaming for steak at about 6 each evening."[11] Ashton insisted that the cast learn the words and movements simultaneously. He would stand in the center of the basement, the cast surrounding him, music scripts in hand, and demonstrate a liquid arm gesture to simulate falling snow or a sinuous swiveling of the knees. He offered a running commentary as he paced about the stage, directing with his left arm while his right hand cupped the right cheek of his large, flat buttocks. He even tried to arrange their facial expressions. "He was very good at it, but this face of mine just wouldn't change," said Beatrice Robinson Wayne. He initially instructed the cast to mimic him precisely, using a choreographic counterpart to Eva Jessye's rote teaching, but he soon realized this was a mistake. After a morning's rehearsal of a scene, Ashton would attempt to set it permanently with a final run-through before the two o'clock lunchtime break. Edward Burra reported, "Hotsy Ashton is becoming frantic as the cast learn everything perfectly before lunch and forgot it all after."[12] When the cast returned at three, Ashton recalled, "I'd say, 'Now we'll go through Scene Two,' and they had never heard of Scene Two." Serving as the collective memory of the cast and fighting a bad case of flu in the midst of this, Ashton adopted a different strategy. "I did a pose or gesture," he said, "and said 'Now do that,' and they would do something quite different but full of the beauty of their own skinny plasticity, and their heads would fall always harmoniously and they were never gawky, and though strange always harmonious."[13]

For all the incongruity between Ashton and the cast, the affection be-

Frederick Ashton and his male dancers (Maxwell Baird, Floyd Miller, Billie Smith) for *Four Saints in Three Acts*, by George Platt Lynes, 1934.

tween them was real. Virgil was "Mr. Thomson" and Gertrude was "Miss Stein"—except in those behind-the-back moments when it was "Miss Thomson" and "Mr. Stein"—but Ashton quickly became "Freddie." "The cast thought he was the funniest thing alive," John Houseman remembered. "Freddie was used to little white dancers, and suddenly here were all these black people. He adored them, and they very soon adored him." Ashton spent time in Harlem after dark—walking the sixty blocks home to avoid paying the cab fare from his meager ten-dollar-a-week pin money— and at parties he liked to imitate Ethel Waters singing "Just can't take it baby." Thomas Anderson recalled that the cast would laugh approvingly as he rehearsed them. "We could see that he could dance, and he tried to cut his ability to dance down to their greatest potential. What could they possibly do? He found it, and that was his greatness."

The cast's familiarity with Ashton grew in part from the fact that he was sleeping with one, or perhaps two, of the male dancers. His homosexuality was known to the cast, as was Thomson's, but that apparently did not disturb them. "It was the strangest and most beautiful production," Ashton later reflected. "I say this though I made it, because I am devout and the Negroes are devout and I am plastic and they are plastic."[14]

NEW YEAR'S EVE

The cast took a brief break from rehearsals to celebrate the year's end. A few snapshots of high bohemians and Harvard modernists on the eve of 1934 reflect the new hopes that accompanied the repeal of Prohibition that December.

Muriel Draper wrote to Mabel Dodge Luhan that the city was "gayer than it has been for years—gayer in spirit, possibly because of Repeal and no more huddling in speakies [sic], but a general and more expansive wine-drinking in red-roped hotel dining-rooms and rather charming little bars." Draper faced a financial crisis as she prepared for her annual New Year's Eve party. She could not afford a plumber to fix her leaking pipes, and friends contributed money to pay her coal bills. One suggested that she charge each person twenty-five dollars to attend the party, but she shunned such an idea and sent out engraved cards as usual announcing that Muriel Draper would be At Home after eleven o'clock. Henry McBride, who attended the evening, claimed that he had never before had the courage to venture into Muriel Draper's maelstrom. "The house is too extraordinary," he reported. "You know Muriel lacks funds and gets along on nothing at all. The house is almost in a state of ruin, and whilst I was chatting with the ex-Duchesse de Clermont-Tonnerre, something hit me on the shoulder and I looked up to see several great yawning holes in the ceiling. It was a bit of plaster that had hit me."[15] This would be Muriel's last New Year's party for several years; a year later she sailed to the Soviet Union to explore Communist society.

For Lincoln Kirstein, New Year's Eve saw his dream for a School of American Ballet assuming concrete form. A month before, he had signed the lease for the fourth floor of 637 Madison Avenue, once Isadora Duncan's headquarters. Kirstein had furnished the classroom from Macy's and four days earlier had polished the mirrors behind the barre. On December 29, George Balanchine had conducted his first class in the space, and on New Year's Eve they threw an impromptu party there. Kirstein brought Persian rugs to make the floor more inviting, Eddie Warburg sent a case of champagne, and Balanchine, looking gaunt after a severe undiagnosed illness, banged on the upright piano. Russian dancers from the rival ballet company—Colonel de Basil's Ballet Russe de Monte-Carlo—dropped in, and the young ballet students brought fruit and nuts.

On the other side of the Atlantic, Gertrude Stein wrote Virgil Thomson her first letter since their contract negotiations about the opera six months earlier. Stein's letter focused on her hopes for the opera: "My brother Mike says will they make a record of it but really perhaps they will make a film and that would be even more exciting as well as everything else."

Chick Austin had received only a few responses promising funds for *Four Saints*. The two biggest supporters, Edward Warburg and Hartford banker Charles Cooley, pledged $500 each. Lord Duveen gave $250, and Kirk Askew, Lincoln Kirstein, and hostess Mrs. W. Murray Crane each promised $100. Contributions fell off drastically from there, and even Chick Austin could figure out that it would take many five- and ten-dollar contributions (like those of gallerist John Becker, society photographer Harry Bull, and Paul Sachs) to add up to $10,000. But anticipation of the event was steadily growing in conversation, newspaper columns, and letters. "That Jack Houseman is putting on Gertrude Stein's *Three Nuns*," wrote one member of America's first avant-garde to another, "(doesn't that remind you of the Arensburg [sic] days)."[16] As far away as Chicago, mentions of the opera appeared in gossip columns. In New York, architect Philip Goodwin was drawing up a list of people to accompany him on private railway cars that would be added to the New Haven Railroad for the opera's opening night—the party would begin at Grand Central Station at four in the afternoon and continue right on through to the return the next morning at seven.

Meanwhile, the largest throng in fifteen years crowded into Times Square on New Year's Eve. Huddled together in the six-degrees-below-zero night, 300,000 people watched the glowing white orb slide down the flagpole atop the New York Times Building. Red lights on all four sides of the building flashed "1934."

| | |

While the opera slowly assumed shape in St. Philip's basement, John Houseman kept track of the production details. He was the paymaster to the cast, coordinator of the rehearsal schedule, and liaison between the technical staff and Florine Stettheimer. As Abe Feder put it, "Florine was from outer space." She tested Houseman's genial nature with her inability to understand why the tiny beads of her stage maquette could not be blown up to large cut-crystal balls, why Saint Ignatius held "a beastly purple book," why the chorus of angels did not drape their trains exactly the way she had dressed her miniature figures ("no style—couldn't make them understand altho—puppet showed the costume," she noted[17]). But Houseman's affability made him the ideal person to meet the conflicting demands of the production crew, the cast, and the designers. "And Houseman is at his best when overworked," Thomson later observed. "He cannot do just one job at a time; he must have two; fatigue excites him."

Of those weeks in the basement of St. Philip's Church, the *Four Saints* participants most vividly remember the goodwill and high spirits. As Thomson said one day to John Houseman, "The show's no good unless everybody is in love with everybody." The situation was potentially volatile: disparate and clashing egos, no model to follow, not much money to spend, and little time to rehearse. Since neither Virgil Thomson nor Eva Jessye was an easygoing personality, John Houseman and Maurice Grosser were particularly welcome presences. Grosser could assuage Virgil's tantrums, and Houseman could deal with everyone else. When they had disagreements, they took them outside. If they did not want the cast to understand what they were saying, Thomson, Houseman, and Ashton would slip into French. As Thomas Anderson put it, "We didn't even know *chevrolet coupe.*"[18]

Well-wishers (and voyeurs) who visited the rehearsals in St. Philip's Church included Henry McBride, Carl Van Vechten, Maxwell Anderson, and Mrs. Ira Gershwin. The most important of these visitors was Harry Moses. After making a fortune in Chicago from manufacturing women's underwear and pajamas, he had become a theater producer at the age of fifty-seven. As Abe Feder recalled it, Moses had embarked on his new profession because of his wife's interest:

> There was an oddball broad who was married to an adoring guy who had stomach ulcers. When shows came to Chicago, his wife used to invite them to her house for dinner, all the cast. She got exposed to all the theater people, she loved it. About twenty years go by. He says to her once, "Honey, I bought tickets, we're going on a trip around the world." She says, "You go, I'm not. I want to go to New York to produce plays." "What'll I do?" "Just keep your mouth shut and put up the money." She was also nuts. He bowed to her like she was a goddess. She gave him a different kind of life he never expected.

Moses had heard about *Four Saints,* for it was already being reported in newspapers across the country, and the buzz that circulated from Harlem to Park Avenue to Times Square had been expertly exploited by Nathan Zatkin. Described by Houseman as "our demon press agent," Zatkin invited Moses to the rehearsal. Having already produced Katharine Hepburn's first Broadway vehicle, *The Warrior's Husband,* Moses thought that *Four Saints* might be a worthy follow-up. He promptly announced that he would produce *Four Saints in Three Acts* on Broadway. He arranged to occupy the Forty-fourth Street Theatre just a few weeks after the opera's Hartford opening on February 8. "He got intellectual prestige out of us, and it didn't cost him very much, only about $5,000, to bring us to Broadway," Virgil observed. "And this affair was very high top intellectual world."

On January 17, Joseph Alsop, then a cub reporter for the *New York Herald Tribune,* visited the rehearsals. Entering the dim, overheated church basement, he found saints marching and countermarching across the floor, while others stood beneath illuminated Sunday school texts singing arias. Saint Teresa felt too exhausted to sing, so Virgil Thomson both played the piano and sang her part, as he had done so many times before in "the Paris productions." Upstairs in the church's Hospitality Room, Frederick Ashton coached the dancers. When the cast sang, "The scene is changing from the morning to the morning," the reporter declared that it "seemed to bring a whole dawn into the Sunday schoolroom."[19] That moment of radiance, however, did not mask his general impression of a dingy stage, a tinny piano, and the rehearsal's air of exuberant disarray and encroaching exhaustion. John Houseman explained to the young reporter, "You see they must fuse, just as the words and music fuse into one general emotion." As if aware that he was not convincing, Houseman glanced around the church basement and added, "It is hard to imagine it now in this place, but I think they will fuse."[20]

|||

Virgil Thomson and John Houseman traveled to Hartford on Thursday, February 1, 1934. A large cache of Picasso paintings had just arrived that day and were already leaning against the freshly painted white walls of the Avery Wing galleries. When civil unrest in France had recently threatened the arrival of several loans, Paul Rosenberg, Picasso's dealer and also the exhibition's informal cocurator, had calmed Austin with a telegram saying, "SOYEZ TRANQUILLE."[21] A few weeks later, Rosenberg personally transported the canvases across the Atlantic on the *Ile de France,* and "Soyez tranquille" became a reassuring password among the Atheneum staff during the harried days before the grand opening. A couple of Harvard modernists and local museum men dropped in to participate vicariously in Austin's adventurous enterprise. Henry-Russell Hitchcock came up from Wesleyan every day, and Jere Abbott responded to a telegram that implored, "FOR GOD'S SAKE DO COME DOWN. WE NEED YOUR HELP."[22] Along with museum directors from Worcester and New London, they came to lend moral support and offer a few suggestions; but most of all they came to see Chick Austin's instincts for juxtaposing paintings.

On the night of their arrival, Thomson and Houseman briefly toured the museum and descended to the basement theater that Houseman would later call "the womb of his theatrical career." Austin drove Thomson and Houseman to his house, where they ate the last full meal they would see for a week. Over brandy, Austin sprung the bad news on them: there

The black cast and the white building: newspaper publicity for the premiere, February 1934.

was no money in the coffers of the Friends and Enemies of Modern Music. Flashing his most disarming smile, Austin wondered aloud if the cast and technicians might wait until the out-of-towners paid for their tickets? There was no alternative. The production was already hundreds of dollars over budget. To maintain momentum, Houseman dug into his own pockets and loaned $150 to the production, soon followed by the Askews' loan of $500.

III

Kate Lawson arrived in a truck on Friday, February 2, accompanied by 1,500 square feet of cellophane. All day and much of the night she directed a crew in hanging the cumbersome piece from the low-lying grid of the Avery theater and gathering it in pouches. On Saturday, in the first ceremony celebrating the completion of the new wing, Chick Austin performed magic tricks in the Avery courtyard for the construction crew. The workers returned to installing the final strip lighting, tacking fabric to partitions, putting final touches on exhibition platforms, as they would until the final moments before the official opening three days later. During moments of exhaustion, Austin lay down on the floor of the museum's Great Hall.

On Sunday, February 4, Frederick Ashton and the cast traveled by bus from New York to Hartford. The Negro Chamber of Commerce greeted the cast and transferred their baggage to the Hotel Avon, and by afternoon the singers began rehearsing in the Avery theater. Ashton began adapting the scale of their movements from the expanse of the St. Philip's basement to the smaller stage of the theater. Houseman, meanwhile, had to tell the cast that they would not be paid their expected $50 until after the box office received money from the ticket buyers. No one complained.

The performers did not stop rehearsing until midnight, at which point the technicians took over. Abe Feder, the chief of the crew, saw the lighting of Florine's cellophane cyclorama as a personal challenge. Feder prided himself on his ability to combine gelatins and floodlights, offstage olivets and border lights, and he would patiently lecture Florine about the nature of theatrical lights. He spent the night relentlessly pursuing the perfect mix. He affixed lights to hanging pipes and beams, all the while muttering that the cyclorama was "a creeping bitch." Florine wanted the string of bulbs in her toy theater to become larger bare bulbs, flooding her decor with what she called "pure white light." When crew member Louis Frankel sliced off the tip of his left index finger at 5 A.M. a day before the final dress rehearsal, Houseman rushed him to the hospital, but not before Feder had chewed him out for bloodying the lighting equipment.

When Feder presented Florine with his expertly mixed lighting, she remained adamant that nothing but pure white light should be used, Thomson recalled. "She said, 'Tommyrot. We are going to have pure white light on that stage because my decor is highly colored and I don't want it darkened or falsified.' She took him to a place where he could buy real white bulbs, and we used real white light on that stage, I think for the first time ever."

The plan to present the cast in whiteface had by now been abandoned. Feder added turquoise and pink gels to the lights to give the dark skin "an aura of cool iridescence."[23]

The final rehearsals were long and harrowing. When Alexander Smallens and his twenty musicians arrived on the morning of Monday, February 5, they could scarcely squeeze into the tiny Avery pit. Smallens discovered that the score was riddled with orchestration errors—hundreds of them, it turned out, due to Thomson's having created the orchestra score without access to instruments. When Smallens realized the magnitude of the problem, he began to shout. John Houseman observed near the end of his life that it was the only time that he had ever seen Thomson seriously shaken. Although he lost face in front of his cast, there was no time for emotions. The conductor called out changes from the podium, and Thomson worked, tight-lipped, penciling changes to the score. His indefatigable energy began to flag. "As a matter of fact," reported Henry McBride, "Virgil looked as though he had just been run over by an automobile truck in Taos in August (August being the dusty month down there)."[24] The cast marveled at the ability of "Papa Smallens," as they called him, to keep musical order during the chaos of corrections. He rapped his baton, shouted instructions, praised the singers, and chastised the orchestra, saying, "The real musicians are on stage."[25] Their flagging performance owed something to the long hours of overtime. Thomson's scoring mistakes resulted in five hundred dollars' worth of overtime.

As Monday progressed, Frederick Ashton saw the liquid movements of his choreography unravel as the acts proceeded and the orchestra struggled with the newly corrected score. Smallens, at the end of his short rope, tugged on his short English pipe and began shouting that the choreographer had placed the performers so they could not follow his baton movements. Tearful and distraught, Ashton stalked up the aisle and out of the theater. "I have worked with Sir Thomas Beecham!" he cried. "A genius! And he never spoke to me as you have!" Since the temperature outside was well below zero, Ashton quickly reversed his dramatic exit, but he continued to worry about glitches.

On Tuesday night, Connecticut Governor Wilbur Cross joined Charles Goodwin, Edward Forbes, architect W. H. O'Connor, and the major of Hartford to open the Avery Wing of the Wadsworth Atheneum. Although Chick Austin was present, he was too exhausted to say anything; the newspaper described it as "a slight indisposition."

On Wednesday afternoon, Florine Stettheimer and Kate Lawson conducted the first dress parade. One performer objected to a headdress she was to wear and flung it at Florine instead of putting it on, but she proved to be the exception. The rich fabrics and spangles on the whole excited the cast; they were unlike anything they had ever worn.[26] Florine reported to Henry McBride that they were acting not only like saints but like angels. The costume inspection was the first time most of the cast had seen Florine Stettheimer, and many were struck by her ladylike manner and her fragility.[27] "She was like a little Dresden doll," Thomas Anderson recalled, visualizing the blue veins on the backs of her hands. Beatrice Robinson Wayne remembered a glow of affirmation when Stettheimer looked at her and softly commented that Saint Teresa looked beautiful. Kate Drain Lawson came to the same conclusion, although Saint Teresa was affronted at her backhanded compliment, "Now you look like a lady!"

Seeing the cast in her costumes, Florine felt a shock: the saints were not wearing gloves. "The naked human hand is not beautiful or elegant," said Florine. "You wouldn't come onstage barefoot, why come on barehanded?" Gloves were an odd thing for Florine to have overlooked. Certainly she wore gloves herself whenever she left the Alwyn Court, and she and her sisters had discussed the long white kid gloves Florine would wear for the opening night. Cheap white cotton gloves studded with rhinestones were quickly ordered for the entire cast, but they were not available until the New York opening. (When compiling a list of the costume's shortcomings, Florine wrote, with uncharacteristic repetition, "Gloves-gloves-gloves.") John Houseman said, "She didn't want those black hands sticking out of her costumes." As a final touch Stettheimer dispatched Henry McBride to purchase two artificial roses for the Commère at the nearest Woolworth's: get the best, she instructed him.

That same night, downstairs in the Avery theater, the final dress rehearsal proceeded with sets, costumes, and full light cues. "Once we started the dress rehearsal, with the orchestra and all," Abe Feder recalled, "Florine sat out there and said, 'Oh, Abe, it's a miracle, it's a miracle.'"

The final dress rehearsal ended in the middle of the night. Nerves were ragged, collective fatigue was high, and the chorus members in the upper tiers complained that Feder's bright lights had blistered their ears. Houseman's faith that everything would fuse seemed only slightly more imaginable. The first public performance was a day away.

Opening
Night

"By Rolls-Royce, by airplane, by Pullman compartment, and for all we know, by specially designed Cartier pogo sticks, the smart art enthusiasts converged on Hartford," wrote café society scribe Lucius Beebe.[1] He exaggerated only slightly. A society columnist from Chicago wrote, "For one day at least, Hartford has been the Right Place and enough of the Right People seem to have known it in time to be there."

The people who invaded Hartford for the opening night of *Four Saints in Three Acts* encompassed two generations of modernists—its artists, writers, collectors, and aficionados. The crowd included Brahmin Boston and Park Avenue New York, university academics and café society. As *Vogue* summed it up, the audience was "the top of the American intelligentsia (and precocity), highly susceptible to sound, colour, form and revolution."

Only those with the most foresight had reserved rooms at Hartford's oldest hotel, the Heublein. The rest had to share Hartford's few hotels with a heavily attended bartenders' convention—the first since the repeal of

Prohibition. Count Roussy de Sales and Harry Bull of *Town and Country* gamely put up in a Turkish bath, while Mrs. Averell Harriman slept in a fleabag hotel. Millionaire poet Annie Winifred Ellerman, known as "Bryher," was determined to be present at the avant-garde event, but only bulldog tenacity and bribery yielded her, at the last minute, a pair of tickets and a bed in one of Hartford's most run-down hotels. The generation of traveling salesmen who had occupied her hotel bed had left hollows that did not conform to her body, and on awakening the next morning she found that the tip of her ear was frostbitten. Bryher assured Gertrude Stein, "We must suffer in the cause of Art."[2]

The pilgrimage to Hartford began on Tuesday, February 6, amid snow and near-zero temperatures. By mid-January, Philip Goodwin had already arranged for private parlor cars to be added to the Hartford–New Haven line, and many of the opera's closest supporters gathered at Grand Central Station to board the four o'clock train. The Family core included Julien and Joella Levy, Alfred and Marga Barr, Kirk and Constance Askew, John McAndrew, and Muriel Draper. They were joined by art dealers Pierre Matisse and Felix Wildenstein and architect Wallace K. Harrison. Food and drink were circulated in the parlor car. On arrival in Hartford, the men changed from traveling clothes to white tie and tails in the lavatory of the Heublein Hotel. Julien Levy overheard Austin's rival Francis Henry Taylor, director of the Worcester Museum, standing in gray flannel underwear and declaiming on Austin's "genius for providing his own earthquakes" but then shaking his head about the "unfeasibility of Chick."[3]

A Hartford insurance executive and quietly brilliant poet, Wallace Stevens, made the short journey from his home on Westerly Terrace to the museum. He surveyed the "people who walked round with cigarette holders a foot long" and declared them "Asses of the first water. After all, if there is any place under the sun that needs debunking, it is the place where people of this sort come to and go to."[4] For Katherine Dreier, the earnest organizer of America's first avant-garde, the opening evoked memories of Marcel Duchamp, Man Ray, and "the flavor of the early days of the Société Anonyme."[5]

The most spectacular guest was Mrs. Harrison Williams, whom *Vogue* described as "a famous beauty and arbiter of gaieties," and Thomson called "the queen of fancy dressers in those days." For the opera's premiere her dress designer had created a glittering bit of sartorial legerdemain. On the train to Hartford, it looked like a beaded, floor-length cocktail dress.

Unidentified man, Dorothy Hale, and Isamu Noguchi in Buckminster Fuller's Dymaxion car, arriving at the premiere of *Four Saints in Three Acts*, February 7, 1934
(photograph by Jerome Zerbe).

When Mrs. Williams reached Hartford, she flashed her famously large
aquamarine eyes, unfastened a small button, and unfurled a train.

Wherever Mrs. Williams went, Lucius Beebe followed. *Four Saints*
was America's first avant-garde event that required not only critics to evaluate the work but a society writer to review the crowd. In his dove-gray
gibus hat, astrakhan coat, and pearl stickpin, the café society scribe was at
once eager and world-weary; he called the opera premiere "the fanciest
and most utterly Bedlamite flag-raising within recent memory."[6]

Just fifteen minutes before the curtain was scheduled to rise, a sleek,
black, lozenge-shaped Dymaxion car pulled up to the Wadsworth Atheneum. Buckminster Fuller emerged from behind the wheel and opened
the car's futuristic side panels. Into the clear, cold evening emerged editor
Clare Boothe Brokaw (soon to be Luce), Dorothy Hale (widow of mural
painter Gardiner Hale), and young sculptor Isamu Noguchi.

From Cambridge and Boston came architect Nathaniel Saltonstall,
art historian Agnes Mongan, the three beautiful Cushing sisters,[7] Edward
Forbes, and Paul Sachs. There were also a few university professors: Agnes
Rindge and John McAndrew from Vassar, Jere Abbott from Smith, Henry-
Russell Hitchcock from Wesleyan. Among the younger crowd were several
future modernist eminences: Sidney Janis (then Janowitz), who would be-

come a prominent art dealer; Harvard student James Laughlin IV, who volunteered free ads for the opera in the Harvard *Advocate* and later founded New Directions, under whose imprint he published many modern writers; Muriel Rukeyser, who was reviewing the opera for her school newspaper and later became a prominent poet. The mixture of local insurance executives and what Lucius Beebe called "snipers armed with thirty-six-inch cigarette tubes" was incongruous.

One of the oldest operagoers was sixty-seven-year-old Henry McBride, who had witnessed *Four Saints'* 'debut at the Stettheimers' in 1929 and closely followed its progress through Stein's letters and Van Vechten's conversations. As Stein's tireless American lieutenant since 1913, McBride saw the ironic dimension of her "sudden" celebrity: surveying the audience at the Avery theater, he observed, "Half of them were of the *avant-garde*, aware that a Gertrude Stein opera was about as advanced as anyone could ever hope to get in this world and fully persuaded, even before the curtain went up, that the evening could not possibly be a failure. One would laugh either against Gertrude or with her. One, in any case, would laugh."[8]

While out-of-town visitors attended a luncheon given by the Hartford museum supporter Charles Cooley and a formal tea given by the James Thrall Sobys, McBride telephoned reports to the New York *Sun* nearly hourly. On Wednesday evening, the diners at the Heublein Hotel included the Barrs, Philip Johnson, Muriel Draper, Mrs. W. Murray Crane, Carl Van Vechten, and Mrs. Averell Harriman, and McBride reported to his editors that the excitement had now "reached a point where it became practically unbearable."

Then the stylish congregation crossed Prospect Street and approached the exterior of the Avery Memorial, a sleeker version of the Italian Renaissance–style Morgan Memorial, to which it was attached. The smooth marble surfaces and the horizontal band of mezzanine windows seemed modern enough, but the door one passed through was adorned with Beaux Arts–style pilasters and ornamental metalwork. "The outside is O.K., as they say, but the inside is special," wrote Henry McBride. Upon entering the Avery courtyard, "at once," observed a contemporary critic, "you feel that this building stands for the freedom of the XXth century."[9]

The eggshell-white walls seemed improbably and elegantly light.

The Avery courtyard, February 1934, with sixteenth-century Mannerist figures by Pietro Francavilla.

Slabs with tapered undersides and stark thin rails gave the impression the balconies were floating over the glass-ceilinged central court. One of the Avery Wing's first visitors described the resistance to the new architectural vocabulary: "But the eye instinctively seeks the appearance of strength, and not finding it, the observer, however small his knowledge of architecture, has the vague feeling that something is wrong."[10] The central court, bounded by sheer pristine planes and topped by a broad skylight, was potentially forbidding; as one visitor put it, "Absolute purity is not very winning."[11] At the center stood an oversized group of figures by the sixteenth-century Italian sculptor Pietro Francavilla. The sculpture's sinuous Mannerist curves provided a perfect foil to the strict geometry that ruled the building. Architectural critic Helen Searing observed that the courtyard "gives the impression of an exterior facade, of the Bauhaus turned inside out."

Even Francis Henry Taylor, who had earlier questioned Austin's practicality, announced that he was impressed. "Walking through the magnificently stripped court," he observed, "it was brought home with feverish insistence that the day of period rooms is not only a relic of a past romanticism, but that we are about to enter a new (and I think equally romantic) phase of clinical asepsis where the work of art will play the role of the isolated microbe on the microscopic slide."

For the gallery walls, Austin had selected the fabrics personally. They ranged from corduroy velvet to silk damask, and he had overseen their dyeing to ensure that the colors were exactly right. Each object was staged theatrically, instead of appearing in the context of a period room. Italian majolica stood against raw silk dyed Guardi blue, and the Rococo room looked as if it had been covered with the material of a Chardin dress. Even the exotic woodwork—white pine in one room, Brazilian walnut in another, white mahogany in a third—contributed to the museum's theatricality. The grille-covered radiators in the gallery floors and the two-foot baseboards evoked the Machine Age. Looking at the wing reminded Philip Johnson of how comparatively "drab and dull" the Museum of Modern Art looked; he declared himself "especially crazy about the imbuya wood" of Austin's office.[12] Paris art dealer Paul Rosenberg exclaimed, "At last there is one genuine modern museum in the world!"

Later the Avery Wing would receive the Architectural League's Silver Medal, but the first reactions from Austin's museum colleagues were especially heartening. The competitive excitement that buoyed that opening night was best expressed by Winslow Ames, the director of New London's Lyman Allyn Museum. "Hartford has the first genuinely (not merely mechanically) modern museum building in this country, an exciting and distinguished job. Just as death is swallowed up in victory, so is the envy that I might feel swallowed up in my applause and congratulations. Experiments are paid for not only in the money but in hard work, opprobrium and small thanks. No honest experiment is melancholy."[13]

The Avery Wing's stark white third-floor galleries provided the only suitable backdrop for the seventy-eight paintings and sixty drawings and prints included in the first museum retrospective in the United States devoted to Picasso. Henry McBride surveyed the walls and rhetorically asked, "Who is there, more than he, who represents modernity?" To McBride's experienced eye the paintings looked like a period exhibition: "Of a truth, the period just past is as unmistakably reflected in the work of Picasso as the Mme. Dubarry–Louis XV period is in the work of Fragonard."

Harry Bull of *Town and Country* photographed everyone, exposing an entire roll on a newly slim Carl Van Vechten and an extravagantly turbaned Muriel Draper. Alexander Calder, in tweeds, a red flannel shirt, and dusty boots, offered a stubborn exception to the high style surrounding him, as did a young man who wore gray trousers instead of black because he felt black was too sad for the occasion. Philip Johnson recalled standing in the beautifully illuminated courtyard and looking around at the assembled friends: "I felt as if I were in the umbilicus—the center of where things were at."

Downstairs the cast crowded into two dressing spaces cordoned off by curtains. The cast's excited rumors about the goings-on upstairs grew giddily distorted: there were millionaires flying in from all over the world, including "the Titian lady from Paris," and tickets were reportedly being sold for as much as a thousand dollars a piece. Beatrice Robinson Wayne remembered Chick Austin bringing her a dozen lilies, which drooped as they made the transition from the bitter cold to the heat of the dressing room. She cried for a moment, hoped it was not a portent of the performance to come, and asked for a shot of muscatel. Peeking between curtains, she saw the shell-pink walls and mahogany trim of the still-empty auditorium. "It seemed so cold out there," she remembered. "You get an eerie feeling in a place like that." She prayed, as she always did before singing. "I went out there that night thinking I've got to make good because Virgil is back in his own home. This will make or break him."

The audience take their seats, February 6, 1934: Henry-Russell Hitchcock sits in the center of the second row, and in the fifth row from left to right are Chick Austin (looking over his shoulder), Helen Austin, Kirk Askew, and Constance Askew.

About 8:30, the crowd of 299 people began entering the theater and walked down the aisles, sometimes more than once. Carl Van Vechten made three entrances; Philip Johnson sat in the second row, directly in front of Van Vechten, Pierre Matisse, and Henry-Russell Hitchcock. In the fifth row were the Austins, the Askews, John McAndrew, Agnes Rindge, and the Levys. Armed with his 16-millimeter Bell and Howell film camera, Julien Levy filmed segments of the performance, which make up a vivid record of the opera. At 8:47, Chick Austin appeared backstage to say that everyone was seated and the performance could begin.

The bright red curtains slowly parted, revealing a proscenium framed by lace. Alexander Smallens signaled the beginning of a long drumroll. A single saint in red velvet appeared, and, as he knelt at the side of the stage, he remembered his firm instructions: "Let the footlights hit your eyes, and you'll be in the right spot." When Feder's intense lights came up again, the stage filled with saints. Two choruses, wearing light blue tunics, ascended a pyramid of risers on each side of the stage. They were followed by the twelve named saints, whose costumes formed a color wheel of intense primary hues: from the two Saint Teresas in cardinal-red velvet, through the purple saint, the yellow saint, and finally to Saint Ignatius in green. The Commère and the Compère stood flanking the proscenium in stylish contemporary clothes and served as intermediaries between the audience and the opera spectacle. Behind them, tufted and semiopaque, the cyclorama looked like a sky made of rock candy.

From the orchestra pit came vigorous oompah rhythms:

> To know to know to love her so
> Four saints prepare for saints.
> It makes it well fish
> Four saints it makes it well fish.

A saint unhooked a curtain from a palm tree to introduce the first of seven tableaux. Saint Teresa II sat on a filigreed throne, framed by an arch of cellophane balls, brandishing a palette in one hand and a brush in the other as she mimed painting the huge pink egg in her lap. Saint Settlement raised the dainty black lace mantilla from an old-fashioned box camera on a tripod, focused, and photographed Saint Teresa II. After the Compère sang, "Leave later gaily the troubadour plays his guitar," Saint Ignatius played a stringed instrument with the neck of a banjo and the body of a lute, accompanied by castanets. Saint Ignatius then presented to Saint Teresa II a bouquet of cellophane flowers, with Henry McBride's two roses from Woolworth's. In the next scene an angel dancer with a bare midriff hovered over Saint Teresa II as Saint Teresa I sang:

> There can be no peace on earth with calm. There can be no peace
> on earth with calm with calm and with whom whose calm and
> with whom whose when they well they well they call it there made
> message especial and come.

The last of the tableaux presented Saint Teresa II rocking an imaginary baby, while Saint Settlement led the chorus, singing, "Summer summer makes a child happening at all to throw a ball too often to please." Exiting

Four Saints in Three Acts production photographs, February 1934.

in slow procession, the saints gaily sang, "One two three four five six seven all good children go to heaven," and the first act ended.

The principals took twelve curtain calls before they were allowed to change and the audience flowed into the Avery courtyard. Chick Austin stood by a punch bowl on a long dark table, while across the room Henry McBride stood in line to congratulate Virgil Thomson. McBride went backstage and glimpsed Frederick Ashton ardently embracing Florine Stettheimer, "both of them in a kind of heaven that only artists know, at the way things were going."[14] Carl Van Vechten held the opinion that "the Negroes are divine, like El Grecos, more Spanish, more Saints, more opera singers in their dignity and simplicity and extraordinary plastic line than *any* white singers could ever be."[15] As one society reporter wrote, "Everyone thought *something* and was earnestly trying to express it."

Gertrude Stein's words were the subject of most controversy. A few worried aloud, "But what is going to happen if we acquire a new species of opera in which the words of the poet do not convey any thought?" Others giddily declared, "Of course it is nonsense, but who cares?" Some commented that, for the first time, they had simply given up on the words and just enjoyed the opera, and a gentleman in tails exclaimed that it was like grand opera but with more sense.[16] Governor Wilbur Cross said, "Well, you can't read the damn stuff, but you certainly can sing it." To those bewildered by the presence of two Saint Teresas, Mrs. W. Murray Crane judiciously responded, "Why such a fuss? After all, some of the leading authorities held that there was something dual in St. Teresa's nature."[17] Press agent Nathan Zatkin slyly comforted the uncomprehending: "Either you get it or you don't—and, really, you shouldn't feel ashamed if you don't."

About the sets, the cast, and the music there was more universal agreement. Some thought that Florine Stettheimer's costumes outdid the Ziegfeld Follies, and one quipped that the sets were "Botticellophane." Some people remarked on the unself-consciousness of the singers, the beauty of their enormous voices in the tiny theater, and the spectacle of choreographed bronze hands against cellophane. Virgil Thomson observed, "They moved, sang, spoke with grace and alacrity, took on roles without self-consciousness, as if they were the saints they said they were." One muttered that Thomson's score was "mere tonal wisecracking," but many took relief in the vigorous music. It suggested familiar tunes and then skipped away from them, always clearly and lightly, without any of the dissonance they expected from modern music. The more common feeling expressed in the Avery lobby, halfway through the opera, was that "in its own crazy way, it's a perfect thing." Van Vechten congratulated Thomson, "You knew exactly who you wanted and I guess you pretty much got it."[18] Between the buzz about the opera and the excitement of mingling in the stylish crowd, the audience refused to take their seats until finally a shrill police whistle was blown. Act II commenced.

|||

The curtain rose on the saints at a lawn party, standing on a bright green rug of grass, under a grove of cerise-colored palms. At the far left stood a ten-foot-high gauzy tent, just large enough to house an enthroned Saint Teresa and a long picnic table graced by brightly frosted cakes and a feathery centerpiece. Saint Teresa had her own tent, a conical transparent pavilion, its entry trimmed in tinsel, which bore a striking resemblance to the canopy over Florine's bed. The cast wore a new array of costumes, and for visual extravagance each outdid the last: white fitted basque and black paillettes, full robes of colored tinsel, tulle ruffles and loose cowls, high combs and black mantillas, sun hats that resembled both halos and cellophane flowers. Although most of the saints went bare-handed that night, at least Saint Teresa I wore rhinestone-studded gloves. Backstage, Frederick Ashton breathed more easily as he saw that the cast members were remembering their movements, cavorting in stylized versions of "ring-around-the-rosy" and "drop the handkerchief."

Then six young dancers appeared, dressed as angels in loincloths, golden wings, and gold halolike hats. (In the audience, Joseph Alsop thought they were "startlingly naked for such a saintly gathering.") Their short ballet, which Thomson described as "the angels' flying lessons," incorporated the swiveling of the Charleston with a variety of dips and swoops, all performed at the breakneck speed of jazz club dancing. Then Saint Plan entered with a long telescope. Kneeling, he directed it toward the overarching cellophane sky, while all the saints turned their backs to the audience, for they too wanted to glimpse "the Heavenly Mansion." On the irregular surface of the cyclorama, a faint projection that resembled the U.S. Capitol appeared as the cast sang variations of "How many windows and doors and floors are there in it."[19]

Without intermission, Act III opened in Barcelona, against walls of faux sea shells, as Saint Ignatius's men mended their fishnets and their leader sat on his bright coral throne. As the men lined up in military formation, Saint Ignatius and Saint Chavez sang about the importance of discipline in the monastic life. Then, as the lights dimmed, Saint Ignatius, in a pale green cassock, somberly walked before his men. He raised his palms toward the heavens and sang what would become the opera's most repeated lines:

> Pigeons on the grass alas
> Shorter longer grass short longer longer shorter yellow grass
> Pigeons large pigeons on the shorter longer yellow grass alas
>   pigeons on the grass

This passage, which Stein had identifed as a vision of the Holy Ghost, became so well known in part because Columbia radio had planted microphones in the cellophane set to broadcast fifteen minutes of the opera's third act across the nation.

Then an offstage chorus of female saints started trilling, "Let Lucy Lily Lily Lucy Lucy let Lucy Lucy Lily Lily Lily Lily Lily let Lily Lucy Lucy let Lily" like a flock of birds taking flight. In stark contrast to the monastic discipline of Saint Ignatius's men assembling in line, three sailors and their Spanish ladies appeared stage front. They performed a stylish tango, more formal than the angels' dance, animated by extravagantly arched backs and linked hands. Feder's masterful lighting invoked a gathering storm as the female saints entered one by one with white birds attached to their wrists. Raised above the others, Saint Ignatius delivered a prophecy ("Around is as sound and around is a sound and around"), and the saints fell on their knees before him.

Late in the third act, the Commère and Compère joined all the saints for the procession. In this scene Ashton's choreographic ingenuity was sorely tested. He had had to block thirty-five people continuously filing across a stage that was only thirty-three feet wide without resorting to circular movement. The saints marched without proceeding under a black chiffon baldachino surmounted by bunches of black ostrich plumes. This scene later elicited praise even from Gertrude Stein for making "a religious procession sway and slowly disappear without moving."[20] The act concluded with a majestic climax that rapturously evoked the apotheosis.

When the curtain rose again, the audience was surprised to discover that *Four Saints in Three Acts* had a fourth act. The saints were now in heaven reminiscing about their happy days on earth. Nearly empty, the stage was dominated by a huge gold cellophane star that Stettheimer called her "sunburst." As the assembled saints sang, "When this you see remember me," a large glass, reminiscent of the eucharistic chalice, was passed among them. Instead of blessed wine, however, the vessel contained a scrap of red cellophane. The Compère's bass voice dropped an octave as he announced, "Last act." The chorus shouted in unison, "Which is a fact." The final curtain fell.

The audience remained silent for more than a minute; then the Avery theater broke into pandemonium. The audience stamped their feet and screamed "Bravo!" and "Viva!" as the red curtain parted and shut. Carl Van Vechten wrote Gertrude Stein that he had not witnessed a crowd more inflamed since the legendary premiere of *Le Sacre du Printemps*, in 1913. Fortunately, Chick Austin had warned the police captain on duty, "You know what these Gertrude Stein fans are." Even Wallace Stevens, skeptical about the glitzy event, was swept along by the music and declared that "the opera immediately becomes a delicate and joyous work all around."[21] Amazed by his feelings of giddiness on the occasion, Alfred Barr looked up, blinked, and said, "Well, I'm not drunk."[22] Henry-Russell Hitchcock was the most demonstrably enthusiastic. At first he cheered, then he stampeded up and down the aisle, smashing his opera hat, and finally he began pulling his stiff, formal shirt to shreds.

Hitchcock led the calls for the opera's collaborators to take the stage. Virgil Thomson took his bow, making pirouette movements in his patent-leather shoes, and kissed the hands of Saint Teresa and the Commère. Alexander Smallens and Maurice Grosser followed him to the stage. Modestly bowing from his seat in the middle of the fifth row, Chick Austin was propelled onstage by the audience, and Frederick Ashton entered late from backstage. Finally, even Florine Stettheimer mounted the stage to take her place under the bright white lights that she had helped engineer. From Henry McBride's perspective, her little bow was carried off with extreme nonchalance. One detail, however, betrayed her overwrought state of mind: she was not wearing her long opera gloves. When the call went up for her to mount the stage, she had looked into the folds of her new dress, made of heavy white silk with gold pinstripes. "I got excited and I didn't find them," Florine explained to her sisters, "until the last moment when I could only carry them with me." So Florine mounted the stage with naked arms, and Ettie would later upbraid her for the awfulness of her public moment: "It was inelegant. . . . It was *inelegant*."

After a half hour of curtain calls, hoarse cheers, and fluttering handkerchiefs, everyone connected with the production had mounted the stage. As the *Hartford Times* concluded its piece, "Only Gertrude was missing."

Among the torrent of telegrams that had arrived throughout the day, there had not been a word from Gertrude Stein. A few days before, she had charged Carl Van Vechten with the responsibility of seeing the opera for her. "The first night is drawing near and I am very xcited," she wrote. "I kind of feel that I am feeling and seeing it through you and that is very comforting."[23] That night Van Vechten cabled her three words—"OPERA BEAUTIFUL TRIUMPH"—and three days later she wrote him, "Yours brought us the good news, and I keep it to be a bookmark and a mascot."[24]

After the hurrahs came tears. They started with Kirk Askew and Julien Levy and soon spread. Lucius Beebe was astonished to behold "little groups letting down their back hair and crying quietly in corners for beauty." Even gruff Alexander Calder admitted that he would have cried for beauty, but it might have diluted his punch.

Why were they crying? The collective exhaustion building up to the climactic event demanded catharsis. Askew and Levy said they had cried because they "didn't know anything so beautiful could be done in America." An extraordinary confluence of artistic currents had come together that evening: the experimental Parisian world of Gertrude Stein, Virgil Thomson's reinvented heartland, the cocoon world of Florine Stettheimer under the bright light of publicity, the movements of Frederick Ashton, all housed in the pristine severity of the Avery Wing.

Henry McBride, who understood the crying best of all, called the performance "a great emotional opportunity for the emotional." He wrote to Gertrude Stein a few weeks later, "The fact of the matter is that everybody connected with the presentation caught an inspiration. All of them had to create and all of them did—so that the word miracle is the only one that describes what happened."[25]

CHAPTER 17

Four Saints
Goes to Broadway

Emboldened and exhilarated by the opera's reception in Hartford, the company now faced the altogether different problems of mounting *Four Saints* on Broadway in less than two weeks. Press agent Nathan Zatkin sent complimentary tickets for the February 20 opening to every New York art critic, music critic, theater critic, fashion writer, book critic, and even sportswriter. He compiled a mimeographed guidebook for the press that included not only reviews and production credits but two apologias, by Carl Van Vechten and Virgil Thomson. They provided critics with an accessible vocabulary for an experience that eluded conventional description. Thomson's rationale for his all-black casting provided the press with a positive spin to the reigning black stereotypes. Among them, Thomson, Van Vechten, and Zatkin targeted their PR impeccably for modernism, fashion, and Negro chic.

Harry Moses booked *Four Saints in Three Acts* into the Forty-fourth Street Theatre, one of Broadway's largest. The production had to be adapted to its wide stage, and the cast had to project their voices to an audience of 1,400, nearly five times the size of the original audience. Accustomed to singing before massive congregations, they had no trouble doing so, and Frederick Ashton relished the opportunity to expand the size of his movements. Virgil Thomson was similarly pleased to add a few new singers to the chorus and a harmonium and strings to the orchestra.

The set, however, posed a nightmarish problem. Stettheimer's cellophane cyclorama reached only halfway up the back wall of the theater, and the set was so dwarfed by the theater's expanse that Lee Shubert, who happened by at midweek, asked when the scenery was arriving. Florine Stettheimer offered no solutions for adapting her design. "I can't do anything I don't feel like doing," she told a reporter. "I mean I really can't."[1] Kate Lawson addressed the problem of scale by renting a black velour portal to mask the stage opening, and she added an inner red velvet curtain. To light the huge cellophane cyclorama for the theater's cavernous expanse, Feder had no one to consult but the electrician at the Forty-fourth Street Theatre. "You have to put four times more light on that cellophane," the electrician advised. "Otherwise it looks like shit." Feder added four more border lights and supplementary blue light. He recalled, "For the first time I could *see* it. I put light behind it. It just shimmered. My Irish electrician friend said, 'That's better, Abe, but maybe you should put more lights.' 'I already got four lights!' I said. 'It's embarrassing!'"

Just when it seemed that production problems were finally solved, fifty hours before the premiere, New York City's fire marshal arrived. Holding a lit match to a swatch of cellophane, he watched the flame and promptly condemned in one fell swoop the cyclorama, the tarlatan trees, and the grass mats. (The week after the opera opened, the Fire Department passed a regulation that prohibited cellophane from ever appearing on Broadway again.) The pale, glum assembly was saved from despair by the theater's janitor, who suggested they try a new fireproofing material called "water glass." Within two hours it had been tested and found effective. An overtime crew spent the whole night on ladders spreading the smelly substance across acres of cyclorama and drying it with fans and projectors. Water glass made the tarlatan trees droop, so Kate Lawson had a duplicate set without water glass fabricated, the treated one to show the inspectors and the untreated one to be substituted just before the curtain rose.

While the water glass was drying, it began to snow. Snow fell on GERTRUDE STEIN and VIRGIL THOMSON, delineated in white lightbulbs on

Four Saints in Three Acts marquee at the Forty-fourth Street Theatre, February 1934, by Carl Van Vechten.

the theater marquee; it fell on city streets and skyscrapers and elevated train tracks. Nine inches accumulated, trains stopped, businesses throughout the city closed. But neither the snow nor a taxi strike, nor the price of the top ticket—at $3.30, the most expensive on Broadway—kept the stylish crowd or the journalists from opening night. As Lucius Beebe reported, "The intelligentsia in tortoiseshell glasses and the representatives of fashion with monocles descended in an avalanche of ermine and broadcloth on the old Forty-fourth Street Theatre." Or as Cholly Knickerbocker's column put it, "Who Says EVERYBODY is in Florida?"

The monied set was represented by Mrs. "Bill" Rockefeller and the Hohenlohe-Schillingfursts, who delayed their exodus to Palm Beach for the opening. The Algonquin crowd included Robert Benchley and Neysa McMein, Alan Campbell and Dorothy Parker. Cecil Beaton accompanied dancer Tilly Losch. Representing the performing arts were opera singer Lawrence Tibbett, George Gershwin, Theatre Guild producer Lawrence Langner, actresses Ina Claire and Helen Westley (who commented, "It's very beautiful, but I like *Elektra* better"). One critic summed up the crowd as "an audience of almost Parisian choiceness and of quite unbearably dazzling intelligence." They dressed *en haute cérémonie*, reported society and fashion columnists, and showed "more originality in their costumes than we've seen in many a fashion show." The men served as a black-and-white backdrop for the women: Blanche Knopf in stunning jet, Isadora Townsend Pell "looking chicer than chic," Lucia Symphorosa Bristed wearing an outsized tiara. Elaborate trains and postilion hats, unruffled chiffon, ostrich plumes, and velvet cloaks rivaled the stylishly formal clothes in Hartford a few weeks earlier. "Individualism was out hey-heying around the other night," one fashion reporter wrote, adding, "It was no mere Greenwich Village brand of individualism, either."

When the curtain rose a few minutes late, many audience members had little idea what to expect—they had come "either [to] have a good laugh or to feel snobbish."[2] Henry McBride reported, "The reception by the house was almost instantaneous. For the first five minutes they laughed at some of Gertrude's words, but soon they were gasping in admiration at Florine's marvelous color arrangements and Virgil's really adorable music."[3]

In the Stettheimers' box sat Virgil Thomson, Henry McBride, and Florine and Carrie Stettheimer. (Ettie cabled Thomson that she could not attend because she was "SWELLING WITH ASTHMA AND CONCEIT AT HAVING

BEEN ONE OF THE EARLIEST ADMIRERS OF YOUR MUSIC."[4]) In the neighboring box sat *Vanity Fair* editor Frank Crowninshield, who joined them after the first intermission. "I could hear him saying, 'lovely, lovely,' to himself, as each new little thing came along," reported McBride, and "I was surprised to see how cool Virgil and Florine were. He is the most unfussed person I have ever met."[5] Gertrude Stein did not attend, but she alone graced the program cover in a photograph by George Platt Lynes.

As *Vogue* put it, "One sat and watched and heard and wondered and laughed and did not understand." Before the evening was out, the audience surrendered to their delight. When the chorus finally ended the opera with "Last Act. Which is a fact," John Houseman, standing in the wings, heard only silence. Then, "with a triumphant roar, through which I could vaguely distinguish the sharper tones of cheers and bravos, it came rushing at us out of the darkness, sweeping over the bright-lit stage, overwhelming the small, solemnly bowing figures of our astounded saints." Carl Van Vechten whooped louder than the rest, and the Countess Ghika became so excited that, for the first time in recorded history, she dropped her monocle. Virgil Thomson bowed at center stage, and Frederick Ashton and Houseman entered from the wings, while Florine Stettheimer bowed from the stage box.[6] As the onstage delivery of flowers continued and the curtain calls hit twenty, voices grew hoarse, Cecil Beaton was in tears, and sculptor Jo Davidson declared it the best thing he had ever seen in New York. The fireman on duty looked around and said, "Jeez, has everybody gone crazy or are they just stewed?" *New York Times* critic Olin Downes described the implications of that night's ovation: "Debussy and the poor old Met were buried last night, buried to shouts of joy and hosannas of acclaim for the new dawn of the lyric drama."

|||

Before John Houseman left the theater that night, he laid his face against the stage's splintered wood and sobbed with exhaustion and joy. Then he went on to a party at Julien and Joella Levy's apartment. Henry McBride reported that the party was a "terrific crush"; he left at one, hoping to sleep. "I passed a *nuit blanche*—the excitement had been too much."[7]

Lucius Beebe predicted that the opera "will be most expressively the vogue for the next few weeks." The subject dominated tea and dinner party chat, conversations about it erupted in automats and subways, and on the street people waved their programs at one another. One reporter observed people "laboring hugely in steam-filled air to convince various bewildered stay-at-homes that it was a cock-eyed, or it was not a cock-eyed, show." George Gershwin declared *Four Saints* "refreshing as a new dessert," prompting Franklin Pierce Adams to quip in "the Conning Tower" column, "Our conviction is that he can't spell." (From the opera Gershwin also drew inspiration for *Porgy and Bess*, produced a year later.) Julien Levy was so excited about the performance that he simply declined to talk to anyone who had not seen it. Among the opera's repeat customers were Arturo Toscanini (twice), Henry McBride (four times), Dorothy Parker (five times), and Alma Wertheim, holding the record at seventeen times. Marianne Moore called it "a blasphemous but talented thing" and declared Saint Teresa's to be the only bearable soprano voice she had ever heard.[8] An inevitable backlash soon set in. "The smart thing among the younger artists is to be violently against it," Paul Bowles wrote Thomson. "Stieglitz decides also to side with them. Most of the defense must be taken for Virgil, against whom they allow themselves to rage for having the audacity to give Gertrude Stein in modern dress."[9]

|||

The most hermetic of operas, oddly enough, managed to enter the broad stream of American popular culture. While *The March of Time* broadcast three minutes on national radio and children across the nation skipped rope to "How many acts are there in it?," a women's club in Bronxville did a parody skit called "Four Paints in Compacts." Realizing that money was to be made in merchandising *Four Saints* chic, Bergdorf Goodman offered a tea gown in five colors, called "Saint" because "it looks like one of the thrilling costumes in the much-talked-of Four Saints opera."[10] Gimbel's featured modernistic, geometrically patterned tablecloths named after lines from the opera, and John Wanamaker promoted $16.95 cellophane and rayon ready-to-wear evening wear ("Four Wraps in Cellophane") with matching handbags for an extra $3.95. Decorated for Easter Sunday, the most prestigious windows along Fifth Avenue evoked Florine's sets: Elizabeth Arden showed Saint Teresa with an Easter egg, Bergdorf Goodman depicted Saint Teresa singing "April Fools Day a pleasure," and Lord & Taylor and others followed suit. There were even rumors that the Republican Party would incorporate bits of the opera into its next party platform.

Gertrude Stein had anticipated this phenomenon in "Composition as Explanation," which she had written nearly ten years earlier:

For a very long time everybody refuses and then almost without a pause almost everybody accepts. In the history of the refused in the arts and literature the rapidity of the change is always startling. Now the only difficulty with the volte face concerning the arts is this. When the acceptance comes, by that acceptance the thing created becomes a classic. It is a natural phenomena, a rather extraordinary natural phenomena, that a thing accepted becomes a classic.[11]

Four Saints provoked views so divergent that one newspaper observed, "The opera has been called everything human ingenuity can suggest." Some called it a masterpiece, others a cheap hoax. Some described it as futurist, while others thought the modernism of Stein's libretto "exhaled an aroma of the quaintly old-fashioned." Some interpreted the opera as a satire of Catholicism, others as a deeply devotional work. A few socialists claimed the opera as an expression of their political position, since it represented close cooperation among artists. Young children thought the people onstage were real angels and that the cellophane set showed how heaven really looked. Some writers tried to find whimsical equivalents, labeling the opera the *Green Pastures of Mattewan* or the *Run Little Chillun of Bedlam*. While not every critic found Stein's words rhythmical, few casually dismissed their lack of sense. Some made no attempt to describe the opera but nonetheless recognized its entertainment value. *Variety's* critic noted, "It is drivel, of course, but the most beguiling, fascinating twaddle one can possibly imagine."

Because of his articulate celebration of the opera in the New York *Sun*, Henry McBride's acquaintances telephoned him for a few quick tips about the opera: What was the symbolism? What was meant by "Pigeons on the grass"? Why two Saint Teresas? Weary of explaining Gertrude Stein to the public, as he had for two decades, McBride wrote her about the incessant queries:

All this is tiresome. After twenty years of cubism and abstract art, it seems that these unfortunate people have not yet heard of it. I loathe explaining any work of art, and always insist that any work of art that can be explained is worthless; yet nevertheless I suppose I must at least bully some of these people into reasonableness. What I really feel is, that people who do not feel greatness in the best things of Picasso and Braque (now being shown here by Paul Rosenberg), do not know what painting is; and those who do not see poetry in your *Four Saints,* do not know what poetry is.[12]

Virgil Thomson summarized the critics' response: the music critics liked the words and not the music, while the literary critics liked the music and not the words. Nearly everyone applauded the contributions of Florine Stettheimer and Frederick Ashton. Talented humorists such as F. P. A. and Ogden Nash had a field day with Stein jokes,[13] while less clever detractors printed sections of the libretto as self-evident commentary. Most striking was the newspapers' generally serious discussion of the opera—their attempts to describe the indescribable to a broad, unsophisticated audience.

Most critics hailed the novelty and effectiveness of an all-Negro cast in a production that was not about Negro life. Although a few singled out the individual lead singers (notably Edward Matthews and Beatrice Robinson Wayne), most critics described the singers as a collective racial entity performing according to the dictates of their musical heritage. *Vogue's* primitivizing response typified the praise, calling the Negro singers "the audible miracle" of the opera. "Whites could never in the world have sung that opera. The very essence of the work demands primal ignorance and native awkwardness of which only the Negroes are capable. . . . I could not help thinking of the triumph of these instinctive dark people over the conscious Miss Stein." Other critics sounded the same notes of "praise": the Negroes were "winning," "joyous," "spiritual," "childish." Some made the point that they combined "intuition with trained technical brittleness." Only one major white critic, Olin Downes of *The New York Times,* challenged the condescension of "the assumption that [the black cast's] naiveté and presumptively unsophisticated minds would enable them to do more with the Stein text, and be less self-conscious about it, than if white singers were engaged." The fine line between celebration and racism was crossed repeatedly. The African-American periodical *Opportunity* summarized the depiction of the cast as simple, intuitive children, then dryly commented, "Just how these simple children were able to memorize the highly complicated, intellectualized libretto in the first place, was never explained."[14]

Critics and audience members struggled for words to capture the ineffable feelings that could be linked to neither psychological identification nor narrative drive nor political sympathy, nor, indeed, anything outside the opera itself. Dance critic John Martin called the opera "a synthesis of the theatrical arts such as we have all been waiting for and talking about for years." Theater critic Stark Young best captured the *sui generis* quality of the opera's delight: "But only now and then in the theatre can we hope for something of the quality of a thing in nature (a tree, a melon, a sheet of water, a flight of birds). The point in such case is not that it is beautiful or not beautiful, but that it lives in itself, and is in essence a constant surprise."

|||

During the Broadway run Virgil Thomson savored the barrage of telegrams and letters he received. Old Kansas City friends wrote, recalling their shared boyhood days of stealing apples, and fellow composers cabled. (One enthusiastically wrote, "BROTHER YOU ARE A CENTRIFUGAL WOW."[15]) Even Gertrude Stein cabled that she was "HAPPY AS CAN BE NEW YORK NEWS."[16] It was her first telegram of congratulations, Thomson noted with irritation, and she had not even sent it to the correct address. He was miffed that Stein was receiving the majority of the publicity but hoped that her celebrity would translate into a longer life for the opera. Throughout the six-week Broadway run, Harry Moses proposed touring the opera—to Boston, to Philadelphia, to London, to Chicago—which excited Virgil. Houseman observed at the time, "Thomson is like any man who, never before having made any money, is dazzled by the prospects suddenly opened to him and determined not to lose any part of it."[17] Not understanding the vagaries of producing the opera or Chick Austin's loose financial style, Gertrude Stein was disturbed at receiving no royalties from the Hartford production. Knowing that Austin was still in debt from the production overruns, Thomson told her not to bother Chick at the moment; Harry Moses had assumed his debt. (Moses never did pay the Hartford royalties to either Thomson or Stein.) When her go-between, Bradley, wrote her that the producers seemed to be reasonable men, she responded, "Moses and Houseman may be alright but you have to remember that they were chosen by Virgil and they may be very easily playing his game."[18] What was his game?

The sticking point was Thomson's insistence that Maurice Grosser be paid a percentage of the royalties as the opera's scenarist and that it should come from the librettist's share. Thomson's point, while valid, was an invitation to conflict. Everyone who had worked for free in Hartford was put on salary when the opera moved to Broadway, except for Florine Stettheimer and Grosser. (The former by choice, the latter not.) Stein simply said no, without explanation, while Thomson interpreted it as "a case of consent 'unreasonably withheld.'" Thomson refused to conduct when the show went to Chicago unless Gertrude acceded to the legal agreement he had spent fifty dollars to have drafted. Gertrude budged not an inch, and Moses ended up paying Grosser a half percent out of the producer's take. Thomson reconciled himself to Stein's refusal by selling a letter from Stein for fifty dollars to offset his legal costs. He considered it poetic justice but did not tell Stein. "I did not care to risk another quarrel," he wrote. "For Gertrude, about money, did not joke."

Thomson did not prosper materially from the Broadway run of the opera as he had expected. He received no new jobs or offers to perform his music, and no music publisher wanted to publish the opera. The only interesting proposal came from Lincoln Kirstein, who suggested that Thomson create a score for a ballet of *Uncle Tom's Cabin*. (When Thomson received e.e. cummings's scenario, he declared it unproduceable.) On the rare occasion when the press solicited his views on music, Thomson seized the opportunity to become the mandarin of the new American opera: "Very few know beans about musical declamation. Practically no Americans, excepting a few of the jazz boys, can be depended on to find a melody that will not only speak the sentiment but also the correct prosody of a simple phrase like 'Lady, Be Good' or 'All Alone by the Telephone.' . . . Our popular style is rich and racy. Our grander language is an uncharted sea."

Thomson did receive offers to lecture in Kansas City, where he made a grand triumphal return. At the Kansas Citian Hotel he gave a ninety-minute lecture on "Music for the Modern World." When a *Kansas City Star* reporter arrived at his parents' Wabash Avenue home, Thomson conducted the interview dressed in black pajamas and a black robe, as if to prove that one could be a sissy cosmopolite and still appear in a midwestern newspaper.

During the opera's Broadway run, John Houseman scraped bottom financially. "Why we have not made a fortune in New York is a profound mystery," he wrote Chick Austin three weeks into the run. "Or rather I think the explanation is to be found in the word Stein."[19] Meanwhile, the Friends and Enemies of Modern Music owed him $350, and Houseman

Virgil Thomson, by George Platt Lynes, photographed for Chick Austin's Hartford Festival, 1936.

owed his agent. (Austin did not pay Houseman back until June, and then only by selling some of his own furniture.) But more important than the money, Houseman felt the enlivening conviction that, at the age of thirty, he had finally discovered his vocation.

Henry McBride reported to a friend, "Florine, as you can guess, is now quite up-stage with all the flattery she has been getting."[20] A New York University student hoped to write his dissertation on Stettheimer's paintings; reporters requested interviews; and Julien Levy reported that dealers wanted paintings that were like Stettheimer's—"féerique and candy box and magical"—and they hoped to give her an exhibition.

Carrie and Ettie Stettheimer expressed their ambivalence about their sister's Broadway success by leaving town. They vacationed in Atlantic City during three weeks of the opera's Broadway run, leaving Florine to care for their mother at the Alwyn Court, where the two lived principally on chicken broth and chicken hearts. To a tea one afternoon during the run Florine invited not only such regulars as McBride, Thomson, and the Askews but also Saint Teresa, the Commère, and another cast member. She wrote to her sisters that the addition of the cast members transformed the tone of the gathering: "They made their entree with an overlife-size great Danse. The conversation was such as never occurs in our salon—childbirth—thoroughly gone into by the three women—when the men joined us (sounds antiquated) stories of French—Paris—brothel life."[21] Such a mixed-race gathering would probably not have occurred had the two other sisters been home; black guests had rarely been received at the Alwyn Court before.

Two years earlier, Florine had written to Henry McBride, "Shall I never be rescued from oblivion?"[22] But when that rescue came, she did not appear to enjoy it. She rejected a *New Yorker* reporter as lacking in knowledge, she pooh-poohed the Easter window displays along Fifth Avenue since she had not been consulted, she dismissed the new interest in her painting and continued to show noncommercially, and she thought the praise of her sets had become "shopworn." And she warned a *Sun* reporter that she would be a difficult interview. "Others have tried it," she said. "They seem to go away and find they haven't anything to write about."[23] About the dissertation writer, Florine noted that he wanted to "discover and analyze me—I shall have to keep a secretary like the star members of our cast."[24] The flip side of fame, invasion, struck her as intolerable.

During the Broadway run of the opera, Harry Moses grew so enchanted with the cast that he planned to form a black opera company that would sing the standard repertory in English. Similarly, Frederick Ashton continued his love affair with the cast and with Harlem, and finally with the whole audience. He said, "Americans make you *feel* it when you've done something well." He danced at uptown parties, once for four hours on end, improvising a pas de deux with a chair. His London friends observed that New York had raised Ashton's energy level and increased his interest in drinking potent Horse's Necks. "He was stirred up," observed a friend. "New York stirs you up." Ashton strongly considered staying. He asked John Martin, *The New York Times'* dance critic, whether he could find work in New York. "You're a classicist," Martin replied. "There's no room for you here." Discouraged and homesick, Ashton recalled that he "suddenly got terribly nostalgic for an English spring." On March 22, he boarded the S.S. *Berengia* on its final transatlantic voyage. He was touched to find a large contingent of the *Four Saints* cast lined up by the gangplank to wish him farewell. "Well duckie, I often think of our triumph last winter," he wrote Thomson after his return to London, "and get very nostalgic indeed."

Four Saints in Three Acts closed two times. The first closing, on March 17, played to a packed house. The opera was already considered a success, since it had doubled the planned two-week run; not only had 45,000 people seen it, but 16,000 tickets had been sold in the final week. *Variety* reported that the opera had already garnered more print coverage than any show in the previous ten years. The audience at the Forty-fourth Street Theatre on March 17 thought they were seeing the opera's final performance, and they cheered and refused to leave until the theater manager came on stage and announced the likelihood of a resumed run in two weeks. Just as the opera's opening had been celebrated by a party at the Levys', so was its closing. Chick Austin performed his "Magic at Midnight," and Joella Levy recalled that he did a trick with a balloon that was actually a condom.

Harry Moses reopened the opera at the Empire Theatre on April 2 and broke a theatrical tradition holding that shows that are brought back usually fare poorly. The opera played strongly through the first week, started the second week at dangerously low levels, and nearly sold out the last three performances. On the final night, McBride went to the Empire Theatre, not to see the opera for a fifth time but simply to bid farewell. "I sauntered in about 10 P.M. to say goodbye to the best of all operas and was surprised to see all three sisters in a box."[25] For the first time in a decade, the three Stettheimer sisters had left their mother alone.

When the Broadway run finally ended on April 14, the red velvet draperies were returned to their owner and Florine's sets went into storage, in the hopes that the show would travel. The collaborators split up. Frederick Ashton had already left; Alexander Smallens was next. The cast resumed their varied workaday lives in Harlem and Brooklyn with the hope that they would be reunited for a tour. Before Virgil Thomson left, on May 19, he ate a last magnificent meal of halibut and lobster in mayonnaise aspic, squab, and gooseberry preserves at the Stettheimers'. He sailed again on the *Ile de France* and found himself on deck with Marcel Duchamp. "As we passed the lower end of Manhattan Marcel said, pointing to the skyline, 'The reason that is beautiful is that nothing in it was built before 1900.'"[26]

After the final performance at the Empire Theatre, John Houseman watched the cast clean out their dressing rooms and dreaded their dispersal. It was the end of their collective lives together and the conclusion of an impossible—and miraculous—collaboration. "With their going I suffered a sentimental and physical loss," Houseman wrote. "I had become accustomed to their warm, rich, world of color and scent and resonance: its sudden withdrawal made the all-white world to which I was returning seem pale and arid and cold."

EPILOGUE

CHAPTER

18

Aftermath

Boarding trains, buses, and an airplane, the *Four Saints* company would assemble one last time for five performances in Chicago. Not all the original group made the trek in early November 1934—Frederick Ashton, Florine Stettheimer, and Chick Austin were absent. But for the first time, thanks to hastily made plans, the opera's librettist was present.

Gertrude Stein and Alice B. Toklas had arrived in New York just a week earlier on the first leg of Stein's American lecture tour. Curtis Air offered them free round-trip flights for the opera's Chicago premiere (a great advertisement for flying), and Carl Van Vechten offered to hold their hands when they got frightened (Gertrude said her only fears were of heights and indigestion). Harry Moses filled the cabin with American Beauty roses and a sign reading, "Rose is a rose is a rose." On takeoff, Gertrude and Alice were beguiled by the airplane's hum and the feeling of mounting. "The air seems so solid," said Gertrude. She looked down on Pennsylvania, her home state, and saw in its shapes the lines of Cubism. In a moment of inspiration she took out a pencil and began to write notes for an opera about America. Although Carl Van Vechten called it the bumpiest ride on record and the plane arrived an hour late, Gertrude and Alice were unperturbed either by the ride or by the hordes of society women and newspaper reporters who had come to greet them at the airport. As they headed off for the historical Auditorium Theatre, an admiring photographer exclaimed, "Nuts! She's the ritziest dame I ever tried to read."

The airplane ride seem to have exacerbated Stein's partial deafness. From her seat in Colonel Harold McCormick's plushly appointed opera box at the center of the Golden Horseshoe, she grumbled that she could not make out her words clearly; she later told Henry McBride "she couldn't hear half of it."[1] But she and Alice both relished the sets' otherworldly brightness and Ashton's choreography; as Stein approvingly observed, "They moved and did nothing." At the first-act curtain they moved to an orchestra seat close to the stage. Now they could discern the words. After the final curtain had come down to thunderous applause, Stein announced to the press, "I think it is perfectly extraordinary how they carried out what I wanted."[2]

After witnessing firsthand how the audience enjoyed her opera, she instructed NBC radio listeners to approach it without fear of incomprehension: "If you go to a football game you don't have to understand it in any way except the football way and all you have to do with *Four Saints* is to enjoy it in the *Four Saints* way which is the way I am, otherwise I would not have written in that way."[3]

|||

But it was not Stein's desire to see or explain *Four Saints* that had brought her to America. She had returned, for the first time in thirty-one years, to experience her late celebrity face to face—and to escape the writing block that had plagued her for more than a year.

Just over a week earlier, on Wednesday, October 24, Gertrude and Alice had arisen at 6 A.M. as their ship, the S.S. *Champlain,* was arriving in New York. Stein dressed in a brown tweed suit with a cherry-colored vest, large, low-heeled, round-toed shoes, and woolen stockings. On her head she wore a Louis XIII hunting cap. The two women ascended to the upper deck, where they watched through the mist as Manhattan's skyline came into view. Gertrude found it disappointingly low. A coast guard cutter filled

Gertrude Stein, Alice Toklas, and Harold McCormick, November 7, 1934, at the Chicago premiere of *Four Saints in Three Acts*.

with a dozen reporters approached from the Battery, and Carl Van Vechten stood on the pier in a bright purple-and-green shirt, his bracelets jangling as he waved. The press formed a ring around Stein in the *Champlain*'s lounge, squatting on the floor and perching on chairs and tables. Stein controlled her anxiety by throwing out the first gambit: "Suppose no one asked a question, what would the answer be?" The reporters quickly fell into line, asking many of the questions she had heard countless times. Stein told them she had come "to tell very plainly and simply and directly, as is my fashion, what literature is." When Joseph Alsop, who had reported on the *Four Saints* rehearsal at St. Philip's Church, asked why she did not write as she talked, Stein demonstrated her deft mastery of the sound bite. "Oh, but I do," she said. "After all, it's all learning how to read it."

Ship-to-shore radio broadcast their arrival, afternoon papers gave them front-page headlines, and thousands of electric bulbs crawling around the New York Times Building spelled out, "Gertrude Stein has arrived in New York, Gertrude Stein has arrived in New York." (Alice looked up and dryly observed, "As if we didn't know it.") Before their first evening was over, they had dined with Carl Van Vechten and the Pathé newsreel company had filmed them in their Algonquin suite. Stein was delighted with the attention she received from anonymous people on the street who called out to her and from shopkeepers who inquired about her transatlantic crossing. Alice reported to Henry McBride, "Gertrude said walking down the street in N.Y. was the realest and unrealest thing yet."[4]

In the wake of her double success, *Four Saints* and *The Autobiography of Alice B. Toklas*, Stein had achieved a level of celebrity that astounded even the most jaded journalists. "For the first time in my experience as a New York newspaper correspondent a celebrity has come to America whose right to fame defies analysis," concluded one. "She has created as great a sensation as would the combined appearance, in their heyday, of Charles Lindbergh, Gene Tunney, and 'Peaches' Browning."[5]

Celebrity had flummoxed Stein and stopped her from writing. Just before her arrival, *Vanity Fair* published her candid description of her crisis:

> What happened to me was this. When the success began and it was a success I got lost completely lost. You know the nursery rhyme, I am I because my little dog knows me. Well you see I did not know myself, I lost my personality. It has always been com-

pletely included in myself my personality as any personality naturally is, and here all of a sudden I was not just I because so many
people did know me.[6]

Stein embraced that public personality over the next five months, as she
and Toklas traversed the country in planes and cars and trains. She spoke
to more than forty audiences—university students, members of women's
clubs, art collectors, and high school girls—and along the way she and
Alice met a number of America's great celebrities. Eleanor Roosevelt invited them to tea, George Gershwin played sections of *Porgy and Bess* for
them, the mayor of San Francisco gave them the keys to the city. In Hollywood they dined with Mary Pickford, Charlie Chaplin, and Dashiell Ham-
mett, who asked how Stein had succeeded in getting so much publicity. It
was a matter of having a small audience, she responded, for "the biggest
publicity comes from the realest poetry and the realest poetry has a small
audience not a big one."

America was a joyous discovery. Observing her obvious glee, Alfred
Stieglitz said to Stein, "I know what it is it is just a Christmas tree for you
all the time." She cherished the privileges and glitz of celebrity, and both
she and Alice were reluctant to leave. Stein's final scheduled lecture was
envisioned as a gala event that would include Virgil Thomson playing and
"the 2 nice saints" singing selections ("the Paris production" plus two).
That evening, of April 29, would have been the only time that Thomson
and Stein were on the same stage together; the sponsor was called, appropriately, the American Arbitration Association. Thomson wrote to Stein, "I
am honored and will be only too delighted." But Stein canceled that
evening, objecting to the fact that admission was to be charged.

Stein's final telephone call, her "farewell to America," came from
Beatrice Robinson Wayne, Saint Teresa, who told her how much the *Four
Saints* cast liked singing her words—"they all did they all said all the words
were such natural words to say."

Carl Van Vechten accompanied Stein and Toklas to the dock on
May 4. After they boarded the S.S. *Champlain*, Toklas descended into a
black mood because she believed that nothing ahead could ever equal
their American adventure. When they arrived in Paris eight days later,
Stein told a reporter, "I was like a bachelor who goes along fine for twenty-
five years and then decides to get married. That is the way I feel—I mean
about America."[8]

After its spectacular 1934 season in New York and its brief revival in Chicago later that year, *Four Saints in Three Acts* settled into a long hibernation. Thomson received proposals to send the opera on tour, to stage it in concert, to mount a puppet adaptation, and even to reconceive it as an opera about the Spanish Civil War. Thomson always acceded to the proposals but remained skeptical about their coming to fruition. "The epoch isn't right," he wrote to Gertrude Stein in 1938. "The original production isn't forgotten enough. All of a sudden one day it will be forgotten and then *Four Saints* will be easy to perform and it will start its natural life as a classic repertory piece which I know will be a long life."[9]

In fact, the epoch would not be right for several decades, and *Four Saints* has yet to become a classic repertory piece. Although many prominent contemporary critics rank *Four Saints* on a shortlist of great American operas (along with *The Ballad of Baby Doe, Porgy and Bess, The Mother of Us All, The Medium*), the opera is seldom performed.[10]

The American National Theatre and Academy mounted the first major revival in 1952, at the Broadway Theatre on Fifty-third Street, and it subsequently traveled to Paris. Rather than conceiving a new vision of the opera, Thomson aspired to re-create the 1934 production. He could now select his black cast from a larger pool of professionally trained performers—singers from the Juilliard School and dancers from the Katherine Dunham School. Only two members from the original cast re-created their roles: Edward Matthews as Saint Ignatius and Altonell Hines, now his wife, as the Commère. Although the musical performance was first-rate, the production unwittingly demonstrated the unrepeatability of the original's peculiar success. The bright colors that had once looked shockingly chic were now called gaudy. The original production had prompted a ban on cellophane in Broadway theaters, and the 1952 synthetic alternative looked greasy and dismal. "It drooped," Thomson sadly explained, "like the Pope's balls." Some critics applauded the playfulness of Stein's words and Thomson's adroit prosody, but other music critics, such as Irving Kolodin, voiced the fear that *Four Saints* was "significant for what it was rather than for what it is."[11] The exhilarating frisson of 1934—thriving on the avant-garde, high bohemia, and Negro chic—could not be duplicated in post–World War II America.

By this time modernism was ensconced in the museums, New York was the world's art capital, and the International Style was beginning to dominate the skyline. New York's social landscape had changed completely. Gone were the Prohibition speakeasies and Harlem music clubs that had offered the arena for hedonistic, racially mixed insouciance. The repeal of the Volstead Act at the beginning of 1934 and the Harlem riots of 1935 had spelled the end of Going Uptown. By the end of the 1930s, the fertile amalgam of bohemia, money, stylishness, and modernity seemed as frivolously anachronistic as an F. Scott Fitzgerald novel. Even *Vanity Fair* went out of style; in 1936 the magazine was folded into *Vogue*, and Condé Nast charged Frank Crowninshield with advising on a new magazine, pitched to the working girl, called "*Glamour* with a 'u.'"

New York's salons decreased in number and paled in spirit. Muriel Draper was the first saloneuse to jump ship—six months after *Four Saints* premiered, she boarded the S.S. *President Harding* and set out to Russia to witness the Communist experiment firsthand. "GO FORTH SAINT THERESA," wired her friend Esther Murphy.[12] Draper would return to New York and a few years later her New Year's Eve At Homes resumed in ramshackle spaces, but many of her guests had dropped away because of Draper's now-dangerous socialist politics.[13] The Stettheimers' gatherings at the Alwyn Court ended when Mrs. Stettheimer died, in 1935, and the sisters moved out. The Askews' gatherings were discontinued in the early 1940s. Kirk ascribed their end to the war, the expense, too much drinking, and age. But Thomson and other friends also ascribed the end to Constance's displeasure. "Constance said to me, 'I'm closing up,'" recalled Joella Levy. "'Last Sunday I turned around and it was all men, not a single woman.'"[14]

III

Four Saints has had a vital underground life, even though it was rarely performed and existed for a long time only in an incomplete 1948 recording. But over time the opera achieved a cultlike status as a landmark event in the history of the American avant-garde. It became a model for performance to come later in the century.

The opera offered no blueprint for new performance—it was too quirky to be successfully imitated—but it suggested new parameters for the stage. After *Four Saints*, it became possible to conceive of a performance as "a landscape," without single focus or narrative progression. Physical relations between objects and sounds might supersede conventional drama. The stage could be reconceived as an arena for hypnotic and layered images, just as words and music could establish new relationships. "Theater was a limited art," said Judith Malina, "and with very few exceptions it hadn't caught up with dance or art or poetry. Everything in the modern theater has been touched by Stein's reorganization of the English language. She freed the theater in every dimension. She simply plowed everything under and it allowed us a wide field to experiment with new forms. And the seeds she planted have continued to grow."[15]

Four Saints taught theatrical producers that Broadway could accommodate both opera and Tin Pan Alley. George Gershwin's *Porgy and Bess* followed directly on the heels of *Four Saints*, opening in 1935, and broke its record as the longest-running opera on Broadway. (Eva Jessye was its choral director and Alexander Smallens its conductor.) Before the practice of opera on Broadway ended in the mid-1950s, the most prominent American operas opened on Broadway, including Gian Carlo Menotti's *The Medium*, *The Saint of Bleecker Street*, and *The Telephone*, Kurt Weill's *Street Scene*, and Marc Blitzstein's *Regina*.

Only one of Gertrude Stein's plays was performed during her lifetime and her stage popularity did not improve after her death. But her influence could be felt in the works of others. Alice Toklas wrote to Carl Van Vechten after Stein's death: "You know what Jane Heap said long ago—Gertrude Stein may not be the most read author—but she certainly is the most stolen author."[16] Her friend Thornton Wilder told Stein in 1937 that the third act of *Our Town* depended on her ideas—"the American's right to remake himself a language from the fabric of the English language"—and described their relationship as a "deep-knit collaboration."[17] In the 1960s and '70s, the theater composer Al Carmines repeatedly turned to Stein for his works *In Circles*, *Dr. Faustus Lights the Lights*, *Listen to Me*, *The Making of Americans*, and *What Happened*. When Carmines saw a production of *Four Saints* after completing his first Stein work, *What Happened*, it confirmed him in the desire, like Thomson decades before, to interweave his melodies and Stein's pared-down words. "She offers the possibility for true collaboration because you are adding an element that Gertrude Stein doesn't have," Carmines said. "She adds precision and scientific pragmatism, and you add love and gentleness and passion and joy and sadness and all the traditions of American music."[18]

For several decades after *Four Saints'* premiere, Thomson's music influenced few important composers. Interest began to revive in the late 1970s, when the minimalist compositions of Philip Glass, Steve Reich, and John Adams were compared to Thomson's work (notably by John Rockwell of *The New York Times*). Shortly after the 1976 premiere of Glass's *Einstein on the Beach*, Tim Page, an early writer on Glass, described his first exposure to *Four Saints*: "I'd found the great, great grandfather/mother of what had gone since. And it didn't sound old-fashioned at all."[19] In the last decade of his long life Thomson enjoyed a circumscribed popularity that had eluded him for most of his composing years.

Four Saints' most lasting influence has been in blurring the lines between various branches of performance. Two hubs of the New York avant-garde in the 1950s and 1960s, the Living Theater and the Judson Dance Theater, both incorporated Stein into their programs. The Living Theater's first performance, a quartet of plays staged in Julian Beck and Judith Malina's living room in 1951, opened with Stein's *Ladies Voices*. James Waring, the éminence grise of the Judson Dance Theater, and choreographer Remy Charlip were deeply influenced by Stein. Closer to the present day, such performing groups as The Wooster Group and Richard Foreman's Ontological Hysterical Theater, and Robert Wilson's collaborations, repeatedly draw from Stein's use of words.

Four Saints prefigured the large-scale interdisciplinary performance works of the 1980s, which were often called operas, a newly popular catchphrase of the period. The most influential figure in the shaping of these new spectacles was Robert Wilson, whose collaboration with Philip Glass, *Einstein on the Beach*, became the landmark event of the era. Both Wilson and Glass have testified that *Four Saints in Three Acts* provided their only model for multimedia opera. In 1996 Wilson realized a decades-old ambition to stage *Four Saints*, producing it at the Houston Grand Opera, the Lincoln Center Festival, and the Edinburgh Festival. Other influential productions that integrated music and performance on a grand scale, in ways that suited neither Broadway theaters nor opera houses, included Lee Breuer and Bob Telson's *The Gospel at Colonus*, Meredith Monk's *Quarry*, and Laurie Anderson's *United States, Parts I–IV*. A new avant-garde "tradition" has been forged.

|||

The death of Rosetta Walter Stettheimer in 1935 released Florine and her two sisters from their joint caretaking and enforced sorority. Soon Ettie replaced her mother as the family invalid, and Carrie never again touched the dollhouse she had worked on for fifteen years. In her diary entry for September 30, 1935, Florine commemorated "The Collapse of Our Home":

> Goodbye Home
> 182 W. 58
> the Allwyn [*sic*] Court
> Salamanders, Crowns,
> Cupids & Fleur-de-lys
> farewell

While Carrie and Ettie moved together to the Dorset Hotel, Florine took up full-time residence in her studio. Her sisters initially regarded Florine's separate quarters as desertion, while her friend Isabel Lachaise described the move "as a release—'a Room of One's Own,' so to speak."[20] To mark the change in her life, Florine destroyed several old paintings and repeatedly redecorated her studio—adding new cellophane drapes and swags, inventing new gilded and beaded bouquets—until it exactly suited her taste. From a niche in her cocoon presided the marble bust of George Washington—"the only man I collect."[21] She attended parties less frequently and declined to join her sisters on their summer travels; as she put it, "The air in my lace bedroom is much better for me."[22] In her late sixties, she focused her dwindling energies on large and ambitious paintings, relishing her daily rhythms. She especially enjoyed painting at her easel, lunching only on brightly frosted pastries ("Things mean their colors," she insisted).

On January 1, 1942, Florine began her last painting, *Cathedrals of Art*, a crowning work that encapsulated on canvas her perspective on the art world. Over the next two years, between long periods in the hospital, she repeatedly returned to the painting that stood taller than she did, giving up only six weeks before her death. Its three richly populated panels depicted the Stettheimers' coterie of friends in the social context of the art world establishment: museum directors Alfred Barr and Chick Austin and art dealers Julien Levy, Kirk Askew, and Alfred Stieglitz are all there. Henry McBride holds signs commanding "Stop" and "Go." Born under photographer George Platt Lynes's bright lights, the painting's protagonist, the infant Art, hopscotches on a Mondrian painting, then ascends a red-carpeted stairway to the high altar. Beneath a cellophane-and-gilt canopy stands Florine, in the guise of *Four Saints'* Commère.

Florine Stettheimer's living area/studio in the Beaux Arts Building on Fortieth Street near Fifth Avenue, photographed by Peter Juley after her death. Stettheimer designed her furnishings. On the easel in the background stands her portrait of the three sisters with their mother.

Kirk Askew repeatedly asked Stettheimer to let him exhibit her paintings and handle her estate. She hoped that the paintings could remain together after her death, but she also wanted them to disappear with her. Shortly before her death, she charged her lawyer, Joseph Solomon, with destroying them all, but she also considered giving her sisters free rein to distribute them. "I have a few unrealistic ideas for their future which I should like to tell you about," she wrote Kirk Askew shortly before her death. But she succumbed to cancer before confiding her fantasies about her paintings' ultimate disposition. She demurred until the end.

Florine died on May 11, 1944. Two weeks later, Henry McBride observed that her death had "passed as unremarked by the general public as did the poet Emily Dickinson's," and he predicted that Stettheimer would eventually hold an equally important position.[23] The first step in her

Cathedrals of Art (1942–44) by Florine Stettheimer, oil on canvas, 97.2 x 51.1 cm., Metropolitan Museum of Art, gift of Ettie Stettheimer, 1953 (53.24.1).

posthumous recognition was a retrospective exhibition at the Museum of Modern Art, arranged in 1946 by two of her oldest friends. Marcel Duchamp selected the paintings, and McBride wrote the catalog that finally situated Florine on the art map. Surveying her sister's collected paintings in the museum, Ettie remarked to a friend, "I think that this is the beginning of something."[24]

Alone now, for Carrie's death had followed Florine's by only six weeks, Ettie was responsible for arranging the disposition of her sisters' art and artifacts. After giving Carrie's unfinished dollhouse to the Museum of the City of New York, Ettie hired Peter Juley to photograph Florine's studio and paintings, collected her stray verses into a slim volume called *Crystal Flowers*, and dispersed her paintings to museums around the country. "Florine will be rediscovered as an important figure," prophesied her friend Pavel Tchelitchew, "a dreamer in the times when no one really dreamed well, when the garden of her life, the magical existence of all of you, is accepted as a reality."[25]

III

After the momentous events of February 1934, Julien Levy said that Chick Austin "might well forever after ride his star trailing clouds of glory."[26] Two years later he organized an event, the Hartford Festival, that aspired to the same ambitious scale and interdisciplinary focus. Students from the School of American Ballet danced in George Balanchine's ballet *Magic*, and Virgil Thomson conducted the American premiere of Erik Satie's *Socrate* against a backdrop by Alexander Calder. For the festival's final event, the Paper Ball, the sleek floating planes of the Avery courtyard had been transformed by Pavel Tchelitchew into three tiers of onlookers painted on old newspaper. Live guests in specially designed costumes made choreographed entrances below, as Austin, aptly garbed as a circus ringmaster, recited poems written for the occasion. Lincoln Kirstein observed, "It was about the last public party in America designed as an illustration of the dominance of a certain scale of grandeur in taste and manners."[27]

But the Depression-era trustees soon lost interest in Austin's grand frivolity, and the frisson of excitement that had spurred his first decade gradually congealed into fear and controversy. His homosexuality became fodder for local gossip. Although Austin continued to treat the Wadsworth Atheneum as his personal staging ground for art, movies, ballet, grand

AFTERMATH: THE HARVARD MODERNISTS

By 1935 **Alfred Barr** had realized his 1929 manifesto for an interdisciplinary Museum of Modern Art, exhibiting, in addition to the traditional fine arts, architecture and design, film, and photography. In 1939, at the opening of the museum's first permanent building, President Franklin Delano Roosevelt declared, "The conditions for democracy and for art are one and the same." Barr was fired in October 1943, but he stayed on without a formal position, sequestered in a cubicle in a corner of the library, furnished with a chair and a sawed-in-half library table. In 1947, he returned to his old office as chairman of the museum collections, and he remained there for twenty years. "Of course Alfred would not leave," said his wife. "It was his Museum. The Museum was his mistress."

On December 6, 1934, **Lincoln Kirstein**'s School of American Ballet gave its first public performance at the Wadsworth Atheneum. Kirstein and George Balanchine created a series of ballet companies: the Ballet Caravan (1936), Ballet Society (1946), and, in 1948 and most enduringly, the New York City Ballet. Kirstein continued as general director until 1989, Balanchine until his death. Ballet in America is unimaginable without their stamp. Around the same time Kirstein founded the ballet, he turned against abstract art and photography and concluded that the Museum of Modern Art was "one of the worst influences on cultural history."

In the spring of 1934, **Philip Johnson** curated an epochal exhibition, "Machine Art," inaugurating the Museum of Modern Art's design collection. After several years' involvement with fascist politics in America and Europe, he returned to Harvard in 1940 to study architecture and found *The International Style* on his required reading list. But the popularization of International Style came only after World War II, when it became a standardized corporate style. Just as he had helped define modernism in architecture during the 1930s, Johnson subsequently helped promote the postmodern aesthetic in the 1970s and showcased deconstructivist architecture in the late 1980s.

Before his death at the age of 83, **Henry-Russell Hitchcock** wrote twenty books and taught at Vassar, Wesleyan, Smith, MIT, Yale, Harvard, and New York University. He was widely considered to be the dean of American architectural history.

The course **Julien Levy** set for his gallery in its first few years continued until its end. He exhibited his stable of surrealist and neo-Romantic painters, including Max Ernst, Eugene Berman, De Chirico, Tchelitchew, and Joseph Cornell. During the war Levy joined forces with **Kirk Askew** to ride out the lean war years together. They closed the gallery in 1949.

balls, and magic, his golden period ended before the decade was out. By the time the United States entered World War II and a newly patriotic atmosphere took hold, Austin's unique combination of playful subversion and avant-garde experimentation went out of style.[28]

At the end of 1944, Austin gave his last performance in the museum as the Great Osram, and two days later he resigned under pressure. "In a way it was curious he lasted so long there," Henry McBride wrote Ettie Stettheimer, "for he ran the museum with a verve that amounted to genius, and the surprises he manged for us so enchantingly would, naturally, confuse and infuriate the stodgy trustees. A museum is never an easy berth for a genius."[29] Some of his Hartford friends thought that Austin had grown bored with the struggle he waged at the Wadsworth Atheneum; others maintained that he had been "crucified" by Hartford's inherent conservatism. "Chick Austin was a kind of victim of the revenge that is taken on the advance-guard," said Lincoln Kirstein.[30] Many of Austin's friends recognized that he had led them and excited their imaginations during what Philip Johnson called "those blazing years." But Johnson also noted the inevitable end of the period: "It wasn't that it left Hartford. It just ceased midair."[31]

With the good fortune that seemed to grace his life, Chick Austin soon became the director of the John and Mable Ringling Museum in Sarasota, Florida. Its distinguished collection of Baroque paintings ideally suited his tastes. "I am really in a delirium about life again after those miserable fallow years," he wrote his friend James Thrall Soby, "and having been afraid for a while that I COULDN'T work again, I now find that I can do more than ever and much more sensibly."[32] In 1946, he reopened the galleries that had been closed since John Ringling's death a decade earlier, and in 1948 he expanded the galleries to include the Museum of the American Circus.

Since Sarasota was off the circuit of his friends, Austin felt isolated. "He knew he had put himself on the front line, done dangerous things," his daughter recalled, "and he needed to be told what he had done."[33] His days increasingly regulated by Dexedrine in the morning and drink in the afternoon, driving around in his secondhand Rolls-Royce, Chick lived out his final years in sunny exile. He died on March 29, 1957, at the age of fifty-six.

The Family friends and museum colleagues gathered on a wet and blustery day in a Windham, New Hampshire, graveyard, on land that

Chick Austin moving from the Wadsworth Atheneum to the Ringling Museum, 1949.

Austin had donated a year earlier. Just as Chick was interred, the sun shone fully for a brief moment; then the storm resumed. Some consoled themselves that Chick would not have liked growing old, and the day after his funeral Constance Askew felt his tangible presence: "I can see him—now—this minute—come into the room,—the laugh, the gesture with his hands, all the mannerisms, and the wonderful divine [story] about what had happened to him ten minutes before."[34] Many simply refused to believe that he had died. "Because Chick in my mythology was immortal," Thomson wrote Helen Austin. "But of course he is because he has always been there whether we were with him or not. His reality was unerasable."[35]

To the Harvard group Austin's death signified the mortality of their invincible generation. "Chick was so much a part of all our beginnings in the modern world," Philip Johnson wrote Helen. "He held it all together somehow. His death seems to mark sort of an end of a whole era."[36] Summoning up Austin's golden moment on the night of February 7, 1934, Jere Abbott listened to his RCA phonograph record of *Four Saints in Three Acts*. "The Saints still sing lovely and beautiful," he wrote Virgil, "and I thought of Chick and nearly wept."[37]

| | |

"That production was absolutely crucial to me," John Houseman said in an interview in 1987, two years before he died. "In *Four Saints* I suddenly discovered what I wanted to do and it changed the whole course of my life."

In the commercial theater the opera was regarded as "maverick" and "highbrow," and it did not lead to Broadway offers for Houseman. His most important break came in the fall of 1935, when the Federal Theatre appointed him head of its Negro Theatre Project. In the wake of Harlem's 1935 riots a few months earlier, many white people were wary about traveling uptown, but Houseman regarded it as a return to the scene of his happiest theater experience. Relying on the counsel of his *Four Saints* cohort Edward Perry to help negotiate the politics of theater in Harlem, Houseman organized more than seven hundred black performers and theater craftsmen into two units. One would perform contemporary plays by and about black Americans, the other would tackle the classic repertory. Virgil Thomson, who shared five apartments with Houseman during this period, constantly counseled him to follow the precedent of *Four Saints*: cast Harlem's performers in plays that were not about black life.[38]

For the Negro Theatre Project's first classic play, Houseman chose the notoriously difficult *Macbeth*, and to direct the production, he invited twenty-year-old Orson Welles. Set in the jungles of Haiti, the production was tagged "the voodoo *Macbeth*." When the production opened on April 14, 1936, klieg lights filled the night sky over Manhattan, ten thousand people milled around the Lafayette Theatre, and Harlem's northbound traffic was stopped for more than an hour. For its ten-week uptown run, every seat was filled, and it transferred to Broadway for an additional two months.

John Houseman remained in the background of the voodoo *Mac-*

beth, as he had in *Four Saints* and as he would for most of his career. He stayed with Orson Welles and helped found the notorious Mercury Theater in 1937. His involvement in *Citizen Kane* led him to movie production, a career that lasted two decades and resulted in such memorable films as Nicholas Ray's debut, *They Live by Night*, Max Ophüls's masterpiece, *Letter from an Unknown Woman*, and Vincente Minnelli's *The Bad and the Beautiful*.

In 1969, at the age of seventy-one, Houseman appeared in front of the camera as Harvard Law School professor Charles Kingsfield in *The Paper Chase*. After winning an Academy Award for this supporting role, he was suddenly in great demand as an actor. The traits Houseman projected onscreen—crusty trustworthiness, competence, and cosmopolitan intelligence—were the same qualities Thomson had intuited on first meeting him in the Askews' drawing room years before. Shortly before he died, at the age of eighty-six, he repeatedly turned back to that pivotal moment in his life: Why had Virgil chosen him? It had made all the difference: "That particular chemistry, that particular miracle that occurred has never been reproduced since."

|||

When Frederick Ashton boarded the S.S. *Berengia* on March 22, 1934, he vowed to return to New York soon, but fifteen years passed before he did. Three years after *Four Saints*, he choreographed his second Gertrude Stein text, set to music by Lord Berners and called *A Wedding Bouquet*. After she met the choreographer, Stein asked Alice Toklas if he was a genius, and she replied, "More likely than any one we have seen for a long time."

Four Saints retained a unique place in Ashton's choreography, and he wrote to Virgil Thomson fifteen years later, "It brings back happy times when we were still in our twenties and when our natures were still passionate."[39] In the intervening years Ashton had created a brilliant repertory of classical ballets, culminating in his masterpiece, *Symphonic Variations*. In the years to come, he continued to choreograph prodigiously. Serving as the director of the Royal Ballet from 1963 to 1970, he was knighted and became a friend of the queen mother and an internationally acclaimed figure. ("Who would have thought this of little Freddie Ashton from Lima, Peru?" he asked friends.) Sir Frederick Ashton choreographed until the age of eighty-one and continued to believe that he had half an hour of choreography left in him. When he died, at eighty-four, in 1988, obituaries frequently observed that his death marked the close of an era in ballet shaped by the three masters Frederick Ashton, George Balanchine, and Anthony Tudor. Ashton had delivered his own epitaph years earlier, when he said to an interviewer, "Choreography is my whole being, my whole life, my reason for living. I pour into it all my love, my frustrations, and sometimes autobiographical details."[40]

|||

Most of the cast members of *Four Saints* never performed again in an opera or on a Broadway stage. They had been anonymous singers in choruses and church choirs, and to those most of them returned. Some, such as Beatrice Robinson Wayne (Saint Teresa), taught music or gave vocal lessons, while others became full-time homemakers or wage earners. A few would perform in productions of *Porgy and Bess*, and Edward Matthews (Saint Ignatius) had a distinguished stage career. Bruce Howard (Saint Teresa II) found more musical opportunities abroad, where, she declared, "I'm a black princess!"

The four cast members I tracked down nearly sixty years after the performance recalled the opera as a central and unforgettable event in their lives. If asked to sing, they usually declined because their voices had deteriorated. But if asked just to recall the words, they inevitably sang them. Words and music had been welded together at the time of the rehearsal, and memory had not separated them. The cast member who remembered the opera most precisely was Thomas Anderson. For the 1934 production he had kept a promptbook, and, as Virgil Thomson wrote, he "knew every move." Anderson could still recall each detail in 1992 and acted bits of it out for me in his living room in Englewood, New Jersey, simulating the conductor's moves and creating scenes in the space between the Naugahyde sofa and the dining table. "Now, why has that stayed with me all these years?" Anderson asked. "I remember it as if it were yesterday."

|||

Abe Feder was among the youngest of the opera's collaborators and the opera's last known survivor; he died on April 24, 1997, at the age of eighty-seven. Early on he had been dubbed the "genius with light," and he lived up to that title right into his eighties. Feder lit more than three hundred

Broadway productions, including the voodoo *Macbeth* (1935), *The Cradle Will Rock* (1938), *My Fair Lady* (1956), and *Camelot* (1960). Believing that lighting extended beyond the stage, Feder lit everything from the altar of St. Patrick's Cathedral to the penguin house of the Bronx Zoo, from the United Nations to Buckminster Fuller's geodesic dome. His slogan was "Push back the darkness!,"[41] and his last desire—unfulfilled—was to light the Sistine Chapel.

|||

When Gertrude Stein returned from her American tour in May 1935, she had achieved her twin objectives of fame and publication. She had encountered celebrity face to face, and her agreement with Bennett Cerf was a writer's dream: each year she would select a previously unpublished manuscript from her store and Random House would publish it. Stein's tour had also provided her a welcome diversion from her crippling writer's block. Once she returned to the domestic routines of Paris and Bilignin, Stein again faced the blank pages of her notebooks. For the next ten years she continued to fill them, circling rudderlessly and obsessively around the theme of the genius's personal identity amid public celebrity. She wrote a novel in desultory spurts over four years and called it *Ida*. Stein called Ida a new kind of saint, a "publicity saint," and critic Donald Sutherland described her as a "combination of Helen of Troy, Dulcinea, Garbo, the Duchess of Windsor, and in particular 'Gertrude Stein.'"[42]

When France entered World War II, Gertrude and Alice entered a five-year period in the south of France, cut off from friends and fame.[43] The exile increased Gertrude's longing for America. At the war's end she conducted a radio broadcast to the United States: "I can tell everybody that none of you know what this native land business is until you have been cut off from that same native land completely for years. This native land business gets you all right."[44]

|||

Despite the hoopla surrounding *Four Saints in Three Acts*, the man who had initiated it and assembled its collaborators reaped little immediate benefit. Virgil Thomson attracted no lecture agent, no publisher, and no opera company to perform *Four Saints*. A dozen years passed before *Four Saints* was recorded (even then it was only half the opera), and he waited fifteen years for the opera to be published.

In the blaze of publicity just after *Variety* reported that the opera had had more coverage than any show in a decade, Thomson thought the opera would sustain him indefinitely. On March 6, he reported, "The prognostic on Broadway is that we will continue doing business (here, on the road, in London, etc.) for at least two years."[45] Before the season was out, Thomson faced the brutal discrepancy between fashionable fame and money in the pocket, and by the fall of 1934 he was down to his last $20. Confronting his bleak finances in characteristically foursquare manner, Virgil stayed in New York and split his apartment rent with John Houseman for the next three years. When he found that musical venues in concert and orchestra halls were closed to him, he opened other doors, soliciting jobs through his Harvard and *Four Saints* connections. Lincoln Kirstein commissioned Thomson to compose *Filling Station*, a ballet that premiered in 1938 at Chick Austin's Wadsworth Atheneum, and Houseman commissioned scores for Federal Theatre productions. Beginning in 1936, Thomson composed music for the movies: Pare Lorentz's *The Plow That Broke the Plains* (1936) and *The River* (1937), and later Robert Flaherty's *Louisiana Story*, which won him a Pulitzer Prize for music.

Thomson gamely composed for any venue open to him: the ballet, the theater, the movies, and the WPA. But he benefited little from the conventional music establishment, left or right. Neither the International League of Composers nor the International Society for Contemporary Music played Thomson's music, and *Four Saints'* commercial success rendered it suspect among music highbrows. Thomson fought back by deriding the various factions of the music world as "the taste boys," "the League of Jewish Composers," "the pseudo-educational rackets," or "the Schoenbergians and the Bang-Bangs." His residual bitterness lasted until his last years, when, at the slightest prompting, he would trot out his anti-Semitic theory that the Jewish mafia had excluded him.

From his position at the margins of the music world, he developed an "economic-aesthetic" theory about the links among money, music, performance, and critical attention—as he put it, "Who Does What to Whom and Who Gets Paid." Thomson set down his opinionated wisdom at length, published in 1939 as *The State of Music*. Although the book sold only two thousand copies, it provided Thomson an ideal platform for his pungent wit. "The book was aimed at the profession and seems to be hitting its mark surprisingly," Thomson wrote a friend. "It's supposed to be just God's truth every word of it and time somebody said same out loud."

The book elicited an invitation to become the chief music critic of the *New York Herald Tribune*, widely considered the liveliest and most literate of New York's eight daily newspapers. When the editor's wife asked Thomson how he liked the idea of being the music critic, Thomson bluntly replied that "the general standard of music reviewing in New York had sunk so far that almost any change might bring improvement."

Within the span of two days in October 1940, the *Herald Tribune* audience got a foretaste of the outrageous, slangy, no-nonsense prose that would appear over the next fourteen years. As if to announce that he was the brightest new bully on the block, Thomson's leadoff review called the popular composer Sibelius "vulgar, self-indulgent and provincial beyond all description" and concluded with Maurice Grosser's remark that he now understood why the New York Philharmonic was not part of New York's intellectual life. He followed up the next day with a descriptive paean to the Boston Symphony Orchestra, which he glowingly described as America's finest orchestra. His first two pieces for the *Herald Tribune* showed both sides of Thomson: the biting and the smitten, the sweet and the sour. His editor, Geoffrey Parsons, praised the Boston piece ("peaches and cream from every point of view") but warned Thomson that his high-handed dismissal of Sibelius had been miscalculated and potentially alienating. He suggested that Thomson would now have to demonstrate that he wasn't simply "a Young Pedant in a Hurry, with a Paris condescension."

At the *Herald Tribune* Thomson shaped musical tastes for two generations. He expanded musical criticism to include everything from Artur Rubinstein playing Chopin at Carnegie Hall to Bishop Utah Smith playing an electric guitar at Newark's Church of God in Christ, from Maxine Sullivan singing in a nightclub to John Cage playing at the New School for Social Research. As the organizer of the New York Music Critics Circle and an employer of critics, he shaped the musical establishment.[46] Music historian Gilbert Chase summed up his influence: "We can only say that he is unscholastic, unacademic, unorthodox, and unregenerate."[47]

His reviews, anthologized in several volumes, provided subsequent generations with an authoritative musical history of the period. Perhaps most pleasing to Thomson, publishers and conductors expressed a sudden interest in his music. "They used to know in advance that they did not want to encourage it," he wrote a friend a year after assuming his critic's post. "Now they know in advance they do. They still don't bother to read it."[48]

Before Thomson reached fifty, it appeared that he had achieved nearly everything he wanted, and at this midlife moment he came into Gertrude Stein's orbit one last time.

|||

In 1934, after their first meeting since the break, Virgil had written Chick Austin, "Gertrude and I have kissed, I wouldn't quite say made up, but kissed." Thomson wrote in retrospect that their quarrel had been "purely Parisian" and not worth keeping up, because "for both of us [it] had long since lost its savor." What he neglected to say was that the friendship, too, had lost its savor. Although Thomson frequently visited Paris in the late 1930s, he rarely saw Gertrude and Alice. Seven months after beginning his post at the *Herald Tribune*, he received a rare, warm letter from Stein: "And I am awfully pleased that success has come to you at last, you were always a believer in longevity, and I must say it is a pleasure, and I know you are liking it."[49] Then the onset of war restricted communication.

Shortly after the war ended, in 1945, Columbia University's Alice M. Ditson Fund for music provided an opportunity for Thomson and Stein to reconcile. Recalling *Four Saints*, the committee members proposed a joint commission for an opera: Thomson would be paid $1,000 for the score and Stein $500 for the libretto. Stein accepted the invitation without objecting to the unequal payment, and the stage was set for a virtual replay of their earlier collaboration. Stein again proposed George Washington as a subject, and again Thomson refused on the grounds that everyone in the eighteenth century had looked alike. Then Stein selected as a protagonist another strong, tenacious woman who had been revolutionary and reviled in her lifetime: the late-nineteenth-century suffragist Susan B. Anthony. Honoring both Anthony and herself, she called the opera *The Mother of Us All*. In the fall of 1945, when Thomson read the first two scenes, he was heartened by Gertrude's transparent identification with the heroine: "When she showed her in a scene of domesticity that might as well have been herself and Alice Toklas conversing about Gertrude's career, I knew that she had got inside the theme and that the work would now be moving rapidly."

Stein, at seventy-two, suffered from fatigue during the fall and winter, but she was buoyed by enthusiasm for *The Mother of Us All* and its inspiring heroine: "I think I did make her quite magnificent." When Thomson received Stein's libretto in late March, he called it "sensationally handsome" and thankfully much easier to dramatize than *Four Saints*. (Since Stein and Thomson had both been so pleased with Maurice Grosser's earlier opera scenario, they again invited him to join the team.) Serving as the opera's narrator, analogous to *Four Saints'* Compère, was a character called Virgil T.

In May 1946, Thomson sailed to Paris, where he threw a dinner party for Gertrude and Alice. In honor of their renewed friendship, he served a jugged hare and a fine bottle of Château Lafitte. Carried away by his high spirits, he jokingly needled Gertrude, but he had miscalculated the fragility of the relationship; Alice jumped in protectively, warning that Gertrude might cry if he teased her. Stein subsequently sought to remove the character of "Virgil T." from the opera. Although Carl Van Vechten persuaded her to restore "Virgil T.," the threat of excommunication continued until the end.

During the final months of her life, Gertrude Stein tied up all loose ends. Picasso's *Portrait of Gertrude Stein* was willed to the Metropolitan Museum of Art.[50] She arranged with librarian Donald Gallup for the rest of her papers to go to Yale University, and she spent part of the winter destroying the materials she did not want to survive. With Carl Van Vechten she had planned an edition of her selected writings, and a month before her death she wrote the "Message from Gertrude Stein" that would introduce it. She appointed Carl Van Vechten to publish her unpublished writings after her death and allotted sufficient money to arrange that.

Gertrude Stein died at 6:30 P.M. on Saturday, July 27, 1946, and was buried in a double grave in Père-Lachaise Cemetery, the burial ground for renowned French cultural figures.[51] The stone was simply inscribed with Gertrude's name and dates on the front, and twenty-one years later, when Alice Toklas died, her name was inscribed on the back.

Two months after Stein's death, Virgil Thomson began composing *The Mother of Us All*, and two months later he had set seven of the opera's eight scenes. The opera's setting in rural nineteenth-century America allowed him to draw from the wellspring of his childhood musical repertory in Missouri, and he incorporated gospel hymns and sentimental ballads, stately waltzes and vigorous marches. Thomson described his musical vocabulary as "the basic idiom of our country because they are the oldest vernacular still remembered here and used."[52]

Before tackling the opera's final scene—an epilogue featuring Susan

B. Anthony immortalized as a marble bust, singing on a pedestal from be-yond the grave—Thomson summoned up Gertrude Stein for one final evocation. On the printed page Susan B. Anthony's last speech echoed Stein's own final concerns:

> In my long life of effort and strife. . . . Life is strife, I was a martyr
> all my life not to what I won but to what was done. Do you know
> because I tell you so, or do you know, do you know. In my long
> life, my long life.

The words became immeasurably moving when set to Thomson's music. Limpid, plaintive, affirming, and intense, the last notes stretch out so long that the listener palpably feels Thomson's reluctance to let the heroine go.

In music and words, Thomson at last achieved his reconciliation with Stein. The competitiveness and rivalry, the quarrels and nit-picking negotiations paled in comparison with Thomson's indelible memory of Stein's revolutionary impact, both on him and on the American lan-guage.[53]

Thomson would live forty-three more years, and into his nineties he continued writing, composing, lecturing, and tidying up his own promi-nent place in the history of the twentieth century. *Four Saints in Three Acts* remained one of the last things he still enjoyed remembering. "I am sorry now that I did not write an opera with her every year," Thomson observed. "It had not occurred to me that both of us would not always be living."[54]

For each chapter, the most-used sources are given at the beginning, and quotations from those sources are not individually cited, whereas other sources are. When a source is cited in short form in the notes, it can be found cited in full in the bibliography. Unless specified otherwise, the Virgil Thomson Collection refers to his collection at the Yale University Music Library.

PROLOGUE: INTRODUCING *FOUR SAINTS IN THREE ACTS*

The primary sources include the author's interviews with Virgil Thomson and the book *Virgil Thomson* by Virgil Thomson.

1. Constance Askew to Virgil Thomson, n.d. (ca. 1948), Virgil Thomson Collection.
2. John Houseman, interview with the author, March 27, 1987, New York.
3. Lloyd Goodrich, *The Nation*, December 4, 1929, p. 665.
4. Lucius Beebe, "Foreword," *Snoot If You Must*, p. x.

CHAPTER 1: THE WORLD OF 27, RUE DE FLEURUS

The primary sources include the author's interviews with Virgil Thomson. Primary source publications are: *Charmed Circle: Gertrude Stein & Company* by James Mellow; *The Third Rose: Gertrude Stein and Her World* by John Malcolm Brinnin; *Sister Brother: Gertrude and Leo Stein* by Brenda Wineapple; *Confessions of Another Young Man* by Bravig Imbs; *Virgil Thomson* by Virgil Thomson; *The Flowers of Friendship: Letters Written to Gertrude Stein*, edited by Donald Gallup; *The Autobiography of Alice B. Toklas* by Gertrude Stein; *The Biography of Alice B. Toklas* by Linda Simon; *Gertrude Stein Remembered*, edited by Linda Simon.

1. Scofield Thayer in *Hemingway*, p. 156.
2. Thomson in Brendan Gill, *A New York Life*, p. 290.
3. Untitled newspaper article, n.d., enclosed in Alice Edwards to Thomson, n.d., Thomson Collection; Auden's description comes from Irving Drutman, *Good Company: A Memoir, Mostly Theatrical* (Boston: Little, Brown and Company, 1976).
4. Samuel L. Barlow, "American Composers, XVII: Virgil Thomson," *Modern Music*, May–June 1941, p. 243.
5. Donald Sutherland, "Alice and Gertrude and Others," *Prairie Schooner*, Winter 1971–72, vol. 45, No. 4, p. 297.
6. Janet Flanner to Virgil Thomson, n.d., Virgil Thomson Collection.
7. Stein to Thomson, February 11, 1938, Virgil Thomson Collection.
8. Mabel Dodge, "Speculations or Post-Impressionism in Prose," *Arts and Decoration*, 3 (March 1913), p. 173.
9. *Chicago Tribune*, February 8, 1913.

10. Robert Coates to Stein, January 24, 1930, in Gallup, *Flowers of Friendship*, p. 242.

11. Carl Van Vechten, in unsigned article, "America Has Literature, Says Tourist Van Vechten," *New York Herald*, Paris edition, September 28, 1928, p. 11; in Burns, ed., *Letters of Gertrude Stein and Carl Van Vechten*, p. 170.

12. Louis Bromfield, "Gertrude Stein, Experimenter with Words," *New York Herald Tribune*, September 3, 1933.

13. Born in San Francisco in 1877, Alice had experienced the privileges of an up-wardly mobile Jewish family: she had traveled to Europe, taken piano lessons, and attended operas. She never enjoyed dolls but was drawn to collecting but-tons, smelling the scents of her mother's flower garden, and tasting the flavors of her mother's cooking. When she reached the age of eighteen, her mother fell ill and died two years later. At the moment when Alice would normally have made her debut in society, she instead became the dutiful housekeeper for her grandfa-ther, father, and brother. She attended concerts and studied to become a pianist, but after performing in two recitals, she judged her talent to be commonplace and gave up her music career. She saw no marital possibilities, although she had demonstrated the domestic expertise that would have been attractive in a wife at the turn of the century. She deflected the interest of potential suitors.

14. Leo Stein to Mabel Weeks, June 1, 1920; quoted in Wineapple, *Sister Brother*, p. 297. Leo's other observations of Alice in the same letter: "She's a sort of all-im-portant second fiddle. She did play first fiddle to Annette [Rosenshine] but I reckon she did it rather badly. Playing second fiddle to Nelly & Harriet, and above all to Gertrude has been her star role. . . . She's capable of great kindliness & great cruelty—because she's really indifferent to everything except her own sat-isfactions. Within her sphere & limits being nice is far more effective & gives more scope than not being so. There's something of Becky Sharp if you can imag-ine, an introverted Becky, i.e. Becky no longer ambitious or keen."

15. Stein, in *Journals of Thornton Wilder 1939–1961*, ed. Donald Gallup (New Haven: Yale University Press, 1985), p. 45.

16. Stein, *Everybody's Autobiography*, p. 119.

CHAPTER 2: VIRGIL THOMSON: ROOTS IN TIME AND PLACE

The primary sources for this chapter include the author's interview with Virgil Thom-son. Primary source publications are: *The Selected Letters of Virgil Thomson*, edited by Tim Page and Vanessa Weeks Page; *Virgil Thomson* by Virgil Thomson; and *Composer on the Aisle* by Anthony Tommasini.

1. Gertrude Stein, "To Virgil and Eugene," in *Painted Lace and other Pieces* (New Haven: Yale University Press, 1955), p. 310.

2. Thomson, "A Conversation with Virgil Thomson" (conducted by John Rock-well), *Parnassus*, Spring–Summer 1977, p. 423.

3. Peggy Glanville-Hicks to Thomson, n.d., Ms. 29A, Virgil Thomson Collection.

4. Thomson, quoted in Geneve Lichtenwalter to Kathleen Hoover, October 1948, Virgil Thomson Collection.

5. Alice Smith Edwards, "Concerning Virgil Thomson, Composer and Author," 1949–50, unpublished manuscript, Virgil Thomson Collection.

6. Alice Smith Edwards, a classmate and friend, recalled asking him what he would do if he should happen to discover a fault within himself. "He thought a minute, and then he reached up and pulled out quite a sizable tuft of his silky reddish-gold

hair—I'll bet he'd give a lot for that tuft now—and holding it at arms' length, he dropped it dramatically, just where a draft caught it and blew it down the hall. Then he wiped his fingers, daintily and with an air of utter finality. The gesture was typical and quite unforgettable." (Edwards, "Concerning Virgil Thomson, Composer and Author.")

7. Thomson to May Thomson, October 23, 1917, Virgil Thomson Collection.
8. Thomson, "Maxims of a Modernist" (1921–1922), Butler Rare Book and Manuscripts Room, Columbia University.
9. Ibid.
10. Thomson to Briggs Buchanan, December 1923, Virgil Thomson Collection.
11. Thomson, "Maxims of a Modernist."
12. Grosser's unpublished memoir, n.p., collection Louis Rispoli.
13. Virgil Thomson, "The Greatest Music Teacher—at 75," *The New York Times Magazine*, February 4, 1962, p. 24.
14. When Thomson read this passage in Grosser's unpublished memoir, he ordered Grosser to strike it out; after Thomson's death, Anthony Tommasini published it in his biography *Virgil Thomson: Composer on the Aisle*, p. 149.
15. Antheil to Kathleen Hoover, April 4, 1949, Virgil Thomson Collection.

CHAPTER 3: VIRGIL AND GERTRUDE WRITE AN OPERA
Primary sources include the author's interviews with Virgil Thomson. Primary source publications are: *The Selected Letters of Virgil Thomson*, edited by Tim Page and Vanessa Weeks Page; *Virgil Thomson* by Virgil Thomson; *Virgil Thomson: Composer on the Aisle* by Anthony Tommasini; *The Autobiography of Alice B. Toklas* by Gertrude Stein; *Confessions of Another Young Man* by Bravig Imbs; *The Third Rose: Gertrude Stein and Her World* by John Malcolm Brinnin; *Words with Music* by Virgil Thomson; *Parnassus*, Spring–Summer 1977.

1. Thomson to Briggs Buchanan, December 27, 1926, Virgil Thomson Collection.
2. Thomson to Stein and Toklas, January 1, 1927, Gertrude Stein Collection.
3. Hemingway to W. G. Rogers, July 29, 1948, in *Ernest Hemingway: Selected Letters, 1917–1961*, ed. Carlos Baker (New York: Charles Scribner's Sons, 1981), p. 650.
4. *Ernest Hemingway: Selected Letters, 1917–1961*, p. 650.
5. Stein, "A Diary," in *Alphabets and Birthdays*, pp. 203, 214.
6. Stein, "Regular Regularly in Narrative," in Stein, *How to Write*, p. 244. I thank Ulla Dydo for bringing this to my attention; see "The Company of Saints," unpublished ms., collection Ulla Dydo.
7. Virgil Thomson, interview with John Gruen, November 6, 1977, Oral History Project, New York Public Library, Dance Collection.
8. Toklas to Minna Curtiss, June 18, 1949, in *Staying on Alone*, pp. 168–9.
9. Stein, in *Journals of Thornton Wilder*, p. 116.
10. Thomson to Stein, April 1927, Gertrude Stein Collection.
11. Thomson's recollections in an interview with the author: "All good things come in pairs: Harvard and Yale, Christians and Jews, Republicans and Democrats, men and women, Macy's and Bloomingdale's, Catholics and Protestants. Like two sides of the same coin. You can treat them as a war between the sexes, or you can show them as at peace between the sexes. But they are still two kinds of things."
12. Stein, "Regular Regularly in Narrative," in *How to Write*, p. 225 (Dover edition).
13. My discussion of Stein's method of creating *Four Saints* relies on the scholarship

of Bonnie Marranca ("Presence of Mind," in *Ecologies of Theater: Essays at the Century's Turning* [Baltimore: Johns Hopkins Press, 1996]); Jane Bowers ("The Writer in the Theater: Gertrude Stein's *Four Saints in Three Acts*," in Michael Hoffman, ed., *Critical Essays on Gertrude Stein* [Boston: G. K. Hall, 1986]); and Ulla Dydo ("The Company of Saints," unpublished ms., collection Ulla Dydo).

14. Stein, "Plays," in *Lectures in America*, p. 112.
15. Ibid., pp. 128–9.
16. Stein, *Four Saints in Three Acts*, in Van Vechten, ed., *The Selected Writings of Gertrude Stein*, p. 585.
17. Thomson to Stein, June 17, 1927, Gertrude Stein Collection.
18. Thomson to Stein, June 20, 1927, Gertrude Stein Collection.
19. Thomson to Stein, June 17, 1927, Gertrude Stein Collection.
20. Stein to Thomson, May 20, 1927, Virgil Thomson Collection.
21. Thomson to Charles Cochran, January 29, 1932, Virgil Thomson Collection.
22. Stein, radio interview, November 12, 1934, printed in "A Radio Interview," *Paris Review*, Fall 1990, p. 95.
23. Ulla Dydo, "The Company of Saints," unpublished ms., collection Ulla Dydo.
24. Wilson, quoted in Bonnie Marranca, *Ecologies of Theater*, p. 12.
25. For example, responding to Anthony Tommasini's questions on April 29, 1983, he wrote, "I have never been able to make much out of my portrait by GS. Have been looking at it lately with some intensity. So has Maurice [Grosser]. Neither of us can get very far. It is grand, but terribly dense. Do let me know what you make of it" (in Tommasini, *Virgil Thomson's Musical Portraits*, p. 10).
26. Thomson to Stein, September 1927, Gertrude Stein Collection.
27. Thomson, *Music and Words*, p. 51.
28. Ward, Kelly Mac, "An Analysis of the Relationships Between Text and Musical Shape and an Investigation of the Relationship Between the Text and Surface Rhythmic Detail of 'Four Saints in Three Acts' by Virgil Thomson," Ph.D. dissertation, University of Texas, Austin, 1978, p. 346.
29. Mrs. Chester Lasell was the mother of Hildegarde Watson, the wife of Sibley Watson, who was the copublisher of the *Dial*. Mrs. Lasell was grateful to Thomson for providing a medical referral in the summer of 1927; for the next three years she sent him $125 a month.
30. Stein to Van Vechten, January 13, 1928, in *The Letters of Gertrude Stein and Carl Van Vechten*, p. 159.
31. Thomson to Stein, June 17, 1928, Gertrude Stein Collection.
32. Thomson to Stein, July 2, 1928, Gertrude Stein Collection.
33. Thomson in Gill, *A New York Life*, p. 290.

CHAPTER 4: A TRANSATLANTIC LOVE AFFAIR

The primary sources include the author's interviews with Virgil Thomson. Primary source publications are: *New York 1930* by Paul Morand; *The Selected Letters of Virgil Thomson*, edited by Tim Page and Vanessa Weeks Page; *Virgil Thomson* by Virgil Thomson; *The Correspondence of Gertrude Stein and Carl Van Vechten*, edited by Edward Burns; *Virgil Thomson: Composer on the Aisle* by Anthony Tommasini; *Four Lives in Paris*, by Hugh Ford.

1. Advertisement for Goodrich tires, *Vanity Fair*, January 1929.
2. Stein, "An American in France," *What Are Masterpieces* (Los Angeles: The Conference Press, 1940), pp. 62–63.

3. Fitzgerald, "My Lost City," in *The Bodley Head Fitzgerald*, p. 25.

4. Malcolm Cowley, *Exile's Return*, p. 119.

5. Arthur Cravan (signed Fabian Lloyd), "To Be or Not to Be . . . American," *L'Écho des Sports*, June 10, 1909, translation by Terry Hale, in *Four Dada Suicides: Selected Texts of Arthur Cravan, Jacques Rigaut, Julien Torma, and Jacques Vaché*, introduced by Roger Conover, Terry Hale, and Paul Lenti (London: Atlas Press, 1995), p. 34.

6. Le Corbusier, quoted in Reyner Banham, *A Concrete Atlantis: United States Industrial Building and European Modern Architecture 1900–1925* (Cambridge, Massachusetts: MIT Press, 1986), p. 228.

7. American Waldo Frank gave expression to the same sentiment in *Our America*: "We are perhaps the only nationally vulgar people. And therein dwells not alone our predicament but our hope" (Frank, *Our America* [New York: Boni and Liveright, 1919], p. 171).

8. Other examples: In 1924, Diaghilev commissioned John Alden Carpenter to compose a ballet score, *Skyscrapers*, evoking New York's verticality and urban energy. Also in 1924, the Ballets Suédois commissioned Edmund Wilson to write a ballet scenario that would involve Charlie Chaplin, a Negro comedian, a movie machine, typewriters, a radio, and a jazz band. George Antheil claimed that his opera *Transatlantic* would be the first "to put America in a grand simple melodic line," and "certainly the first to use a typical American jazz in an American way" (in Ford, *Four in Paris*, p. 63). His virtual identification of "American" and "jazz" was characteristic of the period; when Aaron Copland composed his first self-consciously American piece in 1926, he automatically chose to employ a jazz idiom; Antheil's mixture onstage typified the transatlantic genre: gangsters, the Bowery, a Childs restaurant, the Brooklyn Bridge, newspaper bulletins, moving elevators, and revolving doors. Instruments included banjos and pianos muted by newspaper, and the dominant jazz idiom mixed with burlesque tunes, telephone bells, and typewriter keys. Everything happened simultaneously and loudly, crosscutting in a cinematic fashion that was the most American element of all. Ezra Pound called it a milestone along the "American road."

9. Murphy, quoted in William Rubin, *The Paintings of Gerald Murphy* (New York: Museum of Modern Art, 1974), p. 29, from *New York Herald*, Paris edition, October 25, 1923.

10. Briggs Buchanan wrote Virgil Thomson about the crowd at the New York premiere: "Artists with long curly hair (dirty) and open blue shirts (also dirty); 'debs,' slim and sarcastic; handsome Jews and fragile Puritans; gorgeous Negroes, gay and gaudy; Chinese, ageless and beautiful; misceganetic dream. In Paris one counts Princesses; in New York races" (Buchanan to Thomson, April 11, 1927; Virgil Thomson Collection, Yale Music Library).

11. Charles Prager, "A Riot of Music," *New York Herald Tribune*, April 10, 1927.

12. Flanner in Ford, *Four in Paris*, p. 37.

13. Toklas, *Staying on Alone*, p. 88.

14. Gertrude Stein, *Narration* (Chicago: University of Chicago Press, 1935), p. 7.

15. Stein, "A Radio Interview," November 12, 1934; reprinted (ed. Stephen Meyer) in *Paris Review*, Fall 1990, p. 93.

16. Stein, *Lectures in America*, p. 161.

17. Thomson, *Words with Music*, pp. 52–53.

CHAPTER 5: VIRGIL THOMSON VISITS AMERICA

The primary sources include the author's interviews with Virgil Thomson, and published sources include *Virgil Thomson* by Virgil Thomson, *Composer on the Aisle* by Anthony Tommasini, and *Florine Stettheimer* by Parker Tyler.

1. Thomson to Stein, December 2, 1928; Gertrude Stein Collection.
2. Carl Van Vechten, *Parties* (New York: Alfred A. Knopf, 1930), p. 123.
3. Thomson, "Home Thoughts," *Modern Music*, January–February 1933, p. 108.
4. Coates to Stein, October 11, 1927, Gertrude Stein Collection.
5. All citations of the portrait in Gertrude Stein, "Portrait of Virgil Thomson," *Four Saints in Three Acts* program.
6. Thomson to Stein, February 12, 1929, Gertrude Stein Collection.
7. Van Vechten to Muriel Draper, n.d. (ca. February, 1929), Muriel Draper Collection.
8. Max Ewing to his parents, February 1929, Max Ewing Collection.
9. Geraldyn Dismond, "Social Snapshots," *The Inter-State Tattler*, February 22, 1929.
10. Stein, in Janet Hobhouse, *Everybody Who Was Anybody* (New York: G.P. Putnam's Sons, 1975), p. 144.
11. Bloemink, *Florine Stettheimer*, p. 155.
12. Van Vechten, in Steven Watson, *Strange Bedfellows*, p. 253.
13. Thomson to Stein, February 26, 1929, Gertrude Stein Collection.
14. "Le Berceau de Gertrude Stein, ou Le Mystère de la rue de Fleurus," text by Georges Hugnet, music by Thomson (New York: Southern Music Publishing Inc., 1979).
15. Henry McBride to Stein, May 10, 1929, Henry McBride Collection.
16. Stein to Thomson, May 22, 1929, Virgil Thomson Collection.
17. Before he had even finished composing the opera, Thomson wrote on June 17, 1927, that "Bebe will do decors."
18. Charles Demuth, "Notes on F. ST.," Stettheimer Collection.
19. Florine Stettheimer diary, March 27, 1929, in Tyler, *Florine Stettheimer*, p. 47.
20. The other prominent transatlantic salon, organized by Walter and Louise Arensberg, was common ground for European expatriates associated with New York Dada, the poets associated with *Rogue* and *Others*, and American modernist painters. It operated from autumn of 1915 until about 1920.
21. Ettie Stettheimer journal, October 17, 1916, Stettheimer Collection, in Watson, *Strange Bedfellows*, p. 258.
22. McBride, *Florine Stettheimer*, p. 13.
23. Van Vechten to Thomson, March 29, 1929, Virgil Thomson Collection.
24. Thomson to Stein, March 21, 1929, Gertrude Stein Collection.
25. Thomson to Stein, January 7, 1929, Gertrude Stein Collection.
26. McBride to Stein, May 10, 1929, Henry McBride Collection.

CHAPTER 6: YOUNG HARVARD MODERNS

The primary sources include the author's interviews with David Austin, Sarah Austin, Florence Berkman, John Coolidge, Lincoln Kirstein, Philip Johnson, and Virgil Thomson. Primary source publications are: *Highbrow/Lowbrow: The Emergence of Cultural Hierarchy in America* by Lawrence W. Levine; *Mosaic: Memoirs* by Lincoln Kirstein; "Profiles: Conversations with Kirstein I and II," (conducted by W. McNeill

Lowry), *The New Yorker*, December 15 and December 22, 1986; *Memoir of an Art Gallery* by Julien Levy; *Good Old Modern: An Intimate Portrait of the Museum of Modern Art* by Russell Lynes; *Philip Johnson: Life and Work* by Franz Schulze; *Virgil Thomson* by Virgil Thomson; *A. Everett Austin Jr.: A Director's Taste and Achievement*, published by Wadsworth Atheneum; Julien Levy, interviewed by Paul Cummings, Archives of American Art; and an Oral History by Paul Sachs, Vols. 1 and 2.

1. Edwin Denby, best known as a dance critic, promoted the opera in Darmstadt, where he worked as a dancer and assistant *régisseur* at the Hessisches Landestheater, well known for producing avant-garde musical works by such composers as Ernst Krenek and Paul Hindemith and ballets by Erik Satie and Darius Milhaud. The plan to produce the opera in German was derailed in 1930 as the theater curtailed its production of modernist works. Elsa Maxwell had been engaged to promote hotels and theaters on the newly fashionable Côte d'Azur; although she proposed producing the opera in Monte Carlo in 1929, the plans never went far.
2. Thomas Surette (The Music Fund) to Virgil Thomson, May 18, 1931, Virgil Thomson Collection, Yale Music Library.
3. Henry McBride, "Four Saints for Artists," New York *Sun*, February 24, 1934.
4. Others who figured prominently included Jere Abbott, the associate director of the Museum of Modern Art, 1929–31, subsequently director of the Smith College museum; Agnes Mongan, who worked for Paul Sachs and became an important figure at the Fogg Museum; John McAndrew, who became the secretary at Julien Levy's gallery, taught at Vassar, and became curator of architecture and design at the Museum of Modern Art; Agnes Rindge, who chaired the Art Department at Vassar and became the acting director of the Museum of Modern Art during World War II; and Edward Warburg, one of the founders of the Harvard Society of Contemporary Art, who served on the Museum of Modern Art's Junior Advisory Committee and financially supported the School of American Ballet.
5. Kirstein, "Introduction" to Mitzi Berger Hamovitch, *The Hound & Horn Letters*, p. xii.
6. "Boston Is Modern Art Pauper," *Harvard Crimson*, October 30, 1926, reprinted in Barr, *Selected Writings*, p. 52.
7. "Boston Revolt," *The Art Digest*, September 1928, in Nicholas Fox Weber, *Patron Saints*, p. 3.
8. In addition to these was the Liberal Club, an on-campus organization for like-minded progressive students. Virgil Thomson met Maurice Grosser there; Philip Johnson was a member; and Lincoln Kirstein painted a mechanomorphic mural on its walls. Off campus, students found an intellectually stimulating environment at the Dunster House bookstore, whose regulars included Conrad Aiken, Archibald MacLeish, R. P. Blackmur, Lincoln Kirstein, and John Wheelwright.
9. Henry James, "Charles Eliot Norton," in Leon Edel, *The American Essays of Henry James*, p. 121. Rossetti, in Charles Eliot Norton, *Letters* (Vol. 1), ed. Sara Norton and M. A. DeWolfe Howe (Boston: Houghton Mifflin, 1913), p. 207.
10. Van Wyck Brooks, *New England: Indian Summer 1865–1915* (New York: E. P. Dutton and Company, 1940), p. 40.
11. Sachs inspected the modern collection of Maurice Wertheim and James Loeb, who became Sachs's model of a scholar-patron. He was especially close to Felix Warburg, whom he called his "patron saint," Jacob Schiff, Lessing J. Rosenwald (founder of Sears, Roebuck), David Weill (collector and partner at Lazard

Frères), Philip Lehman, Frank Woolworth and his associate Seymour Knox, and Carle Dreyfus.

12. Charles C. Perkins, "American Art Museums," *North American Review*, Vol. III (July 1870), p. 8, cited in Neil Harris, "The Gilded Age Revisited: Boston and the Museum Movement," *American Quarterly*, Winter 1962, p. 533.

13. Coolidge, in *Avery Memorial*, Gaddis, ed., p. 65.

14. Francis Henry Taylor, *Babel's Tower, The Dilemma of the Modern Museum*, quoted in Dillion Ripley, *The Sacred Grove* (New York: Simon and Schuster, 1969), p. 72.

15. Fry, additional note to Lincoln Kirstein, "The Hound & Horn," *Harvard Advocate*, Vol. 121, No. 2 (Christmas 1934), p. 93.

16. Henry Marston, "Henry Marston's Journal," *The Hound & Horn*, Fall 1927, Vol. 1, No. 1, pp. 9–10.

17. "Conversations with Kirstein II" (conducted by W. McNeill Lowry), *The New Yorker*, December 22, 1986, p. 53.

18. The trustees included Paul Sachs and Edward Forbes of the Fogg; Philip Hofer, a bibliophile and collector of drawings; John Nicholas Brown of Providence, known at birth as "the richest baby in the world," a collector of drawings; Felix Warburg, collector, international banker, father of Eddie; Arthur Sachs, brother of Paul and a broker in the family firm; Arthur Pope, art history professor at Harvard; and Frank Crowninshield, editor of *Vanity Fair*.

19. Agnes Mongan's recollection in her interview with Robert Brown, Oral History Project of the Archives of American Art; interviews over the period June 19, 1979–July 17, 1987.

20. Harvard Society for Contemporary Art, first-year report, Archives of American Art.

21. Barr, application for a Carnegie Grant, January 4, 1927, in Roob, "A Chronicle of the Years 1902–1929," *The New Criterion*, Summer 1987, p. 12.

22. Schapiro, in *Alfred H. Barr, Jr.: A Memorial Tribute*, n.p.

23. Edward King to Margaret Barr, August 30, 1981, roll 3145, Museum of Modern Art Archives.

24. Marga Barr, "The Art World," *The New Yorker*, November 16, 1981, p. 184.

25. Abbott to Marga Barr, July 10, 1981, MoMA Archive, roll 3262, frame 1159, in Barr and Roob, "Our Campaigns," *The New Criterion*, Summer 1987, p. 12.

26. Barr, "A New Art Museum," in Barr, *Defining Modern Art*, p. 69.

27. Barr and Roob, "Our Campaigns," *The New Criterion*, Summer 1987, p. 19.

28. Barr, in Dwight MacDonald, "Profiles," *The New Yorker*, December 19, 1953, p. 42.

29. Hitchcock, "Modern Architecture—A Memoir," *Journal of the Society of Architectural Historians*, Vol. 37, No. 4 (December 1968), p. 227.

30. Philip Johnson, introduction to *In Search of Modern Architecture: A Tribute to Henry-Russell Hitchcock*, ed. Helen Searing (Cambridge, Massachusetts, 1982), p. vii.

31. Hitchcock, "Movie Magazines," *The Hound & Horn*, September 1928, p. 97.

32. Hitchcock to Thomson, April 25, 1928, Virgil Thomson Collection. In the late 1920s, Hitchcock wrote an (unpublished) autobiographical novel called "Passion Is Not All" describing "the achievement of a balance between passion and intelligence."

33. Hitchcock, "The Decline of Architecture," *The Hound & Horn*, September 1927, p. 30.

34. Hitchcock to Alfred Barr and Jere Abbott, April 18, 1928, MoMA Archives.

35. Smith was one of America's first modernist architects: he traveled to Paris in 1927 to work in the office of André Lurçat, and his early designs for houses demonstrated enormous promise. Smith died the next year at the age of twenty-six, and Hitchcock's letters made clear his deep feelings for the young man. Around the time of Smith's death, Hitchcock failed his doctoral exams in art history at Harvard and also shifted his attention to modernist architecture.

36. Hitchcock, "The Decline of Architecture," p. 31.

37. Hitchcock, "Four Harvard Architects," *The Hound & Horn*, September 1928, p. 47.

38. Barr, "Modern Architecture," *The Hound & Horn*, April–June 1930, p. 431.

39. Johnson in Calvin Tomkins, "Forms Under Light," *New Yorker*, May 23, 1977, p. 47.

40. Hitchcock, "The Architectural World of J. J. P. Oud," *The Arts*, February 1928, p. 97.

41. "Conversations with Kirstein II" (conducted by W. McNeill Lowry), *The New Yorker*, December 22, 1986, p. 50.

42. Kirstein: "A Memoir: The Education," *Raritan*, Vol. 2, No. 3 (Winter 1983), p. 35.

43. Ibid., p. 42.

44. Kirstein, "Loomis: A Memoir," *Raritan*, Vol. 2, No. 1 (Summer 1982), p. 35.

45. Kirstein was not alone in these enterprises; Varian Fry helped found *The Hound & Horn* and Edward Warburg and John Walker were cofounders of the Society for Contemporary Art. Kirstein's was the initiating energy.

46. Kirstein, "A Memoir: At the Prieure des Basses Loges, Fontainebleau," *Raritan*, Vol. 2, No. 2 (Fall 1982), p. 48.

47. Ibid., p. 49.

48. Kirstein, "The Education," *Raritan*, Vol. 2, No. 3 (Winter 1983), p. 28.

49. Kirstein, *The New York City Ballet*, p. 16.

50. Austin in "Austin's Work Is on Exhibition," *Hartford Times*, February 11, 1932.

51. Edward Forbes to Charles Goodwin, January 19, 1927, in *Avery Memorial, Wadsworth Atheneum: The First Modern Museum*, p. 40.

52. Austin, *Hartford Times*, March 17, 1928.

53. Austin in Wadsworth Atheneum Archives.

54. Paris dealer René Gimpel's contemporary assessment of Austin's success, although inaccurate, suggests how the Venetian fete was perceived: "He [Austin] is about twenty-four and has been at the museum one year. The town was asleep, his youth and intelligence have conquered all hearts, and he has made the money flow in torrentially. He has obtained about $600,000 for a museum which had nothing. How has he brought about this miracle? By giving a ball in the museum. Everyone enjoyed it and after all they swore by him. Who can say what future may be in store for this institution, thanks to this Don Juan friend of the great masters." (From Michael Fitzgerald, *Making Modernism: Picasso and the Creation of the Market for Twentieth Century Art* (New York: Farrar, Straus and Giroux, 1995), pp. 217–18.)

55. Wadsworth Atheneum Archives, Wadsworth Atheneum.

56. Exhibitions included "Modern French Painting," "Modern Mexican Art," "Modern German Art," and "The Watercolors of Edward Hopper," and they all predated the founding of the Museum of Modern Art.

57. Thomson to Stein, April 15, 1946; Gertrude Stein Collection.

CHAPTER 7: A PERSONAL BREAK, A COMMERCIAL BREAKTHROUGH

The primary source publications are: *The Correspondence of Gertrude Stein and Carl Van Vechten*, edited by Edward Burns; *The Flowers of Friendship: Letters Written to Gertrude Stein*, edited by Donald Gallup; *Charmed Circle: Gertrude Stein & Company* by James Mellow; *The Autobiography of Alice B. Toklas* by Gertrude Stein; *Virgil Thomson* by Virgil Thomson; *Sister Brother: Gertrude and Leo Stein* by Brenda Wineapple; and *Stanzas and Meditation*, in Gertrude Stein, *Writings 1932–1946* (New York: The Library of America, 1998), pp. 1–145.

1. Stein to Thomson, October 26, 1927, Gertrude Stein Collection.
2. Parker Tyler, *The Divine Comedy of Pavel Tchelitchew: A Biography* (New York: Fleet Publishing Co., 1967), p. 347.
3. Stein to Thomson, March 19, 1930, Thomson Collection.
4. Stein to Thomson, September 28, 1928, Thomson Collection.
5. Hugnet's preface to *Morceaux Choisis de la Fabrication des Americains*, quoted and translated in Ulla Dydo, "Landscape Is Not Grammar: Gertrude Stein in 1928," *Raritan*, Vol. 7, No. 1 (Summer 1987), p. 107.
6. Stein to Thomson, April 16, 1930, in Tommasini, *Composer on the Aisle*, p. 212.
7. Stein, "George Hugnet" in Ulla Dydo, *Stein Reader*, p. 540.
8. Gertrude Stein, *Narration: Four Lectures by Gertrude Stein* (Chicago: University of Chicago Press, 1935), p. 51.
9. Stein to Thomson, October 21, 1930, Thomson Collection.
10. Stein to Hugnet, December 17, 1930, Gertrude Stein Collection.
11 Thomson, "Wickedly Wonderful Widow," *The New York Review of Books*, March 7, 1974, p. 14.
12. Thomson to Stein, December, n.d. (1930), in Tommasini, *Composer on the Aisle*, p. 214.
13. Stein to Thomson, December 16, 1930, Virgil Thomson Collection.
14. Toklas to Thomson, n.d. (ca. December 1930), Gertrude Stein Collection.
15. Stein to Thomson, December 26, 1930, Virgil Thomson Collection.
16. Toklas to Thomson, n.d. (ca. December 1930), Gertrude Stein Collection.
17. Imbs, *Confessions of Another Young Man*, p. 298.
18. Stein, "Left to Right," *Story*, November 1933, p. 20.
19. Plain Editions publications: *Lucy Church Amiably* (1930), *Before the Flowers of Friendship Faded Friendship Faded* (1931), *How to Write* (1931), *Operas and Plays* (1932), and *Matisse Picasso and Gertrude Stein, with Two Shorter Stories* (1933).
20. Among those who published Stein: Leonard and Virginia Woolf's Hogarth Press published *Composition as Explanation* in 1926, Laura Riding and Robert Graves's Seizin Press published *An Acquaintance with Description* in 1929.
21. Stein, *The Making of Americans*, p. 261, in Van Vechten, ed. *Selected Writings*.
22. Stein, "Here. Actualities," Stein Collection, partially quoted in Ulla Dydo, "*Stanzas in Meditation*: The Other Autobiography" *Chicago Review*, Vol. 35, No. 2, p. 12.
23. Stein, *Selected Writings*, p. 207.
24. Maurice Grosser, "Visiting Gertrude and Alice," *The New York Review of Books*, November 6, 1986, p. 36.
25. Alice's editing includes, for example, crossing out the following material in ital-

ics: "It was over a thousand pages long and I was typewriting it *and I enjoyed every minute of it.*" (Bridgeman, *Stein in Pieces*, p. 213.) Also, "she handed him the manuscript ["Q.E.D"] and said to him, you read it. *When we return to Paris this autumn, I [Toklas] will read it.*"

CHAPTER 8: GROUP SNAPSHOT 1932: THE HARVARD MODERNS

The primary sources include the author's interviews with Philip Claflin, Henry-Russell Hitchcock, Philip Johnson, Lincoln Kirstein, and Virgil Thomson. Primary source publications are: *Mosaic: Memoirs* by Lincoln Kirstein; *Memoir of an Art Gallery* by Julien Levy; *Good Old Modern: An Intimate Portrait of the Museum of Modern Art* by Russell Lynes; *Alfred Barr: Missionary for the Modern* by Alice Goldfarb Marquis; *A. Everett Austin, Jr.: A Director's Taste and Achievement; Avery Memorial, Wadsworth Atheneum: The First Modern Museum*, edited by Eugene R. Gaddis; *Patron Saints: Five Rebels Who Opened America to a New Art 1928–1943* by Nicholas Fox Weber.

1. David Harris, "The Original *Four Saints in Three Acts*," *The Drama Review*, Vol. 26, No. 1 (Spring 1982), p. 111.
2. Toklas in Stein to Thomson, March 6, 1930, Stein Collection.
3. Grosser freely maintained that his scenario was arbitrary, but it served the music and words so well that it was employed not only for the first production but for most subsequent productions.
4. Interview with Philip Johnson, Museum of Modern Art Oral History Program, December 18, 1990, p. 37.
5. Johnson in Martha Delano, "Making Space for Modern Living," *House & Garden*, May 1934, p. 50.
6. Goodyear, quoted in Dwight MacDonald, "Action on West Fifty-third Street," *The New Yorker*, December 19, 1953, p. 36.
7. Terence Riley, *The International Style*, p. 65. Barr's installation of the ninety-eight works flouted traditional salon-style installation: he hung the pictures lower than usual, in a single row along the galleries' forty-seven running feet, fifty inches from the floor to the center of the picture, didactically installed by chronology or theme rather than size or symmetry.
8. M. P., "The Art Galleries," *The New Yorker*, November 30, 1929, p. 38.
9. Henry McBride, New York *Sun*, November 9, 1929.
10. Ralph Flint, "Concerning the French Invasion," New York *Sun*, November 16, 1929.
11. Barr, "A New Museum," *Vogue*, October 26, 1929.
12. Beaumont Newhall in Museum of Modern Art, *Alfred H. Barr, Jr.: A Memorial Tribute*, n.p.
13. Margaret Barr, "Oral History," Archives of American Art, p. 14. Key players from the Harvard family included Philip Johnson, Henry-Russell Hitchcock, Lincoln Kirstein, and Edward Warburg, along with unpaid assistant Cary Ross, dealer J. B. Neumann, and dynamo Nelson Rockefeller.
14. Johnson in Museum of Modern Art, *Alfred H. Barr, Jr.: A Memorial Tribute*, n.p.
15. *The Ink Well*, published by the Boys' Latin School, Baltimore; written on the occasion of Barr's graduation on June 7, 1918, cum laude, as head boy, quoted in Barr and Roob, "Our Campaigns," *The New Criterion*, Special Issue, Summer 1987.

16. Barr in Hitchcock and Johnson, *The International Style: Architecture Since 1922* (New York: W.W. Norton, 1932), p. 13.

17. Philip Johnson in Museum of Modern Art, *Alfred H. Barr, Jr.: A Memorial Tribute*, n.p.

18. Interview with Philip Johnson, Museum of Modern Art Oral History Program, December 18, 1990, p. 15.

19. Peter Eisenman summarizes this transformation in his introduction to Philip Johnson, *Selected Writings* (New York: Oxford University Press, 1979), p. 15.

20. Hitchcock and Johnson, *The International Style*, p. 68.

21. Levy to Alfred Stieglitz, September 11, 1931, in Maria Morris Hambourg, *The New Vision: Ford Motor Company Collection* (New York: Metropolitan Museum of Art, 1989), p. 283.

22. Levy to Loy, ca. December 1931; the Campigli show had been up for one week.

23. Other dealers who dealt in modern art at that time included Valentine Dudensing, Joseph Brummer (who showed Brancusi), and John Becker, a Harvard graduate who showed photographs in 1930 and provided a venue for some of the Harvard Society for Contemporary Art ventures. Although Stieglitz showed modern work at An American Place, he restricted his artists to his tight circle of six painters. Pierre Matisse opened his gallery in about 1935.

24. Virgil Thomson, "Julien Levy," unpublished manuscript, Virgil Thomson Collection.

25. The Harvard crew who bought works by the neo-Romantics included Virgil Thomson, Henry-Russell Hitchcock, Agnes Rindge, Chick Austin, Kirk Askew, and Lincoln Kirstein.

26. Maurice Grosser, interview with David Harris, October 24, 1981, courtesy David Harris.

27. Julien Levy worked with Lincoln Kirstein on the notorious 1932 show at the Museum of Modern Art, "Murals by American Painters and Photographers," which introduced photography to the Museum of Modern Art; Levy helped select the photographers.

28. The gallery's more peripheral associates were also valuable. Joseph Cornell trimmed the gallery's Christmas tree and Chick Austin (aka The Great Osram) was the resident magician. Even the gallery's first secretaries were distinguished: Levy's Harvard friend John McAndrew (who later became the architecture and design curator for the Museum of Modern Art), Allen Porter (who later became the Museum of Modern Art's secretary), and Eleanor Bunce (secretary of Chick Austin and Alfred Barr and wife of James Thrall Soby).

29. McBride, New York *Sun*, January 28, 1933.

30. *The Hound & Horn's* circulation reached four thousand at fifty cents an issue.

31. Edward Warburg, interview with David Sinkler, November 19, 1987, using Steven Watson's questions.

32. Paul Draper Jr., interview with the author, April 11, 1992.

33. Kirstein, *The New York City Ballet*, p. 16.

34. This was a common in-group expression, noted by both Agnes Mongan and Allen Porter, quoted in Gaddis, *Avery Memorial*, p. 39.

35. Barr to Austin, n.d. (ca. June 1944), Austin Collection.

36. A. E. Austin, "The Lifar Collection," *Wadsworth Atheneum Bulletin*, Vol. XII, No. 2 (October–December 1934), p. 8.

37. "He'd pick things up almost faster than I could say them," Philip Johnson recalled. Quoted in Gaddis, *Avery Memorial*, p. 66.

38. Information about the house is drawn from Eugene Gaddis, "Austin House Declared a National Landmark," *Wadsworth Atheneum Bulletin*, Autumn 1994, p. 1.

39. Press clippings, Wadsworth Atheneum Archives.

40. Austin, letter announcing event of Friends and Enemies of Modern Music, Wadsworth Atheneum Archive.

41. "The Friends and Enemies of Modern Music," Hartford program for *Four Saints in Three Acts*.

42. Benjamin Morris and Robert O'Conner, "Architecture and the Role of the Avery Memorial," *Wadsworth Atheneum Bulletin*, Vol. 12, No. 1 (January–March 1934), p. 10.

43. Austin, address to the trustees, ca. late 1932 or early 1933, A. E. Austin Jr. Collection, Wadsworth Atheneum Archives.

44. Mounting a Picasso retrospective was not so much pioneering as it was strategically difficult. Alfred Barr tried to mount a Picasso exhibition in 1932, but that fell apart for several reasons, chief among them that art dealers were influential in curating the exhibition, and Barr regarded it as a matter of principle to maintain complete curatorial independence from commerce. Chick Austin had fewer qualms about the overlap, and his Picasso exhibition was heavily influenced by Paul Rosenberg. A quarter of the works belonged to him, another quarter came from his scouting in Paris and New York. Only four works came from museums; for complete details, see Michael C. Fitzgerald, *Making Modernism: Picasso and the Creation of the Market for Twentieth Century Art* (New York: Farrar, Straus and Giroux, 1995).

CHAPTER 9: THE WORLD OF THE STETTHEIMERS

The primary sources include the author's interviews with Virgil Thomson. Primary source publications are: *The Life and Art of Florine Stettheimer* by Barbara Bloemink; *Florine Stettheimer: A Life in Art* by Parker Tyler.

1. McBride to Malcolm MacAdam, December 27, 1932, Henry McBride Collection.

2. Florine Stettheimer diary, n.d., Stettheimer Collection.

3. Florine Stettheimer in Marian Murray, "Artist Takes the Stage," *Hartford Times*, January 6, 1934.

4. The source of their money is not known; Thomson believed that the Stettheimers' older brother, Walter, who lived in Redwood City, California, and ran a successful clothing business, had settled enough money on his family that they could live comfortably. In 1922, the sisters' Uncle Sylvain left each of the daughters $10,000, and the Stettheimers invested money in the stock market. Alfred Cook, one of Ettie's former suitors, advised the sisters financially.

5. Their older sister, Stella, and older brother, Walter, escaped the enmeshed family by marrying and moving to San Francisco. The remaining three sisters traveled with their mother to Europe, where social embarrassment was avoided, living was cheaper, and social life with their German relatives was possible.

6. "I am tempted to confide to all interested that I look upon this production of Carrie's as a facile and more or less posthumous substitute for the work she was eminently fitted to adopt as a vocation, had circumstances been favorable: stage design. For stylistic presentation of drama and opera she had the necessary thorough knowledge of music and the visual arts, of architecture, decoration, furniture and costume—of cultural history in a word. Her acute sensitivity to

literature, her originality and wit would have provided freshness and individuality for the immediate visual impact that supplies the clarification or enhancement of dramatic content." (Ettie Stettheimer, "Introductory Foreword," *A Fabulous Dollhouse of the Twenties* [New York: Dover, 1976], p. 12.)

7. Ettie Stettheimer journal, December 5, 1916, Stettheimer Collection.
8. Ewing to his parents, November 18, 1929, Max Ewing Collection.
9. Florine Stettheimer diary, n.d. (1931), Stettheimer Collection.
10. Florine Stettheimer to McBride, August 17, 1932, Henry McBride Collection.
11. McBride to Florine Stettheimer, August 20, 1932, Stettheimer Collection.
12. Van Vechten, "The World of Florine Stettheimer," *Harper's Bazaar*, October 1946, p. 354.
13. McBride, "Artists in the Drawing Room," *Town and Country*, December 1946, p. 337.
14. Florine Stettheimer, *Crystal Flowers*, privately printed by Ettie Stettheimer (1949), p. 56. Although published as "Et Gertrude," Barbara Bloemink discovered that "St. Gertrude" was written in the original manuscript.
15. This is probably a coded reference to Thomson's attraction to black men.

CHAPTER 10: HIGH BOHEMIA AND MODERNISM
Primary sources include the author's interviews with Atwood Askew Allaire, James Amster, Pamela Askew, Paul Bowles, Philip Claflin, Paul Draper Jr., Emily Hahn, John Houseman, Robert Isaacson, Lincoln Kirstein, Philip Johnson, John Bernard Myers, Tonio Selwart, Virgil Thomson, and Edward Warburg. Primary source publications are: *Who Killed Society?* by Cleveland Amory; *Runthrough: A Memoir* by John Houseman; *Memoir of an Art Gallery* by Julien Levy; and *Virgil Thomson* by Virgil Thomson.

1. Clement Greenberg, "Avant-garde and Kitsch," *The Collected Essays and Criticism*, Vol. 1., ed. John O'Brian (Chicago: University of Chicago Press, 1986), p. 11.
2. Thomson to Stein, June 1927, Gertrude Stein Collection.
3. Astor in David Sinclair, *Dynasty: The Astors and Their Times*, (London: J. M. Dent & Sons, 1983), p. 196.
4. Richard Sherman, "Sophisticate 1933," *Vanity Fair*, October 1933, p. 62.
5. F. Scott Fitzgerald described that sea change in manners: "Then [ca. 1920], for just a moment, the 'younger generation' idea became a fusion of many elements in New York life. People of fifty might pretend there was still a four hundred, or Maxwell Bodenheim might pretend there was Bohemia worth its paint and pencils—but the blending of the bright, gay, vigorous elements began then, and for the first time there appeared a society a little livelier than the solid-mahogany dinner parties of Emily Price Post. If this society produced the cocktail party, it also involved Park Avenue wit." (Fitzgerald, "My Lost City," *The Bodley Head F. Scott Fitzgerald* [London: The Bodley Head, 1960], p. 25.)
6. Van Vechten, *Parties: Scenes from Contemporary New York Life* (New York, Alfred A. Knopf, 1930), p. 76.
7. As early as the 1910s, a sprinkling of gilt-edged society began to appear at avant-garde gatherings—notably Gertrude Vanderbilt Whitney and Robert Chanler, but they were artists and thereby exceptions. Their attendance was regarded—and reported in the newspapers—as a renegade act.
8. Three of the collaborators—Stein, Stettheimer, and Grosser—were Jewish. No Jews appeared on Ward McAllister's list of the Four Hundred, although he sug-

gested that "our good Jews might wish to put out a little book of their own." New York's Jewish community felt such an enterprise was unnecessary, and they considered, as one wrote, that Mrs. Astor's society "was based on publicity, showiness, cruelty, and striving." (Anonymous member of "Our Crowd"; quoted in Birmingham, *Our Crowd*, p. 271.)

9. Geoffrey Hellman, "Profiles," *The New Yorker*, November 27, 1942, p. 25.
10. "Luscious Lucius" was Walter Winchell's nickname; both are quoted from "Lucius Beebe: A Biographical Sketch," *The Lucius Beebe Reader*, ed. Charles Clegg and Duncan Emrich (Garden City, New York: Doubleday, 1967), p. 391.
11. Other regular high-bohemian gatherings included Carl Van Vechten and Fania Marinoff's mixed-race parties and Mrs. W. Murray Crane's elegant and earnest "general conversations" about topics of cultural interest, held at 820 Fifth Avenue.
12. Ewing to his mother, December 19, 1932, Max Ewing Collection.
13. Kirstein published sections of this in *The Hound & Horn*, January 1933. Draper hoped to publish it as a book, but this did not happen.
14. Draper, "America Deserta," Muriel Draper Collection.
15. Adapted from Richard Sherman, "Sophisticate 1933," *Vanity Fair*, October 1933, p. 42.
16. Anonymous to Draper, n.d., Muriel Draper Collection.
17. Maud in Max Ewing to his parents, January 1928, Max Ewing Collection.
18. Ewing to his mother, December 17, 1925, Max Ewing Collection.
19. Minna Kirstein Curtiss to Draper, n.d., Muriel Draper Collection.
20. Arne Ekstrom to Draper, n.d., Muriel Draper Collection.
21. Rascoe, "Contemporary Reminiscences," *Arts & Decoration*, n.d., clipping, Max Ewing Collection.
22. Minna Curtiss to Draper, n.d., Muriel Draper Collection.
23. Samuel Courtauld to Draper, August 5, 1927, Muriel Draper Collection.
24. Osbert Sitwell, "New York in the Twenties," *The Atlantic Monthly*, February 1962, p. 40.
25. Luhan, *European Experiences*, Vol. 2 of *Intimate Memories* (New York: Harcourt, Brace, 1936), p. 270.
26. *Town and Country*, n.d., clipping, Max Ewing Collection.
27. Draper to Luhan, June 27, 1933, Mabel Dodge Luhan Collection.
28. Ewing to his parents, April 1, 1931, Max Ewing Collection.
29. Ewing to his parents, June 3, 1925, Max Ewing Collection.
30. Tobey to Draper, n.d., Muriel Draper Collection.
31. Ewing to his parents, November 29, 1929, Max Ewing Collection.
32. Evans to Draper, n.d., Muriel Draper Collection.
33. Bowles, *Without Stopping*, p. 220.
34. Burra, *Well Dearie!*, p. 82.
35. David Richardson, interview with the author, November 22, 1992.
36. Elizabeth Hawes's attempt to establish American fashion that was not dependent on Paris was embodied in her ready-to-wear line, established in August 1933, which ranged in price from $15.75 to $29.50. "These clothes are for those special people who wail aloud in a world of diamond buttons for a good solid brass show hood . . . who prefer an innocent twist of yarn to a satin bow . . . who may want to be different but know that all good clothes are classic" (Hawes, *Fashion Is Spinach* [New York: Random House, 1938], p. 246).
37. McBride to Malcolm MacAdam, January 28, 1940, Henry McBride Collection.

38. Kirk Askew's talk on the occasion of Paul Sachs's seventieth birthday, Pamela Askew Collection.
39. Art historian Richard Offner introduced Constance Atwood to Arthur McComb, who was one of two members of Paul Sachs's first Museum Methods course. He organized America's first major exhibition of Baroque paintings and drawings at the Fogg Museum in January 1929, and in 1934 his book *The Baroque Painters of Italy: An Introductory Historical Survey* was published, influencing American taste for the Baroque. McComb was a guiding light for Chick Austin, and he fostered the taste for the art sold by Kirk Askew.
40. Emily Hahn, interview with the author, June 4, 1985, New York.
41. John Mosher, "The Gallantry of Mr. Land," *The New Yorker*, March 9, 1929.
42. Jane Bowles, in Christopher Sawyer-Laucanno, *The Invisible Spectator: A Biography of Paul Bowles* (New York: Weidenfeld and Nicolson, 1989), p. 206.
43. McBride to MacAdam, October 23, 1934, Henry McBride Collection.

CHAPTER 11: MODERNISM GOES UPTOWN

The primary sources include the author's interviews with Virgil Thomson, Philip Johnson, John Houseman, and Lincoln Kirstein. Primary source publications are: *Virgil Thomson* by Virgil Thomson; *Secret Muses* by Julie Kavanagh; *Keep A-Inchin Along: Selected Writings of Carl Van Vechten About Black Art and Letters* by Carl Van Vechten.

1. Kirstein, "Carl Van Vechten," in *By With To From: A Lincoln Kirstein Reader* (New York: Farrar, Straus & Giroux, 1991), p. 34.
2. Ewing to his parents, May 21, 1929, Max Ewing Collection.
3. Wallace Thurman, *Negro Life in New York's Harlem* (Girard, Kansas: Haldeman-Julius Publications, 1928), p. 17.
4. Seldes, quoted in Lewis Erenberg, *Steppin' Out: New York Nightlife and the Transformation of American Culture 1890–1930* (Westport, Conn.: Greenwood Books, 1981), p. 258.
5. Thomson to Briggs Buchanan, July 3, 1925, Virgil Thomson Collection.
6. Rosalyn M. Story, *And So I Sing: African American Divas of Opera and Concert*, pp. 185–88.
7. Van Vechten, "A Few Notes About Four Saints in Three Acts," introduction to Gertrude Stein, *Four Saints in Three Acts: An Opera to Be Sung* (New York: Random House, 1934), pp. 7–8.
8. Cole Porter's "Love for Sale" was considered too racy a song for a white performer, so it was given to a black actress dressed as a hooker.
9. A few black divas performed opera in the nineteenth century. Elizabeth Taylor Greenfield, "the Black Swan," debuted in 1851; Ann and Emma Hyers organized and sang in their own touring company from the 1870s to the 1890s; Mamie Flowers, "the Bronze Melba," performed in the 1890s; most prominently, Sissieretta Jones, "the Black Patti," sang on stage and in the White House. Others developed their own troupe (as did Sissieretta Jones with her Black Patti Troubadours) or presented their repertoire in concert halls (as did Elizabeth Taylor Greenfield and later Marian Anderson).
10. McBride on Lawrence Tibbett in *Emperor Jones*: "We never saw, at the Opera, such a display of flesh before. Chaliapin once stripped to the waist for such an infinitesimal loin-cloth. It was rather sensational to see Lawrence taking the curtain calls in a state of nature." (McBride to Malcolm MacAdams, January 22, 1933, Henry McBride Collection.)

11. Thomson, Waterbury *Republican*, January 28, 1934.
12. Johnson, quoted in Van Vechten to Stein, October 23, 1933; in *The Letters of Gertrude Stein and Carl Van Vechten*, p. 281.
13. Stein to Van Vechten, August 11, 1927, in *The Letters of Gertrude Stein and Carl Van Vechten*, pp. 152–53.
14. Stein, *Everybody's Autobiography*, p. 279.
15. Baker, in Phyllis Rose, *Jazz Cleopatra*, p. 81.
16. George Chester Morse, "The Fictitious Negro," *The Outlook and Independent*, August 21, 1929, p. 648.
17. Van Vechten, *Nigger Heaven* (New York: Alfred A. Knopf, 1926), p. 89.
18. Yvonne Davidson to Thomson, February 22, 1934, Virgil Thomson Collection.
19. Jacques-Emile Blanche, in Phyllis Rose, *Jazz Cleopatra*, p. 22.
20. Virgil Thomson, "Home Thoughts," *Modern Music*, January–March 1933, p. 109.
21. Calverton, *Anthology of American Negro Literature* (New York: Modern Library, 1929), p. 4.
22. Van Vechten also photographed African Americans, both clothed and nude. He compiled scrapbooks that included double-entendres about homosexuality; he ensured that both the nude photographs and scrapbooks were sealed until twenty-five years after his death.
23. Florine Stettheimer to Thomson, n.d. [ca. June 1933], Virgil Thomson Collection.
24. Stein, in Bradley to Thomson, May 15, 1933, Virgil Thomson Collection.

CHAPTER 12: NEGOTIATIONS AND EXCHANGES

The primary publication source is *Virgil Thomson* by Virgil Thomson.

1. Bradley to Thomson, January 23, 1933, Virgil Thomson Collection.
2. Thomson to Chick Austin, May 11, 1933, Austin Collection, Wadsworth Atheneum Archives.
3. Bradley to Stein, May 6, 1933, Gertrude Stein Collection.
4. Thomson to Bradley, May 6, 1933, Gertrude Stein Collection.
5. Bradley to Thomson, May 15, 1933, Gertrude Stein Collection.
6. Stein to Bradley, n.d., Gertrude Stein Collection.
7. Thomson to Bradley, February 16, 1934, Gertrude Stein Collection. YCAL or Music Box 83, Folder 1.

CHAPTER 13: SNAPSHOTS: SUMMER 1933

The primary sources include the author's interviews with Lincoln Kirstein and Virgil Thomson. Primary source publications are: *The Autobiography of Alice B. Toklas* by Gertrude Stein; "From the Early Diary" by Lincoln Kirstein, in *By With To & From: A Lincoln Kirstein Reader*, edited by Nicholas Jenkins; *Charmed Circle: Gertrude Stein and Company* by James Mellow; and *Virgil Thomson* by Virgil Thomson.

1. Brinnin, *The Third Rose*, p. 309.
2. Tristan Tzara, "Testimony Against Gertrude Stein," *transition*, February 1935, p. 13.
3. McBride to Stein, October 27, 1933; in *Flowers of Friendship*, pp. 270–71.
4. Chick Austin to Helen Austin, July 10, 1933, Wadsworth Atheneum Archives.
5. Chick Austin to Helen Austin, July 11, 1933, Wadsworth Atheneum Archives.

6. Balanchine's works for *Les Ballets 1933* were: *Mozartiana, Songes, Errante, The Seven Deadly Sins*. The season was funded by the eccentric patron of neo-Romanticism and Surrealism Edward James, largely as a gesture to win the love of his new ballerina wife, Tilly Losch.
7. Kirstein to Draper, June 11, 1933, Muriel Draper Collection.
8. Kirstein to Draper, July 13, 1933, Muriel Draper Collection.
9. Ibid.
10. Kirstein to Draper, July 18, 1933, Muriel Draper Collection.
11. Austin, in interview with Paul Cooley, November 1, 1974, in Gaddis, *Avery Memorial*, p. 67.
12. Austin to Kirstein, August 8, 1933, in Richard Buckle, *Balanchine*, p. 69.
13. Kirstein to Draper, August 4, 1933, Muriel Draper Collection.
14. Kirstein, in Tommasini, *Composer On the Aisle*, p. 240.
15. Maurice Grosser, unpublished memoir, n.p. (property of Louis Rispoli).
16. Van Vechten to Florine Stettheimer, August 7, 1933, Stettheimer Collection.
17. Thomson to Austin, July 7, 1933, Virgil Thomson Collection.
18. Thomson to Austin, n.d., Austin Collection.
19. Austin to Thomson, n.d., Virgil Thomson Collection.
20. Thomson to Aaron Copland, July 1933, Virgil Thomson Collection.
21. Thomson to Austin, July 7, 1933, Austin Collection.
22. The initial contributors to the School of American Ballet were: Lincoln Kirstein ($2,000), Edward Warburg ($1,000), Philip Johnson ($500), James Soby ($500), Paul Cooley ($500), Jere Abbott ($200), Chick Austin ($100), Tom Howard ($100) Cary Ross ($50), the Askews ($50), Lucy Goodwin ($50), Mrs. A. E. Austin, Sr. ($25), Josiah Marvell ($25), Drew Bear ($20).
23. Marian Murray, "Plan Ballet School at Morgan Memorial," *Hartford Times*, October 17, 1933.
24. Austin, in Marian Murray, "Plan Ballet School at Morgan Memorial," *Hartford Times*, October 17, 1933.
25. Kirstein, *The New York City Ballet*, p. 21.
26. Kirstein to Austin, n.d., Austin Collection.
27. Austin to Thomson, March 18, 1952, Thomson Collection.
28. Barr to Austin, January 18, 1933, Austin Collection.
29. Austin to Stein, 1933, Austin Collection.

CHAPTER 14: COLLABORATORS: NOT THE USUAL SUSPECTS

The primary sources include the author's interviews with Abe Feder, John Houseman, and Virgil Thomson. Primary source publications are: *Frederick Ashton* by Dominic and Gilbert; *Runthrough* by John Houseman; *Secret Muses* by Julie Kavanagh; and *Frederick Ashton* by David Vaughn.

1. Thomson, *Words with Music*, p. 71.
2. The Woolfs' Hogarth Press had, in fact, offered to publish a collection of his short stories, but irretrievably lost the manuscript.
3. *Lovers, Happy Lovers* with Lewis Galantiere, *Three in One* with Lewis Galantiere, *A Very Great Man* with A. E. Thomas, and *The Lake* with Zita Johann.
4. Houseman, in retrospect, thought that it was his apparent malleability that made Thomson choose him over another Askew regular, Joseph Losey, who had more experience directing theater; at the beginning of his theater career, Losey was more politically directed. He was later well known as a film director.

5. Virgil Thomson, "Scenes from Show Biz," *New York Review of Books*, May 4, 1972, p. 38.
6. Abe Feder, in Joseph Wechsberg, "The Right Light," *The New Yorker*, October 22, 1960, p. 70.
7. Ashton, in T. H. Parker article, *Hartford Courant*, February 9, 1934.

CHAPTER 15: REHEARSALS IN HARLEM

The primary sources include the author's interviews with Thomas Anderson, Leonard du Paur, Abe Feder, Beatrice Wayne Godfrey, John Houseman, Eva Jessye, Kitty Mason, and Virgil Thomson. Primary source publications are: *Secret Muses* by Julie Kavanagh; *Runthrough* by John Houseman; *Virgil Thomson* by Virgil Thomson; and *Frederick Ashton* by David Vaughan.

1. *Run Little Chillun* file, New York Public Library for the Performing Arts.
2. During the run of *Run Little Chillun*, Hall Johnson explained the difference between the styles in this way: "All *folk art* is the result of the attempt of simpleminded (technically untrained) peoples to express aesthetically their emotional reaction toward their experiences and environment. . . . Negroes have originated their own 'manner' in music just as they have in the spoken language." (*Run Little Chillun* file, New York Public Library for the Performing Arts.)
3. Antheil to Draper, n.d., Draper Collection.
4. Eva Jessye to Steven Watson, August 11, 1987, collection of Steven Watson.
5. "Eva Jessye's demand was a penetration that took years to come. And even after it came in this limited fashion, all you could get for a long time was chorus equity; people who deserved full equity status had to settle for a lesser status, lesser salaries. With very little protection from the kickback system which was so prevalent at that time. It was common for a producer to go to someone and say, 'I want you to get the chorus together.' And he would ask for forty-five dollars for the chorus. If they get forty-five, they can kick me back five. Then I would get the lieutenant, the one who represented me in the chorus, to go around and ask for forty-five, five of which comes back. That's the way the conductors made theirs. I think Eva was fighting that. I know it was in vogue when *Showboat* was running." Leonard DePaur, interview with the author, August 29, 1987.
6. Altonell Hines had been dating chorus member Thomas Anderson, but during the rehearsals she began a romance with Edward Matthews that resulted in a long marriage.
7. Thomson, in Tommasini, *Composer on the Aisle*, p. 250.
8. Benchley, *The New Yorker*, April 15, 1933, p. 24.
9. Thomson, Oral History interview with John Gruen, Dance Collection, Lincoln Center, November 6, 1977.
10. Beryl de Zoete, "Frederick Ashton, Background of a Choreographer," in *The Thunder and the Freshness*, p. 34.
11. Burra, *Well Dearie!*, p. 84.
12. Ibid., p. 86.
13. de Zoete, *The Thunder and the Freshness*, p. 37.
14. Ibid., p. 36.
15. McBride to McAdam, January 12, 1934, Henry McBride Collection.
16. Bessie Breuer to Dorothy Kreymborg, ca. December 1933, Alfred Kreymborg collection, Special Collections, University of Virginia. I thank Francis Naumann for bringing this to my attention.

17. Florine Stettheimer's notes on the *Four Saints* production, Stettheimer Collection.

18. Thomas Anderson, interview with author. Lack of French wasn't strictly true; Edward Matthews spoke fluent French and German, and Embry Bonner, another principal, had lived a year in Paris.

19. Joseph Alsop, "Gertrude Stein Opera Comes to Life in Harlem," *New York Herald Tribune*, January 18, 1934.

20. Ibid.

21. Rosenberg, in James Thrall Soby, "The Changing Stream," in *The Museum of Modern Art at Mid-Century: Continuity and Change* (1995), p. 186.

22. Soby, in Eleanor Bunce (Austin's secretary) to Abbott, January 19, 1934.

23. Joseph Wechsberg, "The Right Light," *The New Yorker*, October 22, 1960, p. 71.

24. McBride, *The Flow of Art*, p. 314.

25. Tommasini, *Composer on the Aisle*, p. 258.

26. Madame Pulich, who fabricated the saints' costumes, made costumes for the Ziegfeld Follies, and the fashionable garb of the Commère and Compère were created by couturier Helen Pons.

27. Frederick Ashton, too, called her "the most refined and delicate woman I ever met in my life—she was so petite, and her gestures were so precise and exact. She was tiny and frail and yet at the same time capable of doing these terrific paintings with great passion and observation, and these brilliant colors" (Vaughan, *Ashton*, p. 100).

CHAPTER 16: OPENING NIGHT

The primary sources include the author's interviews with Thomas Anderson, Beatrice Robinson Wayne, Eleanor Bunce, Henry-Russell Hitchcock, John Houseman, and Virgil Thomson. Reviews quoted are collected in a *Four Saints in Three Acts* clippings scrapbook, Thomson Collection. Primary source publications are: *Virgil Thomson* by Virgil Thomson; *Avery, Memorial, Wadsworth Atheneum* by Eugene Gaddis; "Four Saints in Three Acts at Hartford" by Henry McBride, reprinted in *The Flow of Art*, pp. 311–16; and David Harris's "The Original Four Saints in Three Acts."

1. Lucius Beebe, *Snoot If You Must*, p. 168.

2. Bryher to Stein, February 12, 1934, Gertrude Stein Collection.

3. *A. Everett Austin, Jr.: A Director's Taste and Achievement*, p. 36.

4. Wallace Stevens to Harriet Monroe, February 12, 1934, in *Letters of Wallace Stevens*, ed. Holly Stevens (New York: Alfred A. Knopf, 1966), p. 267.

5. Katherine Dreier to Austin, February 14, 1934, Austin Collection, Wadsworth Atheneum Archives.

6. Beebe, "Foreword," *Snoot If You Must*, p. x.

7. The Cushing sisters became famous for their marriages. Barbara ("Babe") married Stanley Mortimer Jr. and William Paley; Mary ("Minnie") married James Fosburgh and Vincent Astor; Betsey married James Roosevelt and John Hay Whitney. On returning from the opera, Nathaniel Saltonstall thought aloud to Agnes Mongan about starting a modernist institution for Boston, which soon came into being as the Institute for Contemporary Art.

8. McBride, *Florine Stettheimer*, p. 34.

9. "Avery Memorial Unique Example of Modern Style," *Artnews*, February 10, 1934, pp. 3–4.

10. W. E. H., "Times Reader Critical of the Avery Memorial," *Hartford Times*, February 15, 1934.
11. Winslow Ames, *Hartford Times*, February 8, 1934.
12. Johnson to Austin, n.d., Austin Collection, Wadsworth Atheneum Archives.
13. Winslow Ames, *Hartford Times*, February 8, 1934.
14. McBride, *Florine Stettheimer*, p. 37.
15. Van Vechten to Stein, February 8, 1934, Van Vechten Collection. Van Vechten wrote to *The New York Times*, February 18, 1934: "After ten minutes it is possible to forget altogether that these are Negro singers. As they fall one after another, into their sublime, if tutored, poses, they become in short order a series of reminders of the genius of El Greco, Zurburan and Velasquez."
16. John Houseman, *Runthrough*, p. 117.
17. McBride, *Florine Stettheimer*, p. 34.
18. Van Vechten to Thomson, February 9, 1934, Thomson Collection.
19. In Florine Stettheimer's original design, the Heavenly Mansion's resemblance to the Capitol would have been exact; Kate Lawson cut off the capitol dome because, in the midst of the Depression, she felt it was important that the Heavenly Mansion not be taken as a thinly veiled political endorsement.
20. Stein, *Everybody's Autobiography*, p. 316.
21. Wallace Stevens to Harriet Monroe, February 12, 1934, in *Letters of Wallace Stevens*, p. 267.
22. Thomson, interview with the author, December 7, 1987.
23. Stein to Van Vechten, February 5, 1934.
24. Van Vechten to Stein, February 10, 1934, in *Stein–Van Vechten Letters*, p. 298.
25. McBride to Stein, March 20, 1934, Gertrude Stein Collection.

CHAPTER 17: *FOUR SAINTS* GOES TO BROADWAY

Reviews quoted are collected in a *Four Saints in Three Acts* clippings scrapbook in the Virgil Thomson Collection. Primary sources include interviews with John Houseman and Virgil Thomson. Primary publications are: *Runthrough* by John Houseman; *Secret Muses* by Julie Kavanagh; and *Virgil Thomson* by Virgil Thomson.

1. Stetteimer, in Dorothy Dayton, "Before Designing Stage Settings She Painted Composer's Portrait," New York *Sun*, March 24, 1934.
2. T. S. Matthews, "Gertrude Stein," in *Gertrude Stein Remembered*, p. 152.
3. McBride to Malcolm MacAdam, February 25, 1934, Henry McBride Collection.
4. Ettie Stettheimer to Thomson, February 1934, Virgil Thomson collection.
5. Both quotations from McBride to MacAdam, February 25, 1934, Henry McBride Collection.
6. When McBride later escorted Stettheimer backstage, she lost her footing and fell. "It was awful," McBride recalled. "She had several necklaces and long dangling earrings and all those things jangled and clanked as she went down. It was like the fall of Chartres Cathedral." (As recalled by Maximilian Miltzlaff, annotated collection of Henry McBride's letters; Collection Maximilian Miltzlaff.)
7. McBride to MacAdam, February 25, 1934, Henry McBride Collection.
8. Marianne Moore to John Warner Moore, March 1, 1934; in Moore, *The Selected Letters of Marianne Moore*, ed. Bonnie Costello, Celeste Goodridge, and Cristanne Miller (New York: Alfred A. Knopf, 1997).

9. Bowles to Thomson, quoted in Christopher Sawyer-Laucanno, *An Invisible Spectator* (New York: Weidenfeld & Nicholson, 1989), p. 154.
10. Tommasini, *Virgil Thomson*, p. 266.
11. Stein, "Composition as Explanation," in *Selected Writings of Gertrude Stein*, p. 515.
12. McBride to Stein, March 20, 1934; Stein Collection.
13. For example, F.P.A. wrote: "Nobody knows the opera I seen; nobody knows but Gertrude" (*Herald Tribune*, February 22, 1934).
14. "4 Saints in 3 Acts," *Opportunity* (May 1934). I thank Cristina Ruotolo for bringing this to my attention.
15. George and Tibbie Newell to Thomson, n.d., Virgil Thomson Collection.
16. Stein to Thomson, n.d. (ca. February 1934), Virgil Thomson collection.
17. Houseman, quoted in Bradley to Stein, April 6, 1934, Gertrude Stein Collection.
18. Stein to Bradley, April 21, 1934, Gertrude Stein Collection, and in Tommasini, *Composer on the Aisle*, p. 267.
19. Houseman to Austin, March 10, 1934, A. E. Austin Jr. Collection.
20. McBride to MacAdam, April 7, 1934, Henry McBride Collection.
21. Florine Stettheimer to Ettie and Carrie Stettheimer, April 11, 1934, Stettheimer Collection.
22. Florine Stettheimer to McBride, August 17, 1932, Henry McBride Collection.
23. Dorothy Dayton, "Before Designing Stage Settings She Painted Composer's Portrait," New York *Sun*, March 24, 1934.
24. Florine Stettheimer to Ettie and Carrie Stettheimer, March 29, 1934, Stettheimer Collection.
25. McBride to MacAdam, April 20, 1934, Henry McBride Collection.
26. Thomson to Jennifer Gough-Cooper and Jacques Caumont, January 29, 1987, Virgil Thomson Collection.

CHAPTER 18: AFTERMATH

The primary sources include the author's interviews with Thomas Anderson, Abe Feder, Beatrice Wayne Godfrey, John Houseman, Eva Jessye, Kitty Mason, and Virgil Thomson. Primary source publications are: *The Life and Art of Florine Stettheimer* by Barbara Bloemink; *Secret Muses* by Julie Kavanagh; *Runthrough* by John Houseman; *Everybody's Autobiography* by Gertrude Stein; *Virgil Thomson* by Virgil Thomson; and *Composer on the Aisle* by Anthony Tommasini.

1. McBride to Malcolm MacAdam, November 16, 1934, Henry McBride Collection.
2. *Chicago Daily Tribune*, November 9, 1934.
3. Stein, radio interview, November 12, 1934, printed in "A Radio Interview," *Paris Review*, Fall 1990, p. 92.
4. McBride to Malcolm MacAdam; October 20, 1934, Henry McBride Collection.
5. Introductory notes to Stein's radio interview, November 12, 1934, printed in "A Radio Interview," *Paris Review*, Fall 1990, p. 86.
6. Stein, "And, Now," *Vanity Fair*, September 1934, p. 35.
7. Thomson to Stein, April 29, 1935, Gertrude Stein Collection.
8. *New York Herald Tribune*, May 13, 1935, in Mellow, *Charmed Circle*, p. 497.
9. Thomson to Stein, July 16, 1938, in Thomson, *Letters*, p. 122.
10. Among the critics who consider *Four Saints* a major work: Andrew Porter, Peter G. Davis, John Rockwell, Tim Page, Anthony Tommasini.

11. Kolodin, in Tommasini, *Composer on the Aisle*, p. 425.
12. Murphy to Draper, August 8, 1934, Muriel Draper Collection.
13. When Muriel Draper returned from Russia in 1935, many could not integrate her championing of individualism with the communal grayness of Russian life. "It excites you to think that every Russian is aware of participating in one of the long strides of history," wrote Gilbert Seldes in 1936, "but you are still an individualist at heart, and the plight of those who feel themselves rejected by the movement of their time still calls for your sympathy" (*Mainland* [New York: Charles Scribners Sons, 1936], dedication). When she died, many of her friends declined to be associated with Muriel's socialism, and they avoided Frank Campbell on the afternoon of her funeral. "The old friends who could take it no matter what were on one side, and the Communist people were on the other" (James Amster, interview with the author). In memory of Draper's salon in Edith Grove, the Schubert C-major cello quintet was played.
14. Joella Bayer, interview with the author, December 3, 1992.
15. Judith Malina, interview with the author, April 8, 1998.
16. Toklas to Van Vechten, November 1, 1946, in *Staying on Alone*, p. 30.
17. Thornton Wilder to Stein and Toklas, July 18 and September 13, 1937, in *The Letters of Gertrude Stein and Thornton Wilder*, ed. Edward M. Burns and Ulla Dydo (Yale University Press, 1997), pp. 156, 175.
18. Al Carmines, interview with the author, March 25, 1998.
19. Tim Page, interview with the author, April 20, 1997.
20. Barbara J. Bloemink, *The Life and Art of Florine Stettheimer* (New Haven: Yale University Press, 1995), p. 211.
21. Ibid., p. 216.
22. Ibid., p. 217.
23. McBride, "The World of Art," New York *Sun*, May 27, 1944.
24. Tyler, *Florine Stettheimer*, p. 189.
25. Pavel Tchelitchew to Ettie Stettheimer, in Steven Watson, "Three Sisters," *Art and Antiques*, May 1992, p. 67.
26. Julien Levy, "Dealing with A. Everett Austin, Jr.," in *A Director's Taste*, p. 36.
27. Kirstein, "The Ballet in Hartford," in *A Director's Taste*, p. 72.
28. A month after Japan bombed Pearl Harbor, Austin outlined to his trustees the fight that nearly overwhelmed him:

> The quest of the last two decades for material luxuries, questionable security, the abandonment of spiritual responsibilities, the insistence on values of mere entertainment, the pedestalling of mediocrity, the fear of offending by conviction or definite statement, the cult of compromise, the marked suspicion of enthusiasm, the many false values engendered by the racket of advertising, the mesmerism exerted by numbers, tables, polls, efficiency as such, and finally and most dangerously, the almost total lack of imagination, have all been the ingredients of the weakened years in increasing force.
> (Austin, "Annual Report of the Director," January 17, 1942; Soby papers, I.3.5, Museum of Modern Art Archives.)

29. McBride to Ettie Stettheimer, October 20, 1944, Henry McBride Collection.
30. Kirstein, interview with the author, July 15, 1992.
31. Johnson, in Gaddis, *Avery Memorial*, p. 68.

32. Austin to Soby, May 31, 1946; Soby Papers, Series I, Box 3, MoMA.

33. Sarah Austin, interview with the author, May 7, 1992.

34. Constance Askew to Helen Austin, April 2, 1957, Wadsworth Atheneum Archives.

35. Thomson to Helen Austin, April 1, 1957, A. E. Austin Jr. collection.

36. Philip Johnson to Helen Austin, April 1, 1957, A. E. Austin Jr. collection.

37. Jere Abbott to Thomson, May 1, 1957, Virgil Thomson Collection.

38. A few years later, Houseman acknowledged Thomson's seminal influence on his development: "I think for three years you were the soil of taste and encouragement and good sense and esprit in which the roots to my activities were able to grow. . . . I know now—and I suspect that you have always known—just how essential your judgements (not so much on specifics but on the far more important ground of relative human and artistic values) were to me in these few years—beginning with *Four Saints*—which are the span of my valid theatrical career." (*Runthrough*, p. 442.)

39. Ashton to Thomson, n.d. (1949), Virgil Thomson Collection.

40. Ashton, quoted in Arlene Croce, "The Loves of his Life," *The New Yorker*, May 19, 1997, p. 78.

41. Mel Gussow, obituary for Abe Feder, *The New York Times*, April 26, 1997.

42. Donald Sutherland, *Gertrude Stein: A Biography of Her Work* (New Haven: Yale University Press, 1951), p. 154. During the remainder of the 1930s, she also wrote *The Geographical History of America*, a long intellectual work about identity; *Everybody's Autobiography*, a memoir about her American tour; *Picasso*, a memoir of her friendship; and *Paris France*, a valentine to her adopted hometown. In addition she wrote short commercial pieces for *The Saturday Evening Post*, prefaces to exhibition catalogs, reviews, and plays which were never produced in her lifetime: *Listen to Me* and *Dr. Faustus Lights the Lights*.

43. When France declared war on Germany, Gertrude and Alice were living in their home in Bilignin. They retrieved two paintings from Paris (Cézanne's *Portrait of Hortense* and Picasso's *Portrait of Gertrude Stein*) that provided a connection to Stein's and Toklas's rich past; the remainder of the collection hung unguarded on the walls. Gertrude and Alice would not see their paintings, their apartment, their friends, or Paris, for five years.

       Wartime life in Bilignin provided Stein a stark contrast to her celebrity in America. The villagers appreciated her primarily for her gregarious conversations as she foraged for food, hoping to wheedle an egg or some milk. Even when the two Jewish women were urged to move to Switzerland, Alice and Gertrude chose to remain in France. Their safety was in part due to their friendship with Bernard Fay, who served as the director of the Bibliothèque Nationale under the Vichy government and used his influence to protect them. Utterly different from their salon life, this community was based on daily events and hardship during war. Stein recalled those years as "the happiest years of my life."

44. Mellow, *Charmed Circle*, p. 546.

45. Thomson to Buddy Bradley, March 6, 1934, Virgil Thomson Collection.

46. Believing that trained musicians made the best music critics, Thomson built up a lively department of stringers and regular music reviewers that included John Cage, Edwin Denby (on dance), Lou Harrison, Paul Bowles, Elliot Carter, William Flanagan, and Peggy Glanville-Hicks.

47. Gilbert Chase, *America's Music: From the Pilgrims to the Present*, Revised Third Edition (Chicago: University of Illinois Press, 1987), p. 525.

48. Thomson to Sherry Mangan, October 8, 1941; in Thomson, *Selected Letters,* p. 170.

49. Stein to Thomson, May 15, 1941, Virgil Thomson Collection.

50. Alice Toklas received the collection, $20,000 in securities, and $6,650 in cash.

51. In the summer of 1946, after Stein described feeling pain, doctors at the American Hospital in Neuilly recommended surgery, but refused to operate until Gertrude had built up her strength. Alice wrote, "She was furious and frightening and impressive like she was thirty years and more ago when her work was attacked" (Tommasini, *Composer on the Aisle,* p. 564). Stein summoned the director of the hospital and ordered him to operate: "I was not made to suffer." Alice wrote of the end: "And oh Baby was so beautiful—in between the pain—like nothing before." On the afternoon of July 27, she lay sedated in bed and uttered her final sentences, which have become part of the Stein legend. "What is the answer?" she asked Alice, and when no response came she added, "In that case, what is the question?" Then they wheeled Gertrude away and Alice never saw her again.

52. Thomson, *The New York Times,* April 15, 1956.

53. Thomson on Stein: "Living through a war takes nothing, as courage, compared to being for forty years a one-man literary movement. And to have become a Founding Father of her century is her own reward for having long ago, and completely, dominated her language" ("The Daily Life" [1945] ms., Virgil Thomson Collection, Rare Book and Manuscript Library, Columbia University).

54. Thomson, jacket notes for *Four Saints in Three Acts,* Nonesuch 79035, 1982.

ARCHIVAL SOURCES

A. E. Austin Jr. Collection, Wadsworth Atheneum Archive

Muriel Draper Collection, Yale Collection of American Literature, Beinecke Library, Yale University

Max Ewing Collection, Yale Collection of American Literature, Beinecke Library, Yale University

Maurice Grosser, unpublished memoir, in the possession of Louis Rispoli

Philip Johnson, Oral History, Museum of Modern Art

Mabel Dodge Luhan Collection, Yale Collection of American Literature, Beinecke Library, Yale University

Henry McBride Collection, Yale Collection of American Literature, Beinecke Library, Yale University

Maximilian Miltzlaff, Annotated Collection of Henry McBride's letters, collection of Maximilian Miltzlaff

Paul Sachs, Reminiscences, Oral History Collection, Columbia University

Gertrude Stein Collection, Yale Collection of American Literature, Beinecke Library, Yale University

Florine Stettheimer Collection, Columbia University

Stettheimer Collection, Yale Collection of American Literature, Beinecke Library, Yale University

Virgil Thomson, Oral History, interviewed by John Gruen, November 6, 1977, New York Public Library, Dance Collection

Virgil Thomson Collection, Yale Music Library, Yale University

Virgil Thomson Collection, Rare Book and Manuscript Library, Columbia University

Carl Van Vechten Collection, Yale Collection of American Literature, Beinecke Library, Yale University

AUTHOR'S INTERVIEWS

Atwood Askew Allaire, November 13, 1989, New York

James Amster, April 10, 1986, New York

Thomas Anderson, June 19, 1987, December 7, 1987, February 2, 1992, February 29, 1992, Englewood, New Jersey

Pamela Askew, July 24, 1985, February 26, 1992, Millbrook, New York

David Austin, May 28, 1992, New York

Sarah Austin, May 7, 1992, New York

Joella Levy Bayer, August 16, 1986, August 17, 1986, December 3, 1992, Montecito, California

Florence Berkman, February 18, 1986, Hartford, Connecticut

Paul Bowles, February 21, 1989, Tangiers, Morocco

Eleanor Howland Bunce, March 18, 1986, Bloomfield, Connecticut

Al Carmines, March 25, 1998, New York
Philip Claflin, July 17, 1985, April 15, 1987, New Paltz, New York
John Coolidge, April 17, 1991, Cambridge, Massachusetts
Paul Draper Jr., March 20, 1986, April 11, 1992, Woodstock, New York
Abe Feder, February 7, 1996, New York
Emily Hahn, March 4, 1986, New York
John Houseman, March 27, 1987, New York
Robert Isaacson, September 24, 1993, New York
Philip Johnson, October 8, 1987, August 6, 1992, New York
Lincoln Kirstein, January 10, 1991, March 12, 1992, August 6, 1992, New York
William Koshland, August 5, 1992, New York
Judith Malina, April 8, 1998, New York
Kitty Mason, July 2, 1987, December 7, 1987, New York
Agnes Mongan, March 20, 1987, Cambridge, Massachusetts
Tim Page, April 20, 1997, New York
Tonio Selwart, May 22, 1991, November 18, 1991, New York
Joel Thome, April 30, 1996, New York
Virgil Thomson, May 27, 1985, July 19, 1985, April 30, 1987, May 7, 1987, September 2, 1987, December 8, 1987, New York
Edward Warburg, November 3, 1987, New York

PUBLISHED SOURCES

Amory, Cleveland. *Who Killed Society?* New York: Harper and Brothers, 1960.
————, and Frederick Bradlee, eds. *Vanity Fair: A Cavalcade of the 1920s and 1930s.* New York: Viking Press, 1960.
Barr, Alfred. *Defining Modern Art: Selected Writings of Alfred H. Barr,* ed. Irving Sandler and Amy Newman. New York: Harry Abrams, 1986.
Barr, Margaret Scolari, and Roob, Rona. "Our Campaigns: Alfred H. Barr, Jr., and the Museum of Modern Art: A Biographical Chronicle of the Years 1930–1944." *The New Criterion,* Summer 1987, pp. 1–74.
Beebe, Lucius. *Snoot If You Must.* New York: D. Appleton–Century Company, 1943.
Benstock, Shari. *Women of the Left Bank: Paris, 1900–1940.* Austin, Tex.: University of Texas Press, 1986.
Birmingham, Stephen. *Our Crowd: The Great Jewish Families of New York.* New York: Harper & Row, 1967.
Blackmer, Corinne, and Patricia Juliana Smith, eds. *En Travesti: Women, Gender Subversion, Opera.* New York: Columbia University Press, 1995.
Bloemink, Barbara. *The Life and Art of Florine Stettheimer.* New Haven: Yale University Press, 1995.
Bowles, Paul. *Without Stopping: An Autobiography.* New York: Putnam, 1972.
Brinnin, John Malcolm. *The Third Rose: Gertrude Stein and Her World.* Boston: Little, Brown, 1959.
Buckle, Richard (in collaboration with John Taras). *George Balanchine: Ballet Master.* New York: Random House, 1988.
Burra, Edward. *Well Dearie! The Letters of Edward Burra,* ed. William Chappell. London: G. Fraser, 1985.
Chaucey, George. *Gay New York: Gender, Urban Culture and the Making of the Gay Male World 1890–1940.* New York: Basic Books, 1994.
Cowley, Malcolm. *Exile's Return: A Literary Odyssey of the 1920s.* New York: Viking Press, 1951.

de Zoete, Beryl. *The Thunder and the Freshness*. New York: Theatre Arts Books, 1963.

Dominic, Zoe, and Gilbert, John Selwyn, *Frederick Ashton: A Choreographer and His Ballets*. Chicago: H. Regnery Company, 1973.

Dzikes, John. *Opera in America: A Cultural History*. New Haven: Yale University Press, 1993.

Fitzgerald, Michael C. *Making Modernism: Picasso and the Creation of the Market for Twentieth Century Art*. New York: Farrar, Straus and Giroux, 1995.

Flanner, Janet. *Janet Flanner's World: Uncollected Writings 1932–1975*, ed. Irving Drutman. New York: Harcourt Brace Jovanovich, 1979.

Ford, Hugh D. *Four Lives in Paris*. San Francisco: North Point Press, 1987.

———. *Published in Paris: A Literary Chronicle of Paris in the 1920s and 1930s*. New York: Macmillan, 1975.

Gaddis, Eugene R., ed. *Avery Memorial, Wadsworth Atheneum: The First Modern Museum*. Hartford, Connecticut: Wadsworth Atheneum, 1984.

Gill, Brendan. *A New York Life: Of Friends and Others*. New York: Poseidon Press, 1990.

——— and Jerome Zerbe. *Happy Times*. New York: Harcourt Brace Jovanovich, 1973.

Gallup, Donald, ed. *The Flowers of Friendship: Letters Written to Gertrude Stein*. New York: Alfred A. Knopf, 1953.

Haight, Mary Ellen Jordan. *Walks In Gertrude Stein's Paris*. Salt Lake City: Peregrine Smith, 1988.

Hamovitch, Mitzi Berger, ed. *The Hound and Horn Letters*. Athens: University of Georgia Press, 1982.

Harris, David. "The Original *Four Saints in Three Acts*," *The Drama Review*, Spring 1982, Vol. 26, No. 1, pp. 101–30.

Hitchcock, Henry-Russell, and Philip Johnson. *The International Style: Architecture Since 1922*. New York: W. W. Norton, 1932. Reprinted 1966.

Hoover, Kathleen, and John Cage. *Virgil Thomson: His Life and Music*. New York: T. Yoseloff, 1959.

Houseman, John. *Runthrough: A Memoir*. New York: Simon & Schuster, 1972.

Imbs, Bravig. *Confessions of Another Young Man*. New York: Henkle-Yewdale, 1936.

Jones, Carolyn. *Modern Art at Harvard*. New York: Abbeville Press, 1985.

Kavanagh, Julie. *Secret Muses: The Life of Frederick Ashton*. New York: Pantheon, 1997.

Kellner, Bruce. *Carl Van Vechten and the Irreverent Decades*. Norman: University of Oklahoma Press, 1968.

Kirstein, Lincoln. *By With To & From*, ed. Nicholas Jenkins. New York: Farrar, Straus & Giroux, 1991.

———. "Conversations with Kirstein" I and II, conducted by W. Lowry McNeill. *The New Yorker*, December 15 and December 22, 1986.

———. *Mosaic: Memoirs*. New York: Farrar, Straus & Giroux, 1994.

———. *The New York City Ballet*. New York: Alfred A. Knopf, 1973.

Kluver, Billy, and Julie Martin. *Kiki's Paris: Artists and Lovers 1900–1930*. New York: Harry N. Abrams, 1989.

Koestenbaum, Wayne. *The Queen's Throat: Opera, Homosexuality and the Mystery of Desire*. New York: Poseidon Press, 1993.

Levine, Lawrence W. *Highbrow/Lowbrow: The Emergence of Cultural Hierarchy in America*. Cambridge, Massachusetts: Harvard University Press, 1982.

Levy, Julien. *Memoir of an Art Gallery*. New York: G. P. Putnam's Sons, 1977.

Lynes, Russell. *Good Old Modern: An Intimate Portrait of the Museum of Modern Art*. New York: Atheneum, 1973.

Marquis, Alice Goldfarb. *Alfred Barr: Missionary for the Modern.* Chicago: Contemporary Books, 1989.

McBride, Henry. *Florine Stettheimer.* New York: Museum of Modern Art, 1946.

———. *The Flow of Art: Essays and Criticisms of Henry McBride,* ed. Daniel Catton Rich. New York: Atheneum, 1975.

Mellow, James. *Charmed Circle: Gertrude Stein & Company.* New York: Holt, Rinehart and Winston, 1974.

Morand, Paul. *New York 1930,* trans. Hamish Miles. New York: Book League of America, 1930.

Museum of Modern Art. *Alfred H. Barr, Jr.: A Memorial Tribute.* New York: Museum of Modern Art, 1981.

Noble, John. *A Fabulous Dollhouse of the Twenties: The Famous Stettheimer Dollhouse at the Museum of the City of New York.* New York: Dover Publications, 1976.

Parnassus: Poetry in Review (A Tribute to Virgil Thomson on His 81st Birthday), ed. Herbert Leibowitz. Spring–Summer 1977, Vol. 5, No. 2.

Riley, Terence. *The International Style: Exhibition 15 and the Museum of Modern Art.* New York: Rizzoli, 1992.

Rose, Phyllis. *Jazz Cleopatra.* New York: Doubleday, 1989.

Schulze, Franz. *Philip Johnson: Life and Work.* New York: Alfred A. Knopf, 1994.

Simon, Linda. *The Biography of Alice B. Toklas.* Garden City, N.J.: Doubleday, 1977.

———, ed. *Gertrude Stein Remembered.* Lincoln: University of Nebraska Press, 1994.

Gertrude Stein. *The Autobiography of Alice B. Toklas.* New York: Harcourt, Brace, 1933.

———. *Everybody's Autobiography.* New York: Random House, 1937.

———. *Fernhurst, Q.E.D., and Other Early Writings,* introduced by Leon Katz. New York: Liveright, 1971.

———. *A Gertrude Stein Reader,* ed. and with an introduction by Ulla Dydo. Evanston, Ill.: Northwestern University Press, 1993.

———. *How to Write.* Paris: Plain Edition, 1931 (reprinted New York: Dover, 1975).

———. *Lectures in America.* New York: The Modern Library, 1935 (reprinted New York: Vintage, 1975).

——— and Carl Van Vechten. *The Letters of Gertrude Stein and Carl Van Vechten,* ed. Edward M. Burns (2 vols.). New York: Columbia University Press, 1986.

——— and Thornton Wilder. *The Letters of Gertrude Stein & Thornton Wilder,* ed. Edward M. Burns and Ulla E. Dydo with William Rice. New Haven: Yale University Press, 1996.

———. *Selected Writings of Gertrude Stein,* ed. Carl Van Vechten. New York: Random House, 1946.

Stern, Robert A. M., Gregory Gilmartin, and Thomas Mellins. *New York 1930: Architecture and Urbanism Between the Two World Wars.* New York: Rizzoli, 1987.

Story, Rosalind. *And So I Sing: African-American Divas of Opera and Concert.* New York: Warner Books, 1990.

Sussman, Elizabeth, Barbara J. Bloemink, and Linda Nochlin. *Florine Stettheimer: Manhattan Fantastica.* New York: Whitney Museum of American Art, 1995.

Thomson, Virgil. *Selected Letters of Virgil Thomson,* ed. Tim Page and Vanessa Weeks Page. New York: Summit Books, 1988.

———. *Virgil Thomson.* New York: Alfred A. Knopf, 1966.

———. *A Virgil Thomson Reader.* New York: E. P. Dutton, 1981.

———. *Words with Music.* New Haven: Yale University Press, 1989.

Toklas, Alice B. *Staying on Alone: Letters of Alice B. Toklas*, ed. Edward M. Burns. New York: Liveright, 1973.

———. *What Is Remembered.* New York: Holt, Rinehart and Winston, 1963.

Tommasini, Anthony. *Virgil Thomson: Composer on the Aisle.* New York: W. W. Norton, 1997.

———. *Virgil Thomson's Musical Portraits.* New York: Pendragon Press, 1986.

Tyler, Parker. *Florine Stettheimer: A Life in Art.* New York: Farrar, Straus and Company, 1963.

Van Vechten, Carl. *Keep A-Inchin' Along: Selected Writings of Carl Van Vechten About Black Art and Letters*, ed. Bruce Kellner. Westport, Conn.: Greenwood Press, 1979.

———. *Letters of Carl Van Vechten*, ed. Bruce Kellner. New Haven: Yale University Press, 1987.

Vaughan, David. *Frederick Ashton and His Ballets.* New York: Alfred A. Knopf, 1977.

Wadsworth Atheneum (no editor listed). *A. Everett Austin Jr.: A Director's Taste and Achievement.* Hartford: Wadsworth Atheneum, 1957.

Watson, Steven. *Strange Bedfellows: The First American Avant-Garde.* New York: Abbeville Press, 1991.

———. *The Harlem Renaissance: Hub of African-American Culture, 1920–1930.* New York: Pantheon, 1995.

Weber, Nicolas Fox. *Patron Saints: Five Rebels Who Opened America to a New Art 1928–1943.* New York: Alfred A. Knopf, 1992.

Wineapple, Brenda. *Sister Brother: Gertude and Leo Stein.* New York: G. P. Putnam's Sons, 1996.

I was fortunate to begin this project in time to speak with a number of remarkable men and women who could tell me stories of their involvement in *Four Saints in Three Acts*: Virgil Thomson, Lincoln Kirstein, Philip Johnson, John Houseman, Eva Jessye, Thomas Anderson, Beatrice Robinson Wayne, and many more. (A full list of these interviews can be found in the bibliography.) Collectively, they evoked a stylish and pioneering era that I was privileged to share secondhand.

I owe a debt to several writers who were models of scholarly generosity: Anthony Tommasini, for his work on Virgil Thomson; Eugene Gaddis, for his study of A. E. "Chick" Austin Jr.; Ulla Dydo, the late James Mellow, and Brenda Wineapple, for their work on Gertrude Stein; Bruce Kellner, for his work on Carl Van Vechten; Julie Kavanagh, for her book on Frederick Ashton; Rona Roob, for her work on Alfred Barr; Franz Schulze, for his work on Philip Johnson.

The Yale Collection of American Literature at the Beinecke Rare Book and Manuscript Library has been my primary archival home for this book. The pleasure of returning to this library reflects the collecting foresight of curators Donald Gallup and Patricia Willis and the spirited desk staff—Maureen Heher, Kevin Glick, Ngadi Kponou, Lynn Braunsdorf—led by Steve Jones, the library's walking memory. At the Yale Music Library, I thank Ken Crilley and Suzanne Eggleston. At Columbia University's Rare Book and Manuscript Library, home of Florine Stettheimer's maquette for the opera, I thank Jean Ashton, Patrick T. Lawlor, Claudia Funke, and Bernard Crystal.

I am also grateful to those who read portions of the manuscript: Mason Cooley, Louise Bernikow, Craig Rutenberg, Eugene Gaddis, David Vaughn, and Robert Marx. My admirable assistant, Catherine Morris, helped marshal order.

For miscellaneous help and enthusiasm over ten years I am grateful to the late Joseph Solomon, Louis Rispoli and Danyal Lawson, Maximilian Miltzlaff, Joella Bayer, the late Allan Stinson, Jay Sullivan, Ronald Smith, Mohammad Moughal, Charles Fussell, Richard Flender, Michael de Lisio, Francisco Drohojowski, Saun Ellis, David Harris, David Del Tredici, Tobias Schneebaum, Cindy Mann, Sostena Romano, Peter Swanson, Robert Gregson, Jane Hammond, the late Dale Harris, Charles D. Scheips Jr., Faith Middleton, Shelley Wanger, Jeremy Tamanini, Matthew Moreno, Nicholas Jenkins, Salleigh Rothrock, Emile Bedriomo, Tom Blewitt, Michael Gray, John Ingle, James Sellars, Rosalind Solomon, Rosemary Morse, and Josh Himwich. I thank my family, Robert and Loranda Watson, John, Janet, and Philip Watson, for their continued support. Diane Cleaver, my agent, who secured the contract for this book, did not live to see it completed. For their support of the documentary *Prepare for Saints: The Making of a Modern Opera*, I wish to thank Mary Jo Kaplan, Michael Nicklas, David Bhagat, and colleagues at Connecticut Public Television, Judy D. Pansullo, Larry Rifkin, and Dana O'Neill. I am grateful to the Yaddo Foundation for providing both an ideal setting and undemanding support.

At Random House, I wish to thank Sharon Delano for acquiring the book, as well as Webb Younce and Sean Abbott. I thank Lynn Anderson for her scrupulous copy-editing, Gabrielle Bordwin for the dust jacket design, Caroline Cunningham for her design, and Beth Pearson and Stacy Rockwood for their attention to editorial production and manufacturing. Most of all I thank my editor, Joy de Menil, for her energetic engagement and her intelligently ruthless editing.

Robert Atkins lived through the dozen years of work on this project, and the stamp of his literary craft is reflected in the final manuscript. I thank him, my critic and my partner, for his scrupulous care and love.

Page numbers in *italics* refer to illustrations.

Morgan, J. Pierpont, 83–84, 154
Morgan State College, 242–43
Morris, Benjamin Wistar, 161
Moses, Harry, 258, 281, 289, 297
Mosher, John, 193
Mother of Us All, The (Stein and Thomson), 302, 319–21
Mountbatten, Lady Edwina, 58
Mouvel, Boutet de, *176*
Murphy, Esther, 188, 303
Murphy, Gerald, 31, 60
Murphy, Sarah, 31
Museum of Living Art, 90
Museum of Modern Art (MOMA), 90, 91, 92, 95–96, 134, *136*, 158, 196, 228, 270
  Barr as director of, 95–96, 113, 137–41, 144, 157
  early exhibitions at, 138–46, 149, 153–54, 205
  film and photography departments of, 90, 96, 150
  financial base of, 140
  founding and opening of, 7, 65, 95–96, 137–41, 177
  Junior Advisory Committee of, 140, 153–54
  "Modern Architecture: International Exhibition" at, 140, 141–44, 145–46, 149, 161
Music Fund, 79
mythology, 42

N

Nabokov, Nicolas, 61
Nadar, 150, 187
Nadelman, Elie, *70*, 74
Narcisse Noir (Grosser), 88
"Narrative of Prepare for Saints, A" (Stein), 46
Nash, Ogden, 288
National Guard, 26
National Negro Opera Company, 201
Native Americans, 62
Natoma (Herbert), 62
Negro, 30
Negro Chamber of Commerce, 261
Negro Theatre Project, 313–14
neo-Romantic art, 52, 150
Neumann, J. B., 95
New Directions, 268
New Haven Railroad, 257, 266
New York, N.Y.:
  Alwyn Court in, 69, *70*, 71, 74, 75, 163, 167, 224
  architecture and skyline of, 58, 63–64, 69, 71, 227, 298
  Beaux Arts Building in, 167–68
  expatriots in, 58, 74–75
  Greenwich Village in, 14, 32, 65, 66, 153, 180, 198
  Harlem in, 5, 6, 68–69, 178, 194, 196, 197–201, 204, 230, 240–52

  mutual attraction between Paris and, 7, 55–60
  Upper East Side of, 7, 146, 194–96
New York Amsterdam News, 242
New York City Ballet, 310
New Yorker, 52, 90, 138, 175, 193, 251, 292
New York *Graphic*, 65
New York Herald Tribune, 177, 179, 258, 318
New York *Sun*, 15, 80, 268, 287, 292
New York Times, 175, 177, 285, 288, 293
Niagara Falls, 56
Nietzsche, Friedrich Wilhelm, 26, 184
Nigger Heaven (Van Vechten), 198, 204, 205
Nijinsky, Romola, 154, 155, 220
Nijinsky, Vaslav, 154, 155
Noailles, Vicomte de, 173
Noguchi, Isamu, 90, *183*, 267, *267*
Norton, Charles Eliot, 82, 190
Nursery Murmurs, 238

O

O'Connor, Robert B., 161
O'Connor, W. H., 262
Offner, Richard, 188
O'Keefe, Georgia, *70*, 71, 74
Olympic, 227
O'Neill, Eugene, 201
Ontological Hysterical Theater, 305
opera, 49
  American, 62, 302, 304–5
  history of, 49
  impact of *Four Saints* on, 7
  society and, 174
opera seria, 42
Opportunity, 288
Orage, A. R., 58, *183*
Oregon trail, 24
Orpheus and Eurydice (Gluck), 236
Osborne, Herbert, 213
Oud, J.J.P., 100, 101, 141
Our America (Frank), 205

P

Pagany, 120–21
Page, Tim, 305
Pans, 26
Pansophists, 25–26
Paper Chase, The, 314
Parade, 60
Paris:
  American cultural influence in, 55–60
  artistic and cultural life in, 19–22, 29–33, 36, 46–47, 51–54, 65, 104
  expatriates in, 6, 9–10, 19–22, 30–31, 32, 55, 65, 104
  GS's apartment at 27 rue de Fleurus in, 9–12, *10*, 13, 16, 18, 19–21, 31, 36, 38–41, 122–24
  homosexual life in, 28, 32, 68
  Left Bank in, 19, 52
  Luxembourg Gardens in, 9, 36, 47–48

Stein, Gertrude (*cont.*)
    revolutionary use of language by, 13–14,
        16, 20, 38, 47–48, 50, 62, 65–66, 71, 93,
        119, 130, 166, 179, 251–52, 278
    "rose is a rose is a rose" phrase of, 18, 297
    self-publication financed by, 14, 125–26,
        128
    soirees and dinner parties of, 9–12, 19,
        21–22, 38, 40–42, 122–23, 202
    theater as conceived by, 45–46, 61, 62
    unpublished works of, 14–16, 20, 41, 126,
        127
    vocal quality and conversation of, 11, 16
    VT on, 11, 12, 20, 37, 41, 50, 53–54, 119
    VT's affinity for works of, 9, 11, 29, 38, 50,
        66
    VT's first meeting with, 9–13, 14, 16, 22,
        33, 36
    VT's personal relationship with, 37, 40–42,
        65–66, 115–16, 121–25, 126, 133, 207–8
    VT's settings of works by, 9, 11, 29, 37–41,
        46–47, 72
    writing habits of, 19, 46, 54
    young male protégés of, 19–22, 116–25
Stein, Leo, 18, 21, 70
    GS and, *10*, 16, 218
Stettheimer, Carrie, 66, 69–72, 74–75, *75*,
    166–67, 179, 224, 305–6, 309
Stettheimer, Ettie, 66, 69–72, 74–75, *75*, 164,
    166–67, 170, 179, 224, 279, 284–85,
    305–6, 309
Stettheimer, Florine, 69–76, *73*, *75*, 163–70,
    165, 179, 188, 257, 280
    art works of, 15, 72–75, 164, 167–68,
        169–70, *171*, 306–9, *308*
    death of, 164, 169, 307–9
    diary of, 164, 166, 167
    family background of, 164–66
    Four Saints sets and costumes designed by,
        3, 5, 6, 73–74, 164, 167–70, *168*, 206–8,
        212–13, 217, 224–25, *224*, 261, 262–63,
        273, *274–75*, 276–79
Stettheimer, Rosetta Walter, 303, 305
Stevens, Wallace, 266, 279
Stieglitz, Alfred, *70*, 74, 148, 167, 286
stock market crash of 1929, 64, 137, 174
Stokowski, Leopold, 236
St. Philip's Episcopal Church, 248–50,
    257–59, 261
Strachey, Esther, 195
Strauss, Richard, 236
Stravinsky, Igor, 33, 34, 36, 49, 86, 95, 112,
    160
Street Scene (Weill), 304
Strozzi, Bernardo, 157
Sullivan, Mary Quinn, 91, 140
Sumner sisters, 111
Surrealism, 19, 33, 81, 125, *136*, 150
"Susie Asado" (Stein and Thomson), 37,
    38–40, 46
Sutherland, Donald, 316
Swanson, Gloria, 103

T

Tailleferre, Germaine, 32
Tandy, Vertner, 248
Tanner, Allen, 42
Tate, Allen, 153
Taylor, Deems, 62
Taylor, Francis Henry, 85, 266, 270
Tchelitchew, Pavel, 21, 42, 44, 120, 150, 188,
    309
Tender Buttons (Stein), 9, 11, 14, 27, 29
Teresa of Avila, Saint, 44, 47, 48, 71
Thayer, Scofield, 15
Théâtre des Champs-Élysées, 36
Théâtre du Châtelet, 221
Theatre Guild, 71, 284
Thomas, Edna, 189, 242
Thomas, Teddy, 235–36
Thomson, Virgil Garnett:
    accompanying and conducting of, 25, 27,
        47, 309
    artistic collaboration idealized by, 29, 54
    audacious manner and egotism of, 11–12,
        23, 25–27, 32, 34, 41–42, 202, 246
    autobiography of, 38
    career building of, 38–41, 46–47, 52–53
    childhood and adolescence of, 23–26, *24*
    collaboration of GS and, 41–55, *43*, 60,
        61–62, 65–66, 74, 79, 113, 115, 118,
        164, 211–16
    complementary pairing "joke theory" of, 44
    compositional methods of, 32–33, 38–39,
        47, 48–51, 62
    compositional studies of, 26, 29, 30, 33, 34,
        35, 37, 40, 53
    concerts of, 37–38, 52–53, 122, 124
    correspondence of, 9, 26–27, 33–34, 37,
        38, 44, 49, 51, 52–53, 63, 66, 72, 76,
        113, 214–16
    cultural politics instinct of, 79–80, 116,
        178, 223
    early compositions of, 12–13, 32–34, 38, 40
    early schooling of, 24–26
    first formal composition of, 27
    GS on, 12, 42, 124–25, 218
    Harvard education of, 9, 11, 12, 26–28, 34,
        40, 76
    homosexuality of, 25, 26–28, 33, 34–36,
        202, 255
    as host, 51
    illnesses of, 123–24
    income of, 28, 51–52, 181
    irreligious views of, 25
    latter day status and popularity of, 27, 305,
        319
    lecturing of, 179, 290
    loneliness and alienation of, 26, 28–29, 33
    on love vs. affection, 34
    military service of, 26
    Missouri birth of, 23
    musical establishment's shunning of, 6, 36,
        42, 52–53
    musical influences on, 25, 33, 50, 61, 62

The photographs and illustrations in this book are reproduced courtesy of those listed below.

STEVEN WATSON is a cultural historian. He is the author of *The Harlem Renaissance: Hub of African-American Culture 1920–1930*, *The Birth of the Beat Generation: Visionaries, Rebels, and Hipsters 1944–1960*, and *Strange Bedfellows: The First American Avant-Garde*.

ABOUT THE TYPE

This book was set in Electra, a typeface designed for Linotype by W. A. Dwiggins, the renowned type designer (1880–1956). Electra is a fluid typeface, avoiding the contrasts of thick and thin strokes that are prevalent in most modern typefaces.